THE PERILS OF INTERPRETING

The Perils of Interpreting

THE EXTRAORDINARY LIVES OF TWO TRANSLATORS BETWEEN QING CHINA AND THE BRITISH EMPIRE

Henrietta Harrison

PRINCETON UNIVERSITY PRESS

PRINCETON, NJ

Published by Princeton University Press
41 William Street, Princeton, New Jersey 08540
99 Banbury Road, Oxford OX2 6JX

press.princeton.edu

All Rights Reserved
First paperback printing, 2023
Paperback ISBN 9780691225463
Cloth ISBN 9780691225456
ISBN (e-book) 9780691225470

Library of Congress Control Number: 2021943817

British Library Cataloging-in-Publication Data is available

Editorial: Priya Nelson, Thalia Leaf, and Barbara Shi
Production Editorial: Karen Carter
Jacket/Cover Design: Layla Mac Rory
Production: Danielle Amatucci
Publicity: Maria Whelan and Carmen Jimenez
Copyeditor: Joseph Dahm

Jacket/Cover art: William Alexander, *Lord Macartney's Embassy to China*, 1793. Courtesy of the Huntington Library, San Marino, CA

This book has been composed in Miller

The Chinese do not really believe, though they so express themselves in the official language of their edicts, that embassadors are sent to their court, with the sole view of enabling them to contemplate with more advantage the sublime virtues of their heavenly-enthroned emperor—they are not quite such drivellers in politics. If, therefore, we are so unfortunate as to succeed in persuading them that commerce is not our object, conquest is the next thing that occurs to them.

—GEORGE THOMAS STAUNTON, *MISCELLANEOUS NOTICES ON CHINA*, 1821

Never now it is past have I regretted undertaking something that not even the most stupid person would have done if they had understood the danger.

—LI ZIBIAO, LETTER OF 20 FEBRUARY 1794 (ARCHIVES OF THE PROPAGANDA FIDE, ROME)

CONTENTS

ACKNOWLEDGMENTS

RESEARCHING AND WRITING this book has taken many years. I am immensely grateful to everyone who has helped me and also to all those friends and members of my family who have been willing to listen and talk for many hours about Li Zibiao and George Thomas Staunton, as well as the people mentioned below who provided inspirational ideas and conversation as well as practical assistance. In particular I would like to thank May Bo Ching of City University of Hong Kong for her ongoing enthusiasm and interest in the project.

For Li Zibiao's story Chai Bin now of Shanghai University and his former students at Lanzhou University kindly helped me to find the places where the Li family came from in Wuwei. Michele Fatica gave me access to the archives of the Università Orientale di Napoli in their beautiful setting. The Archives of the Propaganda Fide not only welcomed me but also kindly provided copies of some of Li's letters. Successive archivists of the General Curia of the Franciscans in Rome, who hold the transcriptions of Li's letters to the Chinese students, were wonderfully welcoming. Li Wenjie of East China Normal University and Cao Xinyu of Renmin University both helped with the search for Qing archive materials and were willing to hold long conversations on Qing officialdom and the embassy. Xia Mingfang of Renmin University recommended me to the First Historical Archives in Beijing and Qiu Yuanyuan of the Chinese Academy of Social Sciences was both helpful and inspiring when I arrived there. In Shanxi Father Zhang of Changzhi diocese arranged interviews for me in Machang and Zhaojialing where Li Zibiao lived in his old age. In England Muriel Hall and Mary Keen both discussed points of Latin translation at great length and gave me many new ideas, while Catherine Keen of University College London helped me with the Italian.

For the Stauntons Peadar O'Dowd of the Galway Historical Society guided my understanding of the Irish background. Gabrielle Lynch Staunton and her family kindly gave me permission to see

George Thomas's bank account in the Coutts Archives. Margret Frenz of the University of Stuttgart helped me with material on Indian interpreters. Jordan Goodman generously lent me his photocopies of Macartney's papers now in the Toyo Bunko in Japan. Xu Maoming of Shanghai Normal University found the Chinese version of Macartney's letter of credentials in the National Archives in London. Lawrence Wong provided detailed and helpful disagreement with several statements in an earlier article. Celia Duncan, who is descended from Hochee, sent me her father's family history, and Janet Bateson of the RH7 History Group checked his immigration status for me. Helena Lopes provided me with reading suggestions on Rodrigo da Madre de Dios in Macao. Hannah Theaker kindly did some research for me in the First Historical Archives when, at the end of the project, I realised that I needed to know about Yuan Dehui's activities in Beijing in the 1830s.

Maris Gillette and her colleagues at University of Missouri–St. Louis commented on an early chapter. Alexander Statman and Max Oidtmann not only read the entire manuscript but wrote wonderful comments. In addition I benefitted greatly from talking to Devin Fitzgerald and Michael Sharkey about translation and other topics. David Cox kindly altered John Barrow's 1796 map to make the route of the embassy stand out. Duke University Library, Keele University Library, and the publishers Adam Matthews all found and provided documents on Staunton. I am also very grateful to the Bodleian librarians and especially Joshua Seufert and Mamtimyn Sunuodula.

Some material was previously published in "A Faithful Interpreter? Li Zibiao and the 1793 Macartney Embassy to China," in "Transformations of Intercultural Diplomacies: Comparative Views of Asia and Europe (1700–1850)," ed. Nadine Amsler, Henrietta Harrison, and Christian Windler, *International History Review* 41, no. 5 (2019).

The Li Family of Liangzhou

Li Zibiao 李自標, also known as Jacobus or Giacomo Ly,
Mr Plum and Jacobus May or Mie 乜

Li Fangji, his father

Li Zichang 李自昌, his older brother, an officer in the Qing
army

Li Jiong 李炯, Li Zichang's son, a Confucian scholar

Francesco Jovino di Ottaiano, also known as Mai Chuanshi
麥傳世, a missionary

The Stauntons of Galway

George Thomas Staunton, also known as Sidangdong 斯當東

Sir George Leonard Staunton bart., his father

Jane Staunton, née Collins, his mother

John Barrow, his mathematics tutor, later secretary to the
Admiralty

Johann Christian Hüttner, his classics tutor

Benjamin, a slave purchased in Batavia to look after him

A Hiue, a boy who was brought to England to speak Chinese
to him

Wu Yacheng 吳亞成 Assing (or Ashing), formally known as
Wu Shiqiong 吳士瓊, who came with the family to London
in 1794 and later went into the trade

Peter Brodie, George Leonard's friend who married Jane's
sister **Sarah** and their children, especially the doctor **Benjamin Collins Brodie** and lawyer **Peter Bellinger Brodie**

Thomas Denman, a cousin, later Lord Chief Justice

George Lynch, George Thomas's heir, and other Irish cousins
from the Catholic **Lynch** family

The Qing

The **Qianlong** 乾隆 emperor, reigned 1736–99
The **Jiaqing** 嘉慶 emperor, reigned 1796–1820
The **Daoguang** 道光 emperor, reigned 1820–50
Heshen 和珅, Qianlong's favourite, in charge of the empire's finances
Fukang'an 福康安, a successful general, and his brother **Fuchang'an** 福昌安
Zhengrui 徵瑞, a tax expert close to Heshen
Songyun 松筠, a Mongol border expert deeply committed to Confucian morality
Liang Kentang 梁肯堂, governor general of Zhili and two members of his staff who escorted the Macartney embassy: **Qiao Renjie** 喬人傑, an official in charge of the salt monopoly, and **Wang Wenxiong** 王文雄, an army officer
Heshitai 和世泰, the Jiaqing emperor's brother-in-law
Suleng'e 蘇楞額, an official with a long career in the Imperial Household Department
Guanghui 廣惠, Zhengrui's successor during the Amherst embassy
Zhang Wuwei 張五緯, Qiao Renjie's successor during the Amherst embassy
Lin Zexu 林則徐, the imperial commissioner sent to suppress the opium trade in 1838
Yuan Dehui 袁德輝, an English and Latin translator
Governors general of Guangdong and Guangxi: **Guo Shixun** 郭世勳, who handled the announcement of the Macartney embassy; **Changlin** 長麟, an aristocrat and his austere cousin **Jiqing** 吉慶; **Wu Xiongguang** 吳熊光, who dealt with the 1808 British occupation of Macao; and **Jiang Youxian** 蔣攸銛, who was very cautious

The British

King **George III**, reigned 1738–1820, but suffered from severe mental illness from the 1780s and was replaced by his son, later **George IV**, as Prince Regent in 1810

William Pitt, prime minister, and his foreign secretary, **Henry Dundas**

George Macartney Earl of Lissanoure, first ambassador to China in 1793

Jane Macartney, his wife, the deaf but politically active daughter of the Earl of Bute

Edward Winder, **John Crewe**, and **George Benson**, Macartney's Irish relatives

William Alexander, the junior artist

William Pitt Amherst, Baron Amherst of Montreal, who led the 1816 embassy to China

Henry Ellis, illegitimate son of the Earl of Buckinghamshire, who accompanied him

Henry John Temple, better known as **Lord Palmerston**, foreign secretary

Charles Elliot, superintendent of trade in Canton during the Opium War

The Catholic Church

Guo Yuanxing 郭元性, also known as Vitalis Kuo, a friend of Li Zibiao's father

Guo Ruwang 郭儒旺 (Giovanni Kuo, alias Camillus Ciao), Guo Yuanxing's nephew

Li Zibiao's Naples classmates: **Yan Kuanren** 嚴寬仁 (Vincenzo Nien), **Ke Zongxiao** 柯宗孝 (Paulo Cho), **Wang Ying** 王英 (Petrus Van), and **Fan Tiancheng** 范天成 (Simone Fan)

Gennaro Fatigati, the head of the College for Chinese in Naples

Giovanni Maria Borgia, only son of the Duke of Vallemezzana, Li Zibiao's friend

Giambattista Marchini, who was in charge of the finances of the China mission in Macao

Lorenzo da Silva, the multilingual servant of a French Lazarist missionary in Macao

Bernardo d'Almeida, a Portuguese ex-Jesuit in Beijing

Rodrigo de Madre de Dios, head of the translation office in Macao

Giambattista da Mandello, a Franciscan, Vicar Apostolic (bishop) of Shanxi, and his successors **Luigi Landi** and **Gioacchino Salvetti**

The Trade

Francis Baring and **William Elphinstone**, chairmen of the directors of the East India Company in London

Henry Baring, **George Baring**, and **John Elphinstone**, their sons whom they placed in the company's offices in Canton

Pan Youdu 潘有度, known as Puankhequa, for many years the senior hong merchant, and his relative **Pan Changyao** 潘長耀, known as Consequa

Liu Dezhang 劉德章, known as Chunqua, and his son **Liu Chengshu** 劉承澍, a financial official in Beijing

Wu Bingjian 伍秉鑒, known as Howqua (or Houqua), who was close to the Americans

Zheng Chongqian 鄭崇謙 (Gnewqua), whose business failed

Antonio, the son of a Chinese linguist, who could speak Spanish

Li Yao 李耀 (Aiyou or Ayew), a brash young linguist

He Zhi 何志 (John Hochee), who moved to England

George Millet, an East India Company ship's captain

Ernest Gower, **William Drury**, **Francis Austen** (brother of Jane Austen), and **Murray Maxwell**, officers in the British navy

Robert Morrison, the first Protestant missionary to China, and his son **John Morrison**

Liang Fa 梁發 (Liang Afa), who was converted by Robert Morrison and his son **Liang Jinde** 梁進德

THE PERILS OF INTERPRETING

Introduction

EARLY ONE MORNING in the late summer of 1793, George Macartney Earl of Lissanoure, Britain's first ambassador to China, dressed in the robes of the Order of the Bath with ostrich plumes nodding over his head, knelt before the Qianlong emperor, and held up in both hands above his head a gold box set with diamonds containing a letter from George III.[1] Qianlong was the descendant of Manchu warriors who had conquered China in the seventeenth century. He spoke Chinese and Manchu and was proud of the fact that he could speak enough Mongol, Tibetan, and Uyghur to receive envoys from those areas without the need for an interpreter, but on this occasion an interpreter was essential.[2]

Macartney, who had made a grand tour of Europe in his youth, spoke in Italian. His words were expressed in Chinese by a younger man kneeling behind him, who had given his name as Plum and was dressed in a British uniform and a powdered wig but was in fact Li Zibiao a Catholic from China's far northwest.[3] Li had been educated in Naples and he spoke Chinese simply, rather than in the formal language of the court, but with deep respect for the emperor and a certain attractive sincerity that was characteristic to him. When he turned to Macartney he conveyed the emperor's remarks in elegant formal Italian. The emperor listened to a brief speech, asked a few polite questions, and presented Macartney with a jade sceptre.

When Macartney withdrew, his place was taken by his deputy George Leonard Staunton, a Jesuit-educated Irishman who was an enthusiast for the scientific discoveries of the age, a follower of Rousseau, a slave owner, a supporter of the recent French Revolution, and Macartney's long-standing friend, secretary, and henchman. The great project of Staunton's life was the education of his son, twelve-year-old George Thomas, who now knelt beside him. Li still interpreted, this time into Latin, but George Thomas could understand both sides of the brief conversation: his father had been speaking in Latin to him since he was three, and since his first meeting with Li the previous year George Thomas had also been studying Chinese. When the emperor asked if any of the British could speak Chinese, his chief minister Heshen, who had met Staunton earlier and had a gift for knowing what might amuse the elderly emperor, told him that the boy could speak a little and called him forward. George Thomas was shy, but when the emperor took a yellow silk purse that was hanging at his waist as a gift, he managed to get out a few words of thanks in Chinese.[4]

From beside the throne three of the most powerful men in the land looked on: the prince who would soon come to the throne as the Jiaqing emperor, Fukang'an, the emperor's favourite general who had recently returned from a successful campaign against the Gurkhas in Tibet, as well as Heshen, who controlled the empire's finances. There was also Songyun, a Mongol who had originally trained as a Manchu-Mongol interpreter and had just arrived back from the northern frontier where he had been renegotiating the Second Commercial Treaty of Khiakta with the Russians. After the audience and the banquet that followed, Qianlong ordered Fukang'an, Heshen, and Songyun to give Macartney a tour of the gardens, and while Macartney found Heshen evasive and Fukang'an arrogant, he had served in Russia himself and enjoyed Songyun's enthusiastic questions about Russian politics and government.

This is one of the most famous moments in the history of China's encounter with the West, and the Qianlong emperor in history, as in life, has always dominated the scene. He was in his eighties at this time, simply dressed in dark robes, sitting cross-legged on his throne, but he had been the autocratic ruler of a vast empire for nearly fifty years. Even Heshen and Fukang'an knelt down when they spoke to him, and he liked to be complimented on the fact that his was one of the most glorious reigns in Chinese history: with

rapid population growth after the century of warfare that had surrounded the fall of the previous dynasty, agriculture and trade were
flourishing, the Qing empire had reached its greatest size with the
completion of the campaigns against the Mongols and Zunghars in
the northwest, and the arts and scholarship were flourishing under
his patronage. Far away on the south coast of China, Europeans
had been drawn in by their desire for China's manufactures: fine
silk and porcelain that could still not be replicated in Europe. More
recently the trade with the British had boomed as Europeans and
Americans acquired a taste for tea, a crop grown only in China.

After the audience Qianlong decisively refused the British
requests for a resident ambassador in Beijing and an island off the
coast as a trading base. Soon people in Europe were saying that
he had done so out of anger that Macartney had merely knelt on
one knee, rather than bowing his head to the ground nine times in
the full court ritual of the kowtow.[5] Ever since, Qianlong has been
blamed for the failure of the embassy: as the Son of Heaven, who
claimed to be ruler of the civilised world and knew nothing of rising
British power, he had failed to realise that Macartney was anything
more than an envoy sent by a distant king to bring him tribute.

However, if we turn our gaze away from Qianlong and look
instead at the other people who were present, the embassy is
transformed. This is a book about the interpreters: Li Zibiao,
who interpreted for Lord Macartney, and little George Thomas
Staunton, who got a lot of the credit because his father wrote the
official English account of the embassy. They are fascinating figures because they were impressive linguists who became extremely
knowledgeable and well informed about the other's cultures and
also came to have a real affection for them. Both first travelled in
childhood and as a result came to understand the other's culture
with a particular fluency. This was intensified because they were
isolated from their natural peer group during crucial periods: Li
because he was much younger than the other Chinese students
at his Catholic seminary in Naples, and Staunton because when
he was sent to work in the East India Company's establishment
in Canton the young Englishmen there resented the appointment
of someone from outside their social circle. This isolation encouraged both Li and Staunton to form unusually strong cross-cultural

friendships as teenagers and young adults, which then shaped the way they saw the world later in life. Both were often homesick, and neither ever thought of himself as other than a foreigner in the other's continent, but after they returned home they were not quite like other people there either.

The stories of Li in his powdered wig and little George Thomas Staunton kneeling before the emperor show us how the encounter between China and Britain was not a clash of civilisations coming into contact for the first time but the result of the increasing global interconnections of the early modern world. The trade in tea that brought the British to China had its origins in the voyages of sixteenth-century Portuguese and Dutch mariners trading spices from Southeast Asia to Europe. In many places this trade had expanded into territorial rule, with the Dutch controlling much of Java and, for a while, a fort on Taiwan, while the Portuguese had trading outposts in Goa, Malacca, and also Macao on the south China coast. The Portuguese had also brought with them the first Catholic missionaries, whose successors were still working as artists, technicians, and astronomers at the Qing court. For nearly two centuries missionaries had been scattered across China: Li Zibiao was descended from a family of early Christian converts and had travelled to Europe through the global institutions of the Catholic Church.

Meanwhile Britain had built up settler colonies in the Americas but lost a large part in the wars of the American Revolution. By the time of the embassy the focus of British expansion had shifted to India, where small trading posts were being transformed into a colonial empire. George Leonard Staunton and Macartney had first met on the island of Grenada in the Caribbean, where Macartney was the newly appointed governor. When Grenada was captured by the French, Macartney found a new position as governor of Madras on the east coast of India, with Staunton as his aide. However, Madras was under constant threat from the expansive military power of Mysore; Macartney and Staunton returned home convinced that the new British Empire in India might fall as the first empire in the Americas had done. Now they had arrived in China on an embassy motivated by the British government's desire to expand the China trade to support and fund expansion in India.

George Thomas Staunton was born in 1781, the year his father set off for Madras, and as he grew up this interconnected world was reshaped by the expansion and consolidation of British power in India. Fukang'an, who had been campaigning against the expansive Gurkha state on the southern frontier of Tibet at the time of the Macartney embassy, had heard of the British as an Indian power, but they were not at that point a significant military issue for him. In the years that followed, however, what had been a string of small, and often threatened, British coastal possessions in India was transformed into a vast colonial state. The same process also brought the great warships of the British navy to hover threateningly off the south China coast in their wars against the French and Americans.

The early lives of Li Zibiao and George Thomas Staunton illustrate the extent to which by the time of the Macartney embassy China and Britain, Europe, and the Americas were already deeply interconnected through trade, religion, and finance. And from Li's point of view the Macartney embassy was a success: there were meaningful negotiations, even if the British did not achieve their original goals, and when the embassy departed both the British and the Qing officials were satisfied with the results and optimistic for the future. However, by the early years of the nineteenth century the position of people with the skills needed to interpret became increasingly dangerous. Staunton became a famous translator of Chinese and a banker for the British trade with China, but after the British naval occupation of Macao in 1808 two of his close Chinese friends were sent into exile, and he himself had to flee when the Jiaqing emperor, Qianlong's successor, began to threaten him personally. Jiaqing also cracked down hard on Catholicism as a foreign religion, driving Li into hiding and expelling the last of the European missionaries who had worked for the court since the arrival of the Jesuits in the sixteenth century. When in 1838 Lin Zexu, who was both intelligent and keen to discover more about the British, arrived to take charge in Canton with a policy on opium that was based largely on available written Chinese sources, he sometimes seemed to know even less than the Qianlong emperor had done. As a result he precipitated a war that many Chinese who had lived overseas or worked with the foreigners in the city must have known could not be won.

This book focuses on Li and Staunton as interpreters and thus on foreign affairs, but set against the backdrop of China's interconnections with the early modern world and its transformation into a world of imperialism and violent conflict. Those conflicts have long been explained by Qing China's ignorance of the outside world and in particular the difficulty of adjusting China's ancient tribute system to the new world of modern international relations. This idea has been deeply rooted since the nineteenth century, when British imperialists first saw it as an excuse for war. Later Chinese nationalists used it to attack the Qing dynasty and justify their own revolution, embedding it deep in the history of the modern Chinese state.[6]

The ideal of the Chinese state as the centre of civilisation to which outsiders would naturally come bringing gifts as a sign of homage was indeed both ancient and powerful. Indeed it has recently been revived by scholars of international relations in China who use it to explain and justify China's current aspirations to exert increasing influence in Southeast Asia and beyond.[7] However, for the Qing dynasty this was often a powerful ideal rather than a representation of the world as it was, at least from the point of view of the emperor. The dynasty was founded by Manchu warriors who conquered China in the seventeenth century, and the institutions they built to run their empire contained elements of their own heritage, which was significantly different from classical Chinese tradition.[8] Well into the nineteenth century decisions on relations with foreign states remained a prerogative of the emperor and his closest courtiers, many of whom were Manchu. As we have learned more of the details of their policy making it has become increasingly obvious that decisions were also driven by the practical politics of the day. The dynasty's changing relations with Korea, long seen as the model tributary, are one example of this, but so is the value of tribute items as a source of revenue to the state.[9]

We have also long been aware of the importance of contacts with Europe and later America: the Jesuit mission to China that began in the sixteenth century and the huge expansion of trade in the eighteenth century. The years after the Macartney embassy marked a crucial turning point in these contacts. Britain's empire, which had seemed near collapse with the loss of the American colonies, had shifted east and moved into a second phase with the consolidation of control in India. Mentally justifying colonial rule in India dramatically changed British ideas about non-Europeans and had a major effect on how they saw China and the Chinese. At the same time diplomatic relations between European states were also being transformed as the result of the French Revolution. For centuries European diplomacy had been negotiated between princes and emperors whose social status was a matter of formal hierarchy, but around the start of the nineteenth century the modern ideal of diplomacy between equal sovereign states was beginning to take hold.[10]

In China too this period marked a turning point, with the death of Qianlong revealing a financial crisis that was to dominate policy making throughout the nineteenth century. While Britain fought against France and accustomed itself to the new technology of a national debt that enabled it to build the massive warships that came to threaten the south China coast, the Qing struggled to raise sufficient finances for its everyday administration and was in no position to make major investments in the military.[11] This crisis drove Qing officials to policies controlling foreign contacts that deeply affected the lives of Li and Staunton. I argue that these policies were part of a wider reshaping of how Chinese saw the world as officials reinvigorated elements of classical thinking, including the rituals of the tribute system, as part of their political response to the British naval threat.

The lives of Li Zibiao and George Thomas Staunton help us to understand these changes because as interpreters they allow us to focus on exactly how contacts between states worked. Lawrence Wong, who sees translation problems as a key to understanding China's early relations with Britain, has written extensively on the interpreters of the period. Although in this book I argue that the threat of British naval power was the driving force behind Qing official ignorance of the West, I share Wong's argument that interpreting is crucial to diplomacy because translation between two languages as different as Chinese and English can never be a simple or transparent process.[12] Diplomatic interpreting is a powerful role, especially in a context with relatively few other people with the necessary language skills. During the Macartney embassy Li translated both into and out of Chinese, and most of the time no one else could understand what he was saying. Even today, when professional interpreters are often women imagined as invisible voices, diplomatic interpreting carries with it power: top leaders may have personal interpreters, and high-ranking diplomats may be called in to interpret for important negotiations.[13]

The power of the interpreter arises from the nature of translation. Today we often talk about flows of information from one place to another, but all information is shaped as it is presented. The translator begins by selecting what is to be made available and must then choose whether to stick closely to the original, in which case the translation is likely to sound exotic, or whether to write the text as if it had originally been written in the reader's language. When the information is being presented to political decision makers, these decisions are often crucial. The most famous example is the term *yi*, which was often used by the Chinese to refer to the British. Both Li and Staunton understood it to mean foreigners, but in the 1830s British writers in favour of war insisted on translating it as barbarian, a term that was widely picked up by British members of Parliament. Staunton complained vociferously that this translation was morally wrong because it "tends to widen the breach between us and the Chinese."[14]

The spoken interpreter must make all the same choices as a written translator but at speed and must also operate in a social context where cultural attitudes may be quite different between the two parties. Even the most accurate and professional interpreter today can convey only part of what is said, unless given a document to prepare in advance. Simultaneous interpreting, where the interpreter listens and speaks at the same time, is a twentieth-century invention. Previously all interpreting was consecutive: the interpreter listened to what was said and then expressed it in the other language.[15] In this context the interpreter's choices and decisions become even more important.

Spoken interpreting is a difficult subject for the historian because in an age before recording, the spoken word vanished instantaneously. We can only guess how Staunton and Li worked as interpreters from their written translations, complicated in Li's case by the fact that these are hard to identify and only fragments survive. As far as we know Li did not take notes, and it is unlikely that he could have remembered what Macartney had said word for word, so as he listened he had to decide what main points he needed to get across. He also had to choose the right tone and manner, which fitted with what Macartney wanted to convey and would be acceptable to the Qianlong emperor. What the emperor and his officials heard and how they responded would inevitably be shaped by Li's choices as interpreter as well as what Macartney had said.

Successful interpreting was far more than a matter of linguistic competence. Like many interpreters of this period, Li Zibiao often acted more as a negotiator than as a translator. Although there was an ideal of the interpreter as someone who simply translated spoken words from one language into another, that was not the normal expectation in the eighteenth century.[16] Interpreting for Macartney and Qing officials in Beijing, Li quite often shuttled between the two sides, who might not even be in the same room. He described this as explaining "the mind of the ambassador" to Qing officials.[17] This gave him a great deal of discretion, most notably to introduce an item of his own into the negotiations.

It was this power that made interpreting so dangerous. The interpreter's language skills were inevitably the result of deep immersion in the other side's culture, and national identity was obviously an issue that caused distrust. However, so were social class, institutional interests, and factional politics: Li was acting on behalf of Catholics rather than from loyalty to either Macartney or China when he added his own item to the British requests. For similar reasons both the British and Chinese governments were extremely nervous about allowing the vested interests in the Canton trade to influence negotiations between the two states. Macartney chose Li Zibiao as an interpreter in large part because he saw himself as acting on behalf of the British government and therefore wanted to avoid an interpreter connected to the East India Company. Much later, during the Opium War, Qing negotiators chose to accept British interpreters they loathed rather than use the Chinese merchants and their employees who could speak English.

The story of the interpreters teaches us the crucial importance of foreign language skills to dealing with another culture, the many problems of trust that this poses, and the dangers faced by interpreters when political tensions between states harden. In early nineteenth-century China that happened as a result of the expansion of British power in India. The argument of this book is that there were quite a few people in China who knew a great deal about Europe, but the British threat made that knowledge so dangerous that it came to be hidden.

The Macartney embassy has fascinated generations of historians in part because it is a puzzle. Macartney's diary is full of complaints that he could not understand why the Chinese officials he met behaved as they did. Today we know much more about Qianlong's official decision making from the Qing archives, but much remains unknown: Why was Macartney asked about wars that were taking place on the frontier of Britain's Indian empire in the Himalayas? What was the role of the dynasty's experts on its north-western frontiers in decision making about the British? How much did they know about the European powers? And how much did Qianlong himself know? We can discover only what was written down and preserved, but in the dangerous world of Qing court politics the closer men came to the centre the fewer private records they kept. Thinking about interpreting is valuable in part because it puts the informal meeting and the spoken word back at the heart of political decision making, and this reminds us how much there is that we cannot know. We remember that knowledge itself is a powerful political tool, and this puts the problem of knowledge back at the centre of our interpretation of China's relations with the West.

In addition, it is important to recognise that deception has always been part of diplomatic negotiations, and even genuine ignorance can be strategic for political decision makers.[18] Both the Chinese and the British wrote that the other side was naturally deceitful. This was not in fact always the case: the trade at Canton was successful because both sides were scrupulously honest in their dealings, and large deals relied entirely on the honour and credit of the merchants involved. However, there is no question that during the course of their diplomatic interactions both sides did at times deceive each other: on the famous question of whether or not Macartney fell to his knees and bowed his head to the ground before Qianlong the Chinese and English, evidence is contradictory: it is clear that some deception must have occurred. Even when we have written records of the negotiations we may not always be right to believe them.

This leads us into another puzzle: why was the Chinese state so badly informed about Britain in 1839 that its senior officials precipitated a war that they had no hope of winning? On the eve of the Opium War Lin Zexu, the imperial commissioner who had been sent to Canton to put down the British-dominated opium trade, wrote to the emperor that a war against the British was likely to succeed because their tightly wrapped legs made it hard for them to bend and stretch so they would be unlikely to fight well on land.[19] This implausible claim was made as part of a crucial decision-making process and after two centuries of intensive contact with Europeans. Part of the explanation is no doubt that, as has long been argued, Chinese elites placed a huge value on their own culture and looked down on the culture of others. It is also true that in China as in Europe elite adult men usually wanted to acquire their learning from books and not from common people like servants and seamen or even interpreters, who might in fact have a wider knowledge of the world.

Looking at Li and Staunton and the worlds in which they lived, we cannot simply say that Chinese people were ignorant of the West in this period. Ultimately readers of this book may still conclude that China in 1839 was isolated and ignorant of the West, but I hope you will be convinced that we need to think harder about who was ignorant and why. What knowledge of Europe existed in China in the early nineteenth century? And why did that knowledge not reach top decision makers? These are questions that are impossible to answer, but thinking about them is no less important for that reason.

Li Zibiao and George Thomas Staunton were asked to interpret because their language and cultural skills made them able to do so. They were not professional interpreters: Li was a Catholic priest and missionary, while Staunton's career in China was in trade as an employee of the British East India Company. However, unlike the professional linguists of the China trade whom we will also meet in this story, they interpreted for major diplomatic occasions, and it is possible to find out a great deal about them. Li wrote about his activities during the Macartney embassy to the Naples College and to church superiors in Rome. In later life he continued to write annual reports for them and also wrote extensively to the younger Chinese students in the Naples College. Staunton was a prolific author wealthy enough to publish seventeen books, mostly at his own expense, which present the versions of his life that he hoped would be handed down to posterity. He cautiously burned almost all his correspondence, but he did preserve his childhood diary of the embassy, and his mother kept his letters from China. These sources lead to others: records of Li Zibiao's brother's career in the Qing military, the letters of Staunton's friend Li Yao written from prison in Canton, and many more.

To put these stories in context, this study uses the archives of the three great institutions that dominated China's relations with the West in this period: the Chinese state, the Catholic Church, and the British East India Company. The lives of Li Zibiao and George Thomas Staunton were shaped by these institutions and have mostly been studied through them. Michele Fatica, who was the first to write about Li Zibiao and his role in the Macartney embassy, did so as an expert on the history of the college in Naples where Chinese were being trained for the Catholic priesthood from the mid-eighteenth century.[20] And Li Chen, who has written extensively on the impact of Staunton's ideas on Western understandings of Chinese law, sets his study in Canton's hybrid legal world in which commercial and criminal cases were constantly being negotiated between the two sides with their different legal traditions.[21]

The vast size and complexity of each of the great archives has meant that scholars have given lifetimes to studying each of them separately. Now the increasing number of archive publications and the availability of digital search engines make it possible to bring these archives together transforming our understanding of China's relations with the West in this period. Studies on the Jesuit mission to China have shown us Qianlong's grandfather Kangxi using his knowledge of Western mathematics to impress his courtiers and the personal networks that linked European and Chinese scholars in Beijing.[22] The vast archives of the Canton trade, which stretch far beyond those of the British East India Company, are also being explored to reveal a world in which hundreds of Chinese came in and out of the foreign warehouses every day, wealthy English merchants dined on turtle soup with their Chinese counterparts, and even elite Chinese spoke English and invested in America.[23] Scholars are now also beginning to uncover the ways in which the scale and value of this trade linked it to high politics in both Britain and China, not only through regular taxation but also through the Qianlong emperor's personal finances and the political influence of private British investors.[24]

In these archives Staunton and Li have a wealth of names that reflect the complexity of naming practices at the time combined with the cross-cultural histories that are at the centre of the this book. Staunton's mother had him christened Thomas, and this was the name he used as a child, but when George Leonard Staunton returned from India he wanted his boy called George like himself. So after his father's death he was usually addressed as Sir George and published as Sir George Staunton. In Chinese he was usually known as Sidangdong. To avoid confusing the reader I use his full formal name, George Thomas Staunton, and call his father George Leonard Staunton. Li Zibiao too I call by his formal name even though he probably never used it: as a child in China he would have been known by a nickname, and his surviving letters are signed Jacobus Ly or Giacomo Li and later in life, after he changed his surname, Jacobus May. The English called him Mr Plum (a translation of Li) but addressed him as Padre (Father) or Domine (Master). He is remembered in the Chinese village where he worked as Father Mie, which may have come from a translation of the English word "plum" back into another Chinese equivalent *mei*, but which also means Father Who (or Mr Nobody) in Cantonese.

The same complications apply to many of the other characters in this book, especially those based in Guangdong, where pidgin English was common. While the book is a biography of Li Zibiao and George Thomas Staunton, it also tells the stories of many others who lived between two cultures. There were young men known by nicknames that became their English names, like A Hiue, who came to England, and another friend of Staunton's, Wu Yacheng, who was known as Assing. Pan Youdu, the senior merchant who was Staunton's patron, is best known as Puankhequa, a business name that he inherited from his father and would pass on to his son, but Pan Youdu was also a Chinese scholar with relatives who were officials in the Qing court. Wherever possible I have used the modern transliteration of their Chinese names, even though these are often not the names by which they are best known. Giving the Anglicised names has the effect of smoothing over the very real differences between Chinese and Europeans and can also have the unfortunate result of implying that Chinese Catholics or people involved in the trade with Britain were somehow not quite Chinese. This is one of the mechanisms that has long excluded these people who lived in between cultures from national histories. I hope that this book will convince the reader that, on the contrary, they are an important part of those national histories.

PART I

Lives That Crossed
the World

CHAPTER ONE

The Li Family of Liangzhou

THIRTY-THREE YEARS BEFORE the Macartney embassy, in the twenty-fifth year of the reign of the Qianlong emperor, a younger son was born into a large family in the north-western Chinese frontier town of Liangzhou.[1] The family was called Li, and they gave their new son the name Zibiao. Since they were Catholics, they also gave their new son the Christian name of Jacobus (James). Many years later George Leonard Staunton commented that Li Zibiao "was a native of a part of Tartary annexed to China, and had not those features which denote a perfect Chinese origin."[2] Presumably the idea came from Li himself. By presenting his background in this way, he emphasized the aspects of life in Liangzhou that would lead to his role as interpreter: the recent rapid expansion of the Qing empire westward and the long history of contact between cultures in this frontier town.

Liangzhou, now known as Wuwei, is one of the towns on the ancient Silk Road. It lies on the edge of the Tibetan Plateau where water from the snow melting in the mountains flows out across a flat fertile plain before disappearing into the sands of the Gobi Desert that stretches across to the Mongolian steppe. Because of its location the town's history is a story of the shifting balance of power between Chinese, Mongol, and Tibetan states over the centuries. In the eighteenth century its mainly Chinese inhabitants looked back to the glories of the Tang dynasty (618–907), when a powerful and expansive Chinese state controlled the western trade routes and Wang Han wrote his Liangzhou Song:

> Fine grape wine in a jade cup that shines in the moonlight,
> I long to drink, but the music of the sitar player on his horse
>   rouses me.
> When I lie drunk on the sand, do not laugh at me, sir,
> Since ancient times how few of those who go out to war have
>   returned![3]

The poem is one of the most famous in Chinese literature, but the grapes, the music, and the jade cup were exotic to Tang readers, and beyond the city walls lies the desert. This is a place where Chinese culture was felt and expressed intensely precisely because it was on the frontier of the Chinese world.

The ancestor of the Li family had arrived in Liangzhou sometime in the seventeenth century, when the Ming dynasty collapsed in a series of destructive wars and was replaced by the Qing, whose Manchu rulers came from the frontier cultures of the northeast. The Li family came originally from Ningxia, another trading town with a long history of interaction between Chinese and central Asian peoples. They might have been merchants or soldiers or simply people fleeing from the fighting. All we know is that they identified as Chinese and that at some point members of the family joined a newly arrived religious sect and became Christians.[4]

Christianity reached this area as part of the expanding Qing state and with prestigious European missionaries whose scholarship ranged from astronomy to ancient Chinese texts, who worked on translating the Bible into Chinese, and who were also part of the imperial court. In 1697 the French Jesuits Antoine Thomas and Jean-François Gerbillon passed through Ningxia accompanying the Kangxi emperor on campaign. The Jesuits had already provided up-to-date European models for the armaments that were being manufactured for the war. Now in Ningxia Thomas predicted a partial solar eclipse. Kangxi had an official announcement sent out and called Thomas to his side to watch the eclipse and demonstrate the scientific instruments he had used.[5]

Just a few years later there was already a small group of Christian families in Liangzhou and in 1708 missionaries arrived there too. They were French Jesuits who also came on the emperor's orders: Pierre Jartoux and Jean-Baptiste Régis were mapmakers for Kangxi. As they travelled they measured the distances they covered and made frequent observations of the sun's meridian. They carried an unusually accurate clock, and by timing these observations, they could calculate their location in terms of longitude and latitude. In Liangzhou they observed a lunar eclipse, which they correlated with observations of the same eclipse made in Europe as a check on the coordinates they had established for the city, and on which they would base their map. They were also impressive scholars in Chinese: Jartoux wrote Chinese-language works on geometry and corresponded with the great German philosopher Leibniz, while Régis was known for having translated the ancient Chinese *Classic of Changes* into Latin.[6]

The Jesuits stayed only a few months in Liangzhou and were replaced by Italian Franciscans, under whom Christian conversions briefly boomed. Giovanni Maoletti made several visits and claimed to have baptised nearly a thousand people.[7] Francesco Jovino from Naples then took over and remained in the town for many years. He was a man of few words, who combined strong spirituality and unwavering obedience to his superiors with a gift for languages and distinctly scholarly interests. All this won him the support of the local Christians even after the death of Kangxi, when the practice of their religion became increasingly dangerous. That year there was a drought, and officials in the town made strongly worded announcements against Christianity, but Jovino was protected by an unnamed Christian prince passing through the town on his way back from the wars. The new Yongzheng emperor who came to power in 1723 condemned Christianity as a heterodox sect and expelled all missionaries who were not working for the court, but nevertheless Jovino was able to remain in the town under the protection of the provincial governor. Eventually he was forced to move to Canton, where he focussed on his studies of Chinese books, but it was not long before he returned to Liangzhou.[8]

Back in Liangzhou Jovino had to live secretly in the houses of the most devoted Christians, very likely the Li family. He wrote home to his family that only his converts' affection kept him going though badly cooked food, sleepless nights, terrible journeys, and even having to pull his beard with tweezers and cover his nose with paste in order to pass as a mule driver. Out of doors he was sometimes taken for one of the local Muslims (with their central Asian looks) and was terrified if anyone asked who he was. Most of the time, though, he was shut up in the house, "more closely enclosed than a nun," working on the massive task of making the first ever translation of the Old Testament into Chinese. No doubt he also spent much time in prayer since he wrote a Chinese manual on Christian meditation.[9] When Jovino died in 1737 he was buried in the Li family graveyard.[10] No further missionary came, and the Christian community quickly declined. In 1746 a crackdown by the provincial governor netted twenty-eight Christians, five of them in Liangzhou. They told him that the foreign missionaries were gone and there had been no recent conversions. In time the total number of Christians in the town dropped from over a thousand to around a hundred.[11]

Meanwhile Liangzhou was booming. As Qing forces then moved further out west, they needed to be provisioned, and much of the business passed through the town. The stability the Qing created also allowed the old Silk Road trade route to be reopened and the irrigation system to be expanded.[12] The townspeople looked back to the glories of the Tang dynasty, but when a sophisticated official from the Chinese heartlands was posted there in the 1740s, he was horrified by the vulgar extravagance of the new rich:

> Today when a Liangzhou association invites friends and relatives, the guests arrive and find milk tea, sesame cakes, and deep fried dough sticks in great dishes piled high on the table, so that they are full even before the drinking starts. When the tea is finished, the table is set again this time with savoury dishes, huge wine jugs and large cups, spread all over it in confusion, so that even before the food is eaten the guests are also drunk. Then they put out five main dishes accompanied by four more plates, and a vast amount of food is left over, so that in the end the guest is drunk and stuffed so full that he throws down his chopsticks and longs to leave.[13]

FIGURE 1.1. Liangzhou in 1910 after the wars of the late nineteenth century had destroyed much of its eighteenth-century glory.

Despite this prosperity, it was more than twenty years before another Catholic priest visited Liangzhou. The man who eventually came in 1758 was suited to the times and a very different type from the quiet and ascetic Jovino. He was a colourful character: charismatic, intensely devout, massively ambitious, a big eater, and a smart dresser. But probably the most notable thing about him for the Liangzhou Christians was that he was Chinese. Guo Yuanxing was in fact from Shanxi, the home province of many of the merchants trading in Liangzhou. He had been born into a wealthy family (one uncle was a county magistrate) but orphaned early in life. At the age of seventeen he had converted to Christianity, and for nearly ten years he worked as an assistant to one of the European missionaries, who was hugely impressed and decided to send him to Naples, where a college had recently been established to train Chinese as priests. There he was an outstanding student and was complimented by the pope on his final examination, leaving him with a very high opinion of himself that was not always easy for later colleagues.[14]

The Li family had remained leaders of the small Christian community and welcomed Guo Yuanxing as they had Jovino. When he came again in 1761 he was able to baptise Li Fangji's new son Li Zibiao, who had born a year earlier.[15] It is possible that it was at this moment that Li Fangji first considered the idea of sending the child to train for the priesthood in Europe. This was a large family, so dedicating Li Zibiao to the church would not deprive Li Fangji of an heir. An older son, Li Zichang, already in his midtwenties, had joined the Green Standard forces based in the town as a regular soldier and embarked on a military career. Li Zichang would have been married by this age, so his son Li Jiong was probably around the same age as Li Zibiao. So Li Fangji already had a grandson as well as, very likely, other sons born in the years since Li Zichang's birth.[16]

Li Fangji's plans for this youngest son were no doubt linked to renewed hopes for the church. The Christian community in Liangzhou had begun to grow again and even acquired a new building to use as a church. It was still easy to get up a riot against the Christians, and the number of conversions was nothing like in the glory days of the 1720s, but nevertheless the church was growing: between the 1760s and 1790s the number of Christians in the town more than doubled.[17] The only problem was that it was so difficult for priests to get so far out west.

Although Li Fangji's ambitious plans were for the church, they reflected the atmosphere in the town at this time. Wealthy merchants in Liangzhou were also funding schools and scholarship through which they hoped to promote their sons to the highest levels of the national government. In the whole of the Ming dynasty only a single man from Liangzhou had achieved the highest *jinshi* examination degree. Now the Qing had declared generous new quotas for students from Gansu province. A purpose-built examination hall was constructed, and during the reign of the Qianlong emperor seven local men passed the highest examination degree in Beijing and earned posts as officials across the empire.[18]

Li Fangji shared these ambitions with other members of the Ningxia Li clan, and it seems likely that Li Zibiao started his education alongside his older brother's son Li Jiong. Since Li Jiong went on to pass the *jinshi* examinations, his education would have been grounded in the traditional Confucian texts. One account of a well-known Liangzhou school teacher at this time described how those who passed his schoolroom in the morning would hear only the teacher reading aloud, the students reciting, and the teacher beating the students. In the afternoon the teacher read while the students practiced writing. If they made a mistake he caned them on the hands so hard that the boys would heat a pebble and grasp it to take away the pain. Piles of pebbles built up outside the schoolroom door.[19]

All this was intensely Chinese, but Liangzhou was still a town at the edge of the Chinese cultural world, a place where there were other cultures with their own sophisticated civilisations. Here in Liangzhou the Chinese used the word *yi*, which would later so anger the British, simply to refer to the Mongols, while the Tibetans were called by another term for outsiders, *fan*. Mongol herders came and went from the pastures that lay between the city and the mountains. And at New Year the schoolboy Li would have seen the crowds of young Tibetan men and women, in their leathers with long strings of beads hanging from their waists, who came down from the mountains to the south not only to enjoy the Chinese folk performances but also to take part in the great Buddhist festivals in which giant masked figures performed terrifying dances to drive out demons.[20]

Interpreting and translation were a natural part of such a world. At the centre of the city was an ancient pagoda said to hold the remains of the fourth-century Buddhist monk Kumarajiva, famous as one of the first people to translate the Buddhist scriptures from Sanskrit into Chinese.[21] And the most powerful person to come from the area in this period was not a Chinese but a Tibetan Buddhist lama who became a diplomat and interpreter for the Qianlong emperor. Changkya Rolpé Dorjé was born in the mountains to the south of the city. As a young child he was selected as the new incarnation of a major Buddhist lama. When Qing forces consolidated their control over the Mongol and Tibetan tribes of the area in the 1720s, he was taken to the court in Beijing, where he studied Buddhist scriptures alongside the future Qianlong emperor. He spent much of his life translating Buddhist texts between Tibetan, Mongolian, Chinese, and Manchu. The emperor's trust in him meant that he also operated for the emperor as an interpreter and diplomat, conducting a series of missions to Tibet and interpreting when the powerful Panchen lama visited Beijing.[22]

The large Manchu garrison in Liangzhou also continued to use the Manchu language: those who passed the official examinations often entered government as translators.[23] But however different the Manchus might seem, it was not safe for Chinese to write about them as foreigners: Li Wenfang, one of Liangzhou's most successful scholars, was executed along with his son after his patron at court wrote a poem in which a single phrase was interpreted as a slur on the Qing dynasty.[24]

In 1771 Guo Yuanxing returned to Liangzhou with the exciting news that he been summoned back to Rome. With his encouragement Li Fangji and the other leading Christians of Gansu composed a letter to the pope requesting their own priest. They hoped that the priest could be a local man because of the difficult journey and harsh climate.[25] The letter reflected Guo's ambition to find a post where he would not be under the supervision of a European missionary, but it also expressed Li Fangji's hopes for his son: with the letter he handed Li Zibiao over to Guo to take to Naples to train for the priesthood. Li Zibiao was only eleven. He left no record of what it was like to set off on such a journey at that age. The only thing we do know is that for the rest of his life he would be loved by almost everyone who knew him. It seems likely that his childhood as a youngest son of a large family had given him a certain confidence and courage to accept his father's decision.

They would travel by sea, so they set off south toward the Portuguese colony of Macao on the south coast of China. The journey took a year, travelling on foot and by boat. Guo was also taking a young man from Ganzhou, further out along the Silk Road, who had been working for him. They were joined by another young man from the provincial capital of Lanzhou, and Wang Ying, from one of the villages near the great city of Xi'an. In Macao the group expanded to include three young men who had come down from Beijing with another priest. Two of them were the sons of officials, including the seventeen-year-old Ke Zongxiao. There was also He Mingyu from Sichuan. Most of the group were already in their late teens and early twenties. Wang Ying and He Mingyu were fourteen and fifteen years old. Li Zibiao was by far the youngest.[26]

In the end Guo did not travel with them to Europe after all; the summons had been a mirage produced by his own hopes and ambitions. Nevertheless, he remained much involved: these boys were still his project, and he wanted it to go well. The church authorities in Macao had been expecting only three students, but he persuaded them to take all eight. He then hurried round sorting out their new European-style clothes and Western cutlery. They needed several sets of shirts and breeches as well as socks, shoes, jackets, and hats. Then for the voyage there was bedding, towels, napkins, cutlery, tea and a bowl to drink it from, as well as ink, pens, and paper for their lessons. With everything finally sorted out, Guo saw them off on two French ships sailing for Mauritius. From there they sailed on round the southern tip of Africa and north toward Europe, where they arrived in Paris, before travelling south across France to Marseilles and on by ship to Naples.[27]

Li Zibiao could travel from Liangzhou to Naples because he had been born into the Catholic Church, one of the great global institutions of the early modern world. It was also a reservoir of knowledge and learning. Christianity arrived in Liangzhou precisely because the Kangxi emperor was making use of the Jesuits' European learning for his military and state-building ambitions. In the context of these close connections with the court, quite a number of the Europeans who chose to go to China as missionaries at this time, especially the Jesuits but also Franciscans like Francesco Jovino, became serious scholars of Chinese. And Li Zibiao was only one of forty Chinese boys and young men who studied at the Naples College during the reign of the Qianlong emperor. They came from Christian communities across China, and Guo Yuanxing was not unusual in wanting to send young men of good family since this was an important marker of status once they arrived in Italy. Coming from Chinese families where study was a key route to success, these young men too expected to improve themselves through study of European languages and learning.

CHAPTER TWO

George Leonard
Staunton of Galway

THE YEAR THAT Li Zibiao set off on his long journey to Naples, 1771, was also the year that George Leonard Staunton and Jane Collins met and married. Their son George Thomas Staunton was not born for another ten years, after two older children died in the Caribbean. Like the Li family, the Stauntons came from a multilingual town on the periphery of an expanding state, but while the Qing was expanding overland, Britain was building a maritime empire: this new empire took George Leonard Staunton from his home in Ireland to the Caribbean and on to India. In his old age George Thomas reflected that his career had been made for him.[1] It was his brilliant, ambitious, excitable father who took all the decisions that made it.

The Stauntons were descended from an English soldier who obtained land near the Irish port of Galway during the seventeenth-century conquest of Ireland. In the aftermath of those wars English laws placed Irish Catholics at constant risk of having their property confiscated and made it impossible for them to hold political office. One of the wealthiest Galway families, the Lynch, evaded these laws partly by marrying their daughters to the Protestant Stauntons. Over several generations Staunton men were Protestants active in the town government, but they were seen as acting in the Catholic interest and their wives were often Catholics from the Lynch family.[2]

George Leonard Staunton came from this complex heritage, an English Protestant by formal identity but also an Irishman with close links to the Catholic Church. A thin, fair, intense boy, he was born in 1737 and spent a happy childhood in what his son later talked about as a castle but was actually a very small fort in a Gaelic-speaking district on the banks of Loch Corrib. George Leonard's father, who was an eldest son, had expected to inherit the estate according to English custom, but the Lynches had drawn up a marriage settlement that divided it between all the children equally, as was the Irish practice, so the fort was sold and the family moved into Galway town.[3] When he was sixteen, like many local Catholics, he was sent to a Jesuit college in France, from which he went on to spend four years at medical college in Montpellier. The Jesuit education was in Latin, so by the end of his time in France he could speak both French and Latin fluently as well as English and very probably also the Gaelic that had been spoken around him in his childhood. His intellectual interests were in the natural sciences, and his political sympathies were revolutionary: he was excited to travel across France with an Irishman who had been tried for rebellion against the English and had later escaped from the Tower of London.[4]

George Leonard's first thought after he completed his medical training was to go to London, but although he made many friends there he was unable to find a position. Instead he set off to work as a doctor in the West Indies, where many of his Lynch relatives had investments.[5] These were the boom years of the sugar plantations of the Caribbean; both English settlers and African slaves were dying of disease in huge numbers. The risks a doctor faced were terrible, but the potential profits were proportionately great.

George Leonard survived, settled in Grenada, which had recently been ceded to Britain by France, and began to send money to his family. His letters home were chatty, and one can hear his Irish accent and his charm as he took an interest in events back home: "I don't think there ever was such doings anywhere as at Galway, one would imagine the men of that Corporation are distracted, sure never was such an Ellection for Wardens."[6] The white settlers in Grenada were mostly French Catholics easily won over by this young doctor with his excellent French and his Catholic sympathies. With their support he became secretary to the new governor, causing uproar in the London press, which supported the new Protestant Scottish settlers.[7]

George Leonard was now convinced that he could make his fortune in a couple of years if only he had the money to invest in an estate. He returned to England to raise the capital and found that one of his London friends, Peter Brodie, who aspired to a career in the church, had rented a cottage in the village of Winterslow near Salisbury to further his friendship with Stephen Fox, son of the Whig political grandee Lord Holland who had an estate there.[8]

Like others in these circles, George Leonard Staunton and Peter Brodie would have heard the inspiring story of George Macartney, who had risen through Lord Holland's patronage and had recently made a spectacular marriage. Macartney was the son of an Irish landowner and had inherited some money from an uncle, a member of the Irish Parliament. Macartney invested this in a grand tour of Europe. In Geneva he met Stephen Fox and gambled with him for stakes he could not afford, but the steady friendship that resulted won him the support of Stephen's father Lord Holland and access to the upper circles of London's elite. With Lord Holland's support, he was given a knighthood and sent to Russia on a diplomatic trade mission to Catherine the Great on the grounds that his good looks and polished manners would be helpful in negotiations with a female ruler. On his return he married Jane Stuart, daughter of the powerful former prime minister the Earl of Bute. They shared a real interest in politics, but she was famously plain and already suffering from quite severe hearing loss. She married him, desperately hoping that he actually liked her. With her father's help, Macartney was then appointed chief secretary to the lord lieutenant of Ireland.[9]

George Leonard Staunton and Peter Brodie always felt that this kind of career was what the world owed them, but in practice George Leonard needed money immediately and there was a wealthy banker in Salisbury with four unmarried daughters. Benjamin Collins was a tough businessman who had made his fortune as a printer and was now the owner of a successful Salisbury newspaper with investments in many of the successful London periodicals of the day. Recently he had diversified into moneylending and now described himself as a banker.[10] Less than four months after arriving in England George Leonard married Benjamin Collins's daughter Jane. She was an affectionate but timid and rather anxious girl brought up by a stern business-minded father and presumably fell for George Leonard's dashing confidence and charm.

Benjamin Collins was a good deal less enthusiastic: he gave his daughter £1,253 as a marriage portion, and an annual income of £400. In addition, and on the wedding day, he presented George Leonard with a mortgage for £4,000 to be used to purchase a plantation that was to be jointly owned with Collins's eldest son and for which he was to pay Collins an annual rent of £500. The marriage portion was less than the rent, and the mortgage was far less than the sum needed to purchase the estate outright. Alongside his charm George Leonard had a fiery temper, and he resented the settlement for the rest of his life.[11] It was not a good start to the marriage.

The young couple set out for Grenada, where Jane soon gave birth to her first child, a little girl called Margaret who died, and George Leonard's financial affairs did not go well.[12] Then George Macartney, who had now been given the title Lord Macartney in honour of his new post, arrived to take over as governor. The two men had much in common and got on well. Macartney's opinion was that George Leonard was a gentleman "of a liberal education, enlarged mind, uncommon industry and information, and one of the best head-pieces I have ever met with."[13] Lady Macartney, who entirely outclassed everyone else on the island in social rank, was also kind to Jane Staunton. Both of them had troubles at this time: Lady Macartney was still childless, while Jane Staunton lost a second child a boy, whom they had called George after his father.[14]

George Leonard had eventually managed to put together the money to buy a plantation by taking out a huge loan and now had an estate on the island with slaves to work it. A few years later when Benjamin Collins began to pursue him for debt over the interest payments on the mortgage of the estate, he agreed to secure them with a mortgage of £617 on his slaves.[15] Faced with criticism of slavery a few years later, he claimed that people have fewer needs in a warm climate and that slaves in the West Indies were little worse off than many European peasants.[16] Such attitudes were not, of course, uncommon. Macartney shared his indifference, but Macartney was a cynic who thought it "too idiotic to give freedom to the French and to negroes."[17] George Leonard was a political radical whose ideas about the Chinese were to prove very different indeed. He never explained what made him think it right to buy, sell, and even mortgage, some people and not others.

The outbreak of the American Revolution was the final disaster that destroyed George Leonard's West Indies ambitions. When the French supported the Americans, war broke out between Britain and France, and in 1779 Grenada fell to the French. George Leonard's estate was looted, and British property was confiscated. He gave some of his property secretly to friends, but it was unlikely he would ever get much of it back. His attitudes toward the Africans he had bought were sharply revealed when he wrote to his parents, "my loss in goods, cattle, slaves, furniture etc was very considerable."[18] Then he and Macartney, as the most senior British officials on the island, were sent as hostages to France. Jane travelled with them and had the horrific experience of looking on as the ship sailing alongside sank in a storm and all those on board drowned.[19] She seems to have decided that whatever her husband might do she was never going to sea again.

The shared experience of disaster cemented the friendship between Macartney and George Leonard. Both of them were heavily in debt and desperate for employment. Macartney set to work to win a position that was coming up for governor of the English colony in Madras and made sure that Staunton would go as his secretary.[20] Lady Macartney was agonised about whether or not to go with her husband, writing to her sister, "Shall I go and make my mother miserable, or shall I stay and totally give up all prospect of cordiality and friendship with Lord M."[21] Jane Staunton was pregnant again and stayed with her parents, though George Leonard urged her to come out to India with Lady Macartney after the child was born.[22]

So George Thomas Staunton was born at his grandfather's house near Salisbury shortly after his father set sail for Madras in 1781. Peter Brodie, who had by now married Jane's sister, wrote to George Leonard with the news.[23] Jane wrote later, enclosing a lock of the baby's fair hair and assuring her husband that the baby looked just like him:

> His forehead is also like yours, his eyes mine, and nose bears I think no resemblance to either, as well as his little mouth, which is too handsome for yours or mine, but in his shape and limbs, which are perfectly well made, he takes after you, and even in many of your ways, for he only wants a book in his hand to compleat the manner in which you used to go to sleep, with his little hand lay'd under his cheek, just the posture you used to read yourself to sleep in, and Mrs Clemson says he wakes also as you do in the morning, which indeed I cannot be so good a judge of, as I was not quite so earlier a riser as herself.[24]

In later life, George Thomas really did look very much like his father, with his pale Irish skin, fair hair, and small frame.

For now George Leonard, who had gone to court with Benjamin Collins over who should bear the costs of the losses in Grenada, was certainly not going to allow his son to be brought up by his wife's family. He had sailed out to Madras from Limerick, which allowed him to visit his family in Galway, and Jane soon discovered that George Leonard had promised his mother that she was to have the baby while Jane herself would come out to India. Jane begged her mother-in-law to wait, writing, "Madam you must not blame me (who have lost two children) for being alarm'd at the idea of his travelling (while an Infant) so far and part of the way by sea."[25] Nevertheless, shortly after his first birthday she sent George Thomas off to Ireland with his nurse. Two years later she was still trying to get him back, but his grandmother who called him "one of the lovelyest boys that ever was" and clearly adored him insisted that she would hand him over only to his mother. Jane was obviously not willing to travel to Ireland.[26]

Meanwhile Macartney and George Leonard were in India. Their experiences there would shape George Thomas's future and many aspects of their later attitudes to China. After living through the capture of Grenada by the French and then the defeat of a British army by a south Indian ruler, they came to believe, as others did at this time, that Britain's overseas empire might easily collapse. They learned that wars are fought on the basis of logistics and provisions and that credit and finances rather than weapons technology can be crucial to victory. And finally, during the negotiations that ended the war, George Leonard became aware of the power of interpreters and came to hope that his son could fill this role.

Behind the situation the two men found when they arrived in Madras in 1781 lay the complexity of the relations between the British government and the East India Company. The company was originally set up as a trading organisation with a monopoly on Britain's trade with the East Indies. During the course of the eighteenth century its power and wealth in India grew to the point where it had its own army and began to acquire large areas of territory. By 1781 it controlled the state of Bengal as well as the major ports of Madras and Bombay. Some British families had made spectacular fortunes and many had profited, but the government wanted to control the opportunities for such splendid patronage, and many British people felt threatened by the existence of so much money and power in the hands of a private company. There were accusations of corruption and abuse of power. Madras was at the centre of these accusations, since British private investors had lent a vast sum of money to a relatively weak local ruler, the Nawab of Arcot, and when as a result of the ongoing wars he was unable to repay them, they had called for the military to help them reclaim the debt. In the midst of these disputes, the previous governor sent out from London had died during a coup members of his council had launched against him with the backing of James Stuart, the senior British military officer.[27]

It did not take Macartney long to realise that matters were far worse than he had expected when he left London. The East India Company was only one among several powerful and expanding states in India that were profiting from the collapse of the Mughal Empire. Their major competitor in south India was Mysore, which had now been drawn into the wars against the British through an alliance with France. Mysore's forces had devastated the land for fifty miles around Madras, while French ships were threatening to interrupt the supply of grain by sea. Macartney found "despondency, almost despair prevailing in every mind, all credit lost, government despised, no resources either of treasure or abilities to support it."[28] Staunton was even more discouraged: "As to public

affairs here, they are in the same uncertain, and, I fear, dangerous state, with the rest of the British Empire. . . . If we have not a
peace soon with the powers of this country, we must, as a state, be
ruined."[29]

Macartney was responsible for funding and provisioning the
campaign against the Mysore army. The general in charge was desperate for provisions and livestock to transport them. He might win
a pitched battle, but he could not force one because his horses were
dying from lack of fodder, and even when he did win he still had
to withdraw because of the lack of provisions. The British problems in logistics and finances were not outweighed by any significant advantages in military technology or discipline. Madras was
saved only when the British government finally accepted American
independence and the war with France ended, which allowed ship-
ments by sea to reach the city.[30]

The war with Mysore, however, continued and as British defeats
mounted tensions in Madras were running high. Macartney and
General James Stuart bickered over who had ultimate authority
over the army, and Macartney became convinced that Stuart was
planning the same kind of coup he had launched against the previous governor. It was George Leonard Staunton who led a company
of Indian soldiers up the stairs of Stuart's house, drawn sword in
hand, and intimidated the British officers into accepting Stuart's
arrest.[31] And when it became obvious that the British could not win
and would need to seek a peace treaty with Tipu Sultan, the new
ruler of Mysore, it was George Leonard who acted for Macartney.
Macartney wrote to him, "Upon your judgment, address, and integrity, I solely rely for the happy accomplishment of this business, in
which not only my reputation and future lot of life may depend, but
the salvation of the British empire in this part of the world."[32]

George Leonard and Anthony Sadleir, one of the senior East
India Company merchants, set off across India to negotiate the
peace treaty, taking with them a train of more than a thousand
people and two elephants. George Leonard was acting on behalf
of Macartney and, ultimately, the British state, whereas Anthony
Sadleir was representing the East India Company and the interests of the Madras trade. Tensions between them blew up over the

issue of interpreting. Written translation of diplomatic correspondence, which was in Persian, was undertaken by David Halibur-
ton, who held the office of Persian translator in Madras, but he was
not able to act as a spoken interpreter of the relevant south Indian
languages and had not accompanied the embassy. To interpret
Sadleir had brought with him one Choleapah Moodely, who was
his *dubash*. The term literally means interpreter, but the *dubash*
combined interpreting with the related roles of advisor and private
investment manager, a practice that the East India Company would
later carry over to those who worked with it in China. In Madras
the interpreters were thus often both powerful and wealthy in their
own right. Moodely was clearly a man of considerable ability, had
a strong personal relation with Sadleir, and soon became the chief
channel of communication with the Mysore agents.[33]

The disputes began when the agents held a series of meetings to negotiate directly with the interpreters, rather than with
George Leonard and Sadleir. An English secretary attended to
write notes, but Sadleir rejected his report on the grounds that
Moodely had given him a different version of what had been said.
The secretary insisted that he had omitted only repetitions and
"compliments agreeable to oriental custom and policy."[34] The
issue, of course, was what part of what had been said should be
considered mere compliment and what was crucial to the negotiations. When Tipu Sultan's representative was asked for his version
of what had been agreed, it turned out that he had no record at
all of various complaints about the ill treatment of British pris-
oners important to George Leonard.[35] George Leonard Staunton
was horrified when Tipu Sultan himself acknowledged Moodely's
importance by asking after him personally as soon as the British
arrived at his camp.[36]

George Leonard thought that Moodely was planning to create
a situation where Tipu Sultan would bribe him, and possibly also
Sadleir, to act against the interests of the British state. However,
George Leonard never suggested that the interpreters as Indians
might not be loyal to British interests for the simple reason that
British interests were not uniform: the interests of the East India
Company and its Madras staff were in direct conflict with the inter-
ests of the British government. Instead he condemned Madras

dubashes as a group on the grounds that their occupation as middlemen was likely to make them prone to corruption.[37]

George Leonard's response to Moodely's power was to propose a quite different role for the interpreters. First he demanded that he and Sadleir should be present at all meetings. The proper behaviour of interpreters was what he claimed had happened at the beginning of the embassy, when the interpreters were concerned "simply in translating every separate sentence or words as it was spoken on either side, but the subjects, the argument, the method, the whole scope of the discussion depended on the principals."[38] The very fact that this idea had to be spelled out as a demand reminds us that it was not what was actually happening.

In the end the Treaty of Mangalore, which ended what became known as the Second Anglo-Mysore War, required both Mysore and the British to return all the territory taken during the war. It was widely criticised in England, where the best that could be said for it was that similar terms had recently been agreed with the French in Europe.

Macartney returned to England to fight a duel with General Stuart, whose arrest he had ordered. Macartney had so little idea about firing a pistol that he had to write instructions for himself in his notebook, but being willing to fight to defend one's honour, like gambling for high stakes, was part of the aristocratic male world that he now moved in. The two men agreed to fire pistols at each other at a distance of twelve paces. Before fighting Stuart he renegotiated the mortgage on his Irish estate and wrote a letter of farewell to his wife. Stuart had to be propped against a tree because he had lost a leg in the war, but taunted Macartney with not knowing how to cock the pistol. Unsurprisingly Macartney missed, but Stuart's aim was better and Macartney was hit in the shoulder. He recovered, though George Leonard, to whom Macartney had entrusted the letter to his wife, was sufficiently anxious to give it to her. She stored it up carefully as evidence, finally, of her husband's affection.[39]

George Leonard was rewarded for his embassy with a baronetcy, making him Sir George, and a pension from the East India Company of five hundred pounds per year. Macartney was building a career on a reputation for incorruptibility, but this did not apply

FIGURE 2.1. *George Macartney and George Leonard Staunton* by Lemuel Francis Abbott, 1785.

to George Leonard, who had used the opportunity to buy up some of the Nawab of Arcot's debts that had been at the centre of the original accusations. With his newfound wealth he bought back his father's estate and the fort by Loch Corrib and had himself painted sitting with Macartney and pointing to a map of India (fig. 2.1).[40]

CHAPTER THREE

Li Zibiao's Education in Naples

LI ZIBIAO ARRIVED in Naples at the age of thirteen in 1773. This was the city where he grew up, a city that he would love and remember for the rest of his life. There he received a classic European education, taught in Latin and training him in rhetoric, philosophy, and then theology. Being so much younger than the other Chinese students, his closest friendship was with one of his Italian classmates. As time went on and other Chinese students returned to China, he longed to go home with an intensity that made him ill, but while that was impossible he came to know the city even better as an adult member of the community.

Naples in the eighteenth century was one of the great cities of Europe. Arriving by sea, the Chinese would have seen Mount Vesuvius in the distance and close by the splendid new buildings on the waterfront (fig. 3.1). After centuries of Spanish rule, southern Italy had become an independent kingdom some forty years earlier and Naples was its capital. Aristocratic families from all over southern Italy came to Naples to be close to the new king and built magnificent houses. The last hundred years had also seen a wave of church building, which had added spectacular baroque buildings to what was already a large number of ancient and medieval churches, so that a single street might have five or more churches. Men, women, and children talked loudly in the streets, and the wheels

FIGURE 3.1. *Panoramic View of the Bay of Naples* by Gaspar Butler.

of carriages and carts rattling on the lava-paved streets (unlike the dust and mud of most towns) added to the racket. As the newly arrived Chinese walked higher up the side of the hill, the streets became narrower and darker, with only a small strip of sky visible high above. The houses in these new sections of the city were solid stone constructions five or six stories high, many of them owned by different religious orders. The old aristocracy tried to maintain their wealth and power by restricting the number of their children and grandchildren who could inherit, encouraging their other sons and daughters to enter religious orders. There they expected to live comfortable and leisured lives, provided for by their families, while their presence and lifestyles attracted other members of the upper classes to the same way of life.[1]

The College of the Holy Family of Jesus Christ, known to everyone as the Chinese College, was this type of establishment. It had originally been built as a private residence with fine views and a large enclosed garden that stretched up the hillside behind. Some forty years earlier the missionary Matteo Ripa had returned to Naples from the court of the Kangxi emperor convinced that the Jesuits were going about mission in the wrong way and that the best way to evangelise China was to train Chinese themselves for the priesthood. So he had recruited the first Chinese students and established a religious congregation to teach them.[2] Later, the college also accepted local students, whose fees became an important

FIGURE 3.2. The Chinese Church and College in the early nineteenth century. A man is entering the college's chapel, while the arched gateway leads into the college itself. Over the entrance is a sunny roof terrace with a garden looking out across the city and the bay.

part of its income.[3] When Li and his classmates arrived, they joined seven Chinese students, four from the Ottoman Empire, and fifteen members of the teaching congregation. The community as a whole consisted of perhaps fifty or sixty persons, ranging in age from schoolboys of eleven or twelve to the superior Gennaro Fatigati, who had been a close friend of Ripa and was now in his sixties.[4]

Although the college's aim was to train priests for evangelism, it was also a school. From the hall, with its frescoed entrance, the new Chinese students would have been taken upstairs to a large dormitory on the building's main floor, which they would share with the other Chinese.[5] Some weeks later there was a ceremony in which they were dressed in their new uniform: a black cassock with red bands.[6] There were four hours of classes on weekdays and regular study periods as well as daily mass and morning and evening prayers. In the middle of the day time was set aside for relaxing with the other students, a siesta, and a free period during which the students were encouraged to go out for a walk (though they were supposed to be accompanied by an adult member of the

FIGURE 3.3. The entrance hall of the Chinese College. In the centre of the emblem are the Chinese characters for the Holy Family and round the outside is the Latin motto "Go out into the whole world, and preach the gospel to all peoples."

community and were strictly banned from riding horses or visiting Mount Vesuvius), before they came back for their afternoon classes.[7]

The Chinese students were special for the college and also for the city, which was still influenced by ideas of China as a model of benevolent monarchy, ancient civilisation, and high philosophy. The fashion for such ideas, and the fanciful chinoiserie decorations that accompanied them, was declining elsewhere in Europe, but in Naples, with its powerful monarchy, it continued to be strong. To symbolise the importance of the Chinese Gennaro Fatigati, the superior of the college washed the feet of the Chinese boys when they first arrived and slept in their dormitory room. New students were presented at court, and the king was a major patron of the college. Members of the aristocracy visited from time to time and the students would be given the day off to entertain them and show them the Chinese objects in the college's collection.[8]

Classes began with basic Latin taught by one of the senior Chinese students.[9] Efforts to encourage schools in Naples to teach in Italian had begun a few years earlier, but Latin remained the language of education, the legal system, and much scholarly publication for the city well into the 1790s.[10] Li was young and picked up the language quickly, so that soon he knew enough to enter the college's regular classes.

There he found boys his own age and began to make friends. The boys from the Ottoman Empire were a tight-knit group and tended to resent the college's preference for the Chinese.[11] Instead Li made friends among the boys who came to the college to study from across southern Italy. These boys came because of the quality of the college's education: many of them were from wealthy and aristocratic families and were not destined for the priesthood.[12] Li's closest friend was Giovanni Maria Borgia, only son of the Duke of Vallemezzana. Li would later remember "that joining of our souls which began in our earliest years," and Borgia was the only person he continued to address all his life with the informal words for "you."[13]

Alongside these boys Li received the classical education that bound together the European elites of this period. Giambattista Vico, whose writings have often been used as a statement of the

FIGURE 3.4 A AND B. Chinoiserie porcelain boudoir created for Queen Maria Amalia in the royal palace at Portici in 1759. The Chinese writing is real, unlike that in most European chinoiserie. The Chinese students provided texts for the craftsmen to copy. Here a "distant minister" (*yuanchen*) presents praises to King Carlo.

philosophical foundations of a humanistic education, had been professor of rhetoric at the university of Naples. The education he described was not far from the education Li and his classmates actually received. They began with basic Latin grammar and arithmetic, then moved on to the study of rhetoric, reading all the major classical texts beginning with Cicero's speeches, then the poetry of Vergil and Ovid and even Lucretius's poetry on atoms. They were taught the art of public speaking by Felice Cappello, who published two of the textbooks he composed while at the college. The one on rhetoric urges the general importance of training in public speaking for careers in both the church and the law, though it ends with a section on the use of gestures and pronunciation for giving a sermon. The boys also studied Latin verse composition: a surviving notebook left by an unknown Chinese student is full of long Latin poems in various metres on topics ranging from the religious (choosing Christ over the world), through the political (a poem praising the queen, Maria Amalia of Saxony), to the romantic (the story of Cadwallader, king of Britain, who renounced his throne to save his kingdom).[14]

Because they were destined to return to China as missionaries, it was important that the students also continued to study Chinese. When Matteo Ripa had founded the college, he had brought a teacher from China, but by this time the arrangement was for one of the older Chinese students to teach the younger ones.[15] This role was soon taken over by one of the new arrivals Li Rulin, the son of a military official in Beijing who had received a good education there before he left for Naples at the age of nineteen.[16] The choice of texts seems to have been entirely conventional: the two books we happen to know were used in the college were a seventeenth-century literary anthology widely used as a textbook in China and a much later essay-writing manual for the civil service examinations.[17] A few years before Li's arrival the archbishop of Naples had threatened to close the college down if the students were not properly prepared for mission, which, in his opinion, required a good knowledge of the Chinese histories and chronicles, so presumably these were on the syllabus too.[18] The students also wrote essays on Christian themes: the surviving student notebook includes some rather poorly written Chinese meditations on death and on the nativity of Christ.[19]

Living with a small group of Chinese and studying from his older classmates would not have given Li Zibiao the skills to write Chinese well, but it was enough to maintain the fluency of his spoken Chinese and provide a basic training in the literary language.

Around the age of seventeen, Li Zibiao moved on to the specialist education needed for his future career as a priest. This consisted of courses in philosophy, then dogmatic theology, and finally moral theology. Dogmatic theology is the study of Christian doctrine. Moral theology is the study of ethics, and in this period involved debating ethical problems in order to prepare to hear confessions.[20]

Naples during this period was famous for the high emotion of its Catholic faith, but Enlightenment rationalism was also an important force in the church, and it was this that played the greater part in Li's education. Two of the archbishops of Naples had strong scientific interests, and this influenced the type of clergy who prospered in the city. Serafino Filangieri, who became archbishop in 1776, was an enthusiast for the works of Isaac Newton and had previously held a chair in experimental physics. He saw scientific research, especially physics, as a way of understanding the universe and therefore increasing understanding of God.[21] The impact of these rationalist influences on the education offered by the Chinese College can best be seen in a textbook by Felice Cappello titled *Catholic Sacred Instruction for Boys*. While this was published after Li had returned to China, it presumably reflected the type of teaching that Cappello had been engaged in since he joined the college many years earlier. It is a work of history and scholarship: a discussion of the origins of the tonsure quotes at length from Pliny writing about Christians in Bithynia in the first century as well as various then recently published Roman inscriptions. Moreover, although Cappello comes to the orthodox conclusions of his time, this is a text that values debate: his book presents arguments and counterarguments on all the major issues. On the subject of clerical celibacy he not only engages with the varying positions of the church fathers and Protestants but also speaks to the contemporary political debates of the day about the relations between population growth and the economy. The subtitle, *The Holy Teaching Concerning Clerical Orders Arranged in the Form of an Examination*, suggests that the textbook was intended for students preparing for examinations, and the implication is that in order to do well they would need to be able to explain the debates and their position in them.[22]

Alongside this fairly standard training, Li Zibiao was one of a small group of four Chinese and two students from the Ottoman Empire who arranged to study an extra year of metaphysics, a subject that sat on the borderline between philosophy, the new natural sciences, and theology.[23] He probably also studied Greek and Hebrew: Cappello uses quotations in Greek and Hebrew in his textbooks, and one of the other Chinese students complained about a classmate writing letters in elegant Hebrew but with no content.[24] Wang Ying, the student concerned, was academically much weaker than Li, so if he was studying Hebrew it seems likely that Li was too.

Li was an outstanding student. The school provided annual reports on each of the Chinese students to Rome, and when Li was sixteen Gennaro Fatigati wrote that he was "a boy younger than all the others but better than them all at Latin."[25] Two years later he described him as "a young man of excellent ability, wonderfully hard working, prudent, devout, exemplary" and a year later as "the best talent among all the Chinese, Levantines and Europeans, devout, wise, prudent, studious, observant."[26] He also wrote that he loved Li because he was always cheerful.[27]

The elderly Fatigati was a man of deep Christian spirituality, and from the moment of his arrival Li was his favourite student. Men who joined religious orders in Naples during this period often did so because their families wanted it or as their best option for a career, or simply for an easy life, but there were also some whose lives were entirely shaped by their faith, and Fatigati was one of these. He was hugely admired for having turned down the status and financial rewards of a bishopric in order to remain at the college and train the Chinese students.[28] His letters show him as someone who was always gentle, even when issuing a rebuke, and intensely biblical in his choice of language. His affection seems to have encouraged Li to internalise the values that he represented: Li's own later correspondence echoes Fatigati's spiritual style, something very unusual among the Chinese students, and suggests that he too came to speak easily in this way. The cheerful sincerity that others found so attractive in Li and his easy assumption that others would always respond well to him may have had its origins in his early years in Liangzhou, but it was also built out of his relationship with Fatigati.

Li's growing spiritual commitment seems likely also to have been shaped by his close friendship with Giovanni Borgia, who was struggling with a powerful sense of religious vocation in the teeth of strong family disapproval. As an only son and the heir to a dukedom, the same family strategies that pushed many young men into the priesthood decreed that he must marry and produce an heir. He eventually received royal permission to enter the priesthood, but not until long after Li and the other Chinese.[29]

Few of the other Chinese students shared Li's close relationships with Italian teachers and friends. Fatigati thought that Ke Zongxiao was arrogant, quarrelsome, careless, and not very bright.[30] An even more problematic student was Fan Tiancheng, who Fatigati kept trying to convince himself had overcome his tendency to dissipation.[31] With the pressures on large numbers of young men from wealthy and powerful families to enter religious orders, it was common for priests in Naples to have mistresses or indulge in occasional sex. Moreover, the poor housing on the hillsides round the college made it a regular haunt of prostitutes. Visiting prostitutes was not regarded as a particularly serious problem: Matteo Ripa's rules are clear that Chinese students should not be expelled from the college for sins against chastity.[32] Li's reputation as a model student implies that he never did so, but his caution and ability to handle people, which was noted all his life, also meant that if he had been inclined to have a mistress he would almost certainly not have been found out.

Li was ordained a priest in 1784 at the age of twenty-four, which should have marked his return to China. Several of the other older students had left the previous year, but Li was left behind with the youngest group.[33] Fatigati died, and the new superior later wrote that Li and three other students were still at the college only because there was no money to pay for their return journeys to China.[34] Travel to China was extremely costly, but in addition to having financial problems the college also needed to have Chinese students in residence to justify its existence. The state was trying to reduce the number of clergy in Naples, and there were regular drives to close down any group that was small or no longer fulfilled its original aims. To face this threat the college had to have Chinese students in residence, but in the last few years hardly any new students had arrived. For the superior there was thus little alternative to keeping Li and some of the other Chinese students they already had.[35]

With his friends leaving, Fatigati dead, and a rather harsh and critical deputy temporarily in charge, Li, who had always been so perfect, became ill. Wang Zhengli, one of the students who had left, sent a poem to console him:

Now the body loses its energy and strength,
And the pleasures enjoyed as a youth no longer please.
Sometimes you are in the square, sometimes in the dense shade of the portico,
Now the shade calls you back, and you seek Portici,
Where the warm winds strengthen body and soul.
May the spirit put itself at the service of your duties.[36]

These lines are taken from the poems written by the Roman poet Ovid in exile on the Black Sea coast, lamenting his sufferings in a barbarian land.[37] They come from three different sections, and Wang has adjusted them to fit Li's situation, capitalising "portico" so that it refers to Portici, a seaside town where the college owned a house and the school, along with much of the Naples elite, went for their summer holiday.[38] The direct message of the poem Wang has constructed is to encourage Li by telling him that he will feel better when he goes to Portici and that it is his duty to recover. But through his choice of Ovid's poetry, Wang is also comparing Li's situation to that of Ovid in exile in a barbarian land, except that the situation is reversed: Ovid is sick with longing for Rome, but for Li it is Italy that is the barbarian land and he is homesick for China. In time Li recovered and settled down to life as an adult member of the college.

Three years later Francesco Massei, the new superior, wrote that he needed nothing more to make him a good missionary, excelled in prudence, and had a deep and genuine courtesy.[39] When six new Chinese students arrived in 1789, as the senior student he presumably became their Latin teacher. The close relations he developed with these younger students lasted for the rest of his life.[40]

The Chinese who remained in the college after their ordination were free to go about the city. They also had the money to do so since they were now free to receive gifts and could earn money by saying masses.[41] Getting to know the senior members of the college as colleagues rather than as students drew the Chinese further into the life of the city. Some local men were ordained only as deacons, so that in the future they could leave and marry, and others remained only until they found a better position. Filippe Cozzolino, who became a friend of Li's, entered the college at seventeen and left five years later.[42] Some of the remaining senior members specialised in teaching, and the occasional one went off as a missionary to China, but most lived the ordinary lives of clergy in the city, saying masses, preaching, and acting as confessors. They were supposed to spend at least three days each week in the college, but it was not always easy to get them to comply. Indeed one report claimed that it was difficult to find a time to hold a meeting because they were hardly ever all in the building at once. Even when they were in the college they had many guests, who came to meals in the refectory, where wine was said to flow freely.[43]

In January 1791 Li's career in Italy reached its highpoint, when he, Wang Ying, Ke Zongxiao, and Yan Kuanren went to Rome for the final examination in theology that was conducted in the presence of the pope, the senior cardinal of the Propaganda Fide, and other leading clerics before they set off as missionaries. The examination went well: all five scored the top mark of "excellent" and were praised by the pope. They attended a solemn mass sung by the pope and had the opportunity to go to his palace and kiss his feet. They also went sightseeing and received gifts of relics of Saint Francis Xavier, the missionary famous for first reaching China. Li wrote a couple of short letters back to the community in Naples, expressing his amazement at the huge size of the churches in Rome, promising to tell them all about it when he got back, and sending his greetings specially to Giovanni Borgia.[44]

After nearly twenty years in Naples Li and his companions had completed with success every requirement set for them to be missionaries. They were fluent speakers of Latin and Italian as well as Chinese, who shared in the cultural world of the European elite, but they had been trained specifically to work in China, and all were intermittently smitten with homesickness and longed to return to their families and homeland.

CHAPTER FOUR

George Thomas Staunton's Peculiar Childhood

GEORGE THOMAS STAUNTON had a very different education. After George Leonard returned from India in 1784 he threw all his energies into shaping his son, determined to keep him apart from all other influences and educate him for a new world. These were the years leading up to the French Revolution, years that also saw the beginnings of the Industrial Revolution in England. George Leonard's methods were shaped by the popular educational philosophies of the time, especially the ideas of Rousseau. They were not very easy for the child: in old age George Thomas would quote Edmund Gibbon's comment that while other people might speak of the happiness of boyhood, it was a happiness he had never known. He also regretted that although he was a fluent speaker of Latin he had not learned to write Latin poetry. Latin verse composition was important because it bound together the men of the European elite and continued to do so long after the grand tours, gambling, and duels of Macartney's generation had been abandoned.[1] What George Thomas missed out on, what would always later make him a peripheral figure in British society, was precisely the kind of classical education that Li Zibiao had received.

George Leonard had begun making plans for his new son as soon as he heard of his birth. He wrote back from Madras to his family in Galway that "all my energies will centre in him."[2] His ideas were a mix of fashionable educational philosophy that encouraged the separation of the innocent child from the evils of the world with plans for George Thomas (then known as Thomas) to learn a host of subjects he thought important.[3] As a start, George Leonard instructed his mother to "have Tommy thought to spake, read and write the Irish language" (as she reported to Jane in spelling that reflects her Irish accent).[4] Was this the result of Irish nationalism, enthusiasm for language learning, or, as his mother hoped, a plan to return to live in Galway? However, she died just a few months later, and George Thomas was taken in for a while by her close friend Mistress Lynch. He was only three and could not understand what was happening, asking over and over again why his grandmother was still sleeping. Then his life was suddenly transformed again when he and his nurse were put on a public coach to travel back to his mother in Salisbury.[5]

George Leonard arrived back from Madras shortly afterward and settled in London with his wife and child. He now had enough money to live comfortably but no immediate prospect of employment, so his main occupation was George Thomas's education. Since he had a quick temper and was not used to looking after a small child, it was not an easy transition for George Thomas, who on one memorable occasion said that his father should be sent back to the "ship-house" in Madras.[6]

They began with Jane teaching George Thomas to read, but George Leonard would not allow her to do so from the popular children's books that her father had made his fortune publishing (*Tommy Trip's History of Birds and Beasts with . . . the History of Little Tom Trip Himself, of His Dog Jouler, and of Woglog the Giant*).[7] Instead he bought her the new textbooks of Anna Barbauld, which taught reading in a constant stream of instruction ("Do not spill the milk. Hold the spoon in the other hand. Do not throw your bread upon the ground.").[8] George Leonard tried to control his temper and set a good example. After a while he found that threatening to put his own hand in the fire was an effective way to make the little boy behave.[9] With his father's constant supervision George Thomas, who seems to have inherited his mother's gentle nature and some of her timidity, became an extremely obedient child.

A few days before George Thomas's fifth birthday his father began to speak to him in Latin, refusing to give him anything until he said "si tibi placet" (if it pleases you).[10] Latin was a standard part of education at this time and also the international language of science, but for the vast majority of English boys it was a language learned from grammars in school. George Leonard's Jesuit education had given him an ability to speak it for everyday purposes, which was unusual in England, and his decision that his son should learn Latin from the start as a spoken language was regarded as extraordinary. By the time George Thomas was eleven years old, his father was speaking to him entirely in Latin "even on the most trivial topics," which was reported in the newspapers as something amazing and must have drawn attention to the shy boy every time they went out.[11]

The newspaper reporting suggests that George Leonard's education of his son was intended as a public experiment that would bring him recognition, but although it occupied his time he was becoming increasingly anxious about money. He needed a job, and the prospects were not good. He and Macartney had felt that the treaty they signed with Mysore was a great achievement that saved the British Empire, but in London what was more obvious was the military defeat. Moreover, by the time they got back to England William Pitt was prime minister and Macartney's prospects for patronage from Lord Holland had collapsed. Instead Macartney attempted to present himself as an apolitical and professional figure and relied on his wife's political connections: it was Jane who arranged for George Leonard to meet Pitt to make the case for Macartney.[12] In the end Macartney was offered the job of governor of Bengal, but without the backing he needed to succeed, and he refused and retired to his estate in Ireland.[13] George Leonard had neither an estate nor the backing that would enable him to live for years deeply in debt as Macartney did.

One prospect that came up and excited George Leonard was a new plan for a British embassy to China. As a boy in a French Jesuit school he would have heard about this land where Jesuit

missionaries were influential at court and learned men were valued and employed by a wise emperor. That, of course, was scarcely
the reason that Pitt planned to send an embassy. He was concerned primarily about the same issues that had led to Macartney being sent to Madras: the problems of East India Company
rule in India and especially its finances. Customs duties on Chinese tea were a significant source of finance for the state. The
company was also a major London employer, an important investor in shipping and other industries, a source of safe and reliable
dividends for investors, and also on occasion a provider of large
loans to the government. All this was important, and the war with
Mysore and territorial expansion in India had nearly bankrupted it
even while its employees made private fortunes. Pitt's government
had put in place a rescue package but combined it with the cre-
ation of a Board of Control, headed by Henry Dundas, that would
begin to bring the company under government control. They also
cut import duties on tea with the idea that the trade would then
expand. Increasing trade with China could finance the company
and fund its rule in India. In order to achieve this, the government
hoped to use the embassy to obtain a trading base in China and
a representative at the Chinese court. Although they did not say
so, this was a strategy that had been successful in expanding their
operations in India. It would also have the benefit of increasing the
government's control over the company. The company's directors
naturally resisted the plans as far as they could, trying to reduce
the expenses and pointing out that the Chinese saw embassies as
acknowledgments of inferiority.[14]

George Leonard put himself forward to head the new embassy,
but he and Macartney were far from popular with the company.
In Madras Macartney had acted forcefully to strengthen government control over the company. More recently George Leonard had
become friendly with Edmund Burke, who came from a very similar Irish background and was then preparing his great attack on
the corruption of the company's rule in India. He had even taken
George Thomas to stay with him.[15] The position of ambassador to
China went instead to a less controversial candidate: Charles Cathcart, an army officer and member of Parliament with close ties to
the government.[16]

To add to this disappointment for George Leonard there was bad news from France, where the king's government was reaching a crisis. George Leonard set off for Paris but had to turn back. That winter he had a collapse: he spent his days sitting by the fire too tired even to get up for his meals or write to his closest friends.[17] He could no longer bring himself to teach George Thomas. Instead he employed Leonard Wilson, a young Irishman with a French seminary education similar to his own, as a Latin-speaking servant to look after the boy, though he did maintain enough interest to send George Thomas off for lessons with a specialist on mosses and lichens.[18]

But then it seemed that perhaps the world was changing after all. In 1789 dramatic political changes began to take place in France. George Leonard, now recovered, rushed off to Paris, and although he was taken aback to see the head of a man carried on a pike through the streets he still felt sure (when writing to Ireland) that "a most wonderful Revolution is brought about in favor of the people."[19] Soon afterward his financial affairs improved when the legal case he had been fighting against the Collins family over his losses in Grenada was brought to a conclusion and Jane inherited £5,477 from her father's estate.[20] It also turned out that Charles Cathcart had died on the voyage to China, so that plans for a British embassy had to start again. This time Macartney was put forward as the ambassador, with the idea that George Leonard would go as his deputy but take over and remain in Beijing after the embassy left.

George Thomas was now eight years old. The Latin-speaking servant Wilson had not turned out well: one night he put George Thomas to bed then went off drinking, taking with him an exceedingly expensive gold watch decorated with diamonds specially designed to tell the time in the dark, which Jane had hung on a peg in her bedroom. He was caught and tried, but despite pressure from the court George Leonard, who had trusted him, declared the watch to be worth much less than its true value so that the theft could not be prosecuted on a capital charge. Instead Wilson was sentenced to transportation to Africa.[21]

George Leonard, now back to his normal excitable self, decided that George Thomas should begin to learn ancient Greek too as a spoken language. Finding someone to speak Latin was not particularly hard in late eighteenth-century London, but a tutor who could actually speak ancient Greek was another issue altogether. George Leonard wrote off to a professor in Leipzig, which was known for its study of Greek, asking him to recommend a tutor. The professor wrote back in Latin recommending Johann Christian Hüttner, who set off from Germany to London, where he lived with the Staunton family and taught George Thomas Latin and Greek.[22] Meanwhile, George Leonard had also found a part-time tutor for mathematics: John Barrow had been educated at a grammar school, apprenticed to an iron foundry at the age of fourteen, gone to sea on a whaler for a year, and along the way taught himself enough mathematics and navigation to get a position as a teacher at a school in Greenwich. His grammar school education meant that he was also able to teach in Latin, which George Leonard required. Barrow, like Hüttner, appreciated George Leonard's friendly style and later remembered his assurance that George Thomas was "a lively, animated boy, with more than average abilities, and great docility."[23]

Meanwhile plans for the new embassy to China were developing and were being closely linked to the promotion of British exports. So the next year, when George Thomas was ten, George Leonard decided to advance his practical education by taking him on a tour of England and Scotland with a focus on manufacturing. The little boy's diary records how he set off with papa and mama, his tutor Mr Hüttner, and a visiting Swedish professor of botany (fig. 4.1).

George Leonard was in his normal energetic and enthusiastic form starting the journey with a visit to the astronomer William Herschel, where George Thomas was struck with "the great size of the telliscopes" and was allowed to look through one of them.[24] As they moved north they toured newly built canals, a factory making pins, and another making stockings ("a most complicated machine").[25] In Birmingham they dined with Matthew Boulton and James Watt, whose development of the steam engine is now seen as one of the founding inventions of the Industrial Revolution and was one of the items that it was hoped would be demonstrated to the Chinese.[26] Later on in the journey they saw one of the new steam engines operating a cotton-spinning machine. George Thomas and his father went down a salt mine in a bucket, terrifying poor Jane.

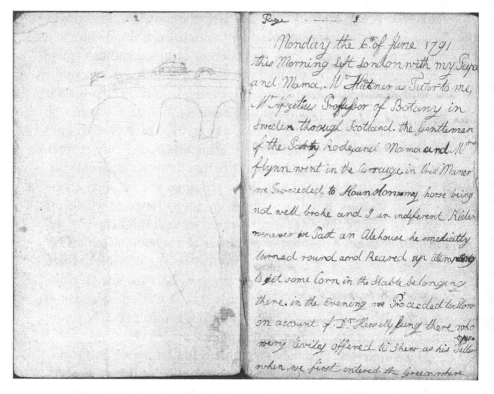

FIGURE 4.1. The first page of George Thomas Staunton's diary, written as a kind of homework. He has drawn a canal boat being pulled by a horse over an aqueduct.

They met a blind mathematician and botanist, and George Thomas was fascinated by the board he used to calculate and record the weather. The journey was explained as part of George Thomas's education, and he tried hard to keep up, but he was only ten and he often got tired. Mostly what shines through his diary is his father's enthusiasm for the new scientific inventions of the age.[27]

All this was on the cutting edge of scientific knowledge and educational theory, but what struck most people was that it was also an extremely odd way of bringing up a child. George Leonard loved showing off his son and wrote to his friend the botanist Sir James Smith about how at Bakewell they looked at fossils and identified bamboo, "and my boy thought he could distinguish another impression to be that of the *Dodecatheon Meadia*" but "my little fellow is too great a novice in conchology to ascertain the species of

FIGURE 4.2. George Thomas Staunton aged eleven by Thomas Hickey. George Thomas is pointing to China on the globe. The open book is a copy of Euclid's *Elements* in Greek to show his unusual linguistic and mathematical abilities.

the shells."[28] When they got to Glasgow, another botanist enjoyed catching up on all the news with "that demi-maniac Sir George Staunton," but joked to Smith that George Thomas was such an odd child that the Chinese would probably keep him as an example of a rare species—"Lord what a hodge podge of ideas the infant must have."[29]

George Leonard was well aware that education played a central role in socialising the young, but he had decided to prepare his son for a new world that he hoped was coming into being. Li Zibiao's classmates in Naples could expect him to recognise the subtexts in Latin poetry, while Macartney could compose Latin verse to while away the time on a sea voyage.[30] Their classical education bound them into the European elite. George Leonard's ideas about children's aptitude for learning languages and science by observation and immersion were very different and far from conventional. George Thomas did learn Latin, and he would carry an interest in science through later life, but his education would always separate him from men of his own class and background.

PART II

Li Zibiao and Lord Macartney's Embassy

CHAPTER FIVE

Finding an Interpreter for an Embassy to China

ONCE MACARTNEY WAS offered the position of ambassador for the new embassy, one of his first tasks was to appoint the members of his retinue, and finding a suitable interpreter was much the most difficult challenge. The trade in Canton inevitably required commercial interpreters, and Macartney intended to take some gifts for the Jesuits in Beijing, who he expected would act as interpreters there, but he was dubious about employing someone from either of these groups. He wrote to Dundas,

> Prudence however requires not entirely to trust, if possible, to interpreters, now either at Pekin or Canton. They might have local views and connections, or feel themselves under too much awe, to be able faithfully and completely to render the sense of the most decent representations. It were therefore desirable to find in Europe a good Chinese Interpreter, who might communicate a variety of hints and instructions, and even some notions of the language, whilst onboard of ship, and above all might contract in the necessary intimacy of a long voyage, an attachment which would ensure fidelity and zeal in the service. His sentiments at least and real character could not fail of being discovered, and of shewing what degree of dependence should be placed upon him; in all events, he would serve as a check upon the resident missionaries.[1]

This was not simply a question of finding someone with the necessary linguistic skills. What mattered was trust, and this was something Macartney hoped he could develop during the journey.

At first the best prospect seemed to be to find a French missionary who had returned from China, so it was decided George Leonard should go to France. His trip would be paid for by the East India Company, and he was excited to see what was happening in the revolution. So in January 1792 he set off for Paris, taking with him George Thomas and his tutor Hüttner. Once there he met with church organisations and did find one former missionary, but he had returned twenty years earlier and flatly refused to go back to China. Meanwhile, the Stauntons also went to watch the meetings of the radical Jacobin Club and the National Assembly, which bored George Thomas, who could not understand French. More dramatic was a trip to the ruins of the Bastille, where George Leonard could teach his son about the "unfortunate wretches . . . in deep dungeons, loaded with chains, having nothing but bread and water for support, to serve the caprice of kings and those above them."[2] In addition to instilling revolutionary ideas in his son, George Leonard was wondering about the risk of buying property in Ireland since "it is not quite certain that any property, real or personal, will be long permanent anywhere."[3]

Failing to find an interpreter in Paris, George Leonard decided to extend their trip into Italy and go south to the college for Chinese in Naples. He had already made a lengthy stay in Paris, and the more costly the expedition, the more important the interpreters became in justifying it. He wrote to the British ambassador in Naples, who replied that he knew the superiors of the college well and was confident that they would agree, but that the Chinese students were afraid that if they went to Beijing they would be arrested and executed for having left the country without permission.[4] This was indeed a law, but one that they must have known was almost never enforced. Nevertheless, when George Leonard arrived in Naples, he told the college that the interpreters' duties would be to instruct the British in the customs and language of China on the voyage, and they could then leave the embassy in Macao. He knew that he needed an interpreter who spoke Mandarin, the northern Chinese dialect used at court. Among the students who had completed their studies at the college, Ke Zongxiao had grown up in an official family in Beijing and Li Zibiao too came from the north of China, so they were chosen to return to China with the embassy.[5]

George Leonard actually wanted the interpreters to do much more than instruct the British on the voyage: he wanted them to come with the embassy to Beijing. So from Naples he went to Rome, where he encouraged Li and Ke to seek permission for their connection with the embassy. The two of them felt strangely important hurrying round the Vatican palace to make the arrangements. They happened to meet one of the college's patrons, now a cardinal, who arranged for a private audience with the pope, who gave his personal approval for their participation in the embassy. Then George Leonard himself approached the cardinals. Li was impressed that they treated him as an eminent person and benefactor, giving him a precious copy of a handwritten Chinese-Latin dictionary and a letter to the bishops in China asking them to assist the embassy.[6] During these days in Rome Li began to think that acting as an interpreter for the embassy might be a task he was undertaking for the good of the church.

He and Ke also had a more immediate goal: they wanted to arrange for two more of their classmates, Yan Kuanren and Wang Ying, to get back to China. Wang Ying was the boy from Xi'an who had travelled down to Macao with Li and Ke so many years ago. He had never been much of a success at the college, but he was their classmate and they did not want to leave him behind.[7] Yan Kuanren was quite another matter: he had arrived at the college some years later at the age of twenty and had turned out to be an exceptional student. After four years Fatigati commented that his Latin was better than that of many Italian literati.[8] When Li and Ke asked, George Leonard agreed that the embassy would take Wang and Yan back to China for free, saying only that they should be sent to London by the quicker (and cheaper) sea route. The cardinals of the Propaganda agreed to this plan, so the college could scarcely refuse.[9]

From the start George Leonard had treated Li and Ke with courtesy. He bought a separate travelling carriage for "the two Chinese gentlemen" (instead of expecting them to travel with his servants), and now he had agreed to take their classmates too.[10] Li wrote back to Naples that "the English gentlemen we are with are really considerate and approachable."[11] He and Ke ate with the Stauntons and Hüttner and, since the conversation was in any case in Latin for George Thomas, they had no difficulty communicating, though they had to get used to the English taste in food: bread and butter with milky tea or coffee and ricotta cheese for breakfast and supper. In the middle of the day the English ate meat, but George Leonard, who was constantly aware of Li and Ke's needs as Catholics, arranged for them to have fish or eggs during Lent. He also found time for them to celebrate mass and even arranged for them to do so at the great pilgrimage site of Loreto, which delighted them.[12] George Leonard was both sympathetic to the Catholic Church and naturally sociable, but he was also following Macartney's plan. From his experiences in India he knew that a trustworthy interpreter was crucial to successful diplomacy, and like Macartney he believed that this kind of trust could be built on the basis of friendship. Even so at times Li felt that, however friendly George Leonard was, "it is wearisome because like the Samaritans and Jews we live together but with differences of wealth and customs."[13]

Then George Leonard learned that the starting date for the embassy had been postponed, and he also came down with a painful attack of gout, so the journey slowed down. He decided to avoid the dangers of crossing France and take George Thomas back along a more interesting route via Venice and Germany. In Venice Li and Ke went sightseeing on their own, which Li preferred especially for visiting churches. He admired the palaces on the main canals and went to hear the famous girls' choirs, though he did not think much of these—they were too like actresses. He also went shopping, looking for a small missal and a textbook on canon law. But his letters also sound as if he had been talking to George Leonard about European politics, something that clearly interested him.[14]

George Thomas was supposed to be listening to Li and Ke speaking Chinese to each other so that he could get accustomed to the sounds of the language. His father had decided that he too should come on the embassy and presumably become the interpreter that George Leonard had imagined during his difficult negotiations in India: simple, utterly loyal to his father, and a transparent medium for the language. Only his mother back in London resisted this plan: she was so desperate when she thought of the dangers of the voyage that she asked her brother to write to George Leonard and try to dissuade him.[15]

From Venice they travelled north across the Alps into Germany, up the Rhine Valley, making a detour to visit Frankfurt, then on to Cologne. By this time the first of the great wars that followed the French Revolution had broken out on the frontier between France and the Austrian Netherlands. Li wrote back to Naples with news of the Battle of Mons: there were fleeing French soldiers and nobles everywhere. Two of them entered his room at the inn one morning and took his purse with a few coins in it but fortunately left their other possessions.[16]

In May the party reached Brussels. This was the last major city they would stop in before they reached England, where Catholic practice was still strictly limited and Li and Ke would no longer be able to wear the habits of the Naples College, so George Leonard bought them new clothes. Li thought these most suitable and was pleased that George Leonard was "no less concerned about our proper modesty as priests than we are ourselves."[17] Li also sent his classmates a long disquisition on the recent politics of Catholicism in England and Ireland, which emphasized the new parliamentary act allowing Catholics to practice their religion, run schools, and enter the legal profession. This can only have come from George Leonard who seems to have told Li that it would soon be followed in the English Parliament by a proposal "for the bringing up of the people and the lowering of the nobility."[18] Li's own politics were much more conservative: he was pleased to see Frenchmen wearing the king's cockade on their hats because he hoped for the defeat of the revolution and restoration of the French monarchy.[19]

Li and George Leonard had their differences about religion too, but it is clear that by this stage they were discussing the matter at a much deeper level than they had at the start of the journey, and that Staunton had revealed the extent of his links to the Catholic Church, attending devoutly when Li and Ke said their daily prayers. It seems that Li even urged him to convert because he wrote that Sir George was "both good hearted and generous, learned without arrogance or excess . . . but he is obstinate in his religion and does not want to change it even though his mother was Catholic and he was also taught religion by the Jesuits."[20] All this was a matter of real trust, because George Leonard's Catholic background was always a significant risk for his career. Indeed his mother's Catholicism is something that the lengthy biography that George Thomas later published about him entirely omits.[21] Li clearly appreciated something of this, for he mentions it only in his letter to the superior of the Naples College and follows it with a request that he will write to thank Sir George for his kindness to them.

When they arrived in London Li and Ke stayed with the Staunton household for four months over the summer. They got on well with Jane, who Ke wrote was "very kind to us even though she is Anglican, she even said she was sad that European women cannot go to Peking."[22] The house on Harley Street was the third rented property the family had occupied in two years.[23] Nevertheless Li was impressed by all the new development in the area, writing to Giovanni Borgia, "The city of London is perhaps the finest and biggest in Europe. Since it is not walled it is constantly growing. Every year 500 mansions are built, all large and magnificent, and to the same design, which creates very harmonious streets and beautiful prospects. The houses are clean and comfortable with furniture in the English style."[24] He went on to talk about the shops full of merchandise, pleasant parks, carriages, horses, and street lighting. George Leonard arranged for them to attend Catholic mass, where Li liked the music of the boys' choir. "Only the weather is bad. It just never stays the same, one moment hot the next cold, and hardly ever good all day."[25]

Li and Ke were wearing the dark knee-length coat and breeches, which they had acquired in Brussels, as well as the shoes (two pairs) and shirts (twelve each) that Staunton provided them with for the voyage. "We also have a neck cloth to wear which is wrapped twice round the neck."[26] Li wrote about the clothes to assure his classmates in Naples that he and Ke were behaving properly as priests, but they also mattered to him. He and Ke were certainly Chinese but in eighteenth-century London their clothes also marked their social class as gentlemen and their identity as Catholic priests.[27]

Living with George Leonard Staunton's family brought Li and Ke into contact with the circles in which he moved. His Saturday night conversation parties were said to be inferior only to those of the great naturalist and patron of the sciences Sir Joseph Banks.[28] Of course the embassy to China was the great topic of conversation. One of those Li met was Edmund Burke, who was Irish and like Staunton "tho not a Roman Catholic he was as *near being* one as a legal protestant could be" (as Macartney put it).[29] The novelist Fanny Burney met Burke shortly afterward at a party. They had argued over his hostility to the French Revolution, but when he sat down to tell her about the embassy and the two Chinese, whom "he described minutely," and when he spoke about the aims of the embassy "in high and perhaps fanciful terms, but with allusions and anecdotes intermixed so full of general information, and brilliant ideas" she soon felt her enthusiasm return.[30]

George Leonard had also taken Li and Ke to see Macartney. With him they could speak Italian, which Macartney had learned on his grand tour, as well as Latin. Macartney had been doing a lot of reading in preparation for the embassy, and Li and Ke were impressed. They were particularly pleased to see a set of engravings of the emperor's palace in Chengde made by Matteo Ripa the founder of the Naples College. Macartney was cautious. He did not want to tell the interpreters the real purpose of the embassy until he was sure he could trust them, but Li was interested and knew that his friends in Italy would be too.[31] A month later, writing to Giovanni Borgia to report the safe arrival of Yan and Wang in London, he added what he had been able to find out about the motives for the embassy, though, as he pointed out, he was hampered by his lack of experience and not being able to speak English. He now believed that "the ultimate aim of this embassy to the Emperor of China (though it is concealed as is usually the case with affairs of great importance) is to be able obtain some port near Beijing where only the English will be allowed to trade, so that they will be exempted from the demands of the company of merchants in Canton, can do their business freely and increase their profits."[32] Much later writing has pictured the Macartney embassy as an attempt to establish modern international relations between Britain and China, but Li's analysis was acute. Behind the scenes Francis Baring, the chairman of the directors of the East India Company, was already debating with Dundas over whether any territory the embassy succeeded in obtaining should belong to the Company or the British state.[33] A radical, seeing the embassy in the light of the slave trade and the expansion of British rule in India, warned the Chinese against the embassy in verse,

> And when, with hollow hearts and honeyed tongues,
>> These slaves of gold advance their blood-stained hand,
> Shrink from the touch—Remember India's wrongs–
>> Remember Afric's woes—and save your destined land.[34]

But at the same time as understanding that the embassy's ultimate aim was to obtain a port so that the English could increase their profits from the trade, Li could not help feeling deeply indebted to Macartney and the Stauntons. Yan and Wang were having a difficult time, living with an English Catholic priest and worrying about the cost of everything, while he and Ke were generously supplied. In addition George Leonard told him that Macartney had agreed to take Yan and Wang to China without payment, not for the benefit of the Catholic mission, but solely because he and Ke had requested it.[35] It was impossible for Li and Ke to repay all this generosity: the formal announcement of the embassy to the Qing court had already been sent off in English and Latin. There was talk of Li and Ke helping to select some of the valuable gifts that the embassy would present at court alongside the examples of British manufactures, but the kind of item likely to appeal to senior Chinese officials as a gift was a topic on which the East India Company was likely to be far better informed than two young men who had spent the previous twenty years in Naples.[36]

One thing that the Chinese could do was to give language lessons to George Thomas, which Ke undertook to do. Because Ke came from an official family in Beijing he could be expected to speak the language of the court, and because he was in his late teens when he left China he had more Chinese education. The British understood that he had a better knowledge of Chinese than Li, but they still preferred dealing with Li. Ke was much less flexible and was finding their life in London considerably more difficult.[37] When John Barrow showed him a Latin version of the Anglican Book of Common Prayer, he threw it on the floor, saying, "It is a diabolical book."[38] Years later Barrow also remembered Ke being a very bad-tempered teacher for George Thomas.[39]

Ke was much happier talking to an Italian named Antonio Montucci, who had managed to get a letter of introduction to George Leonard explaining that he was "a student of the Chinese language" and wanted to enjoy a little conversation with the Chinese.[40] Montucci's knowledge of Chinese came from the works of Etienne Fourmont, a Frenchman whose interest in Chinese was driven by the idea that Chinese characters might be a universal language. Fourmont had spent some time talking to a young Chinese man who had come to Paris to study for the priesthood but then married a French woman, but nevertheless his ideas about the Chinese language came almost entirely from his laborious efforts to decipher Chinese dictionaries and printed texts from first principles. Montucci too was interested in the structure of Chinese characters, so Ke used a Chinese dictionary to explain the system of radicals according to which the characters were organised. George Leonard had taken Ke and Li to see the Chinese books in the British Museum, so Ke was also able to provide Montucci with an introduction there. On the basis of these meetings and what he could learn from the dictionary, Montucci went from being an Italian language teacher to a career as an expert on the Chinese language. He wrote of Ke with gratitude years later, but he never really got to the point of being able to read a Chinese text.[41]

By this time Italian missionaries had been learning Chinese for two centuries: Francesco Jovino who had lived with Li's family in Liangzhou was hardly the greatest scholar of the China mission but was nevertheless able to write books in Chinese. Montucci's difficulty in learning Chinese reminds us that it was not only in China that there were curious absences in knowledge of distant cultures: in England too some knowledge was confined to particular groups or social classes or simply forgotten. There were Chinese books in the British Library, but no one who could read them. Moreover, Macartney was learning about China from works written by the early Catholic missionaries a hundred years earlier: knowledge of China's recent court politics, which was crucial for diplomacy, was entirely absent.

The Chinese language was the key to any further knowledge, but it was not something that was readily acquired by European scholars reliant on published books. The early missionaries had compiled wordlists and grammars but had little incentive to make them available to a wider audience.[42] There had been three English boys who had been taken to China some years earlier with the idea that they would pick up the language. The best known was James Flint, who had survived and learned enough Chinese to go on to work as an interpreter for the East India Company. However, he had ended up being imprisoned for three years and then expelled after he fronted a failed attempt by the British to extend their trade to the city of Ningbo. Flint never returned to China, and by the time plans were being made for an embassy this one Englishman known to have had a reasonable knowledge of the Chinese language was dead.[43]

There were also in fact Chinese living in London: seamen regularly died on long voyages and needed to be replaced. So despite bans by both the British and Qing states, there had been Chinese seamen in London for at least ten years. They lived in the poor area around the docks, and like other sailors came to the attention of elites mainly when they ended up in fights or destitute. When one of the Chinese seamen took a case to court a few years later after he got drunk and was robbed of his wages by a prostitute, another Chinese, known as John Antony, appeared as interpreter. Antony had left China as a boy of eleven, had been shipping in and out of England since the 1780s, and had also been back and forth to China. By the time of the court case he was married to an English woman and ran a boarding house for Indian and Chinese sailors. The East India Company was paying for the boarding house, so they must have known about him, but no one considered these Chinese seamen as possible sources of information. Of course most of them would have been illiterate speakers of the Cantonese dialect, but John Antony was wealthy enough to wear fashionable pantaloons and literate enough to own a leather pocketbook. Someone looking further afield might have found William Macao, a Chinese man who arrived in Britain as a servant in the 1770s and was making a career in the Scottish Board of Excise.[44] In any case, even an illiterate Chinese seaman might have been able to assist a scholar who was otherwise trying to decipher a Chinese book as if it were a code.

Li and Ke, meeting Macartney and discussing rare books in Latin and Italian, were recognised as elite men and absorbed into their social circles. Their knowledge of the Chinese language was appreciated as something rare and valuable, while that of the Chinese seamen at the other end of the city was invisible. Historians who have looked at the rise of scientific knowledge in Britain in this period have argued that many new ideas came to be accepted through social relations of trust between gentlemen: class, status, and personal connections mattered to who was believed and who was not.[45] In the same way Li's education and appearance as a gentleman was crucial to how the English treated him and how they valued his language skills.

CHAPTER SIX

Crossing the Oceans

TOWARD THE END of August 1792 the members of the embassy to China gathered in Portsmouth, where they would board the ships to China. The voyage was indeed as dangerous as Jane Staunton feared. Its dangers would draw Li Zibiao and even little George Thomas into the fellowship that, as Macartney was expecting, developed between the members of the embassy as they faced and survived those dangers. It would also give them a sense of the extent of British naval power and political influence and then, once they reached Southeast Asia, the extent of Chinese migration.

Portsmouth was a major centre for the British navy, heavily fortified, and with great ships being built in the shipyard for the war with the French that everyone now expected. The embassy's ships, HMS *Lion*, a sixty-four-gun warship, and the *Hindostan*, a great East Indiaman, were anchored well offshore as it was difficult for the ships of this size to manoeuvre into the harbour. When George Leonard took his party out to visit them, Li and Ke came along and were able to meet up with Yan and Wang who were already staying on the *Hindostan*. Getting on board meant clambering up the moving side of the high ship on a rope ladder as it rocked on the swell: George Thomas could not manage it and had to be hauled up on a chair. They went on to the *Lion*, which would carry the ambassador and the members of his suite he wished to spend time with, including Li and Ke. Macartney was to have the captain's cabin, with Gower and George Leonard occupying the smaller rooms alongside it and the rest of the gentlemen of the embassy crowded in below.

George Thomas found that he had a little cubicle made of canvas off one of the larger cabins.[1] The *Lion* was the height of contemporary military technology: a floating battery that could manoeuvre easily, sail across the world, and blast to pieces other ships or coastal fortifications. Rows of massive cannons occupied much of the space on the upper decks, projecting into the cabins. The canvas cubicles were designed to be quickly stowed away when the ship was cleared for action. After seeing the town and touring the ship, Li could not have failed to realise something of the scale of Britain's naval power.

Back in Portsmouth, the members of Macartney's suite began to get to know each other. The gentlemen of the embassy were said to have been selected on the basis of their skills and abilities especially in science. In fact, most were close personal connections of Macartney's: he had three secretaries and took his discreet personal secretary Acheson Maxwell for the actual work. The other two secretaries, Edward Winder and John Crewe, and the captain of the guard, George Benson, were the sons of cousins.[2] Ernest Gower, captain of the *Lion*, had commanded one of the ships defending the grain convoys to Madras when Macartney was there. He was experienced in that he had made two voyages of exploration across the Pacific, but less encouragingly in one of them his ship had been wrecked on the southern tip of South America and was rescued only after six men rowed 315 miles to the Falkland Islands to fetch help.[3] George Leonard, as secretary to the embassy, was allowed to take not only eleven-year-old George Thomas but also George Thomas's tutor Hüttner and John Barrow, who came as the embassy's comptroller. Barrow was teaching George Thomas when he found out and burst out excitedly, in Latin, "Not many men get the chance to go to Peking."[4] Thomas Hickey, nominally the embassy's artist, who painted nothing in China, had recently done portraits of both Macartney and George Thomas (fig. 4.2).[5] There were also two doctors, both apparently friends of George Leonard's. A scientist, James Dinwiddie, who was not a personal connection but had been employed to demonstrate the scientific gifts, wanted to be regarded as a mathematician, but Macartney insisted on referring to him as a machinist.[6]

The only gentlemen not selected by Macartney were those sent by the East India Company. William Mackintosh, captain of the

Hindostan, was independent, wealthy, and hugely experienced. This was his tenth voyage to China, and he would have paid a large amount for the post, money that he expected to get back on the profits of his own trade during the embassy. In the hold of his ship were furs from the Pacific coast of America, which he hoped to sell in Beijing. But like most British ships trading to China, the *Hindostan* was taking out only a small cargo compared to the amount of tea that she would bring back, so there was plenty of space for the magnificent gifts for the Qianlong emperor and for some of the junior embassy staff as well as Yan and Wang. Francis Baring, chairman of the directors of the East India Company, had also sent his sixteen-year-old son Henry to keep an eye on proceedings.[7]

Gathered in Portsmouth, the members of the embassy waited for the wind to turn.[8] Huge square-rigged sailing ships like the *Lion* and *Hindostan* were relatively safe out at sea and could carry large amounts of cargo, but they were hard to manoeuvre and almost impossible to sail against the wind. This meant that they had to sail with the ocean currents and prevailing winds caused by the rotation of the earth. Gower planned to sail south, then follow the winds westward across the Atlantic to Brazil, then the current that runs down the coast of South America till he reached the powerful current that circles the Antarctic, which would carry him back east into the Indian Ocean. From there he could follow the trade winds north to the Dutch East Indies (today Indonesia), and then the annual monsoon wind north to China. The whole voyage would take nearly a year.

Once the *Lion* set sail, everyone was living in very close quarters. There were 350 sailors on board and 56 members of the embassy, including soldiers, servants, and musicians. Li and Ke were counted among the ten gentlemen belonging to the embassy who, along with the naval officers, formed the ship's social elite. Macartney addressed them as *padre* (father), a respectful term for a Catholic priest, and William Alexander, the embassy's junior artist, referred to Li as *dominus* (master), a form of address usually used for teachers. As members of this group they would have taken their meals together with Macartney and Captain Gower and when they went up on deck they were allowed to walk on the side of the quarter deck reserved for the captain and his senior officers.[9] They had

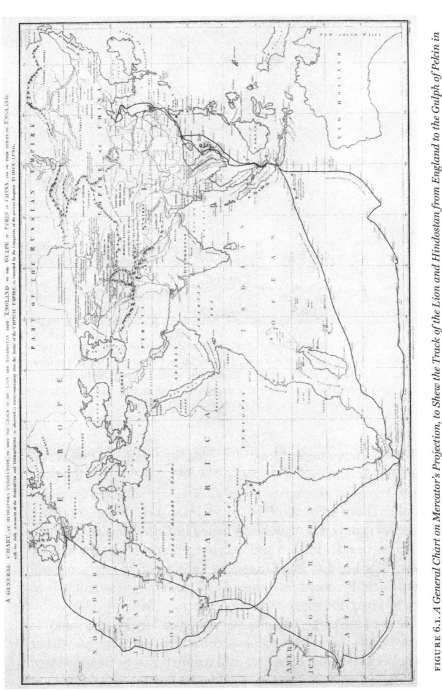

FIGURE 6.1. *A General Chart on Mercator's Projection, to Shew the Track of the Lion and Hindostan from England to the Gulph of Pekin in China, and Their Return to England with the Daily Statement of Barometer and Thermometer as Observed at Noon; Containing Also the Limits of the Chinese Empire, as Extended by the Conquests of the Present Emperor Tchien-Lung by John Barrow.*

FIGURE 6.2. *HMS Lion* by William Alexander. Alexander was sketching from on board the merchant ship *Hindostan*, which sailed more slowly and was usually behind the *Lion*. As well as the magnificent sails that gave the warship speed and agility, he has brought out the highly decorated stern cabin that Macartney occupied as ambassador and the two rows of gunports for the sixty-four great cannons.

picked up a few words of English during their time in London and could talk Italian to Macartney and Hickey, but they mostly spoke Latin. The other gentlemen would all have studied Latin in school, and the various accounts of the voyage make it clear that quite of lot of random conversation was conducted in Latin because of Li and Ke's presence. Hüttner, a serious young man whom they already knew from London as an excellent Latin speaker, was a natural companion. Frequent references in his account of the embassy to things Li had said suggest that they became friends.[10]

Unlike Li, George Thomas was not given much opportunity to make friends. There were plenty of other boys his age on board, but his father's system of education still required that he be supervised at all times. He was also timid: when he saw the midshipmen of the *Lion*, junior naval officers, some of whom were his own age, climbing the rigging, the first thing he said was (in Latin), "What if their mothers saw them now!"[11] George Leonard arranged for him to go down and drink tea in the bowels of the ship, where the midshipmen slept in hammocks over the stinking anchor cables, but the event was not repeated.[12] Later in the voyage, he was occasionally sent to study with the midshipmen, who had lessons in how to manoeuvre the ship and in navigation. He enjoyed mathematics, and afterward his diary began to look like the kind of ship's log that the midshipmen were supposed to keep, but an attempt to climb the rigging as they did was not a success: "I tryed to ascend the shrouds, but found it a very difficult and dirty business."[13] In any case he had little time: for most of the journey he was kept to a strict timetable focussed on Chinese lessons: after breakfast he had two hours of Chinese with Ke, a break, and then a Greek lesson with Hüttner. Then he just had time to change into his good clothes for dinner. After dinner he had another hour of Chinese, and "the rest of the day I had to myself."[14] From time to time one of the adults might attend the Chinese lessons, but the adults making the most effort were sailing on the *Hindostan*, where they had asked Yan and Wang to teach them, so George Thomas was on his own with Ke.[15]

About two weeks after leaving Portsmouth, the embassy arrived in the Portuguese colony of Madeira off the coast of Africa, where ships stopped to load up with wine and other provisions for the Atlantic crossing. There and in the later places where they landed Macartney as the British ambassador went ashore to the sound of gun salutes for several days of formal receptions with the governor.[16] Gun salutes were fired with real ammunition, shook the whole ship, and made such a noise that at times Macartney could hardly bear them. This intimidating display of powerful weaponry was conventional whenever a British warship entered a port as well as when Macartney went ashore. Li and Ke, as members of Macartney's suite, stayed in the same house as the Stauntons and were expected to take part in the formal receptions. George Leonard liked to go exploring, taking George Thomas with him. On this occasion he went up into the hills with Barrow. It rained and although Barrow enjoyed himself philosophizing about meteorites, George Thomas found the end of the day "long and dreary."[17]

The long expanses of time also enabled conversation as they crossed the Atlantic toward Brazil. Sailing for days across an empty sea, Macartney relaxed: in the evenings he liked to stand by the railings at the back of the ship watching people on the quarterdeck walking up and down in little groups chatting in the moonlight. He also had long conversations with Li, who smoked as they talked, and Ke, who snacked on watermelon seeds.[18]

Macartney bought wine for himself and his suite in Madeira, while Captain Gower loaded up a few days later in Tenerife with cheaper wine for the crew. Water stored on the ship quickly tasted bad, and the amount of wine drunk was considerable. Sometime later, Macartney made of a list of how much port, Lisbon, madeira, claret, hock, malmsey, tenerife, arrack, gin, shrub, porter, ale, cider, and perry he had in hand, a list that still included eighteen hundred bottles of claret. Drinking together smoothed over frictions and added to the sense of fellowship in the confined all-male world of the ship.[19]

George Thomas, on the other hand, enjoyed the entertainments when the ship crossed the equator for the first time. For British seamen this meant that they were entering the vast southern oceans, a dangerous and unfamiliar world. A sailor dressed as Neptune, dripping wet and holding a trident and accompanied by another man dressed as his wife, climbed over the prow of the ship and demanded to know what ship this was encroaching on his dominions. Those of Macartney's suite who had not crossed the equator before were allowed to pay a forfeit, but those who did not were seized, shaved, and ducked in water. The day ended with a big meal, bagpipe music, and lots of liquor. The ceremonies, the violent duckings, the meal, and the drinking were yet another activity that bound all those on the ship together.[20]

In December, three months after leaving England, the embassy reached Rio de Janeiro. Here they found the Portuguese to be anxious and apparently hostile to the embassy. Portugal was allied to Britain, and the embassy had been welcomed in Madeira, but the expansion of British trade to China was also a threat to Portuguese Macao. George Leonard took George Thomas to see a collection of butterflies, a waterfall and flour mill, plantations of corn, pineapples, coffee, oranges, cocoa, sugar, and cotton, and a cochineal garden where insects were processed into dye. Macartney laughed at George Leonard for his enthusiasm, but for once George Thomas shared it: he was delighted with the butterflies and the waterfall.[21] Meanwhile the Chinese priests were living in comfort in the wealthy Benedictine monastery overlooking the harbour since the monks, who were also very much interested in the embassy, had invited them to stay.[22]

Captain Gower spent his time in Rio preparing for the dangers of the voyage through the southern oceans: loading enough water for two months, having cattle butchered, resetting the rigging, replacing some of the masts, and strengthening others by fastening planks round them.[23] As he had expected, the ship met rough weather almost as soon as they left, and in January they were caught up in a great gale that swept them along for three weeks. By this time they were far down in the South Atlantic following the current that runs around the Antarctic in an area famous for its wild seas. The timbers creaked so loudly as the ship was pounded by the wind and waves that George Thomas was sometimes convinced that the whole ship would break apart. At other times he thought they would be overturned: "The ship rolled more than ever she did as if she would over-set and the sea was mountains high."[24] Everyone was wet all the time. The cabins were awash with water, which came streaming down through the hatches and leaked through the timbers. One huge wave went right over the ship. For days George Thomas was holding tight to the table with his legs during meals to stop himself falling. Then there were no regular meals at all, just whatever cold food could be found.[25] Gower's logbook, which mostly just noted "gales," breaks forth into description at the height of the storm, when he wrote, "the sea high and irregular the ship rolled very much, at 3 o'clock the wind shifted suddenly to the NW and blew very hard, furled the main sail and hauled up NE to keep the ships head to the sea."[26] A wave hitting the ship from the side at such a moment would have sunk her, but climbing the rigging to furl the sails in such conditions was extremely dangerous. Three days later, when the weather was finally calm, he had all the midshipmen running up and down the rigging to practice. By this time the ship was leaking eight inches of water each hour because the pump that was normally used had been broken in the storm. They had also lost track of exactly where they were.[27]

For days they were hoping to see the island of Amsterdam, a tiny speck in the middle of the southern Indian Ocean halfway between the southernmost tip of Africa and the westernmost point in Australia (labelled New Holland on Barrow's map fig. 6.1). When early one morning John Ommanney, the young lieutenant on watch, shouted out that he had seen land, George Leonard was so excited that he walked out of his cabin in his night shirt: pale and thin, the long red ribbons of his night cap streaming in the wind, and a voluminous nightgown trailing behind him. Ommanney picked up the speaking trumpet and shouted down it in the voice used for giving orders to the crew, asking, "what he was and whence he came, whether a spirit blest, or Goblin damm'd with airs from Heaven, or blasts from Hell."[28] George Leonard took a moment to see the joke, then went off into a fit of laughter. Macartney, who like everyone else had come out to see what was going on, enjoyed the scene as well. The explosive laughter feels like a reaction to the dangers they had all so recently gone through, but the teasing too is a sign of growing friendship between those on board. The loud and eccentric Ommanney would be a friend of George Thomas's into old age.[29]

Soon after this they reached the trade winds that blow northeast across the Indian Ocean. From here they sailed extraordinarily fast, at one point covering 230 miles in twenty-four hours. And thus two months after they left Rio de Janeiro, they reached the straits between Java and Sumatra in what is now Indonesia. They began to see birds, then sighted the first of many small islands. Then there were other boats around and Malay canoes were offering them chickens, fruit, and turtles for sale.[30]

They had reached Batavia (now Jakarta in Indonesia), a crossing point for trade from Europe, North America, and China. In the harbour there was even more shipping than in Rio: huge cargo ships that carried the trade of the Dutch East Indies company, which ruled the city and much of the rest of Java; British ships trading to India; large Chinese junks; French ships whose seamen had taken the recent revolution to heart and were demanding to dine with their officers; and going to and fro among them Malay canoes and sailing boats. In the city, the streets were thronged with people, not the Dutch who kept themselves apart, but Armenians, Persians, Arabs, merchants from north India, Chinese, Javanese, and Malays

FIGURE 6.3. William Alexander's portrait of Benjamin who was purchased by George Leonard Staunton in Batavia. Alexander, like several other members of the embassy, was shocked by the slave trade, and his sympathetic portrait reflects this.

all in their different clothes.[31] There were also slaves: this was also a centre of the Southeast Asian trade in people, and George Leonard, who wanted a servant to help look after George Thomas, went out and bought a slave, a tall, thin, dark-skinned young man whom he called Benjamin.[32]

Batavia was also a very Chinese city. They saw rich Chinese men in long satin gowns with their queues hanging almost down to their ankles and many more poor Chinese in loose trousers and short jackets. George Thomas looked at the Chinese shop signs and could recognise some of the characters he had been learning with Ke. And Captain Mackintosh picked up five Chinese pilots from Macao who could speak some English. Chinese merchants had been encouraged to come to the city by the Dutch so that they could deal in Chinese products outside Qing restrictions and taxation, but since then they had also come to dominate much of the trade within Southeast Asia as well as operating as tax collectors for the Dutch and establishing mines and plantations. The Chinese merchants did not socialise with the Dutch, but some were rich and ran businesses that needed an extensive understanding of the Dutch and their operations.[33] Afterward Macartney worried that it was the Chinese rather than the British who were likely to take over from the Dutch, who he thought were in decline since without the Chinese business would be impossible, and concluded that "they will soon be the masters."[34]

As elsewhere there were formal receptions for the British ambassador and his suite, but the Dutch East India Company was the major competitor of the British and new British trading arrangements in China were a significant threat, so the display was far more spectacular. The ceremonies began at the gate of the Dutch fortress with a gun salute, military parade, and refreshments. Everyone was in European formal dress and the heat was stifling. Macartney's suite were then taken to relax at the house of one of the Dutch merchants. Here the Dutch took off their velvet jackets and heavy wigs before they all sat down to a dinner of boiled and grilled fish, chicken curries and pilaffs, turkeys and capons, joints of beef boiled, roasted, and stewed, soups, puddings, custards, and all kinds of pastries, all served at once. A band of Malay musicians played outside. Afterward there were Chinese pastries, fruits, and sweetmeats.[35]

Then there was a ball at the governor's country house. When the English arrived Chinese operas were being performed on one side of the entrance and Dutch amusements on the other. Painted Chinese lanterns linked together with wreaths of flowers decorated the gardens behind. George Thomas noticed how the light from the lanterns was reflected in the pools and canals of the garden. He also enjoyed the spectacular Chinese fireworks ending with showers of stars and suns descending and each exploding in turn. Later in the ballroom the British found the local wives and daughters of the Dutch, dressed in the Malay style, covered with jewellery, their dark hair scraped back and decorated with jewelled pins. At midnight there was another meal, with political toasts one after another, and some of the gentlemen "were not a little affected by the fumes of the wine," as George Thomas put it, before he could go back to the house where they were staying, yet again "very tired."[36]

Despite the parties, the atmosphere was hostile and Macartney was feeling ill. He hurried the embassy back on board the ships, where at least they would benefit from the sea breezes.[37] At first this was a great relief to the Chinese: Yan Kuanren wrote back to Naples (with a swipe at George Leonard), "Such a journey is really enjoyable for the rich and curious, but to us who are poor and longing for our fatherland it is truly tedious."[38] As they waited for the winds, the tightly packed conditions on the ship meant that dysentery and other infections picked up in Batavia spread easily. George Leonard came down with a fever. Men, already weakened by scurvy, were seized by sudden violent spasms and died. Yan, who attended the dying Catholics, noted that six seamen had died before the *Lion* left Java. Macartney began a list of those who had died or run away in his notebook, but his writing got smaller and smaller until he ran out of space and stopped. The monsoon winds were late in coming, and the ships crept slowly north through the Indonesian archipelago. More men died than had in all the earlier storms.[39]

Yan Kuanren was worried because Li too had become ill, with swellings on his back and chest and a high temperature. The doctors reassured him that the swelling was due to scurvy and that Li was not in danger of death. They knew that scurvy could be cured by eating fresh food, but Yan could not help worrying when Li had such severe swellings and was in such pain. He prayed that God would heal Li and preserve him for the mission, "since he is our greatest hope and dear to all of us."[40] Drinking and dining together created bonds between the gentlemen on board the ship, but there were always differences as well: between the naval officers and the members of the embassy, the rich young men and George Leonard's scientific friends, and also between the British and the four Chinese who were bound together not only by their nationality but also by their education, their hopes for the Catholic mission, and their affection for one another.

CHAPTER SEVEN

Other Possible Interpreters

AS THE EMBASSY sailed up the coast of Vietnam then on north around the coast of China, they first began to need interpreting into Chinese, but it was only as they set off for the final stage of their journey overland that Macartney decided to use Li as his only interpreter. Up until that point the interpreting and translation had nearly all been done by other people, but these men either refused to take the risk of going to Beijing or had interests that could play into the negotiations. Macartney had come to know Li on the long voyage and believed he could trust him. So in the end Li was chosen not because of a lack of other possible interpreters but because for Macartney finding someone he could trust outweighed concerns over particular linguistic abilities.

The first interpreter was Yan Kuanren who, unlike Li, had received a full education in China before setting off for Naples as well as being a gifted linguist. He had grown up in a wealthy merchant family in the Chinese coastal city of Zhangzhou, which had a long history of foreign contacts and emigration. Coming from the family of a notable early convert to Christianity had expanded these cosmopolitan links: he was the second generation of his family to study in Naples and had a relative who was a priest in Thailand and another who had considered studying for the Catholic priesthood at a college in India.[1]

FIGURE 7.1. William Alexander's portrait of Yan Kuanren, which he labelled "Dominus Nean—A Chinese Missionary of the Propaganda Fide at Naples who attended the Embassy as Interpreter."

It was almost certainly Yan who produced a draft Chinese translation of Macartney's letter of credentials that survives in the British archives. The letter was a formulaic document, normally handed over by an ambassador at his first royal audience: the English king complimented the emperor, introduced the ambassador and his deputy with all their titles and honours, and requested that the ambassador be allowed to remain at court. The Chinese translation is competent and covers the major points. What is most striking though is that what, in English, was merely conventional Christian content has been greatly emphasized: God the Creator, whose titles are elevated above the main line of the text along with the emperor's, is made the ultimate cause of the embassy. The main body of the text is heavily abbreviated, but the letter ends with the English king, whose name is not elevated, writing from the palace of Li's patron saint, Saint James.[2]

With Li sick, Yan also acted as the embassy's interpreter, since no one thought the bad-tempered Ke was suited to the task. As the ships approached the southern tip of Vietnam, a party was put ashore on an island to try to buy fresh food. People came out onto the beach, and various Chinese dialects were tried without success, but when Yan took out a notebook and wrote in Chinese characters, which were also used for Vietnamese, one of the islanders took his pencil and wrote an answer. A woman who could speak Chinese arrived, and Yan explained what the British wanted. It seemed to go well, but when they returned the next day they found the village deserted and a letter explaining that the people were too poor to provide these things. Yan translated it into an effective piece of Latin prose pleading with the British to spare the villagers. It seems unlikely that this is a precise translation of what the villagers wrote; rather it is a piece of rhetoric of the kind he had studied in Naples intended to persuade the British to depart peacefully. He was successful, and the ship sailed on.[3]

Events in Vietnam also illustrated the risks of interpreting. By the time the *Lion* reached the port of Da Nang about a week later, there were so many sick that the reduced crew could scarcely sail the ship. What the Vietnamese saw, however, was four heavily armed ships sailing into the midst of an ongoing civil war. The faction that controlled Da Nang were backed by the Qing, who had recently sent an army to support them under Fukang'an, the Qianlong emperor's nephew and favourite general. European warships seemed likely to come from their opponents, who were backed by French missionaries, so they assembled their troops.[4] The British sent a small party ashore with Yan to interpret. Yan, conversing slowly in writing, allayed their fears and arranged for the sick to come ashore while the ship was cleaned and disinfected and for the British to buy meat, fruit, and vegetables. All went well, and the next day the British were invited to a dinner with a great variety of dishes "which they relished extremely."[5] The *Lion's* huge cannons remained at the forefront of everyone's minds: the Vietnamese assembled their troops and presented ever larger gifts, including a hundred tons of rice. Macartney responded with weapons and cloth. When one of the British naval officers began to explore the river, he and his men were seized as spies and put through a terrifying mock execution. It was Yan who had the dangerous task of going ashore to negotiate their release.[6]

Li, who was now recovering from his scurvy with the fresh food, faced a difficult decision. He, not Yan, was the one who had agreed to be the embassy's interpreter. Everyone was well aware that when in 1759 James Flint was imprisoned for presenting a petition requesting the extension of the British trade, his Chinese collaborator Liu Yabian had been publicly executed. Interpreting for the British was officially limited to those Chinese employed in the trade and registered with the government, who could then be held responsible for their actions. As a warning of the risks faced by interpreters who ignored these rules, Liu Yabian's execution was not an event that was easy to forget.[7]

So Macartney pressed Li to continue with the embassy "not as an interpreter but as a friend, because he said he could not find anyone else he could trust in such an important matter."[8] He even promised, as George Leonard had in Rome, that he would act like a papal diplomat and try to obtain advantages for the Catholic mission from the emperor. And he assured Li that he need not be anxious, as he would be expected only to listen to what was said and act as a secret advisor.[9] Writing to his friend Giovanni Borgia, Li explained how hard Macartney had pushed. What the others did not know was that in agreeing to Macartney's demands Li was making a personal sacrifice: he had planned after so many years in Europe to meet his brother Li Zichang, who was now based on Hainan Island, in Macao. Li Zichang had proved to be an outstanding junior officer when the Liangzhou brigade was sent to fight against rebels in the Jinchuan mountains of Sichuan. He was promoted and posted to

Xinjiang and then Guangdong. Then in 1788 he was transferred to the campaign against a rebellion in Taiwan, where he took the lead in perilous forays through jungle and precipitous mountains. Fukang'an, who was in charge of this campaign before being transferred to Vietnam, mentioned him in his despatches, and at the end of the war he was decorated for his courage and given the honour of escorting the captured rebel leader to Beijing. The last four years he had spent as a brigade commander of the Qing naval forces on Hainan.[10]

Tales of virtuous officials who put their responsibilities above the opportunity to see their families are a commonplace of Chinese morality, and Li had always been a model student. Having decided that he could not refuse Macartney, he put on an English uniform with a sword and cockade and decided to use the name Plum, an English translation of his Chinese surname.[11] Yan was amazed: he reassured the superiors at the Naples College that Li "doesn't fear any danger for himself, for he is so ingenious he can change into another person like an actor."[12] When they reached Macao, Li stayed aboard the *Lion*, while George Leonard went quietly ashore with Ke, Yan, and Wang. His plan was to meet with the East India Company staff and European missionaries in Macao and through them to find another interpreter to replace Ke.

There were plenty of Portuguese-speaking Chinese in Macao who could have helped the embassy with interpreting. Some forty years earlier a Chinese official responsible for the town had described how the people there adopted the foreigners' dress, converted to their religion, and even married into their families. As a result they picked up Portuguese and could interpret or translate when needed.[13] Indeed the town's Portuguese administration had an official translation office with a staff of five who translated the documents for their communications with Qing officials.[14] Macartney had brought the painter Thomas Hickey, who was a Portuguese speaker, with him almost certainly with this in mind, but he and Staunton also worried that an interpreter from Macao was likely to oppose the embassy's aim of obtaining an independent British base.

George Leonard's first meeting in Macao was with Henry Browne and the two other senior merchants, who told him how they had gone with the senior Chinese merchants Pan Youdu and

Cai Shiwen to submit a letter sent by Francis Baring announcing the embassy. The letter had been addressed to Fukang'an, the governor general, but by the time it arrived he had been transferred to lead a military campaign against the Gurkhas in Tibet, so it was received by Guo Shixun, the Guangdong provincial governor. Baring had sent the English with a Latin translation, but both versions were in complex, formal prose and the content was opaque, carefully avoiding any clear statement of the embassy's goals of getting a resident at court or obtaining a new port where the English could trade. Guo Shixun sent the Latin version to the Macao translation office, but he also wanted to check the contents of the English version. So, to the consternation of the English, he sent them off with Pan and Cai to an adjoining room to come up with a Chinese translation themselves.[15]

The result was both simplified and misleading: George III's grandiose claim to be king of Great Britain, France, and Ireland came out as a long string of transliterated syllables, merchants played a leading role, and the primary purpose of the embassy appeared to be to bring birthday greetings to the emperor.[16] Although the English spoke no Chinese, Pan and Cai, who had grown up in the trade, did understand English, though they did not read it. The normal practice in the trade was for one side to explain a document and the other to write down the translation.[17] The problem was that in this case the English merchants would have needed to explain what was implied by such vague phrases as "improving the connection, intercourse and good correspondence between the courts of London and Pekin" and "increasing and extending the commerce between their respective subjects" to the very men who stood to lose most from the changes the embassy was seeking.[18] They had no intention of doing this, and the result was confusion that they then blamed on the merchants' poor understanding of English.[19]

The translation from the Macao translation office was shorter and more formal. It conveyed the general meaning of the letter but focussed on diplomacy between kings and omitted the merchants. The Macao translators were in general quite precise, so the abbreviation must have been the result of a conscious choice and was presumably related to Portuguese anxiety about the embassy.[20] Both the originals and the translations were sent off to Beijing, where the European missionaries at court (also Portuguese) provided a second translation of the Latin. This was shorter still, concentrating on two key points: that the intention was to congratulate the emperor and the fact that the English intended to sail directly to Tianjin.[21] All three translations were highly abstracted and used conventionally exalted terms for the Chinese emperor, but the primary cause of their limitations was not so much linguistic difficulties as the translator's decision as to what points to present.

Browne claimed that these events had prompted him to arrange some Chinese lessons, though it is more likely that he knew how critical Macartney had been of the East India Company for its employees' failure to learn Chinese. The teacher they had found was one of the Chinese linguists registered to handle the paperwork for the British merchants. A few lessons in Macao were certainly not going to enable the British merchants to interpret, but Browne was able to tell Macartney that the teacher's son was available and excited at the idea of going to Beijing, maybe even seeing the emperor. This young man, who was known to the British as Antonio, had lived in Manila, which had a sizable Chinese population, and could speak Spanish as well as Mandarin, the language of officials. By the time George Leonard arrived, Antonio had already been sent off on a ship that Browne had sent to look for the embassy, where he was treated as a guest, dining respectably with the captain.[22]

While he was in Macao George Leonard also went to meet with Giambattista Marchini, who was in charge of the finances for the papal mission to China. Marchini was horrified when he heard of Li's decision to remain with the British as an interpreter: he was sure Li would be discovered as a Chinese priest with grave consequences not only for him but for the whole Catholic mission in China. However, George Leonard had impressive letters from Rome, and Li's classmates insisted that it would be useless and painful to order him to disembark as nothing would make him change his mind. When George Leonard asked for another interpreter, Marchini suggested he apply to Claude Letondal, the procurator of the competing French mission. Letondal offered his servant Lorenzo da Silva, who could speak Chinese, Latin, Portuguese, and

French.[23] Silva's surname, occupation, and language skills suggest that he may have been of mixed race from Macao and had initially trained for the priesthood. This also suggests that he was more than a personal servant, but the English had been told he was a servant and treated him as one.

When George Leonard left, Marchini was quick to get in touch with Li Zibiao's brother, Li Zichang, who was known to him as one of very few Catholic officials left in China. Li Zichang must have realised the dangers his brother was likely to face and decided to go immediately to Beijing himself. He needed permission from his superiors to do this, but his most recent promotion the previous year had been accompanied by a summons to Beijing, so, assuming that he had delayed this to wait for his brother's arrival, he had a plausible excuse. Ke Zongxiao, who came from Beijing, was able to travel north under his protection, which may well have been what they had planned for Li.[24]

Meanwhile the embassy sailed north up the coast, and Antonio, Lorenzo da Silva, and Li were all at different times sent ashore to interpret. There were now five ships, the three that had set out from Portsmouth, a brig Macartney had bought in Batavia, and the ship that Browne had sent to look for them. They sailed first for the Zhoushan islands, which lay off the major trading town of Ningbo. The British had previously traded at Zhoushan with considerable support from provincial officials, but some thirty years earlier the Qianlong emperor had decided that the state's interests were best served by confining the trade to Canton.[25] It was for demanding the reopening of this trade that in 1759 James Flint had been imprisoned and Liu Yabian executed.

The East India Company's brig was the first to reach the islands, where Ma Yu, the Zhoushan naval commander, went aboard and questioned Antonio. Antonio said he came from the Philippines and explained that the ship had been sent to look for the embassy. Ma made careful notes of the different types of guns and cannons on the ship and told Antonio that the British must not continue north. A few days later when the winds changed that is exactly what they did. When they next came into port to ask for pilots it was not so easy for Antonio: the officials he dealt with threatened to hold him responsible and punish him.[26]

FIGURE 7.2. William Alexander's sketch of Ma "the
Admiral of Chusan" writing notes on board the *Hindostan*.

About a week later Ma Yu went out again, to meet a second ship
that had sailed into the Zhoushan harbour and fired a gun salute.
This time Li was interpreting, along with one of the pilots they had
picked up in Macao. Li was feeling shaken because he had very
nearly been knocked overboard by the boom of the main sail when
the ship spun to avoid a rock. Everyone had laughed at him because
in his fright he had exclaimed, "Most Holy Mary, it's a miracle! A
miracle!" while one of the sailors who had also nearly been hit just
swore at the boom.[27] Ma Yu offered fruit and questioned Li, who
called himself Don Plum and explained that the ship was indeed
part of the embassy.[28]

They went ashore where Ma provided another interpreter: Guo Jiguan, whose father had done business with the English and who still "retained somewhat of the English language."[29] Guo was a success with George Leonard: he could remember the names of the British merchants, blamed the ending of the trade on the influence of Canton, and was eager for the British to return. Ma, however, continued to be focussed on the embassy's armaments. His superior, the Zhejiang governor Changlin, passed on his report that one of the ships had forty-two cannons, while the other had thirty-two iron cannons, thirty-two brass cannons, and more than six hundred muskets and six hundred swords. Guo discouraged any further gun salutes, pointing out to George Leonard how dangerous it was that the British did not point their guns in the air when they fired, and how much this had harmed the trade on earlier occasions when people had been killed as a result.[30]

The following day there was a formal meeting with the county magistrate. The English were given seats facing the Chinese and offered tea. The magistrate made a long speech "uttered with a variety of tones, and accompanied by gestures."[31] No doubt these were intended to help the foreigners to understand, but in practice the length of the speech made it very difficult for the interpreter, who had to listen to the speech, remember as much as possible, and then express it in another language. George Leonard received only the gist, which was that the magistrate could provide pilots for the coast of this province but no further. When George Leonard threatened to appeal to higher officials in Ningbo, the magistrate pointed to his official hat and gestured to show that in that case he would be dismissed. They ended with a compromise: two local merchants who had been to Tianjin were ordered to accompany the embassy. After the English left Changlin had the unfortunate Guo Jiguan placed under house arrest to prevent any further contact with the British and informed Qianlong, who ordered that he should be brought to Beijing for questioning.[32]

The British sailed on round Shandong province, anchoring briefly off the Miaodao islands, where the Penglai prefect came aboard and spoke to Macartney. This time Lorenzo da Silva acted as interpreter. Macartney found the prefect "courteous, intelligent, and inquisitive," while the prefect himself reported the interpreter's satisfyingly appropriate language.[33] Clearly Silva was a smooth and effective interpreter.

A few days later Silva was also sent with Hüttner, whose fluent Latin made him a useful collaborator, to handle a major meeting to discuss the embassy's travel to Beijing at the Dagu fort, which guarded the approach to the city of Tianjin. Liang Kentang, the elderly Zhili governor general, attended this meeting in person with a large entourage, three of whom were introduced as having been sent by the emperor to greet the embassy. Silva and Hüttner observed that, curiously, it was the man whose hat finial showed that he was of the lowest rank who appeared to be the principal. This was Zhengrui, a Manchu who had recently taken over the administration of the massively profitable salt monopoly based in Tianjin. His low rank was the result of a series of demotions following accusations of corruption: in the past two years alone he had paid fines to the emperor of nearly 36,000 taels. The unwilling respect with which he was treated was the first hint of the court politics that would shape the reception of the embassy. For the present it was Liang who spoke, questioning Silva about supplies for the seven hundred men on the five ships, the best way to transport the embassy's gifts, and how many men would attend the ambassador to Beijing. He also asked if the members of the embassy had brought merchandise to sell in Beijing, assuring the English that the emperor had no objection.[34]

The two other officials who had been appointed to supervise the embassy's journey sailed out to visit the *Lion* the following day. Liang had chosen two of his subordinates: a soldier and a tax expert. Wang Wenxiong was a professional military officer. He was a tall, muscular man who came from the mountains of southwest China. Like Li Zichang he had entered the army as a common soldier and had first been promoted in the Jinchuan wars. His scars from hand-to-hand fighting later impressed the British. Since then he had risen to be the commander in charge of Tongzhou, one of the main access points for Beijing. The other official was Qiao Renjie from Shanxi who had come up through the examination system, though he too was an active man who had been keen on martial arts in his youth.

Qiao was now one of the circuit intendants for Tianjin with an interest in finance and very considerable personal wealth: he had

FIGURE 7.3. Wang Wenxiong. Alexander's portrait shows him as a large, powerful man looking directly out at the viewer.

recently had to pay a fine of 10,000 taels to the emperor after he was held responsible for errors in the taxation of merchants in Anhui, which was less than Zhengrui had paid but still a huge sum. As William Alexander's portraits of them suggest, Qiao was a serious character conscious of his dignity as an official, but Wang was open and enthusiastic, someone who would later win national fame for his success in leading soldiers in battle (figs. 7.3 and 7.4).[35]

FIGURE 7.4. Qiao Renjie by William Alexander,
who sketched him in formal dress holding a
tobacco pipe.

Because of the shallow water in the bay, the *Lion* was anchored some fifteen miles off shore. When Wang and Qiao arrived and had been lifted up the side of the vast ship with its rows of gun ports, they turned out to be friendly and surprisingly informal. The British, who had rather expected senior Qing officials to be serious and severe philosophers and had thought they might well be suspicious of the embassy, were delighted. Wang and Qiao even explained that Zhengrui should have come too but was afraid of going so far out to sea. They had been afraid too, but they were Chinese not Manchu, so they had to come! George Leonard soon concluded that Chinese officials were like men of rank in France before the revolution with "an engaging urbanity of manners, instantaneous familiarity, ready communicativeness, together with a sense of self-approbation, and the vanity of national superiority piercing through every disguise."[36]

For the present, since Silva had not yet returned, Li interpreted, and as George Leonard later recalled, "Much of the stiffness which generally accompanies a communication through the medium of an interpreter, was removed by the good humour of the parties, and the ardent desire they felt of making out one another's meaning. Their discourse by no means partook of the guarded intercourse of strangers suspicious of each other. Sometimes before the explanation was given of the expressions used, the occasion itself suggested what was intended to be said, and gesture often came in aid of words."[37] Soon there was more than one conversation going on, and George Leonard thought he would try out George Thomas, who they discovered could both listen and speak comprehensibly. George Leonard was delighted, though George Thomas's abilities were still limited: a few weeks later Zhengrui reported that Macartney had said that they had only two interpreters, Li Zibiao and George Thomas, who "is only twelve and is not really familiar with the pronunciation."[38] Barrow had also been applying himself seriously to the language, but he was older and even less successful: throughout the embassy his efforts turned out to be mainly a source of amusement to Wang and Qiao.[39]

This cheerful meeting must have given Macartney confidence in the decision he had taken to dismiss Antonio and Lorenzo da Silva and take only Li to Beijing as interpreter. Behind the scenes Macartney was having a battle with Captain Mackintosh, which had redoubled his distrust of those with vested interests in the trade. Mackintosh knew that embassies were usually allowed to trade tax-free, and as well as the furs, he and his crew had brought watches, scientific instruments, and even a coach. When Macartney realised this he was horrified: he was an ambassador, not a merchant. Despite Liang Kentang's evident expectation that the embassy would trade, Macartney issued an announcement banning any trade until the negotiations were complete. Mackintosh was furious. Macartney tried to placate him by purchasing, for the immense sum of £773, the great lens he had brought with him to sell. Furious arguments continued over several days, recorded by Macartney in tiny crabbed notes in the draft of his journal, but carefully removed from the version that was later circulated.[40]

When George Leonard first listed the people who would go on to Beijing, Silva was listed among the servants as the interpreter, while Li was included alongside Maxwell and Winder as "Andrew Plumb 3rd Secretary."[41] But Macartney, now suspecting that Silva was spying for the Portuguese, decided to send him off with Captain Gower as interpreter for the *Lion*.[42] Antonio was not a problem because after the incident requesting pilots he had lost his nerve and did not want to continue.[43] And thus it was that Li Zibiao alone continued with the embassy to Beijing.

CHAPTER EIGHT

Li Zibiao as Interpreter and Mediator

AFTERWARD LI ZIBIAO explained how it felt to take over as the "interpreter of words," dressed in his English uniform and wig, coming with Hüttner from the summer sunshine into the dark of the temple of the sea god where Liang Kentang was waiting to receive the British.

> Taking precautions in this necessity, I appeared and began to confront all the officials, as if I were coming out of some secret hiding place. I was fortunate at the start because the governor general of Zhili, who came to the shore to meet us, by some mistake stood up when I spoke as if I were one of the leaders of the embassy. And the three other high officials, two of whom were with us all the rest of the time, always treated me as the person third in rank after the ambassador. Nor did the ambassador, once he understood what had happened, seem to need greater honour, since everything was done as he wished and he was treated as someone in authority.[1]

There is a certain exhilaration in these words heightened by the sense of risk. The Latin terms he uses in the first sentence suggest an animal, flushed from its lair in the hunt, and throwing itself in the way of danger. Those dangers lie on every side, not only from the Chinese officials but also from Macartney. And yet at the same time

Li's words show a confidence in his own acting ability and a sudden sense of power and status as interpreter. It was a heady mix.

For this first meeting, he and Hüttner had evidently worked out together how they would proceed. They began by entreating the officials "to be so good as to answer our questions exactly, and without interrupting us or talking confusedly together" as they apparently had in the previous meeting which Hüttner had handled with Silva.[2] The Chinese agreed and from then on Hüttner spoke in Latin and Li translated his words into Chinese. Nevertheless, it is clear from Hüttner's report to Macartney that the two of them were in fact working together. They had decided that the key point was to avoid moving the embassy's valuable gifts too often since they might easily get broken. So when they were told that boats large enough to go out to sea would not be able to get up the river, Hüttner and Li "turned therefore (after their own example) our questions, evaded their answers and suggested reasons for the contrary, as many as we could."[3] The conversation went on for more than three hours late into the night. They were offered tea, slices of watermelon, and fans to cool themselves, but it must have been exhausting for Li, who was interpreting in both directions while also trying to work out what was going on. A key piece of information came quite incidentally when one of the officials told him that there was no hurry as the emperor's birthday was not for another two months.

The Qianlong emperor received reports on this meeting, as he had on almost every event as the embassy sailed up the coast. Because of the late summer heat he was up in the mountains beyond the Great Wall. Despite an exceptionally long and prosperous reign, he was anxious about many things: the harvest, factions and corruption at court, appointments of incarnate lamas in Tibet, war with the Gurkhas—and the British embassy. Looking at poems and paintings of expeditions when he was younger to watch the sunset or admire the moon calmed him:

> True self expression always arises in the moment.
> I used to climb Red Sky Peak to admire the mountain view,
> From time to time I would write a poem or paint a picture,

So I keep each of the scrolls to remember the scene.
Recently my heart has been ravelled with cares and I have little
    leisure,
So I spread out the scrolls to drive away my worries for a while.
I watch the late summer shower with anxious thoughts,
As one difficulty retreats another approaches. I miss the quiet
    green hills.[4]

Qianlong's prolific poetry was intended for the eyes of his ministers, who edited it (and probably sometimes also wrote it), and this poem displays him as a virtuous ruler concerned with the cares of state. The notes explain that the hot weather has been oppressive and he has been longing for rain and "also because the English envoy is about to arrive I have to give directions for everything which is why I have no leisure."[5]

Liang Kentang and Zhengrui had both written to the emperor secretly and without agreeing on the line they would take. They were not only very different characters but also on opposing sides of the major factional divide at court. Liang was the same generation as Qianlong and one of the very few Chinese who had risen through the examination system into the emperor's inner circle. His account of the meeting was practical and the content very close to what Hüttner told Macartney.[6]

Zhengrui was Manchu who had spent his entire career in the Imperial Household Department, which ran the emperor's personal finances, and was said to have paid the chief minister Heshen a huge sum for his salt monopoly post. His report was full of compliments to the emperor but both less detailed and less honest than Liang's. He amalgamated the two meetings, the first with Silva and the second with Li, and implied that the discussions were with Macartney himself. (As Qiao Renjie and Wang Wenxiong had told the English when they arrived on the *Lion*, Zhengrui had been supposed to come with them.) He confined the lengthy discussions about the boats on which the embassy was to travel up the river to a couple of sentences and focussed instead on a remark made by Silva about the sickness on board the English ships and their need for fresh food, which he interpreted as the English being on the point of starvation. He assured the emperor that he had addressed this crucial issue by sending a large amount of food.[7]

The appointment of two tax experts, Zhengrui and Qiao Renjie, to handle it suggests that the embassy was seen from the start in terms of the revenue from the British trade and that Heshen, who controlled government finances, was involved. Because the Imperial Household Department received all gifts to the emperor, it was customary for its members to escort foreign embassies to court, but it was also responsible for much commercial taxation, including the bulk of the taxes on the trade with the British. The tea trade was a significant source of revenue for the Qing as it was for the British, but this was less well known because most of the revenue went to the Imperial Household Department, which was staffed by Manchus close to the emperor and shrouded in secrecy. Regular taxes, which included customs duties, were controlled by the Board of Revenue, whose revenue from trade had hardly increased during the eighteenth century. Its accounts were more or less public: Qiao Renjie even provided Macartney with a summary for the previous year. However, in addition to these regular customs duties, there was an additional quota known as the "surplus," and this, along with "donations" by merchants, and the voluntary fines known as "guilt money" paid by officials like Zhengrui and Qiao, went to the Imperial Household Department. A significant part of this commercial income came from the trade with the British and had been increasing rapidly. Since the accounts of the Imperial Household Department were concealed from the British, as indeed from Chinese members of the regular bureaucracy, Macartney had been told that these sums were simply corrupt additions to the regular taxes that he should try to end by appealing to the emperor. Meanwhile Heshen was actively trying to increase the rate of the surplus taken from the British trade.[8]

The immediate result of Zhengrui's analysis of the discussions with Hüttner and Li was that Qiao and Wang arrived on board the *Lion* with vast quantities of fresh food. Thus supplied, Macartney immediately invited them to dinner, where they "though at first a little embarrassed by our knives and forks, soon got over the difficulty, and handled them with notable dexterity and execution upon some of the good things which they had brought us."⁹ Macartney was still well supplied with liquor, and they all settled down to some heavy drinking, working their way through gin, rum, and arrack as well as shrub, raspberry, and cherry brandy. After all this Qiao and Wang shook hands "like Englishmen" when they left.¹⁰

Macartney and his retinue finally disembarked in China on 6 August 1793, a year after leaving England. They were received by Liang Kentang, and there were compliments on both sides: Liang expressed the Qianlong emperor's pleasure at their arrival, while Li, speaking for Macartney, emphasized the distance they had come and expressed their gratitude for the kind reception. Macartney, looking rather than listening, was struck by Liang's unpretentious manner and the kindness and courtesy with which he treated his subordinates and servants, an aspect of Chinese life that was significantly different from the more rigid class hierarchies in Britain at the time.¹¹

But if the Chinese of this period lacked the British hierarchy by social class, they did have a powerful sense of the hierarchy by culture. Classical texts depicted China as the centre of civilisation and its emperor as a cosmic ruler. This cultural hierarchy was acted out when the emperor received envoys from the peoples beyond the frontiers who brought gifts as an expression of their submission. There has been much discussion by scholars over many years of how this "tribute system" actually worked during the Qing. It was, however, very satisfactorily modelled for the Chinese by regular embassies from Korea, which shared the same classical texts and where submission to the distant centre of civilisation was a long-standing part of politics.¹²

The expectations of the tribute system played an important role in how the embassy was received; the *Collected Statutes* of the dynasty, which detailed the various ceremonies with which tribute missions were to be received in Beijing, included a prominent role for the interpreter. When the members of the embassy were sorted out into boats for the journey up the Hai River, Macartney, George Leonard, and Li each had his own boat, while the remaining gentlemen were put together in groups of three or four.¹³

Li had his own boat because interpreters were understood within the tribute system as officials. The Qing had inherited from

FIGURE 8.1. Boats carrying the embassy up the river toward Beijing by William Alexander. The small flags at the top of the masts had written on them the character *gong* meaning "tribute."

the Ming dynasty a set of central government institutions that were intended to provide officials responsible for translation and interpreting for diplomatic encounters. Qianlong had conducted a major reorganisation of these, getting rid of posts for languages that were dealt with by other offices in the central government and others that were better handled on the frontier. He had merged the rest into a single Interpreters and Translators Institute focussing on Arabic, Tibetan, Thai, and Burmese, with a focus on his own pet project of collating foreign language vocabularies, although in theory they were still supposed to provide interpreting for embassies. In practice interpreting was provided by the foreign state sending the embassy. Missions from Korea and the Liuqiu Islands (today Okinawa) brought interpreters with them, who were understood as officials of those states. These interpreters, like those who arrived from Southeast Asia, might be Chinese resident in the relevant state, but this was overlooked. In theory moving overseas was a criminal offense, but in the Ming dynasty occasional interpreters had even petitioned successfully to remain in China.[14] Thus the protocol of the tribute system gave interpreters a prominent role and ignored their ambiguous identity.

The system also tended to shift discussions away from practical negotiations on subjects like taxation and to concentrate minds instead on protocol and the grandeur of the emperor. It was, perhaps, designed for this purpose, but in this case both sides showed considerable flexibility over the protocol. The gifts brought by the British were labelled *gong*, a term for gifts given to the emperor and usually translated as "tribute," which was written on small flags at the top of the masts on the boats carrying the embassy upriver towards Beijing. Li told Macartney what the flags meant, but Macartney decided not to respond unless he was pushed to do so. Qianlong was quite clear that Macartney should be described as an envoy bringing gifts (*gong-shi*), but when this term was not used he decided that the interpreter was probably responsible and chose not to make an issue of it.[15]

There was more difficulty over the expectation that the envoy would go down on his knees before the emperor and bow his head repeatedly to the ground. This is the ritual known in Chinese as *koutou* (literally "to knock the head"), which Macartney usually referred to as a prostration. The instructions in the dynasty's *Collected Statutes* for the reception of tribute missions in Beijing included repeated kowtows by the envoy and his retinue.[16] Macartney had told Henry Dundas before he left England that he would be flexible on "genuflexions, prostrations and other idle oriental ceremonies."[17] On the other hand this was an important issue for the British public: before Macartney left England there had been a biting cartoon by James Gillray that showed him on one knee offering trinkets to a reclining oriental potentate while behind him his gentlemen were kneeling with their heads on the ground and their bottoms in the air. So when Zhengrui came to discuss protocol, Macartney evaded the question. The problem he faced was how any action would be regarded in Britain on his return: in his notebook he wrote pointedly, "Timagoras, an Athenian being sent Embassador to Persia adored the king there after the Persian manner, for which after his return he was condemned to die."[18]

But the formalities of a tribute mission were not the only issue that interested Qing officials. To Macartney's surprise, Wang and Qiao began to ask him questions about British conquests in India and possible British intervention in the recent Qing campaign against Gurkha incursions into Tibet. Macartney's account of this has puzzled scholars since Chinese writings at the time show very little knowledge of India and certainly do not suggest that Qing officials knew about the expanding British Empire there. Fukang'an had written to the British governor general in Calcutta about the Gurkhas, but the Tibetan term for the British was different from that used in Canton for the English, and no connection was made until after the embassy had left, and then it appears to have been forgotten.[19]

So where does this enquiry about the British in India come from? Perhaps Fukang'an guessed more than he had written to the emperor and was prompting behind the scenes.[20] More likely the information had reached Wang and Qiao from Li. Wang and Qiao were responsible for the day-to-day management of the embassy and Li was the only Chinese speaker, so they must have been talking to each other, but there are hints in Macartney's diary that the relationship had developed beyond that. For one thing, Macartney had become aware that Wang and Qiao disliked and resented Zhengrui. He wrote in his diary that "they have scarcely disguised their sense of the Emperor's partiality to the Tartars in preference to his Chinese subjects" and that they thought him crazy and morose.[21] Given the pressure Zhengrui was under, with the emperor constantly rebuking and demoting him and Heshen requiring huge financial gifts, it would not have been surprising for him to be somewhat absorbed in his own problems. This was more than a passing joke about Zhengrui being afraid of the sea and suggests that Wang and Qiao's conversations with Li had gone beyond the immediate practical arrangements for the embassy. Li had just spent a year and a half with the British and was interested in politics; he had talked at great length to both Macartney and George Leonard, he had met Edmund Burke at the height of his campaign against the corruption of East India Company rule in India, and he had sailed round the world with the British with plenty of discussion of maps and charts. He could scarcely have failed to know something about British conquests in India or to be aware that the British were worried the Qing might be influenced against the embassy by knowledge of them. Wang would probably have known enough about the recent victories in Nepal to see a connection. We cannot know what was said but not written in the past, but possibilities emerge: that Fukang'an had suspicions, that Li himself had concerns about a British threat to China, and that

Wang and Qiao were using their contacts with Li to find out about the British.

Military anxieties were no doubt exacerbated by Macartney's display of British artillery when they disembarked from the boats at Tongzhou. Macartney had brought a military guard and a set of lightweight brass cannons mounted on easily manoeuvrable gun carriages. Now he insisted on holding a demonstration in which they fired off several rounds. Wang put on a good show, speaking lightly of the British weapons as if they were nothing new, but Macartney was told, presumably by Li, that he actually felt mortified because the Chinese had nothing as good.[22]

Later that day Zhengrui came with Wang and Qiao to try again to persuade Macartney to kowtow. They demonstrated the actions themselves, rather impressing Macartney who suffered from painful joints because of his gout. When he continued to refuse, they turned the pressure on Li who replied cautiously that he would do only as Macartney directed. Macartney, not quite sure what Li would say, was delighted.[23] However, Li's behaviour was apparently acceptable to Zhengrui too: his status as interpreter was confirmed when, for the final stage of the journey to Beijing, he was provided with a sedan chair along with Macartney and George Leonard, while the rest of the gentlemen were loaded into much less comfortable carts.[24]

Then, when Macartney and his suite finally arrived at their destination, there was a lengthy dispute over where they should be housed, which Li ended up negotiating. The accommodation allocated to them was a garden residence some miles north of the city, near the Yuanmingyuan palace where the British gifts were to be displayed. Macartney, however, was still planning a permanent British residency in Beijing and thought the house totally unacceptable for this because it was outside the city, too small, dilapidated, and to his mind unfurnished. His retinue, exhausted from their journey in the uncomfortable carts, found themselves standing in a corridor with nowhere to go. Eventually, "they all marched in a body in quest of his Lordship and Mr Plumb, whom they found disputing with the mandarines about the appartments not being sufficiently spacious."[25]

FIGURE 8.2. "The vehicles in which we entered Pekin" by William
Alexander. A wooden-wheeled cart and a more comfortable sedan chair.

Everyone had assumed that once the embassy arrived in Beijing
the European missionaries there would take over the formal interpreting. Qianlong had appointed the Portuguese José Bernardo
de Almeida and had promoted him for the purpose. Meanwhile
the Frenchman Jean Baptiste Grammont had written to Macartney seeking to be made interpreter himself and warning against
Almeida. Macartney, entirely agreed: he was convinced that as
interpreter Almeida would be hostile to the British and support the
Portuguese interest in Macao.[26]

The result was a most uncomfortable meeting between Macartney and a group of missionaries in the presence of Zhengrui. In
order to reinforce his demands for a French interpreter, Macartney
had ordered the members of his suite not to speak Latin, which was
the only language in which they could communicate with Almeida.
So when one of the missionaries addressed the embassy's doctor in
Latin with the simple words "Do you speak Latin, sir? Surely you
do!"[27] they had to pretend not to understand. This was demeaning

because speaking Latin was a such an important marker of status as a gentleman. It was also infuriating because, with Li busy interpreting for Macartney and George Leonard, the other members of the embassy had been unable to speak to the Chinese and were now longing to meet these famous European experts on China. With Macartney refusing to speak Latin, the interpreting had to go through a third language before Almeida interpreted into Chinese for Zhengrui. Meanwhile Li, whispering to George Leonard in Latin in the background, told him that Almeida was not really backing the demand for a house in Beijing and had implied that Macartney said this only because he did not really want to set off into the hills to meet the emperor.[28]

The discussions went on for several days and, as tempers frayed, Li tried to keep out of the way. His letter to Naples explains what happened next:

> A sharp dispute arose between the Officials and the Ambassador. When the negotiations were forcefully disturbed, the two Senior Officials who accompanied us, called His Excellency Qiao and His Excellency Wang, came hurrying to find me demanding in a great state of excitement that I would set out openly the Ambassador's opinions and reasons, which I knew full well, so that I could explain the original cause of his excited behaviour, which would certainly remove the reason for the present dispute. I did not do so, saying that I was really tired from the previous days and quite exhausted by the work I had done, which was not my job, and that I was not an interpreter if they could find another, and that if I had done it from time to time it was not because it was my job but out of necessity. But they would not accept my arguments at all, but at length made great progress, so that I gave in to them not because they were right, but because I was overcome by their demands. I came from where I was to the President of the Board, and explained the Ambassador's thinking to him and why he so much wanted to stay in the city of Beijing, and that certainly as soon as his things were all safely arranged in whatever place was decided on, he would be able to leave quickly for the Emperor, who was then staying in Rehe, and that it was certainly not the case that there was anything wrong with the house in Haidian or that it was unworthy of such an important Ambassador.[29]

FIGURE 8.3. "View in the Ambassador's residence at Pekin" by William Alexander. This is the new residence in the city. Quite a few Chinese and Western figures are scattered round the gardens. Macartney is in the foreground, with George Leonard behind him holding George Thomas by the hand.

The striking feature of this account is that the task of the interpreter, as Li saw it, was to explain why Macartney thought as he did and then use persuasion to reach an acceptable solution. In pursuit of this goal he had no qualms about stating the precise opposite to Macartney's opinions: Macartney did indeed think that the house was inadequate and unsuitable for him as ambassador, but this was scarcely a tactful thing to say. Li's tactics worked: the president of the Board of Works offered an alternative residence in the city, inviting Li to visit it first.[30]

A few days later a letter arrived from Heshen appointing Li interpreter to the embassy for the imperial audience. Wang and Qiao told him that this was for the sake of minimising controversy. In other words, they too thought that the interpreter's task was to mediate as well as translate. Li was flattered by Wang and Qiao's good opinion. He explained that "the senior Grand Councillor His Excellency Heshen relying on the account given by the officials made me interpreter to the Emperor and rejected all the others."[31]

With the housing issue solved, Macartney turned back to the problem of protocol for his audience with the emperor. He wrote a letter to Heshen proposing a compromise: he would kowtow to Qianlong if a Qing official privately did the same to a portrait of George III. Getting this letter translated into Chinese became a major issue. Zhengrui refused to allow his staff to assist at all. Li said firmly that he "was utterly unacquainted with the stile necessary for the Palace; and in writing Latin and Italian had lost the habit, during his stay in Europe, of writing the complicated Chinese character."[32] Fortunately, now they were living in the city, where many elite Chinese were visiting their residence to see the English and their gifts; it was easier to get a message through to the French missionaries. One of them, Nicolas Raux, arranged for his Chinese secretary to help them, but only on condition that neither his writing nor his secretary's appeared.[33]

In the end it was George Thomas who was asked to write out Macartney's letter. He had now been studying Chinese intensively for more than a year, and as a child hearing it spoken all round him his ability to understand the language must have been rapidly improving. Since the embassy landed Li Zibiao had been the only interpreter available to the hundred members of Macartney's entourage all full of curiosity and problems. Inevitably they asked George Thomas to say things; even though his Chinese was still limited, the opportunities to practice developed his skills. In Beijing his father found a boy to speak Chinese to him. The boy was terrified, but his family was poor and George Leonard would pay them well, so he stayed with the embassy and George Thomas could speak Chinese all day. Now Hüttner translated the letter into Latin, Li explained the content to Raux's secretary, who wrote it down, then George Thomas copied it out as carefully as he could in his childish Chinese handwriting. George Thomas, as would happen so often later in his life when he wrote Chinese, was safe as the English son of the deputy ambassador, but the secretary, who knew the scale of the risks involved for Li and himself, insisted that his original draft was destroyed before he left the room.[34]

Li wrote to Rome that in complaining about the house Macartney was behaving "as if drunk with too much honour" because the Chinese had been so generous.[35] And Barrow wrote later that, except for issues related to his Christian faith, Li "still manifested a predilection for the customs of his country in every other respect."[36]

Qianlong shared Li's opinion of Macartney's behaviour, but even so, and although Heshen had personally authorised Li's employment as interpreter, it would have been difficult for Qing officials to trust him.[37] Someone like Li who comes from one group but has lived in another is likely to understand both, and when called upon to mediate may well remove the passion from complaints and achieve a reconciliation. These are the insights of nineteenth-century German sociologist Georg Simmel, who also pointed out that in such cases it is very difficult for either side ever to know the inner equilibrium of such a person and that, as a result, very often both sides will doubt him.[38] With the arrival of Fukang'an back from Tibet and as the emperor came to understand the embassy's true goals, the dangers that Li faced were about to intensify.

CHAPTER NINE

Speaking to the Emperor

FROM BEIJING MACARTNEY and his suite travelled up into the hills beyond the Great Wall to Chengde, where they would meet the emperor. This was the high point of the embassy: the moment when the British came into contact not only with the emperor but also with China's leading statesmen and presented their requests. It was the moment for which Li had been planning, the moment when he risked everything to serve China's Christians. And for George Thomas, this moment when he was twelve years old brought him fame for the rest of his life, but was something that he never afterward wanted to discuss.

Macartney took with him to Chengde only a carefully selected group: his interpreter, his personal secretary, his three cousins, George Leonard Staunton with George Thomas and his tutor Hüttner, Hugh Gillan the doctor, and Captain Mackintosh of the East India Company, plus musicians, soldiers, and servants. He left the two artists in Beijing (painting decorations for a tent), which suggests that he was already planning a compromise on the kowtow and wanted to make sure he had full control of how his actions were depicted.[1] For the trusted few who went the atmosphere was relaxed. One vignette in Macartney's diary describes Li amusing them one evening with an account of an official who had come up to him and asked rather mysteriously if he might see the gifts. Apparently news sheets in Tianjin had reported that the embassy was bringing a coal-eating chicken and an elephant the size of a cat. Macartney thought this was just like the English press.[2]

Li had also become closer to Wang Wenxiong and Qiao Ren-jie. When some porcelain vases were stolen from one of the lodges where the embassy were staying, Wang and Qiao had the low-ranking Manchu responsible beaten. Afterward the man insisted that a Chinese could not beat a Manchu outside the Great Wall. Wang, exasperated, turned to Li and said "A Tartar will always be a Tartar."[3] Any kind of anti-Manchu slur could lead to terrible reper-cussions, so this apparently offhand remark suggests trust and per-haps also a certain degree of complicity. Li said afterward that all the mandarins treated him kindly "even though they knew that I was Chinese."[4] This was presumably fairly obvious. What is not clear is how much more he might have revealed: there might have been advantages in hinting to Wang that he had a brother who had also fought in the Jinchuan war and was now an officer of similar rank.

Six days after leaving Beijing the embassy caught their first glimpse of a vast expanse of palaces, gardens, and temples spread out across the hills to the north. This was the emperor's summer retreat built to impress visitors from the northern and western frontiers of the empire, but in recent years also used to receive envoys from Southeast Asia as well. They arrived in formal pro-cession, with musicians playing, and Benjamin the slave from Bata-via in a turban bringing up the rear. As the English settled into their lodgings, Li, who as usual had been meeting with Wang and Qiao, came to tell Macartney that the emperor had seen the pro-cession from the park and was pleased.[5]

Qianlong did not know that the British were still refusing to perform the kowtow; Heshen, who did, was getting anxious. He summoned Macartney that evening to discuss the protocol issues in person. Macartney decided instead to send George Leonard with written documents: a translation of his letter of credentials from George III and his proposed compromise on the kowtow. The meeting was a public affair: Heshen sat on a silk-covered platform between two Manchu and two Chinese officials, while a crowd of other officials stood around. Warm milk was served and George Leonard was given a seat, but Li and George Thomas had to stand.

George Leonard presented the translation of the letter of creden-tials that Yan Kuanren had made, now also copied out by George Thomas. Then Li explained the many reasons Heshen gave as to why Macartney's proposed compromise on the kowtow was unacceptable. At the end of the meeting, George Thomas was asked to sign the Chinese version of the letter of credentials to verify that it was indeed his writing.[6] The British were pleased at this opportunity for George Thomas to prove his abilities, but for Li, whose friend Yan Kuanren had in fact made the translation, the polite request held in it a veiled threat.

As a result of this meeting the British refusal to perform the kowtow became widely known, and the letter provided the court with its first real information as to the aims of the embassy. Qianlong himself did not see either of the documents Macartney submitted but was briefed on the meeting and later saw another translation of the letter done from the Latin version by Almeida. Almeida's Chinese was inferior to Yan's, and as Macartney had suspected, he was unwilling to convey the English point of view so skipped a lot of the content. However, his translation was extremely humble, and no doubt Heshen thought it more appropriate for the emperor's eyes. The original English was opaque, leaving the translator with many choices to make, and on one key point Yan's version was much more explicit: it says clearly that Britain wishes to have an official resident in Beijing so that he could speak directly to the emperor. (Almeida's version says that this person would be there to control British people and answer the emperor's questions.)[7] The text of Yan's translation that survives in the British archives is a copy of a draft, which might have been used by Li and then given to George Thomas. If Li did follow this text, it suggests that he was respectful in his interpreting but quite clear about the embassy's ultimate aims.

Qianlong was angry about the kowtow: he wrote immediately to order that the British should receive lower status treatment on their journey home. However, his letter ends with a question: "Agui usually has an opinion. What does he think?"[8] Agui was the elder statesman of the faction at court that opposed Heshen, so it appears that at this point Qianlong began seeking proposals for a different approach. He also wrote to the governors of the coastal provinces telling them to be cautious: Fukang'an was about to arrive and would receive a personal audience to discuss the matter.[9] Fukang'an not only was Qianlong's nephew, the son of one of his best loved ministers, and his favourite general, but had been governor general in Canton and was just now returning from the campaign against the Gurkhas. Clearly Qianlong was now considering the embassy as more than simply a congratulatory tribute mission.

Two days later Li, who had evidently not found the meeting with Heshen easy, was hovering anxiously around when Zhengrui appeared and unexpectedly agreed a compromise on the kow-tow. The nature of this compromise was something that naturally neither side was keen to publicize, but according to Macartney it included accepting that he could kneel on one knee. This was nor-mal European etiquette, so the only question for Macartney was whether the second knee touched the ground, and this might be concealed behind the robes he planned to wear. Li wrote to the Pro-paganda in Rome that Macartney was given the great honour of being allowed to perform the same ceremony as is done in Europe for kings. However, in his most private letters written to the Col-lege in Naples, he also said that in the end both sides partially conceded.[10]

This cleared the way for a very different meeting with Heshen. Now Macartney found himself discussing not protocol but Britain's relations with India and Russia. The meeting took place privately in an interior part of the palace, and Heshen was accompanied by Fukang'an's brother Fuchang'an. There were tensions between Hes-hen and Fukang'an, but all three men had begun their careers as members of the emperor's bodyguard and were now part of a Man-chu clique on the emperor's Grand Council. Heshen's questions struck George Leonard as penetrating and acute. Macartney found himself explaining that the object of the British was "the extension of commerce for the general benefit of mankind" and that although the Mughal Empire in India had collapsed the British had not removed the native tributary princes.[11]

Russia was a new topic and suggested that someone had made sense of Macartney's career from his letter of credentials that men-tioned his time as ambassador to Catherine the Great. The Qing had long-standing diplomatic relations with Russia, forged as the two states expanded into Siberia and needed to negotiate a border. Now Heshen asked how far England was from Russia, and Zheng-rui followed up with a question about British relations with Russia, to which Macartney replied that Britain had prevented Russian encroachment on the Ottoman Empire. When Macartney rose to leave, Heshen took his hand and said he would be happy to know him better.[12]

After this Qianlong announced that the British envoy regretted his former behaviour and had been respectful to Grand Council members, so the embassy could do some sightseeing when they got back to Beijing.[13] He also ordered additional gifts to be given to embassy members: as interpreter Li was to receive five bolts of different types of silk and satin, four porcelain dishes, ten silk fans, four boxes of tea, a box of tiny pressed blocks of rare tea, a box of dried melon from Xinjiang, and three purses. Li was also sent for to help put together the telescopes that the British had brought as gifts. Since Li knew nothing about telescopes and the emperor had skilled craftsmen of his own, it seems likely that there were other reasons for speaking to the interpreter as well.[14]

Concessions over protocol were possible because, unlike the strict protocol for the reception of tribute missions in Beijing, the emperor's birthday celebrations in his beautiful gardens in Chengde were relatively flexible. Moreover, the focus in Chengde was on the culture of the steppe rather than the strict Chinese protocol. The bowls of warm milk, the yurt in which the emperor would receive Macartney, the performances of wrestling, and the Tibetan Buddhist temples were all part of this. Nevertheless, the act of kneeling before the emperor was still important: the emperor's birthday ceremonies were a celebration of his personal rule, and Macartney's resistance to the kowtow was now known at court.[15]

The audience at which Macartney would be received was to be a very public performance. It began long before dawn, when he and his gentlemen were taken to an area of Mongolian-style parkland beyond the main palaces where crowds of senior officials were assembling in the dim light, gradually taking their places in a great circle that was forming around the emperor's yurt. Macartney and his gentlemen were ushered in, leaving their servants and guard outside the screened enclosure, and taken to a small yurt that had been set aside for them. As they waited there, visitors dropped by: the elderly Liang Kentang, two of the emperor's sons, and an Arabic-speaking Mongol from Russia. The future Jiaqing emperor may well

FIGURE 9.1. This picture, titled *Giving a Banquet at the Wanshuyuan*, was produced by Jesuit artists under Qianlong's personal direction and shows the moment of the emperor's arrival to feast leaders of western Mongol tribes in 1753. The emperor is in the foreground, seated on a sedan chair carried by sixteen bearers. Officials and behind them the Mongol envoys kneel to receive him.

have been one of the princes visited and was almost certainly present among the ranks of courtiers celebrating his father's birthday.[16]

The emperor arrived at sunrise carried in a golden chair. From his point of view this was the climactic moment of the ceremonies as all those present dressed in their formal robes of office acted out their obeisance to his imperial presence.[17] As he approached the English were led out to form a line opposite a crowd of officials and nobles. In the final version of his diary, which was intended to circulation to the East India Company and George III, Macartney wrote, "As he passed we paid him our compliments by kneeling on one knee, whilst all the Chinese made their usual prostrations."[18] George Thomas wrote in his diary, "As he passed we went upon one knee and bowed our heads down to the ground." Then he crossed out the last three words.[19] George Leonard's published account of the embassy omits this moment altogether.

The emperor entered his great yurt, and Macartney was invited to follow him, attended only by George Leonard, George Thomas, and Li.[20] Here, to Li's astonishment, they were allowed to ascend onto the dais where Qianlong sat on his throne surrounded by his ministers, including the newly arrived Fukang'an. It was here, out of sight of the crowd, that Macartney went down on one knee holding the gold box containing George III's letter over his head. Qianlong expressed his good wishes and presented Macartney and George Leonard each with a jade sceptre. George Thomas was given an embroidered silk purse for which he stumbled through his thanks in Chinese. Li too received a purse from the emperor and was deeply moved to be treated with such dignity. At the banquet that followed the four of them sat on cushions inside the yurt, in solemn silence except when Qianlong addressed them or offered them wine. Outside there was wrestling, tumbling, tightrope walking, and opera.[21]

As soon as Macartney and his suite got back to their lodgings, everyone wanted to know what had happened. Macartney could not easily be pressed, George Leonard talked only about the emperor's interest in his son, but George Thomas must have had a harder time. His father had always been very strict about the importance of telling the truth: it was when George Thomas had told a lie that he had threatened to put his hand in the fire. The many crossings out in his diary over the next few days suggest that George Leonard was using it to teach his son how to describe what was happening. After crossing out that the English bowed "to the ground," he also crossed out the words "At last the Emperor got up from his throne and went away in his chair," and added a sentence describing his speaking Chinese to the emperor which was at the centre of his father's version of the story.[22] Two days later he wrote, "We bent one knee," then an insertion "and bowed down to the ground" and "we repeated this ceremony nine times with the other mandarins except that they. . . ." The final five words are hopelessly illegible with insertions and crossings out.[23] After this he resorted to, "We made the ceremony as usual."[24] For the rest of his life he would never feel comfortable discussing that day's events.

Working out what to say was not easy for the adults either. Captain Mackintosh said firmly that Macartney *would* have agreed to the kowtow if necessary.[25] Macartney's cousin Edward Winder wrote, in his private notes, "We paid our respects in the usual form of the country—by kneeling and bowing 9 times to the ground."[26] He preserved these notes along with a letter from a friend from 1797, the year George Leonard's account was published. From the letter it appears that Macartney had told Winder "to keep your mind to yourself," and his friend reassured him that he knew Winder was a sincere person but urged him to obey Macartney because of his knowledge of the world but also "because of the obligations you owe him."[27] Whatever exactly caused this letter, it is clear that Macartney was requiring Winder to live with something he knew to be a lie and was using Winder's dependence to enforce this.

For the Chinese, since about three thousand senior officials had seen the emperor's arrival, the compromise was easier to explain. Indeed the court poet Guan Shiming, who was a protégé of Agui, succeeded in turning both the dispute about the kowtow and its outcome into a neat compliment to the emperor. His poem reads,

> There is a distant land from across the sea that offers treasure,
> Their hearts like wild deer, untamed and stubborn against the court rituals,
> But the moment they enter the imperial presence both knees are on the ground.
> The power of the Heavenly One can make all hearts submit.[28]

He added a note: "The tribute envoy from England in the Western Ocean was not accustomed to kneel. When compelled he only bent one knee, but when he was brought into the presence of the emperor he fell on his knees to the ground in submission."[29]

Qianlong appeared satisfied, but he had also decided that the embassy needed different management. That evening he produced a poem that begins, "In the past Portugal presented tribute, now England is paying homage," but a bad-tempered note, very clearly by the emperor himself, cuts across the verbiage, contrasting "literati making words about marvels" with "real cartographical enquiry," which everyone knew was one of the tasks the court's European missionaries had performed.[30] He also shifted the control of the embassy from Heshen and the Imperial Household Department, who were normally responsible for tribute missions, to his new Grand Councillor Songyun, who had recently returned from conducting successful trade negotiations with the Russians.

The following morning the English were again roused early and taken to the park. When the emperor arrived with his ministers, Macartney was ushered up to speak to him. Qianlong announced that he was going to a temple, but since the British did not worship this god he had told his ministers to show them the gardens. Macartney, Li, George Leonard, and George Thomas were provided with horses and sent off with two of the most powerful men in China, Heshen and Fukang'an, Fukang'an's brother, and the emperor's new border expert, Songyun.[31]

Heshen had lost interest and Fukang'an was hostile. When Macartney approached the emperor, Fukang'an had tugged at his sleeve, then put his hand on Macartney's hat. Macartney swept off the hat, but it seems more likely that Fukang'an had intended to indicate that he should kneel. Fukang'an then turned to Li, who went down on his knees to interpret, so that the speaker was kneeling even if Macartney was not. When Macartney asked permission for Mackintosh to return to his ship, Fukang'an refused. Macartney tried to flatter him by praising his campaigns in Taiwan. Li, who was the actual speaker, presumably had an interest in these since his brother had won glory fighting in them. However, this too failed.[32] The reasons for Fukang'an's hostility are unknowable: perhaps after campaigning on the Tibetan frontier with India he knew more about the British than he wrote to the emperor, but perhaps he was just affected by the pain he had been suffering in his stomach as he made the long journey back in the summer heat and torrential rain.[33]

Songyun seemed more flexible to Macartney, but then his background was very different from that of the great Manchu aristocrats like Fukang'an. He had grown up in Beijing, but in a family that spoke Mongol, and as a boy he had been prepared for specialist examinations for interpreters between Mongol, Manchu, and Chinese. These languages were crucial for the Qing state, which controlled an empire that spread far beyond the Chinese heartlands and much of which was administered in Manchu. The examinations were practical (the set texts for Mongol translation were Qianlong's own essays rather than Confucian classics) and intended to identify students who could actually speak the languages. When he was sixteen Songyun passed and went to continue his studies in the household of Nayantai, who had been on the Grand Council for many years as its Mongol language specialist. From there he was appointed to the Court of Colonial Affairs and then as one of the Grand Council secretaries, both positions where his linguistic skills were valuable. When he was put in charge of one of the Board of Revenue vaults where silver was stored, he began to attract attention as the first Mongol to hold a post previously restricted to Manchus.[34]

Songyun's Mongol identity was strong, and he never studied for the Chinese examinations, but as an adult he was famous for both the sincerity of his Confucian morals and his Buddhist devotion. After his father's death when he was fifteen he had been left under the authority of an extremely difficult uncle. This man, who was once described as being worse than a tiger, took over his property, shouted at him, and drove him around like a servant at home even when he was already a high-ranking official. All this was well known, and Songyun had a reputation for being exceptionally good natured about it: it was said that on one occasion when his uncle ordered him to pick up the cooking pot himself, Songyun just smiled and took it. He was a model of the Confucian virtue of filial piety, but no one thought it was easy or indeed that his uncle's behaviour was right. So when Songyun was appointed to a post in

Mongolia Heshen offered to hold back part of his salary in Beijing rather than handing it over to his uncle. This would have given him some money of his own, but at the cost of undermining the joint family and putting him under an obligation to Heshen. Songyun refused and insisted that all his salary be paid over to his uncle. So he was not close to Heshen, but on the other hand he was also an outsider to the opposing faction, which consisted mainly of Chinese who had come up through the examination system. Young, competent, and positioned between the two great court factions, he was useful to the elderly emperor.[35]

For the last six years Songyun had been in northern Mongolia, where he had successfully negotiated what is now known as the New Commercial Treaty of Kiakhta, which in 1792 reopened the profitable trade between China and Russia that had been closed for several years due to disputes over border raids and other issues. The trade produced large tax revenues for the Russians, and while the Qing exempted the northern Mongols from this commercial taxation, doing so was an important means of holding the loyalties of tribes on the Russian frontier.[36] When Songyun returned to Beijing Qianlong gave him an extraordinary series of promotions: making him simultaneously a member of the imperial bodyguard and Grand Council, and a minister in the Imperial Household Department.[37]

The negotiations in Kiakhta had required Songyun to develop a certain degree of familiarity with European diplomatic practices. At one point Qianlong heard that a Buddhist monk had turned up in Qing territory with a Russian letter inviting the Torghut Mongols, who had migrated from the Volga region of Russia to submit to the Qing twenty years earlier, to return to Russia where an army was being assembled. Songyun doubted this but had to suspend his negotiations until the Russian Senate in Saint Petersburg had written formally to the Court of Colonial Affairs in Beijing to confirm that the letter was a forgery. (Macartney knew about this since the British ambassador to Saint Petersburg, who distrusted Russia's intentions in Siberia, had managed to get hold of the Russian Senate's reply.) When the two sides finally came to an agreement, the Russians laid on a banquet for which Songyun crossed over into Russia, something that Qing officials had previously avoided. Once there he was pleased that, despite the extreme cold, the Russians took off their hats to him, and that when he sat down to dinner he had his back to the portrait of Catherine the Great.[38]

Songyun talked to Macartney about Kiakhta and "seemed very intelligent and asked many proper questions relative to the riches and power of Russia."[39] Each was trying to find out how much the other knew. A year earlier the Russians had sent an intelligence agent who informed the senior Qing administrator in Mongolia about the planned embassy and warned him about British conquests in India.[40] Songyun was out on the frontier at the time, but, as we will see in Canton, even secret government correspondence often circulated quite widely and Songyun might well have come to know of it.

They toured palaces with pictures of the emperor's victories and saw some of his collection of European astronomical instruments and musical automata. They dismounted from their horses and were rowed out to a palace on an island in one of the lakes. By the time they finally got back to their lodgings at three in the afternoon Macartney was exhausted. Li had been interpreting for both sides for nearly twelve hours, but he was exhilarated: he gave "such a favourable account of the general aspect of the negotiation, as to elevate the hopes of everyone concerned in the issue of it."[41]

For several days there were more brief meetings with the emperor and more tours of the garden. The English attended the birthday celebrations, which included a spectacular opera, chosen to fit the theme of people coming across the seas to congratulate the emperor: it ended with a great whale spouting water. George Thomas preferred the acrobatic displays, especially a man who lay on his back spinning a huge jar round on his feet while a little boy climbed in and out of it. Qianlong gave a speech and presented Macartney with a curio box for the English king.[42] In the afternoons Songyun took Macartney, with Li, the Stauntons, and Hüttner, riding up into the hills to visit the great Buddhist temples. The temples were a trial for the Catholic Li, and he flatly refused to interpret any questions about the deities. He was more comfortable asking about the golden roof of one of the temples, which Songyun assured him was covered in real gold leaf.[43]

What Qianlong did not do was to allow Macartney to speak to him about the aims of his embassy. Discussions of trade were beneath the dignity of kings and aristocrats in both China and England. However, the immense profits of the Canton trade had fiscal and military implications for the Qing as well as Britain, so that does not mean that the emperor was entirely unaware of the issues. The spectacular palaces and the gold-roofed temple were all paid for by the Imperial Household Department. Macartney did find out that a meeting held to discuss the response to the embassy had included both Fukang'an and a former superintendent of the Canton Customs.[44]

It was only with Songyun that Macartney was able to discuss these topics. While Macartney skirted round exactly what he meant when he asked for somewhere for the British to remain all year and store goods, Hüttner's Latin translation is perfectly clear that this is a demand for the Qing to "concede some small place to the English merchants not far from Zhoushan, for example a small island nearby."[45] In addition to this and a resident ambassador, Macartney had decided on four other items to try to obtain at this stage: the freedom to trade at Zhoushan or Tianjin, a warehouse in Beijing, a reduction in transit duties for British merchants travelling between Macao and Canton, and a written schedule of taxes.[46]

Macartney was too cautious to present his goals in writing, something he did only back in Beijing when it became clear the embassy would have to leave.[47] So the six British requests were conveyed orally by Li, who took a huge risk and added a seventh: "Christian laws are not at all harmful or contrary to the Chinese state, because men who know God become better and more obedient to control. So I ask your Imperial Majesty to let Christians who are scattered within your borders live peacefully, following their religion without unjust persecution."[48] We know that he did this not only because he said so in his letters to Rome, but also because the request was refused in the emperor's formal response.[49] When Li agreed to interpret for the embassy, it had been on the understanding that Macartney would act as if he were also an ambassador from the pope. Quite what this was to consist of is unclear, but however great Li's sense of identity as a Chinese or his friendship with the British, his first allegiance was to the Catholic community he came from in Liangzhou. What is less clear is exactly how Li added this request. He could have done so in the process of interpreting Macartney's discussions

FIGURE 9.2. William Alexander's reconstruction of the imperial audience has George Thomas in the centre. Macartney wears a plumed hat and George Leonard his Oxford cap and gown. The small figure of Li Zibiao standing behind George Thomas and also dressed in the embassy's uniform is the only picture we have of him.

with Songyun, as he was almost certainly not interpreting sentence by sentence, but taking what Macartney said and explaining it to Songyun. This would have made it possible, though nerve-wracking, for a clever interpreter to add another request and deal with the response without either side being aware of the deception.

It is also possible that Li added this point afterward by making additions to a note he translated from Macartney and delivered to Heshen. Heshen had authorised Li to act as interpreter in Chengde, and there were hints of further possible favours. Macartney wanted to ask that Captain Mackintosh be allowed to travel back to his ship. The request was addressed to Heshen, and Li was able to find someone to help him translate it, though George Thomas was still assisting as copyist. Then Li volunteered to deliver it. The

English were not supposed to wander around, but he talked his way through, found Heshen's residence, and delivered the letter to a secretary. Macartney was delighted at this display of courage and loyalty to the British. Li, on the other hand, said that Heshen always treated him very well and that when he "saw that I was a little sad, he told me through his secretary to be of good heart, and that I should come to his house to receive a gift, which I did."[50]

Once Macartney's demands were clear Qianlong decided to reject them all. A formal written response was composed, and the English were dismissed.[51] Back in Beijing, Macartney and George Leonard described the audience to William Alexander so that he could paint it. His first sketch showed Macartney on one knee in front of the emperor and several of the English who had actually been left outside the tent. This was of course inaccurate, and instead George Thomas was told to kneel to demonstrate his posture. In the final version only Macartney, Staunton, Li, and George Thomas are present. As in George Leonard's published account Macartney has vanished into the background and it is George Thomas who is on one knee in the centre of the picture, with everyone staring astonished as he speaks Chinese to the emperor.

CHAPTER TEN

Becoming an Invisible Interpreter

LI ZIBIAO'S TIME at court had made him much more aware of the risk involved in interpreting for the British: as he said later it was something that "no one, not even a complete idiot, would have undertaken if he had understood the danger."[1] The risks continued after the embassy left court and began its journey south. After a nerve-wracking moment when it looked as if his introduction of the request for toleration of Catholics would be discovered, Li began to efface himself, speaking more and more in Macartney's voice rather than explaining what Macartney wanted, which he understood as becoming an interpreter of words rather than an interpreter of things. Stepping back in this way made him less visible, but not necessarily less influential: the choices he made in his translations still affected the negotiations. And his anxiety provided a strong motivation to interpret in ways that would achieve a positive outcome.

When he was back in Beijing from Chengde he heard that his brother had arrived. Li Zichang soon visited the embassy, presumably passing without difficulty in his formal robes among the other military officers who came seeking gifts of the sharp Birmingham steel sword blades the British had brought with them. Even so it was dangerous for him to be there: he had brought Ke Zongxiao in his retinue and was carrying a letter from the East India Company merchants to Macartney, both actions that could have led to his arrest.² The meeting between the two brothers was secret: the British do not describe it, and there is no hint in the Qing sources that the British interpreter might have been Chinese. Even so, it is hard to imagine that a secret meeting would have been possible without Wang or Qiao's connivance, or that Li Zichang was not fully aware of the risks his younger brother was taking. Marchini in Macao heard that Fukang'an had said to Li Zibiao, "You're one of us. You'll pay for it. Your family depend on me and they'll pay for you."³ Li Zichang had built his career under Fukang'an so this threat was by no means implausible. If in the early stages of the embassy Li Zibiao's willingness to work on behalf of the Qing in the negotiations had been shaped by a sense of Chinese identity; after meeting his brother he must have been constantly aware of the dangers of the task: Fukang'an was no minor enemy.

Moreover, it soon became clear that the compromises over protocol that had been possible out beyond the Great Wall were no longer acceptable to either side in Beijing. When Qianlong went to inspect the British gifts on display in the Yuanmingyuan palace the English did not attend.⁴ Macartney was summoned to the palace to receive Qianlong's formal response to George III and complained that he was kept waiting three hours. The emperor's letter lay wrapped in yellow cloth on a throne, and no doubt Macartney was under pressure to show his respect.⁵ Li was caught between the two sides as the situation deteriorated. He blamed Macartney, who "acted with less and less courtesy so that nearly all the officials came to hate him" and felt that his own survival was little less than a miracle: "In this truly difficult situation I should have been afraid of the danger hanging over me, since I and I alone was speaking with everyone and handling everything, even what was offensive to the senior Ministers, but God miraculously protected me in the many and varied storms around this mission."⁶

After a final meeting with Heshen and Fukang'an when the British received a second sealed letter with the answer to Macartney's specific demands, the embassy set off back to Canton. The letter answered the seven requests as introduced by Li during the discussions in Chengde rather than the six written requests Macartney had recently submitted, but because it was addressed to the king and sealed, the British did not initially know what was in it.[7] Qianlong sent Songyun to escort them south, awe them with Qing military might, and persuade them to accept its contents.

Qianlong had also ordered that military camps along the route should be put on parade and for the first few days Songyun simply allowed the endless lines of soldiers to make their effect. George Thomas wrote about the guns, rockets, and firecrackers that they fired off in salute even at night.[8] And one of the few surviving Chinese poems about the embassy records the severe escort "so they gaze on the splendour of the military and our mountainous defences."[9] The emperor had also ordered coastal defences put on high alert and had stressed the importance of not giving the English any pretext for military action, but that was kept secret.[10] What the British saw was an extraordinary display of the size of the Qing military, which continued for the length of their journey.

Soon Songyun summoned Macartney to his boat for a formal meeting at which he read aloud the emperor's letter appointing him to escort the embassy. His letter to Qianlong, to whom he sent regular reports, names Li, who he assumes the emperor will remember, but not Macartney: he says that he ordered Plum to translate the emperor's edict to "the envoy."[11] They made arrangements for the English to meet up with HMS *Lion*, which was anchored at Zhoushan. According to Songyun, the English said, "This really is the Great Emperor showing consideration to men from afar and being extraordinarily sympathetic."[12] Neither the Chinese terminology nor the fulsome thanks seem likely to have come from Macartney, who was still in a bad mood, so it seems probable that this too is Li speaking. Afterward Songyun went over to Macartney's boat, bringing his attendants including the secretary, who had drafted Qianlong's response to the British. This time they talked about Russia and then the different European and Chinese conventions for ambassadors. After a while Songyun left, and Li was no doubt relieved to be allowed to sit down, which Songyun did not permit anyone but Macartney to do in his presence. Wang Wenxiong and Qiao Renjie remained chatting for the rest of the evening.[13]

These lengthy conversations continued every few days for the month it took to travel slowly south to Hangzhou and covered a variety of topics. Macartney came to trust Songyun, thinking that

FIGURE 10.1. William Alexander's picture of the embassy crossing the Yellow River. Note the Qing soldiers lined up on parade.

he had "such an air of candour, frankness and amity that if I am deceived in him, he must be the most consummate cheat in the world."[14] This sincerity was one of Songyun's great assets in diplomacy, and he was clever at giving Macartney the impression that he knew more than he did: Macartney was struck that he knew about the scandalous accession to the throne of Catherine the Great, but Songyun later gave Macartney himself as the source of this information.[15] Captain Mackintosh was still pushing for the *Hindostan* to be allowed to trade as a tribute ship tax-free. As Macartney had feared, when he raised this it undermined his earlier emphasis on relations between courts (Qianlong scribbled amused notes about "petty profiteering") and made the embassy seem less of a threat.[16]

Eventually it appears that Songyun felt confident enough to provide Macartney with a Latin translation of the response to his requests made by the French missionaries in Beijing. Macartney was startled to discover that whereas he had ultimately submitted six written requests, the emperor had refused seven and that the final request was for toleration of Catholics. His version of the conversation that followed was that he insisted that he had never made this request and the English thought all religions equally pleasing to God.[17]

According to Songyun, however, rather than immediately denying the demand, the English returned the following day and clarified it, saying, "The only thing in the emperor's letter that we still do not understand is the item that refuses the practice of religion. Our original request was to beg the Emperor to bestow on the Europeans living in China permission to continue to practice their religion, we certainly did not mean that we wanted English people to practice their religion in the capital."[18] It appears that Li had first given himself time to think, then decided to reformulate the request safely (the Europeans already had permission to practice their religion). Songyun replied at some length, explaining that China had its own teaching and it would be wrong for the emperor to allow the common people to be disturbed. He then reassured the English, or rather the nervous interpreter: "You have handled the matter quite correctly today, and if it is as you have explained then you have no need to be afraid."[19]

Macartney, however, insisted on sending written clarification to Heshen, in a note that laid out his own universalistic religious beliefs and asked for an investigation of the translation error.[20] This was a moment of high risk for Li, who definitely did not want an investigation, which would probably have focussed on the European missionaries in Beijing. Fortunately, as he recounted later, "His Excellency Song is a mild man with an indulgent nature, so he did not accuse the European interpreter of the letter of treachery, but excused it on the grounds of lack of skill in a foreign language, adding at the same time that this interpretation was absolutely not correct, but said that the ambassador should listen to his own spoken words heard from the mouth of the emperor."[21] This emphasis on the spoken word suggests Songyun's awareness of the power of the interpreter, and indeed in the same letter Li describes Songyun himself as "the interpreter of the words and wishes of the emperor" to the embassy.[22]

After this Li disappears from the Chinese record of the embassy. Accepting that his efforts on behalf of Catholics had failed, he appears to have effaced himself by becoming, as he would have put it, an interpreter of words. Songyun began to record speeches as being made by "the envoy."[23] Two weeks later he used Macartney's name for the first time, though the courtesies that follow sound much more like Li than Macartney.[24] This disappearance minimised the risks Li faced, but that did not mean that he ceased to affect the outcome of the negotiations, as is apparent during the trade discussions that took place on the next stage of their journey

Songyun had come to the conclusion that the British were not an immediate military threat, so when they reached Hangzhou he handed over the role of escort to Changlin, whom Qianlong had transferred to replace Fukang'an as governor general of Guangdong. Changlin was an experienced south coast administrator with a reputation for competence and clean government. He was a member of the emperor's own clan, a great lover of luxury who owned a vast palace in Beijing but had chosen to enter the bureaucracy through the regular examination system and was engaged in a long-running feud with Heshen. The best known story about him was that as governor of Fujian he had once gone incognito to the market and eaten all his meals in a noodle shop to find out what people were saying. Years later he explained to a sceptical friend that the story was true, but his aim was not to find out the gossip but for the story to get out and scare people a bit. For Qianlong he was a convincing choice to address problems in the management and taxation of the British trade. He was also very good company: to his Chinese contemporaries he was also someone whose conversation could make you forget you were tired.[25] Macartney, also enjoyed the conversations and found him "perfectly well bred, and the whole of his manner candid and gentleman-like."[26]

With Changlin in charge the long meetings continued, but their atmosphere was much more informal and the topics shifted from diplomacy to the details of the British trade. He insisted that Wang Wenxiong, whom he knew as a former subordinate and brave soldier, and Qiao Renjie should sit in his presence. This meant that Staunton could do so too, and Li too was noticeably more relaxed. On one occasion Changlin arrived at eight and stayed chatting till midnight, while Qiao took notes. When Changlin got out his pipe, Macartney took out a phosphoric bottle to light it for him. Such bottles were a common enough domestic item in England, but new to Changlin. Macartney gave him the little bottle as a gift, and the conversation flowed happily on science and British inventions.[27]

Meanwhile Barrow was persevering in his efforts to speak Chinese, and Wang was beginning to develop a personal relationship with him as he had earlier with Li. Wang even tried speaking a little English, always calling out "Pallo, how do?" as he passed Barrow's boat.[28] The British were not supposed to wander around the towns they passed through, but in Hangzhou Barrow was taken to inspect the barges they were about to travel in so that he could see the city, and Wang took him out sightseeing on the city's famous West Lake. Later Wang invited Barrow to a party on his boat, where Barrow found Changlin and Zhu Gui, who had been tutor to the future Jiaqing emperor and was now the newly appointed provincial governor of Guangdong with his wife and two other elegantly dressed ladies. Li escorted Barrow to this occasion but did not stay: to attend a party with women in China was quite unacceptable for a Catholic priest. Barrow could not really communicate, but the women offered him tea and cakes, laughed at him trying to speak Chinese, and sang for him.[29] He was coming to the conclusion that, at least for "the respectable class of society" and "the upper ranks," "in our estimation of the character of the Chinese, on leaving England, we were far from doing them that justice, which on closer acquaintance we found them to deserve."[30]

As he fostered this informal atmosphere, Changlin was also thinking about the British demands for changes to trading arrangements. He began by asking Macartney to provide a list of the points he wanted to raise, but since, according to Li, neither Changlin nor Macartney really knew how the trade worked they agreed to postpone negotiations until they reached Canton.[31] Meanwhile Changlin explained the difficulties he was likely to face in making changes and the likely opposition from Heshen and Fukang'an. The risk of accusing a predecessor of corruption made sense to Macartney after his experiences in India. He knew Changlin was manipulating him but concluded that "from a sense of our land forces in India, and of our strength everywhere by sea, the British nation was felt to be too powerful not to require some management even from this proud empire."[32]

Changlin also hinted at possible future concessions by suggesting that Macartney propose another embassy to the emperor as evidence of Britain's friendly intentions. According to Li, Changlin already knew that any such embassy was unlikely to happen soon because Britain was now at war with France. HMS *Lion* had attacked a French ship, which took refuge in Macao, as soon as this news came through. Unlike Changlin, Macartney did not yet know this but was cautious, agreeing merely that there might be a new embassy at some point in the future if there was something to be gained from it. This pleased Changlin, who said that he would report it to the emperor and asked Macartney for a complimentary note to go with his letter. Qianlong approved but emphasized the distance and dangers of the voyage and said that there was no need to fix a date.[33]

As it happens we have both the Chinese text of Qianlong's response and a Latin version titled "Interpretation of the Words of the Emperor's Response from Governor General Changlin's Dictation" in Li's handwriting.[34] Macartney confirms that this was made from a spoken version of the edict.[35] Comparing it with the original Chinese text shows how Li worked toward a positive outcome for the embassy even when he was acting strictly as an interpreter of words.

The Latin follows the Chinese original sentence by sentence, but there are also changes. Some of these are probably just the result of Changlin reading aloud. For example the abbreviation *dufu*, meaning "governor general and governor," is rendered in Latin with the sounds of the two full Chinese titles (*zongdu* and *xunfu*). These would have made no more sense to the British than the original, so it seems as if Changlin was explaining some of the formal language to the interpreter as he went along. Other changes, which make the letter more acceptable to the British, might have been made either by Changlin speaking or by Li translating, as when the Latin omits Qianlong's references to Changlin "controlling and escorting" the British and his warning that a future embassy should not "forcibly demand" to come to Beijing.[36]

There are also changes that can only be the result of translation choices made by Li, and all these avoid terms that might provoke trouble in favour of alternatives more acceptable to the British. Thus the word *gong* is translated as "gifts" (*munera*) rather than "tribute," and *yi* as "foreigners" (*externi*) rather than "barbarians," and Macartney is referred to throughout as the ambassador (*legatus*). Even more interestingly, the repeated references to the English as happily and respectfully submitting (*yue fu gong shun*) are translated with two different phrases, both of which remove the idea of submission. One describes the English as "content and peaceful" (*animo contento et pacifico*), and the other says that the emperor is aware of the "great good will" (*magnam benevolentiam*) of the English king. This is only one of several references to the *benevolentia* of the English king. While this Latin word means "good will," it is cognate with the English term "benevolence," which implies a degree of condescension by the British that then balances the Chinese emperor's condescension. Overall the translation has a much stronger sense of cultural relativism than the original, introducing several references to Chinese customs (*mos et consuetudo Sinica, Sinicis moribus*), where the original speaks only of customs and institutions.[37]

These changes are examples of the kind of choices that any translator must make, and each choice is a small one, but taken together they give a certain atmosphere to the text. The Latin loses the straightforward tone of the Chinese and acquires a sense of balance between Britain and China: the Chinese abide by their own customs, and the British king is full of benevolence as well as the Chinese emperor. Macartney summed the letter up by saying, "As it was explained to me it seems conceived in very friendly terms, if the king should send a minister again he would be well received. But in such a case it is desired that he should come to Canton."[38] Macartney realised that this implied "a sort of disapprobation" of the British having sailed directly north, but this is very much gentler than Qianlong's reference to "forcible demands."[39]

According to Macartney, by this time George Thomas could both speak and write Chinese "with great readiness, and from that circumstance has been of infinite use to us on many occasions."[40] As George Thomas listened to Li and copied out the embassy's Chinese letters he too was learning to make similar translation choices. The best example is a very simple letter he wrote in Chinese on behalf of Macartney asking a high official, probably Changlin, to convey their thanks to the emperor. It is signed by him, though the correct grammar suggests that it was written with some assistance. George Thomas refers to the English king's "respectful submission" (*gong shun*) and says that the king will "listen to" (*ting*, a word that also means to obey) the emperor's instructions in future.[41]

When the embassy reached Canton, Macartney put together a list of British demands for the trade and submitted it to Changlin, who arranged a debate in Macartney's presence in which he put the arguments in favour of changes, while Suleng'e, the superintendent of customs, set out arguments against. In the end Changlin refused the British demands for fixed tariffs, on the grounds that a decision had already been made by the emperor, but he used detailed information provided by the British to check tax records and crack down on the corruption he was perfectly aware also existed. He also found ways of granting several British requests: he declared that some of the fees paid by boats going between Canton and Macao were illegal, expressed his agreement with the unproblematic statement that no innocent man should be held responsible for a crime that he had not committed, promised to put on file that the British were not the same as the Americans, and issued announcements ordering people not to cheat foreigners or extort money from them. He also responded flexibly to a request that the English merchants should be allowed to leave their business premises for exercise, setting up arrangements, which lasted through to the 1830s, for them to visit the gardens owned by Chinese merchants. The permission to do this was a matter of social class: neither side wanted British seamen wandering around.[42]

Macartney had also asked that the English should be allowed to study Chinese, a request that also had the happy effect of foregrounding George Thomas's achievements and pleasing his father. Changlin as a Confucian scholar said that he was shocked that studying Chinese could have been banned. He investigated and discovered, unsurprisingly, that there was no ban; the problem was merely with employing teachers who were not part of the system of government control. He ruled that the British could study Chinese but only with the official linguists or other existing employees.[43]

The day before his departure Macartney signed off a formal report which he ended, very much as Qianlong had hoped, on a positive note: "There is indeed a likelihood of a permanent as well as a complete redress of every grievance, whenever a familiar access to the Viceroy shall be established, and the difficulty overcome of communicating freely with him in the Chinese language."[44] Then Wang Wenxiong and Qiao Renjie went out to dine on HMS *Lion*, where, presumably after more heavy drinking, everyone got emotional and shed tears at parting.[45] As the *Lion* sailed down river to Macao, Macartney pondered the possibilities for a British naval assault on Canton, but this was no more than he had done for every major port they had visited since they left England.[46] Li wrote that after Changlin's public announcements Macartney left Canton with a happy heart.[47]

Li too could be satisfied. His attempt to win an imperial edict allowing Christians to practice their religion had failed, but he had been accepted by both sides and his identity had not been revealed. His strategy of acting as an invisible interpreter of words while using translation to bring the two sides together had been a success. At the moment of departure almost everyone praised him.

Macartney and Staunton were pressing Li to return to England with them and offered to get him employment in London.[48] This

reflected his inclusion by this stage, despite his problematic identity, in the inner circle of the embassy. James Dinwiddie, the experimental scientist who was excluded and resented it, called Li "an
ignorant, bigoted priest" and complained that he "puts questions
frequently different from the intent of the proposer."[49] But that
was not Macartney's view; he wrote that Li "possest a firm strong
mind—neither to be daunted by danger, nor seduced by delight."[50]
Barrow praised his courage, and George Thomas remembered him
later as "a man of very respectable talents and amiable manners, as
well as of sound judgments and the highest integrity."[51]

On the Chinese side, Li writing to Rome returned to the image
he had used of himself as a hunted animal emerging from hiding
and transformed it. He ended his description of events at court by
saying that not only did the emperor give him a gift with his own
hands, but the other officials, even Heshen, were singularly kind to
him, "nor did I think to hide from them like a snake in the grass,
because the outcome proved them to have placed such trust in
me."[52] As he left Guangdong he reported that "many of the officials
among my friends" repeatedly urged him to promise to return to
China with the next embassy.[53] Changlin even said that he hoped it
would be conducted by George Leonard, accompanied, as Li put it,
by the present "interpreter of words and things."[54]

CHAPTER ELEVEN

Li Zibiao after
the Embassy

ARRIVING IN MACAO, Li had to face the procurator Marchini, whose anxiety had been exacerbated by the news that he had arrived in Canton.[1] This could easily have been the beginning of a downward spiral for Li, as happened all too often to Chinese priests who got on the wrong side of European superiors. Li, however, went on to a successful missionary career based on his gift for friendship, the depth of his religious practice, and his continuing ability to operate between Chinese and European culture. Sent to a remote part of north China, he not only continued to write to his friends in Europe but was supported in doing so by the Chinese Catholics he served. During the difficult years when the wealth and security that had marked the reign of Qianlong began to collapse, he was able to build up a successful Catholic mission.

In the short term, however, Li was rescued by Macartney and Staunton and their plans for another embassy. The war between Britain and France meant that HMS *Lion* was to convoy the fleet of merchant ships, whose cargoes were worth five million pounds, back to England, so the British spent several weeks waiting in Macao. After Li dined privately with him, Macartney followed up with a series of meetings with Marchini. Meanwhile George Leonard provided Marchini with a large interest-free loan as well as agreeing to take a relative of Yan Kuanren's and another young man

Li had found who wished to study at the Naples College back to Europe at the embassy's expense.[2]

George Leonard also hired two other young Chinese to come to England so that George Thomas could continue to speak Chinese. One of these, a boy known as A Hiue, spoke good Mandarin Chinese but came from a poor background: his parents had agreed a huge price of three hundred dollars for two years' service in England and sent him down to Macao with a Chinese Catholic. He may have been the frightened boy George Leonard had hired in Beijing to speak to George Thomas, but he could also have come from Canton and learned Mandarin from northern parents or working as a servant for officials. The other young man was Wu Yacheng, a Cantonese speaker from the county adjoining Macao where people had long-standing connections to the European trade. He was educated and in his early twenties, and presumably looking for an opportunity to build up his English language skills for a career in the trade.[3] Macartney and Staunton wanted these four Chinese, just as they wanted to maintain their good relations with Li, as part of the Chinese language skills and the connections they would need for the next embassy.

Meanwhile, Marchini had come to trust Li so much that he asked him to copy confidential correspondence. He also wrote to Rome that he wanted to change what he had written about Li. He now understood that Li had gone to Beijing only for religious motives, although he had not obtained the agreement for religious toleration he was seeking. And he had been much praised by the British both for his role in the discussions with officials and for his exemplary and edifying behaviour.[4] Marchini did not, however, feel that he could allow Li to go to Hainan, which was where Li Zichang was based. Two Christians had arrived from the island explaining that no priest had visited the Catholic communities there for thirty years and requesting Marchini to send someone. Li Zibiao pressed hard to be allowed to go, but Marchini pointed out that he knew no Cantonese, Hainan had a famously unhealthy climate, and he was supposed to be going to the north.[5]

So Li set off back to Gansu with the Catholic merchants who came down from the northwest for the next trading season. Rather than going north along the river route where he might have been recognised, they went across the highlands of western China. Eventually, in the pouring rain and thick mud of the late summer of 1794 they came down out of the mountains into the isolated valley of Hanzhong in Shaanxi province, where they were due to meet Li's new superior Giovanni Battista da Mandello. Because of the weather Mandello did not go out to meet them. Instead he sent a message telling Li to go not to Gansu but north into Shanxi province.[6] And so Li crossed the Yellow River and the precipitous Taihang mountains and arrived finally in Lu'an (today Changzhi), which would be his base for the rest of his life. He believed in the virtue of obedience and later wrote back to Naples that he arrived there "most willingly," but not to be allowed to visit his family first could not have been easy.[7]

Catholicism in Lu'an, where he arrived, dated back 150 years to the Jesuit Alfonso Vagnone, who had built up a centre of Catholic publishing in nearby Jiangzhou. When Li arrived there were about two thousand Catholics scattered across the plain and surrounding hills. Machang, the village where he settled, was close to the main roads, with water, good agricultural land, and a history of trade. Beyond this his mission covered the whole of southern Shanxi province. He was expected to spend most of his time travelling so that each of the hundreds of Catholic communities he was responsible for would see a priest over the course of the year. There were only two other priests in Shanxi: Luigi Landi, an Italian living near Taiyuan, the provincial capital, and the elderly Guo Ruwang, whom Li had known when he first arrived in Naples as a small boy.[8]

Li lived in hiding. He changed his surname to Mie and like the missionaries he had known in his childhood, he lived in the homes of his wealthier parishioners, who would set aside an inner courtyard or room for him. This was where the unmarried daughters of the family lived, so the arrangement required him to behave strictly as a priest at all times: he once described a colleague as "a plague to have living in a Christian's house."[9] No one ever complained about Li.

That first year, however, was a hard one. Li Zichang had suddenly died of an infection: the tropical climate of Hainan was indeed as dangerous as Marchini had feared. Changlin sent a brief notice of the death to Beijing, but the news that reached Li Zibiao was worse than this: his nephew Li Jiong had got into a dispute with the Catholic clergy in Guangdong, decided to take his father's coffin back to Liangzhou, and, in defiance of Catholic regulations, performed the full Confucian rituals for the funeral. In later years Li Jiong became well known for saying that crows disgorge food to feed their parents and otters make them offerings of fish, so how could he do any less? However, in the process he had broken with his family and their Catholic faith. He was almost certainly in a position to betray his uncle if he chose. As had happened before under stress, Li Zibiao succumbed to ill health and was unable to work for many months.[10]

It was not until 1797 that Li returned to Shaanxi to try to get permission from Mandello to visit his family in Gansu, but while he was in Hanzhong the forces of the White Lotus Rebellion swept down out of the mountains. He wrote to the Chinese students in Naples, describing in heavily biblical language how the rebels burned every place they passed through, took the young men with them, and put the weak to the sword, leaving weeping and desolation throughout the land. The rebellion had begun among lay Buddhist groups repressed by the state whose members came to believe that the end of the world was coming. If Li saw copies of the government gazette, he might have known that Wang Wenxiong was in the thick of the fighting and had already been rewarded for his valour as Qing forces pushed the rebels up into the mountains. Once there the rebellion had swelled with the grievances of the poor and desperate, and it was these renewed rebel forces that Li had now encountered. In Europe Li had seen soldiers fleeing in the aftermath of battle, but those were wars fought between professional armies; away from the battlefields ordinary people continued with their lives. What he experienced in Shaanxi was something quite different: an uprising of the dispossessed, whose violence was chaotic and utterly terrifying. Li abandoned his plans and fled back north into Shanxi.[11]

The Qing court too was shocked at the violence, and how to respond to it became the great political question of the day. In 1799 Qianlong died and his son Jiaqing, who had spent four frustrating years as a kind of trainee emperor under his increasingly forgetful father, consolidated his power and the policy changed. By this time Qing forces were exhausted and Jiaqing had come to the conclusion that the underlying problem was not really a religious sect that needed to be stamped out but rather poor government and official extortion that had driven people to rebel. He also thought that vast sums of money spent on the campaign had been embezzled by generals who had no incentive to end the war.[12]

Jiaqing's accession to power marked the end of the Manchu grandees who had dealt with Macartney in the early stages of the British embassy. Fukang'an had died campaigning against an earlier rebellion. Now Heshen was made to commit suicide and those associated with him were blamed for the culture of corruption: Fuchang'an and Zhengrui were both sent off to work at Qianlong's tomb. Meanwhile, their opponents at court were promoted in a move that would be seen later as a turn toward Chinese who came up through the examination system and a new emphasis on Confucian moral values. In practice the changes were as much factional as ethnic: the Mongol Songyun and Manchu Changlin were both also recalled from distant postings. Songyun was put in charge of two of the provinces worst affected by the rebellion, though his tenacious demands for economic assistance when he met the emperor so exasperated Jiaqing that he was briefly banished to Xinjiang.[13]

The new policies also had a huge impact on Li's life in Shanxi. Because Jiaqing saw corruption as the problem that had caused the rebellion, he was much less inclined than his father to blame religious believers. Since, from the point of view of most Qing officials at this time, there was little difference between Buddhist sects and Christianity, the new policies brought a degree of tolerance for Catholics. In 1801 the Machang Catholics went to court over being compelled to take part in the local temple cult. To everyone's amazement the Lu'an prefect ruled in their favour and there were similar judgements in other cases. The results were immediate: Li wrote that his parishioners were cleansing themselves from their unacceptable former practices, giving themselves to good works, and seeking refuge for their souls in the light of the Gospel. There were also conversions: in Dunliu county up in the hills a hundred families were "inclined towards the Lord," many heads of household had been baptised, and some were fired up to convert their relatives and acquaintances.[14] The next year he reported delightedly that the emperor was not hostile to Christianity and had even announced that no one should be troubled by the law because of their religion.[15]

In this context Li became a successful fundraiser. With Britain and France fighting at sea and rebellion across central China, there was no way of getting financial support from Europe. At first he had lived on mortgage payments on a building bought by the earlier Jesuit missionaries. He thought that Mandello had given permission for this but ended up being accused of setting a bad example. So the next year when Marchini did offer to send money, Li refused. Soon not only were his living expenses entirely funded by the local Catholics but he also began to raise funds for the benefit of the diocese as a whole. By 1803 he and Luigi Landi, who was based in the centre of the province, had collected a total of three thousand taels. This stunning figure was by far the largest amount to come from the Shanxi mission until the twentieth century.[16]

Marchini thought that some of the money came from fines, known as penances, paid by those who married their children to non-Catholics, worked on Sundays, gave their sons a Confucian rather than Christian education, and so on.[17] The Catholics in the Lu'an area included a fair number of wealthy and educated families: merchants, landowners, and degree holders had all joined the church over the years. Penances, understood as donations, made it possible for such men to combine their religion with their local obligations, but they were not unusual at the time and do not explain the scale of the donations.

Li's initiative appears to have been to establish a group of donors with whom he had close personal relations. This was an association of twelve men with whom he met once a month for dinner, religious conversation, and good works. The idea comes from Naples but also fitted with Chinese expectations for elite men. The result was a community in which Li's exemplary priestly behaviour could be combined with his gift for friendship to produce impressive donations. The group lasted long after his death and was still in existence in the 1840s, when each member was making an annual contribution of fifteen hundred copper coins and considerable reserves had built up.[18]

Li himself thought it a "near miracle" to have collected so much from those who had so many needs of their own.[19] However, it is hard not to wonder whether perhaps some of the men he dined with knew about his experiences at court. Did he ever show any of them the purse Qianlong had given him? He had sent a length of red silk back with the embassy for his friend Giovanni Borgia to have made up into festival vestments for the Naples College, but what became of the other gifts he received?[20] Even if he himself never spoke of his visit to court, did people perhaps hear rumours from the Catholic merchants who travelled each year to Canton?

The successful fundraising transformed Li's life. He and Landi established a seminary outside the banking town of Qixian in central Shanxi and spent part of each year teaching there. There was a large compound with rooms for the students, a chapel, and spacious garden. The remaining money was invested to provide living expenses for the teachers and twenty students. Life in the seminary took Li back to the familiar routine of the Naples College with daily mass, weekly spiritual discussions, and recreation after meals. The education, however, was much simpler than in Naples: Latin grammar, Bible reading, catechism, and basic theology, then Chinese texts taught by one of the senior students in the evenings. There were also many interruptions: Li would leave the older students in charge when the call came to attend the dying.[21]

The money was probably also what made it possible for Li to send so many letters to Europe. He wrote regularly to the Propaganda in Rome, to the superior of the Naples College and the Chinese students there, as well as to personal friends: Borgia, Macartney, and George Thomas Staunton. The surviving letters may reflect simply what was archived: his letters to Borgia survive only when Borgia became head of the Naples College, and a brief fragment of a translation shows that although the letters we have are in Latin or Italian he did also write in Chinese.[22] Sending letters across the world was slow: a reply would take at least two years, and many letters were delayed or entirely lost. "But," as Li wrote after several years when no letter from Europe had got through, "whatever happens Your Excellency should be sure that although I may not manage to write, I am committed right through to my fingertips to standing firm and acting properly and everything I learned."[23]

Working deep in China's interior and isolated by war and rebellion, Li still cared about his friends in Europe. This letter was written after he had heard a rumour that Naples had fallen to the French revolutionary armies and the Chinese students carried off to France. There was a gap of two years until he finally heard from the college, and this 1801 letter begins by saying that their letter dated December 1799 rescued him from great distress when he learned that the college was unharmed. "I give infinite thanks to my God for keeping our family unharmed and rescuing me and mine from constant fear and anxiety."[24] He also sent family news to the Chinese students in Naples, especially Zhu Wanhe, who came from Qixian where the new seminary was located.[25]

These relationships were strengthened by Li's belief in the power of prayer. When he wrote formally to the college about his terrifying experience with the White Lotus rebels, his letter ended, "I beg you of your kindness, my Father Superior, that you stretch out your spirit to me and keep me in your heart and prayers, for I am weak in both body and spirit."[26] These requests echo through all his later correspondence: "I cannot get round the whole mission in a year," or whatever his most recent problem was, "because I am physically weak and utterly lacking in virtue, so I ask Your Reverence to keep me always in your prayers."[27] He also believed that the prayers of friends and colleagues in Europe were helping him, writing to the Chinese students in Naples that he would have nothing better in difficult negotiations he was facing than their prayers and intercessions on his behalf.[28]

His correspondence with members of the Macartney embassy was touched off in 1801 when George Thomas Staunton returned to Canton. George Thomas seems to have written to Li enclosing a letter from Macartney asking how he had found his family in Gansu. Li was touched and replied.[29] Later, when George Leonard died, Li wrote a letter of condolence to Macartney that begins, "Most Excellent Sir, It is now eight years since I was separated from your most pleasant society, and there is nothing I hold more in my memory than your singular kindness and generosity to me, so that my gratitude and longing for your company can never cease until my life ends."[30]

All this time the campaign against the White Lotus rebels was continuing. Wang Wenxiong became a national hero when he was ambushed after leading a night attack on the rebels. He continued to fight despite being wounded, until his arm was broken and he fell from his horse. It was said that the rebels, angry that he had killed so many of their commanders in the past, then hacked his body to pieces in a cruel torture that lasted all day.[31] When the war finally ended the state too had suffered greatly and the imperial treasury was empty of the vast reserves built up in the previous century.

For Li, the end of the war in 1804 meant that ten years after his return to China it was finally possible to travel to his family in Gansu. His colleagues Landi and Guo Ruwang backed his request to go by writing to Mandello, but the journey was still dangerous and Mandello decided to send not the highly competent Li but his former classmate Fan Tiancheng. Soon Mandello began to receive complaints about Fan's behaviour with women: that he did not take the mass seriously, that he demanded payments, that he was going out and spending his time with nonbelievers, that he had recruited a female servant and touched the Chinese virgins and spied on them as they dressed and bound up their feet. (These were women who had sworn Christian virginity but continued to live at home with their families.) At this point Mandello finally told Li to go to Gansu to find out what had happened.[32]

Li was horrified: this was not a reunion with his family but a scandal that required him to operate within the global bureaucracy of the church and was likely to involve him in the tensions between his Chinese and European colleagues. On a previous occasion when Fan got into trouble Mandello had told the local Catholics that he would rather believe the devil than the Chinese. On the other side was Guo Ruwang, the other Chinese priest in Shanxi province, who wrote Li several letters commending Fan. Li's letters hardly ever mention the tensions between Chinese and Europeans, but he did once urge the Chinese students in Naples to study by saying, "I wish you to know, my dearest ones, that up to now the indigenous or Chinese priests are ridiculed by the European fathers who say that when brutes go to Europe brutes return."[33] It was not an easy situation and got worse.

When Li arrived in Liangzhou it became clear that the root of the problem was Fan's sexual exploitation of several young women, which had then led him into financial difficulties as he tried to pay them off. Li had no doubts as to the right course of action, for "What use is it to hide crimes that are being sung abroad like songs in the marketplace?"[34] Fan's actions were "neither apostolic, nor religious, nor Christian, but offensive to many, a squandering of souls, a provocation of divine justice, and a gateway to vice."[35] He decided to make a formal report to Rome and get Fan removed from his post. So he interviewed six of the women and persuaded them to provide brief statements that included the precise detail that would be necessary to church bureaucrats in Rome: two of the women stated that Fan had told them that their acts were not wrong because they created love.[36] When Li included this he was accusing Fan of false doctrine, that is, not accepting that what he had done was wrong, which was a far more serious charge than any of the individual offenses.

Li then settled down to handle his colleagues. He sent a full copy of all the materials to Guo Ruwang, who had heard about Fan's behaviour a few years earlier but had said nothing. He also wrote to another older Naples-trained Chinese priest explaining what had happened. Then he informed the college, arguing that it would not damage their reputation to amputate a rotten limb for the good of the whole body.[37] Landi, who took over as bishop after Mandello's death that year, was impressed: he wrote to Rome, in colloquial Italian, that Li "really has his hands in the pasta" (meaning that he had a lot of influence with everyone involved).[38] Then they sent Fan back to his family in Beijing during the lengthy process that would lead to his suspension.[39]

With Landi as bishop, he and Li worked closely together. Li was punctilious in making an annual confession of his sins to Landi, and Landi sought Li's advice and put him in charge of any priests who had problems. On one occasion when one of these simply vanished after Li had refused him permission to say mass, he informed Landi of the man's departure in a letter that ended cheerfully, "This is one of the best reasons for happiness in this vicariate."[40]

Then in 1805 a church courier was arrested carrying a map that had been sent to Rome by one of the missionaries in Beijing as part of a dispute as to which religious orders and nationalities should control the Catholics in parts of north China. Jiaqing suspected foreign spying and there was a crackdown in which the brothers of Li's classmate Ke Zongxiao were arrested in Beijing, and Ke himself fled to Shanxi. Gioacchino Salvetti, who had been sent by

Landi's home monastery to assist him, was arrested as he entered the country and imprisoned for three years in chains in Canton. A new imperial edict against Christianity followed, and Li wrote to Rome that everyone had been terrified for a whole year.[41]

Unlike many missionaries who blamed the lack of conversions in this context on the Qing state or on Chinese culture, Li never adopted a stark vision of differences between China and Europe. Instead he saw the process of conversion as part of a much larger picture of God's grace and divine action in the world. He wrote to the Chinese students in Naples that the lack of conversions was not due to the new law but because of "the lack of faith, which, since it is a gift of God, is rare and difficult."[42] Writing to Rome he explained that even though there are plenty of Christians hardly any "give a public example of Christian faith by behaving as Christians" but since "the growth of the Divine Religion is a true gift, which is usually denied to the idle and given to those who trust and seek after it" he would continue in his duties as a priest so as to move God's mercy for "the inactivity of the Missionaries and the faithlessness of the Christians."[43]

As a missionary in Shanxi, just as when he acted as interpreter to Macartney, Li clearly identified as Chinese, but he hardly ever spoke in terms of Chinese versus European culture. The depth of his Christian faith and his long experience of both Chinese and European culture meant that his theology of prayer and conversion, just like his participation in the Macartney embassy and in the bureaucracy of the church, was part of a much greater divine work that encompassed the whole world.

PART III

George Thomas Staunton and the Canton Trade

CHAPTER TWELVE

George Thomas Staunton Becomes an Interpreter

BACK IN ENGLAND MACARTNEY was widely criticised for failing to achieve his negotiating goals, but George Leonard Staunton remained optimistic about a future embassy. So he continued to have George Thomas study Chinese, speaking it at home and spending many hours memorising characters and learning to read. When in time he returned to China he turned out to have enough Chinese to be able both to interpret and to translate at a basic level. However, it was in Canton that he learned from the senior Chinese merchants and their staff of the social and political complexities of translation. Under their instruction he developed a style of translation that aimed above all to conciliate and to negotiate agreement across the two cultures.

In London George Leonard had his wife painted by the fashionable portrait artist John Hoppner in a tableau that represents George Thomas's return to his mother who had spent the time while they were away staying with her family in Salisbury. George Thomas is fourteen now and a little taller than his seated mother. Their stiff, reserved expressions as he crosses the room and grasps her hand are typical of the period, but even so he seems awkward. Behind him stands a Chinese boy, holding a box, who

FIGURE 12.1. John Hoppner's portrait of George Thomas returning to his mother after the embassy. The Chinese boy behind him, who is probably A Hiue, is holding a box on which is written a Chinese title for the picture: "Sketched on a Winter's Day in Salisbury."

looks somehow more relaxed. This is probably the Mandarin-speaking A Hiue. Wu Yacheng, who was a few years older, may well have written the Chinese title of the painting that is on the box (since A Hiue was illiterate and the writing is much better than George Thomas's efforts), but he did not last long living with the Stauntons and in 1796 returned to China. Social boundaries between employers and servants were much sharper in England than in China and unlikely to be accepted by a serious young man from an educated background. Jane Staunton did not much like A Hiue's behaviour either, but he came from a poor family and had less choice. He was also a lively boy closer in age to George Thomas who could be relied on to plead his case when there was trouble with his mother.[1]

George Leonard is not in this picture because shortly after they returned he suffered a stroke that left him partially paralysed. Even so he continued to direct his son's education in science and languages.[2] As well as speaking Chinese to A Hiue George Thomas was memorising words, presumably from the Chinese-Latin dictionary that had been presented to his father in Rome. He may also have studied Chinese primers, since many years later his library included *The Thousand Character Text* (*Qian zi wen*) and the *Three Character Classic* (*San zi jing*) as well as *Domestic Sayings in the Mandarin Dialect* (*Jiating jianghua*) used to teach Cantonese to speak the language of the court.[3]

In 1795, as part of his father's plans for another embassy, George Thomas translated a letter from the British government into Chinese. This is largely his own work: the Chinese just about makes sense, but it seems unlikely that Wu Yacheng or any educated Chinese could have been helping. The letter also contains north China dialect terms, which suggest perhaps a joint effort with the illiterate A Hiue. When George Thomas was complimented on it he said he was afraid "the difference between the English and Chinese idiom might cause many mistakes that I could not be aware of."[4] He was quite right: when the letter arrived in China Zhu Gui, now the governor general in Guangdong, reported to the emperor that even though it was in Chinese "the structure of the writing has mistakes so that it is hard to read," so he had ordered one of the linguists to make a new translation.[5]

The following summer, away from his father's supervision for the first time at the age of fifteen, George Thomas made the friends who would be closest to him for the rest of his life. He and A Hiue were sent off to stay with his cousins, in the village of Winterslow, where George Leonard's old friend Peter Brodie had ended up as rector. There were seven children, and Brodie was educating them at home. It was scarcely a holiday since the children studied eight hours a day beginning at six thirty in the morning. But this was not a problem for George Thomas, who revelled in the freedom: a delighted letter to his parents says how much he enjoyed a family dance for Margaret's twentieth birthday. Margaret, the oldest child, had been taught alongside her brothers and now taught George Thomas astronomy, botany, and Italian. Soon he was close friends with Peter and Benjamin, who were about his own age and played chess, shared his scientific interests, and took him walking. A Hiue enjoyed himself with the older boys: he made and painted a Chinese kite for sixteen-year-old William and went off on a visit to Salisbury with Thomas Denman, another cousin who had also come to study for the summer.[6]

Thomas Denman had the conventional education that George Leonard had not given his son. Until recently he had been boarding at Eton, where the older boys once woke him up at night, ordered him to make a speech, and when he refused burned him on the leg with a red-hot poker. The scar, and the story, remained with him for the rest of life.[7] They might shock but they also bound him into a community of elite men formed through such experiences. After a happy summer with his cousins he went on with his peers to Cambridge. Soon George Thomas was studying at Cambridge too, but he never became part of that world. He was younger than the other students and stayed not in the halls but with his parents in the town. The family arrived in January, so he missed the first term, and when in the summer he got top grades in mathematics but did not win a prize, because he did poorly in Latin verse composition, his father was so angry with the university that he removed him.[8] The result was that his summer with the Brodies in Winterslow remained George Thomas's only real experience of spending time with other young people his own age before he was plunged into the world of the East India Company in Canton.

George Leonard had written to the East India Company offering George Thomas's services on the grounds of his proficiency in Chinese. Posts in China, which became available only every year or two, were valuable property, so this provoked a fierce rebuke from Francis Baring, the chairman of the board, who had a son of his own to place.[9] George Leonard's response was to put his son at the centre of the meeting with the Qianlong emperor in the *Authentic Account of an Embassy from the King of Great Britain to the Emperor of China*, which he published in 1797, making it appear as if George Thomas had done much of the interpreting. He then sent copies to a list of powerful aristocrats who could influence the decision, took George Thomas on visits, and with this support successfully pushed the directors into appointing the boy to a post in China.[10]

And so in 1799 George Thomas sailed back to China to take up a post as a writer in the East India Company's Factory (warehouses) in Canton. He was well aware of the pressure his father had exerted, sure that his Chinese was not good enough to interpret, and anxious about what would happen when he arrived. He resolved to speak to A Hiue only in Chinese on the voyage, though he realised that even "if I possessed his whole stock of knowledge in the language it would scarcely enable me to converse or interpret correctly with the Mandarines."[11] So he also began to read a Chinese novel, *Romance of the Three Kingdoms* (*Sanguo yanyi*), practised his Chinese hand-writing, and did translations. Henry Baring, Francis Baring's elder son who was returning to Canton on the same ship, told him discouragingly that Chinese language might be pleasant enough as an amusement but would be no use at all for the company.[12]

Once they arrived, George Thomas spent his days copying letters into record books in Henry Baring's office, where he was soon joined by Henry's younger brother George.[13] If they stayed long enough each could expect to rise to the role of president of the committee that ran the Factory, who dealt with the hong merchants licensed by the Chinese government. Below the hong merchants were other Chinese who were in and out of the Factory all day: compradores who provided provisions and materials for the ships, linguists who handled the interactions with the Chinese authorities, servants, cooks, water carriers, gatekeepers, and many others. Along the waterfront were the warehouses of merchants from Europe, America, and India, who exported tea and porcelain and imported furs from North America, spices from the Dutch East Indies, rice from Vietnam and Thailand, sandalwood, cotton, and (illegally) opium from India. And during the trading season there were thousands of British seamen and their officers living on board their ships.

The local language was Cantonese, but people soon heard about the English boy who could speak Mandarin, the northern dialect used by officials. A few days after George Thomas's arrival the hong merchants paid a formal visit to the Factory. The conversation was in English and the hong merchants spoke what today we call China Coast Pidgin. Native speakers often laugh at such contact languages because they break the rules of formal speech, but George Thomas was respectful, saying later that the merchants spoke English "with great fluency though in a corrupt jargon."[14] As he stood in the background trying to make out what was being said he heard his own name, and one of the merchants began to speak to him in Mandarin. To everyone's surprise George Thomas understood and could reply.[15]

The speaker was Liu Dezhang, an ambitious outsider to the trade from Tongcheng county in Anhui, which was famous for its Confucian schools and the number of officials it produced. He himself spoke Mandarin fluently, and his son was a senior administrator in the Beijing government. For English, he used his brother as an interpreter, but his inability to speak English himself hampered his relations with the company. As he chatted politely to the anxious but increasingly delighted George Thomas, it was obvious that George Thomas's linguistic abilities could be an opportunity for Liu to compete with the local English-speaking merchants and expand his business.[16]

A few weeks later an incident occurred that enabled Richard Hall, the president of the committee that ran the English Factory, to test George Thomas. If the boy succeeded, perhaps he could be used to undermine the power of Pan Youdu, the senior hong merchant who normally interpreted personally, and if he failed no doubt Francis Baring would be pleased.

A sailor keeping watch on a British naval schooner had heard a small boat paddling round in the dark. Thinking that someone was trying to steal the ship's anchor, he fired off a musket, which badly injured one of the Chinese boatmen. This was a serious incident: foreign warships were not allowed to enter Chinese coastal waters, and a Chinese subject appeared to have been killed. George Thomas thought it hardly surprising that the Chinese wanted the sailor handed over. This, however, was something that the English Factory had refused to do ever since 1784, when a sailor had been executed for what the English had regarded as an accidental killing. Instead Hall instructed the schooner's commander to work out a good story and make sure that everyone stuck to it. Then he summoned the senior naval officer in the area, Captain Dilkes. At the same time he flatly denied to the Chinese that he had any inside knowledge of the incident or any authority over the naval officers.[17]

Although there were linguists (*tongshi*) whose job included explaining documents written in Chinese to the English,

FIGURE 12.2. Pan Youdu wearing his official robes in a portrait designed as a presenta-
tion gift, but which also gives a sense of the charm and sense of humour that lay behind
this serious pose. A copy of this portrait was one of George Thomas Staunton's most
treasured possessions in later life.

interpreting for negotiations like this was too important to leave in their hands. Instead Pan Youdu interpreted personally, going between the English Factory and the senior Qing officials, explaining the governor general's statements to the British and trying to persuade them to hand over the sailor.

Pan Youdu's ability to speak English and interpret on these occasions was one of the sources of his power, as both Richard Hall and Liu Dezhang were well aware. His father, Pan Zhencheng, came from Fujian province up the coast, which had long-standing trading links with the Philippines, and had gone to work in Manila as a young man. There he learned enough Spanish to read and write as well as to speak. Back in China Pan Zhencheng moved the family to Canton where he built up a business empire partly by making an early decision to work with the newly arrived British merchants, for which purpose he also learned to speak English. He also used his growing wealth to give his sons the best possible education for the examination system. Pan Youdu's older brother had achieved the highest *jinshi* degree and had recently retired from a prestigious post working at court on the Qianlong emperor's great book collection project. Pan Youdu himself had received a good classical education and that with his brother's position gave him the status to speak easily with high-ranking officials, but he had also learned English from a young age as he was groomed to take over his father's business.[18]

When he interpreted Pan was constantly shaping impressions of what had been said, suggesting possible concessions, and using all his tact, intelligence, wealth, influence, and linguistic abilities to persuade the two sides to adjust the texts of their letters until an acceptable compromise could be reached. Many years later John Elphinstone, the idle son of one of the directors of the East India Company, summed him up by saying that he was "a very clever able man" and he preferred dining with him to doing business with him.[19]

On this occasion, however, when Governor General Jiqing (a cousin of Changlin who accompanied the Macartney embassy) agreed to send a member of his personal staff to meet with Dilkes, Hall announced that George Thomas was to be the interpreter. Interpreting was very different from polite conversation, and

George Thomas was to interpret for the first time in front of all the hong merchants and senior members of the English Factory. If he failed he would be utterly humiliated, and that was what he expected to happen. However, when the day came he was rescued from a quite unexpected quarter: "As the Mandarin was a man of obliging manners and desirous of understanding and making himself understood, I was able to carry on the dialogue much better than expected."[20] A series of meetings followed after which the official, a man named Chu, approved of George Thomas's Chinese and "said I might acquire sufficient perfection in the course of three years."[21] The final accolade came when Chu announced that the hong merchants need not attend a meeting since he had become used to George Thomas's foreign pronunciation.[22]

Meanwhile, it was agreed that Captain Dilkes would take the seamen involved into the city of Canton for a trial at the court of the provincial judge, and George Thomas went as his interpreter. They were thrown out after Dilkes began shouting over the judge, but George Thomas was delighted to enter the walled city for the first time and fascinated to observe a Chinese law court.[23]

After this Hall tested George Thomas by making him translate Chinese documents, first from Chinese into English, and when he proved able to do that from English into Chinese. He was made to do one translation into English at sight during a meeting. This was a set of simple extracts from the laws on accidental wounding, which Jiqing had produced and sent over to the British.[24] Mostly, however, written translation provided an opportunity for various Chinese people to advise him, object to his translations, correct them, and in doing so teach him.

One of the first documents he was asked to translate was a statement by Jiqing, which Pan Youdu had already explained to the English. When George Thomas wrote a translation, the language that emerged was, quite unlike Pan's explanation, "neither agreeable or expected by the committee."[25] Pan disputed the translation, and George Thomas was summoned to explain himself. He went expecting to admit that he had made a mistake, but Pan's objections were not so specific. Hall ended up putting George Thomas's translation in the company records. However, when George Thomas wrote to his father he explained that the problem was due to "the formal and arrogant style in which their official communications with foreigners are generally written" rather than coming from Jiqing, "who is a man universally esteemed and respected."[26] Jiqing did indeed have an impressive reputation, but scarcely among the British who knew little about the personalities of the various governors general: apparently someone had been explaining things to George Thomas.[27] He was learning that translation was a matter not just of individual words but also of writing in a style that would fit with the character and reputation of the author.

He was also learning to write Chinese documents in forms that would be acceptable to the recipients. Captain Dilkes had departed, leaving a forty-page rant addressed to Jiqing that Hall asked George Thomas to translate into Chinese. George Thomas, who much preferred translation to copying letters in Baring's office, announced that this would take him two weeks. Pan Youdu said that if the English explained the contents to him he could write up a Chinese version in the usual way. But instead Hall sent a message explaining that it would take time because "Mr Staunton was not yet sufficiently familiar with the Chinese Language to perform the present task without constant reference to his books."[28] A few days later, however, George Thomas had to admit that books were not enough: he went back to Hall to say that he needed to consult an intelligent native speaker. Hall recommended one of the compradores to go through George Thomas's Chinese with him, before he copied the final version out in his best Chinese handwriting. When the letter was delivered, Jiqing commented approvingly on how the text was laid out on the page: George Thomas had raised the characters referring to the Chinese emperor highest into the top margin, put the English king lower, and Jiqing himself below but still above the margin.[29]

This case was a great success for George Thomas, who was convinced that the East India Company would now welcome his skills. However, behind the scenes it had almost certainly been engineered by Liu Dezhang. Liu had the capacity and connections needed to persuade Chu to accept George Thomas as an interpreter. It was he who arranged for the wounded boatman to be taken in and nursed long enough to survive the forty-day limit on culpability for a shooting, and who bribed his family by paying for the funeral when he died. Afterward George Thomas realised that as Liu had become friendly to him, Pan Youdu had become hostile.[30]

The success mattered because George Thomas had no friends in the Factory and was finding life there very hard. When he arrived there were eleven English men in the Factory, all living on site and dining together. He was the youngest and most junior. He was shocked by their wild behaviour and knew that he was unpopular; they resented his appointment and made him aware of it. They were nearly all the sons of the directors, and several were also the heirs to aristocratic titles.[31] Since they were paid a commission on the trade whatever their abilities, they were seldom the most able even in their own families. John Elphinstone, who arrived in 1801, was typical: he was sent out after getting into trouble, boasted of his own laziness, despised trade, and envied his brother in the army. It seems likely that it was also at this time that he developed his later addiction to opium, the fashionable and expensive new drug that the English were privately importing.[32] The other young men enjoyed drinking, gambling, and when possible physical sports. When they felt their honour was at stake they fought duels: Pan Youdu even wrote a little poem about the extraordinary way in which the English gamble with their lives by firing guns at each other to display their courage.[33]

Only in his own rooms could George Thomas get away from them. He had three rooms, one of which was supposed to be for his servants, but he liked to be alone and in any case with all his meals provided he could not really think what to do with two servants. He could not cut his own hair, but A Hiue was no good at that either. He had asked to have A Hiue as his head servant, which was a formal position in the trade, but was told that because A Hiue was still illiterate in Chinese he could be only a personal servant. Instead Wu Yacheng, who had got a job with the Company after his return from England, took on the role of head servant.[34] George Thomas also began to get to know some of the other Chinese young men working in the Factory, quite a few of whom lived on site. The intelligent compradore recommended by Hall to help him with his translations could have been Li Yao, flashy, ambitious, very open, and a couple of years younger than George Thomas, who we know first met him around this time.[35] Another possible friend was He Zhi, a clever, competent, and ingratiating young man from a relatively wealthy family who seems to have been employed by one of the lesser hong merchants who was heavily in debt to the British.[36] These young Chinese were not George Thomas's friends in the way that Benjamin and Peter Brodie were, but at least they did not resent his very existence and despise his interest in learning Chinese. Wu Yacheng and A Hiue knew his family, and unlike the other British young men all of them understood something of what it really meant to live between two cultures.

That summer, when the trade was over for the season and the English retired to Macao, George Thomas applied himself to improving his Chinese. He still had to dine with his colleagues in the evenings, but he could rise early to ride and bathe in the sea and spend the long hot days studying. He also arranged lessons. In Canton the British required licenses and guarantors for anyone they hired and language issues were the responsibility of the linguists, who had busy jobs and considerable opportunities to make money on their own account.[37] In Macao, however, Marchini was eager to help, and George Thomas acquired a Catholic teacher, who he wrote humbly was probably not much of a scholar in Chinese but "very capable of giving me all the instruction I have occasion for."[38] They met, in the residence of the French missionaries, for two hours each day to talk and read Chinese. Mostly they read the *Peking Gazette* (*jingbao*), a regular digest of the most important reports and correspondence handled by the government in Beijing. Through this George Thomas, who had also been writing to Li Zibiao, followed the White Lotus Rebellion, the fall of Heshen, and the Jiaqing emperor's new policies. In addition he looked for texts that might be of particular interest to the East India Company, translating a chapter on the cultivation of cotton from an agricultural compendium and an order against importing opium.[39]

Over time George Thomas developed a style of translation that aimed to minimise differences and make the text acceptable to its readers. Back in Canton officials, who were under pressure to raise money for the campaign against the White Lotus rebels, imposed a huge fine on Pan Youdu's relative Pan Changyao when English sailors from a ship he had guaranteed were caught smuggling woollen cloth. Pan Changyao called in debts due to him from an

Armenian merchant in Madras with British backers who refused to pay. In the resulting dispute George Thomas provided translations of official statements and the business correspondence, which he rendered into the standard business English of the day. He also worked under instruction by Liu Dezhang and other hong merchants on the translation into Chinese of letters to the authorities. The English thought Liu was behind the fine imposed on Pan Changyao as he tried to get control of the trade from Pan Youdu, so they pressured him to find a solution. Part of this was ensuring that George Thomas wrote the company's letters of support for Pan Changyao in terms that would be acceptable to the Qing authorities.[40] Thus George Thomas learned to write translations in the same way that he was learning to interpret, aiming to get the meaning across effectively rather than seeking to render each word or phrase into the other language.

At this point news arrived that George Leonard Staunton had died and that George Thomas was to return to England for a while to arrange his affairs. He left A Hiue, who was not keen to return to England, and agreed to take two students for the Naples College so he could continue to practice his Chinese on the ship.[41] Two years in Canton and a lot of hard work had greatly improved his Chinese. They had also shown him that he preferred written translation to interpreting. He knew now that the innocent child interpreter of his father's imagination was a mirage. Interpreting in trade as in diplomacy was inevitably a matter of negotiation, and dealing with people was not something that came naturally to George Thomas.

CHAPTER THIRTEEN

Sir George Staunton, Translator and Banker

AT TWENTY GEORGE THOMAS was now Sir George Staunton baronet. The five years that followed were the high point of his career as a translator and interpreter and also the time when he made his fortune. Later generations would look back on this as the golden age of the Canton trade, when Chinese and Western merchants at the centre of an immensely profitable global tea trade visited each other's residences, dined together, and invested in each other's countries. Staunton was at its heart, indeed his translations helped create it.

However, the first thing George Thomas needed to do after his father's death was to rescue his mother. George Leonard, still angry with his wife's family, had left her just enough to live on and stated that the family's house should be sold.[1] George Thomas changed the will and spent the next two years living with his mother in Marylebone. When he returned to China he gave her authority over his London bank account.[2] His friendship with her nephew Benjamin Brodie also deepened. Benjamin, who was training as a doctor, shared many of Staunton's scientific interests and like him was struggling to make friends. Benjamin was living with his brother Peter in Lincoln's Inn, where Peter was studying law with a friend of George Leonard's the eminent Catholic lawyer Charles Butler. George Thomas became part of this group so that his interest in

Chinese law was soon combined with an interest in the latest British legal theories.[3] He also went out to Galway to take over his father's property there. As an eligible young man and a potential patron in the East India Company, he was feted by "my numerous relations in all the remotest degrees of consanguinity and affinity" with dinners and splendid balls, all of which and especially the dancing he enjoyed immensely.[4]

Then in 1804 he sailed back to China on the same ship as a newly appointed company surgeon Alexander Pearson, who was excited by Edward Jenner's recent discovery of vaccination against smallpox and hoped he could introduce it to China. The Chinese had long practised inoculation by blowing powder from smallpox scabs into the nostrils of a child in order to induce a mild case of the disease that would then provide immunity. This was risky because smallpox was still a very dangerous disease. Jenner's new technique of vaccination used matter from the much less serious cowpox but still provided immunity. So Pearson and Staunton produced a Chinese booklet, *The Extraordinary Story of the Newly Discovered English Method of Inoculation*. The East India Company records describe this as being drafted by Pearson and translated by Staunton with the help of a Chinese doctor and Zheng Chongqian, one of the Chinese merchants, but the content suggests that it was written collaboratively. It begins with the story of Jenner's discovery and its spread, but the procedures for vaccination are clearly written with an awareness of traditional Chinese methods of inoculation, and the book ends with a suggestion that rice congee is a suitable food to eat afterward.[5]

This text was replaced within a few years by others written entirely by Chinese doctors, but the introduction of vaccination was remarkably effective. Cutting the skin to introduce the vaccine was alien to traditional Chinese medicine, but people could be reassured by the involvement of the great Chinese merchants: the booklet explaining the new technique was published under the name of Zheng Chongqian, one of the first children to be vaccinated was Liu Dezhang's niece, and Pan Youdu and others funded a vaccination clinic in their imposing guild hall. Both Pearson and Zheng then trained Chinese doctors to use the new technique. The result was that vaccination was absorbed into local medical culture (the cuts were soon being made at acupuncture points) and spread in Guangdong at almost the same time that it was spreading in England.[6]

Meanwhile Staunton continued to translate in a very conciliatory style for a new round of diplomatic correspondence between Britain and China. Tipu Sultan, whose armies had confronted the British so successfully when Macartney was in Madras, had finally been defeated in 1799 as the Napoleonic Wars transformed the balance of power in India. The British then discovered that the French had been planning to occupy Goa and decided to preempt this by seizing Macao and other Portuguese colonies. In 1802 the governor general of Bengal sent three ships and five hundred soldiers to take over Macao. The Portuguese appealed to Governor General Jiqing in Canton who ordered Pan Youdu to make it very clear to the East India Company merchants that a British occupation was not acceptable. After a nerve-wracking two weeks, during which British warships remained off the coast but no troops landed, news arrived that France and Britain had made peace. The British ships sailed away and Jiqing decided not to report the incident to Beijing.[7] Meanwhile, war broke out between the British and the Maratha Empire, the last remaining major military power on the Indian subcontinent.

The news of the threat to Macao did eventually reach the Jiaqing emperor because the Portuguese in Macao sent a letter to the court through the missionary Almeida that emphasized the threat from the ongoing British conquests in India. Jiaqing was annoyed that he had not been told, but beyond that merely ordered the new governor general to find out what was going on.[8] Jiqing's tragic death also hung over everyone involved. He had been impeached by a subordinate on an unrelated issue and the emperor had ordered an investigation. When Jiqing was brought to his palace to hear the emperor's words read to him by one of his subordinates, berated, ordered to dress in prison clothes, and deprived of his servants, he was so angry at the humiliation that he drew his sword to kill himself. When his arm was grabbed, he pulled out a small snuff bottle and swallowed it, which led to his death.[9] Since Jiqing was not only a famously upright official but also a member of the imperial clan, this was clearly no time for further accusations against him.

In London, the Board of Control of the East India Company decided that a letter and some gifts from the king to the Chinese emperor might help improve relations. Staunton carried this letter back to Canton on his return in 1804. There officials demanded a Chinese translation. Staunton did not want to do this, telling his colleagues that his Chinese would not be as good as that of the missionaries at court. Under pressure from his superiors he did produce a translation, which they explained to London was "the sense of the original rather than a literal translation," and this was read and accepted by Woshebu, the new governor general.[10]

Staunton's translation of this letter is missing, but the style of his translation and the kind of adjustments he was willing to make can be seen from an English translation he produced of one of Woshebu's letters to court. Woshebu had reported that the Portuguese were afraid of the British who were particularly fierce and that the war between Britain and France was likely to have an impact on revenues from the trade. Staunton translated this letter, which he probably obtained from the *Peking Gazette*, into English. In his translation James Drummond, whom Woshebu had called the *yimu* or "foreign headman," became "the chief of the English nation," while the explanation that the people of Macao feared the British because they relied on force to get their way (*shiqiang*) was rendered as "that nation . . . being distinguished by its strength and power."[11] Unsurprisingly the English concluded that the letter was "respectful and flattering to the national character."[12]

By this time the senior English merchants were pleased with Staunton's linguistic abilities. They reported that they were confident in "his thorough knowledge of the characters and perfect ability to translate, with some delay perhaps, into the Chinese, where their forms and customs require so much attention, but at all times with the utmost facility and correctness into the European languages."[13] They frequently informed London that the advantage of using him to translate was that unlike the Chinese merchants he spoke out boldly and did not use "servile and degrading expressions."[14]

In actual practice, however, Staunton had been taught by those same merchants, and his writing too aimed to follow forms acceptable to Qing officials. In 1805 he wrote on behalf of a British naval captain who had captured a cargo of valuable bird's nests (used to make bird's nest soup) and then lost it in a shipwreck. In this letter Staunton makes the captain refer to himself as an "official from afar" (*yuan guan*) and appeals in very Confucian terminology to the dynasty's compassion on men from afar. The English captain is made to say that he is trembling and dares to approach the governor general only because something very unjust has occurred. The letter is laid out, as Staunton had learned when he first arrived in Canton, to give the greatest honour to the Qing dynasty and refers to George III, who is placed at a lower level, as "my country's king" (*wo guo wang*).[15]

Meanwhile Staunton was beginning to make money. The East India Company paid well, but real fortunes were made from the opportunities the position provided. After a few years in Canton, the young men would usually be invited to join one of the agency houses that traded with India, but that never happened to Staunton, whom they still resented. However, the sums passing through his London bank account (fig. 13.1) show that he nevertheless made a very substantial fortune and that his big break came in these years: he appears to have brought his first large sum back to invest in 1809.[16]

At this point we reach the realm of conjecture, but it seems most likely that Staunton made his fortune by exploiting the difference between interest rates in China and England, that he increased it through financial transactions, and that his major patron was Pan Youdu. Pan Youdu's father had been innovative in his early use of British remittances, and the Napoleonic Wars were a good time to make money through financial transactions because they caused repeated dramatic fluctuations in the value of currencies and national debt. At the same time, acting as Staunton's patron also enabled Pan Youdu to avoid Staunton's potential power as an interpreter and translator being used against him by either the East India Company or his rival Liu Dezhang.[17]

When Staunton first arrived in China, Henry Baring had suggested instead that he hand over his salary and commission payments to be lent to Pan Changyao. At first Staunton had worried about the morality of lending money at interest rates of 15 to

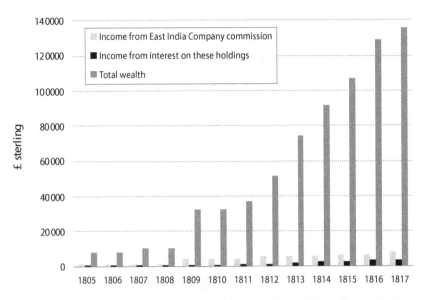

FIGURE 13.1. George Thomas Staunton's growing wealth in British stocks and bonds as recorded in his London bank account in comparison with his income from the East India Company and the interest payments on the investments.

18 percent, but then he became intrigued. He suggested that his father borrow money in England, where interest rates were lower, and send it out for him to invest. He explained that the loan would be secure because if one of the hong merchants failed his debts would be paid by the Chinese government. It was, in fact, illegal for the hong merchants to borrow large sums from foreigners, but these could easily be hidden by the financial transfers necessary to the trade, while the Qing government's decision to enforce repayments of debts to foreigners in order to ensure the security of the trade acted as a loan guarantee.[18] Staunton also asked his father to send him two business accounting textbooks that would teach him how to calculate exchange rates, annuities, interest, and so on.[19] He had always enjoyed mathematics. Applying those skills to transactions in Canton could make him rich, but he needed money to invest.

George Leonard evidently thought the risk too high, but after his death Jane, whose own father had been a banker, and George Thomas went into banking as a partnership. He gave his mother authority over his Coutts account, and she bought silver worth three thousand pounds in London (taking advice from Barrow and from her brother who was also a banker), insured it for the voyage, and sent it out to China. When one of the senior British merchants retired, George Millet, the captain of the ship on which Staunton had first sailed to China, decided to invest through him. East India Company captains bought their positions and operated as major investment syndicates, so this was a big breakthrough. Staunton gave his bond to pay 10 percent interest on twelve thousand pounds; any additional sums he made would be his own. With this he began to act as a broker lending to the Chinese merchants he knew on behalf of British investors who wanted to take advantage of the high interest rates available in Canton. As time went on when he was back in London he also began buying and selling British government short-term debt at various discount rates and terms of maturity, risking large amounts of his capital for the sake of relatively small profits on each transaction. These were the years in which the private trade in Canton began to shift from being funded by silver shipped from country to country to operating on the basis of paper credit instruments. Staunton's activities in London suggest that he was probably also dealing in credit when he was in Canton. The Bank of England records refer to him as Sir George Thomas Staunton Banker.[20]

Staunton's increasing wealth made it easier for him to enter into the social life of the English in Canton, and for one summer he even joined his colleagues in gambling.[21] Although he would never be an insider, he began to make friends. As well as Pearson there was Samuel Ball, a cheerful young tea inspector. Ball had been at school with Thomas Manning, who had taken it into his head to learn Chinese and offer his services to the Chinese emperor as an astronomer. Staunton found Manning a tutor, but Manning, who was already in his mid-thirties and had been studying in France with scholars who had theories about Chinese but little actual knowledge, did not learn much. The court rejected his offer, and he disappeared off to try to enter China through Tibet.[22]

When Robert Morrison arrived in Canton in 1807, Sir George Staunton appeared simply as part of the "the princely grandeur of the English who reside here."[23] Morrison had grown up as a child labourer in Newcastle and had been inspired to come to China by the new Protestant missionary movement. He had begun studying Chinese in London, sharing rooms with a Cantonese man, Rong Sande, who had come to England to study English and was at a boarding school in Clapham. Later Rong would return to Canton and a position in the trade from which he could act as Morrison's patron, but Morrison arrived in Canton with almost nothing but a letter of introduction to Staunton. Staunton helpfully provided a Catholic teacher, although Morrison found it very strange to be taught by "a native from the bosom of the Romish Church."[24] The two young men were about the same age and had many shared interests, but Sir George was a wealthy baronet while Morrison was always aware that he had begun life working fourteen-hour days in his father's workshop.

In these years Staunton's interests in diplomacy, trade, and translation came together in a growing fascination with Chinese law. His early involvement in the case of the unfortunate Chinese boatman had first sparked this interest, and his friendship with Peter Brodie had encouraged it. Now another major case arose, which these interests enabled him to negotiate remarkably successfully. Afterward the directors of the East India Company in London finally acknowledged the value of his Chinese language skills and gave him a formal appointment as Chinese interpreter with a significant additional salary.[25] As a result he embarked on the immense project of translating the Qing legal code into English, for which he is still known today.

This new case began because at the height of the trading season each year there were thousands of British seamen living on ships just off shore. Rowdy parties would come up to the suburbs after many months at sea, with their newly paid wages in silver, wanting drink and women. As in other ports, they were often cheated and robbed and were ripe for disputes with the local dealers. In 1807 one of these disputes blew up into a major riot in which fifty or sixty drunken British sailors from a ship called the *Neptune* fought on the waterfront, with a much larger crowd of local Chinese. The British merchants looked on from their balcony and thought it all very amusing. However, afterward one of the Chinese died. The Qing authorities demanded that the man responsible for the death should be handed over, imprisoned the senior hong merchant for his failure to get the British comply, and then suspended all trade.

This was a difficult case with serious risks for all involved. It was very unlikely that anyone really knew exactly who struck which blow during the chaotic brawl. Officials did not want to report a riot to Beijing, so they needed to deal with the case as murder. The senior English merchants and naval officers did not want to hand an Englishman over to trial in a Chinese court. The ships were already due to leave, so every day that the trade was suspended increased the risks of the voyage and the financial losses. And in addition to all this there were thousands of British seamen off shore who might well be infuriated if one of them was handed over for a murder he might not have committed, so there was always the possibility of further violence and yet worse problems.[26]

Staunton interpreted for the lengthy negotiations that followed. Tensions were high on both sides, and Staunton was no innocent interpreter of words but a key player using his growing knowledge of Chinese law to intervene. On one occasion the Qing official for whom he was interpreting threatened that if the negotiations failed they would hold him responsible. Staunton lost his temper: he translated what had been said into English, then announced in Chinese that "the faithful and distinct interpretation of their respective sentiments to each other" was equally desirable for both parties, and if they wanted him to continue they had better stop threatening him personally.[27]

The result of these tough negotiations was a jointly managed trial of the British seamen, one of the proudest achievements of Staunton's life. A Chinese oil painting of it, which later hung in his house, embodies his vision of the trade and his role in it.[28] The English merchants sit opposite their Chinese counterparts as equals, able to achieve a successful settlement for the British sailors, who are contrite, but not kneeling, in front of the Chinese judge. Staunton himself sits just below the leading merchants, brought forward because of the importance of his unique language and cultural skills. In fact this joint trial was more symbolic than real. In the end the case was solved by a fabricated story that one of the English seamen had dropped something from a window, killing the victim accidentally. The man held to be most responsible was

FIGURE 13.2. The trial of the *Neptune* sailors in the English Factory, 1807. The city prefect seated at the head of the room is questioning one of the English sailors with a linguist interpreting. The senior British naval officer sits on one side, with the senior East India Company merchants all with pot bellies from their fine dining and then Staunton in striking blue trousers. Opposite them sit Pan Youdu and the senior Chinese merchants in their official robes.

then confined by the British until he could be sent back to England. Staunton thought that the seamen should all have been punished, though for riot rather than murder, but that the outcome was "substantial justice."[29]

That summer Staunton sat down to translate the Qing legal code. He described the project as "an agreeable occupation" for his leisure hours, but this was a serious undertaking, especially in the days before the existence of a Chinese-English dictionary.[30] The text he was working on was titled *Statutes and Substatues of the Great Qing* (*Da Qing lü li*) and was nearly three thousand pages in length, although he decided at an early stage to omit most of the substatutes.[31] The code was arranged according to the ministries of the government in Beijing, and Staunton saw his book not so much as a handbook to the law but as a description of the workings of the Chinese state: on the title page he quoted Cicero: "The mind, and the spirit, and the strategy, and the way of thinking of a state are all located in its laws."[32]

He enjoyed working at Chinese texts on his own in his library and had built up an impressive collection of Chinese reference works: more than four hundred volumes of dictionaries as well as hundreds of volumes of law codes from the Qing and earlier dynasties, legal manuals, and books of cases.[33] However, there is no way that his project could have been completed alone: understanding subjects such as the detailed workings of the salt monopoly or how surplus revenues were treated in the taxation system would have been impossible without long discussions with well-informed Chinese. Only hints of these conversations emerge in his text, as when his note on the salt tax mentions that the present chief salt merchant is thought to be the richest man in Guangdong province. Another footnote is drawn from a letter from Li Zibiao in Shanxi describing food shortages there.[34] In the introduction Staunton apologises that sometimes "no effort of attention was adequate completely to reconcile the apparent sense of the words, when considered individually, with their collective meaning, such as it was unanimously declared to be, by the most intelligent of the natives whom the Translator had the opportunity of consulting."[35]

This was not a translation created with an assistant but rather one that grew out of an entire social world. Pan Youdu, like other hong merchants, invited English merchants as well as eminent Chinese literati to parties in the magnificent gardens he was creating outside the city. Other British and American merchants were usually invited only to entertainments with lots of food and drink where they spoke English to each other and to their host, but Staunton, who could speak Chinese, also attended quite different social occasions where he had the opportunity to meet elite Chinese guests. In fact at the very first dinner Staunton was invited to by one of the hong merchants a high-ranking official said that he remembered seeing Staunton when the British embassy was in Beijing and asked if Staunton did not remember him, leaving Staunton embarrassed as he had no recollection of the man at all.[36] Now, several years later, Staunton's questions about the structure and details

FIGURE 13.3. This engraving was one made by Thomas Allom from a set of Chinese drawings that Staunton owned of the Canton merchants' magnificent gardens. Even many years after leaving China Staunton was able to identify this picture with the women of the household feeding the ducks in the foreground and men chatting on the veranda above them as Pan Changyao's garden.

of Qing government for his translation would have made suitable polite conversation on such occasions.

There were also more informal occasions. Years later in England Staunton published a short essay on Chinese drinking games and how an experienced Chinese can nearly always beat a foreigner at them. Pan Changyao sometimes joined the English for an evening's gambling, and the eccentric Thomas Manning had to be talked out of wearing Chinese dress when Lord Amherst arrived. At the end of his life Staunton donated to the Royal Asiatic Society along with his books a collection of Chinese clothes, a set of official robes of the sort foreigners often acquired, but also ordinary clothing for an upper-class man.[37] It is hard not to imagine Staunton in Canton chatting and drinking the wines he imported each year from England with Chinese colleagues in his rooms at the Factory, perhaps even dressing in Chinese clothes in the hot summer evenings.

Staunton was rewarded for his contributions to the *Neptune* case with the privilege of a visit to England. He left Robert Morrison to fill the new position of interpreter and finished his great translation on the ship home. He gave it the title *Ta Tsing Leu Lee; Being the Fundamental Laws, and a Selection from the Supplementary Statutes, of the Penal Code of China*. It was the first book ever to be translated from Chinese directly into English and made Staunton's name. It was reviewed in all the major journals, was rapidly translated into French and Italian, and continued to be used into the late twentieth century when a new translation was finally made.[38]

Staunton's translation had a major influence on later views of Chinese law and has been extensively studied. Scholars have noticed the complexity of his own position as part of the East India Company establishment in Canton and that he aimed to make the text readable and Chinese ideas acceptable to an English audience.[39] Practices such as polygamy and slavery that were likely to offend an English reader disappeared in careful choices of vocabulary or were explained away in the footnotes.[40] Instead the Chinese are presented as having a legal code, something that progressive English legal scholars were then arguing should replace English common law, arguments he would have been familiar with from his friendship with Peter Brodie and legal circles in London.[41]

However, Staunton's translation of the *Ta Tsing Leu Lee* was also an expression of his personal history as an interpreter. Not only had he learned Chinese through friendships with Chinese his own age, but like all interpreters he had been compelled to engage seriously with the other side's point of view, to speak in their language. Conciliation and explanation were at the heart of his role. Through these experiences he had come to believe, as he states in the introduction to the book, that "a considerable proportion of the opinions most generally entertained by Chinese and Europeans of each other" are due either to prejudice or to misinformation and neither side has "any violent degree of moral or physical superiority."[42] The Chinese lack science and Christianity, but they too are civilised and have "some very considerable and positive moral and political advantages" over the British, which he lists beginning with a sacred regard to ties of kindred and ending with avoiding foreign conquests and having comprehensive and uniform laws.[43] Back in

England he developed a fascination with his own ancestry, travelling to Nottinghamshire to see if he might be able to purchase an ancient Staunton estate.[44] Many English gentlemen of this period were fascinated by their medieval ancestry, but for Staunton a regard for ancestry and kindred was a value that he also saw exemplified in China.

CHAPTER FOURTEEN

The British Occupation of Macao and Its Aftermath

IN 1808, WHILE Staunton was in England, British forces again threatened to take Macao, and this time the Jiaqing emperor became aware of the situation. Jiaqing was China's central decision maker, but that very fact meant that his knowledge was limited as his courtiers manoeuvred around him. Key decisions were debated in terms derived from China's ancient history, which reduced the novelty of the British threat. And officials were cautious in what they told him because even the most senior courtiers could be sent into exile if they displeased him. Nevertheless, despite the limits on his knowledge, in the aftermath of the British occupation of Macao Jiaqing was sufficiently aware of the threat to decide to send Songyun, who knew about the British from the Macartney embassy, to check on Canton's defences, and Songyun used his relationship with Staunton to find out more. However, the fragile balance of the past few years had been broken. As Elphinstone put it privately to his father, "The kind of negative character partaking of both nations which we held while Puankhequa [Pan Youdu] managed the foreign affairs here is no longer possible."[1] Staunton and his Chinese friends were caught between the two sides and began to come under intense pressure.

In September 1808 Rear Admiral William Drury arrived off the coast of China with three hundred troops from Madras and occupied Macao. The British desire for a base off the coast of China was long-standing, but as in 1802 the immediate cause lay in the ongoing wars between Britain and France. The French had just invaded Portugal, opening the Portuguese trading colonies in Asia to British attack, and the British authorities in Bengal had again decided to seize Goa and Macao.[2]

The British assumed that the Chinese would accept the occupation since it was Portuguese territory. This was not, however, how the Qing thought of Macao, and the event precipitated a major crisis for Governor General Wu Xiongguang. Macao occupied a narrow, fortified promontory, which made it very hard to retake from the mainland, and Wu knew that it would be impossible for Chinese junks to take on the British warships with their immense firepower. The situation became even more serious when Drury sailed three of his ships up to Canton and threatened to bombard the city.

Wu Xiongguang understood that the only card he held against the British was his ability to control the trade. He ordered the senior English merchants to make Drury leave. When that failed, he stopped the trade but assured the English that it could start again as soon as their forces left Macao. When Drury still refused to go, Wu banned deliveries of supplies to the British warships and then to the English Factory. Finally, he threatened to set fire to the East India Company's immensely valuable merchant shipping already docked near Canton.[3] This would have been catastrophic for his tax revenues, but the British were also well aware that "the fleet could not resist an attack of this nature."[4]

Wu Xiongguang held to this line in the face of furious but impractical orders from Jiaqing to drive the British out. Jiaqing was reading Wu's letters carefully as well as the correspondence from the customs superintendent and a letter from Drury himself, so he knew about the wars and alliances that lay behind the British action. He also learned that the British had brought in thin, ragged, dark-skinned troops from Bengal whom they had forced into their army, which he declared "an exceedingly hateful trick!"[5] The one thing Wu dared not fully explain, though he touched on it, was that Qing water forces simply could not deal with the British warships.[6]

Jiaqing's own policy statements were conventionally expressed in classical terms: "These feuds and mutual slaughter are quite normal among the outer barbarians; the middle kingdom does not concern itself."[7] However, the real issue for him was the empire's territorial integrity. When Wu Xiongguang's successor said that he had rebuked the senior company merchant, who had explained that the British intended to protect Portugal, with the words "Macao is within the limits of the Heavenly Dynasty's territory," Jiaqing commented, "These words go to the heart of the matter."[8]

After two months Wu Xiongguang's policy succeeded, but he had sacrificed his own career. The day that Drury began to remove his troops was the day that Jiaqing lost patience and referred Wu to the Board of Punishments. In Canton Wu, who was one of the rare senior Han Chinese officials, was said to have told his staff that he had no regrets because any other policy would have exposed his country to harm. When he got to Beijing, the official interrogating him reported that all he would do was crawl on the ground and beat his head and say that he handled it all very badly and deserved heavy punishment. He was sent into exile in Xinjiang.[9]

The company directors in London were no happier with the outcome, and Elphinstone blamed the problem partly on poor interpreting. With George Thomas away, this task had fallen to Rodrigo da Madre de Dios, who headed Macao's Translation Office. He was also an agent for the British who paid him large sums for passing on information and translations of Chinese government documents. After Drury left he was arrested by the Chinese. The British and Portuguese got him released, but only on condition that he left the country.[10]

Robert Morrison took over as interpreter, but he had arrived in Canton only two years earlier and still had problems understanding the language. He preferred to have things written down, and even so he could not translate on sight.[11]

Morrison's attitude to translation was also very different from Staunton's. Staunton spoke several European languages and had learned Latin by speaking it as a child. He seldom looked for one Chinese word as the equivalent of an English one, thinking that precise synonyms were rare even between European languages and "the more remote the two nations are from each other, and the

more dissimilar they may happen to be in their habits and characters, the smaller, of course, will be the proportion of words in their
respective languages, that are strictly synonimous."[12] His general
practice was to take the overall meaning and try to get that across
in a way that would be acceptable to his audience. Morrison by
contrast had learned Latin from grammar books and was studying
Chinese to translate the Bible. He believed that for this sacred text
"paraphrase is not to be admitted."[13] As the first stage in this task
he was writing a Chinese-English dictionary so he was constantly
searching for synonyms in the two languages.

In 1810 he was more successful interpreting for Captain Francis Austen in yet another case of a Chinese man killed in a brawl
between English sailors and locals, but even so the negotiations
were frustrating for everyone. Unlike Staunton, who only ever
spoke Mandarin, Morrison was also learning Cantonese from
his servants. He had problems understanding officials speaking formal Mandarin and complained that they were "extremely
haughty, overbearing and clamorous" and sometimes shouted
over one another at him.[14] It was easier for him to communicate
with the witnesses: local shopkeepers and tradesmen who spoke
simple Cantonese, and even this he felt was a great achievement.
Several of the younger English staff began studying Chinese with
him.[15] They could imagine achieving what Morrison had in a way
they could not with Staunton's childhood fluency. Morrison was
also much more willing to teach, so it was he, not Staunton, who
trained the next generation of British interpreters and diplomats
and shaped their translation practices.

The result of Morrison's limited language skills and his determination to translate every word separately was that his early translations made Qing officials sound very strange indeed. Here is part of
his translation of a letter from the governor general complaining,
as it happens, about Morrison's written Chinese: "Respecting the
address that was presented; the manner of the composition was not
perspicacious, the body and cut of it also was not perfectly suitable.
I compassionately consider that the foreigners do not understand
the middle charming empire's manner of composing; I therefore do
not make a deep enquiry into the address (by demanding) (1) three
prostrations but return it."[16] The governor general had written in

particularly simple terms, but even so Morrison's search for synonyms is a problem: "middle charming empire" is a translation of *Zhonghua*, a standard term for China. To this Morrison added his own preconceptions about China: when he came to the term *kou*, which means "to knock" but also, by extension, "to enquire," he added "by demanding" in parentheses and then a footnote about prostrations to officials. The result is that the governor general, who had said only that he was not going to make any objection to Morrison's poor Chinese, appears quite wrongly to be assuming that the British should kowtow to him.

When Staunton got back to China and translated one of the last documents in the case, the contrast was obvious. With Morrison in the office Staunton's translation was somewhat more literal than it had been before: he writes "king of that country" rather than "George III." However, he still makes the Chinese officials express themselves in conventional English, so that what they are saying sounds far more reasonable. His translation ends, "In the meantime the name of the responsible merchant must be duly stated to us and the rest of our orders obeyed with the greatest promptitude."[17]

The smoothing effect of Staunton's translations was only one part of his world that was under threat. He arrived back to find Elphinstone, son of one of the company's directors and leader of the other English young men, promoted to president of the Select Committee in charge of the company's operations in Canton and his friend Wu Yacheng in prison. Wu's problems had begun when the merchant Zheng Chongqian became insolvent, bringing Wu's employer down with him. This had left the East India Company facing an unpalatable choice between accepting a reduced number of registered Chinese merchants, which would threaten the company's monopoly advantage, or giving the failed merchants the money to pay their taxes and continue in business. On previous occasions officials had used this dilemma to extract tax increases from the trade. Now the English decided to resist by appointing someone to run Zheng Chongqian's business under their control and thus pay off the debts. Wu Yacheng accepted the job.[18]

When officials realised what was going on they were swift to act. The occupation of Macao had made clear that to lose control over the trade could be catastrophic and in any case it was unacceptable to put debts owed to foreign creditors on an equal footing with tax arrears. The focus of the investigation was on Wu Yacheng, who was repeatedly interrogated and beaten to extract details of his relations with the British. He was then sentenced to be displayed for three months in a cangue at the scene of his crimes, which presumably meant near the foreign factories, then exiled to Xinjiang.[19]

As Staunton looked on and his friend was displayed day after day as a criminal with a heavy wooden board clamped round his neck, news arrived that a new governor general had been appointed. This turned out to be Songyun. The emperor had called on Songyun and Changlin, both of whom had been involved with the Macartney embassy, to deal with these new British problems. Changlin, now blind, was to advise on new commercial regulations, while Songyun was sent to Canton. Songyun was also famous for being willing to speak openly to the emperor whatever the personal risk, and this was one of a series of brief postings where he was given full administrative powers evidently as a way for Jiaqing to find out what was going on. Jiaqing ordered him to inspect the sea defences and especially the river passage up to Canton. He was also to persuade the Canton merchants to make a massive donation for river conservancy works: another of Jiaqing's problems was the state's inability to collect sufficient taxation for infrastructure.[20]

Shortly after Songyun arrived he was handed a petition from the foreign creditors of one of the failed merchants. He asked who had translated it into Chinese. To the immense surprise of everyone present he then announced that he remembered the father of this Englishman called Staunton. Why had he not sent his respects? The English had just arrived in Macao for the summer when Staunton received a flurry of excited letters telling him that he must come back to Canton immediately. Elphinstone provided formal letters congratulating Songyun on his appointment and agreed that Staunton could act as he thought proper, but it is clear he had no idea of what Staunton was planning.[21]

Staunton's meeting with Songyun began with mutual compliments about the embassy: Songyun asked after Macartney, whose name he remembered, and told Staunton about Wang Wenxiong's death. Staunton had prepared a response ahead of time and could say that Songyun's virtue and benevolence were widely known in

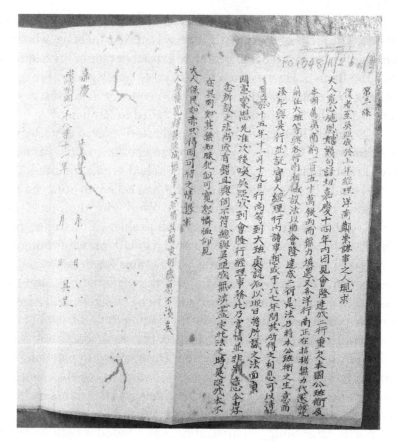

FIGURE 14.1. The final page of Staunton's statement to Songyun. It shows
Staunton's best Chinese handwriting. At the end he has written the dates
according to both the Jiaqing emperor's reign period and the Western calendar.
Someone has crossed out the Western date in Chinese-style loops using a pencil.
Is this perhaps Songyun's correction to the form of the text?

England through his father's book. He handed over Elphinstone's
letters. Songyun glanced at them and passed them on to the customs superintendent sitting beside him.[22] Then Staunton handed
him another paper, explaining that it was a speech he had planned
to make, but he was nervous he "might not be able to deliver myself
on the occasion, so fully and clearly as the importance of the subjects required."[23]

The speech was in Staunton's writing and worded as a formal
request from the East India Company, but evidently composed

by Staunton with the help of Chinese colleagues, probably Wu Yacheng's friends. It consisted of three requests. The first two were perfectly conventional: First, he wanted the East India Company merchants to be treated as people from honourable families with government connections, not like private merchants or ships officers. Second, he requested a reduction of taxes on the Chinese merchants dealing with the British since the current situation was affecting their creditworthiness. Though he did not say so, Staunton had a personal interest in this as he had been buying up their debts (his holdings ultimately brought in about £20,000), which was no doubt also why he had written the petition that caught Songyun's eye. The third request was different: in much stronger language he begged Songyun to reconsider Wu Yacheng's punishment. He assured Songyun that the only aim of the arrangement had been to pay back the debts and Wu Yacheng had no intention of doing anything wrong. He ended by pleading with Songyun as an official who treated the common people like his own children to have mercy on Wu and his family.[24]

Songyun read slowly through the three pages. Then he went back to the beginning and read the whole document over again. The ability to remember documents seen only once was a highly prized skill in Qing court politics; it was always safer to remember the contents of a document than to keep it where others might see it. Songyun did not show this document to the customs superintendent but instead called Staunton over. He said he could agree to the first two requests, but not the request to reconsider Wu Yacheng's case. This section must be removed, and there was one small point that needed changing, which he marked for Staunton. Then he said that Wu's case had already been settled by his predecessor and ratified by the emperor. When the customs superintendent intervened to point out that the English would not expect to reverse their king's decision, Songyun agreed but said it was a pity. Staunton, encouraged by this, began to plead with him, saying that Wu Yacheng had thought the arrangement had been officially approved and asking if perhaps Songyun could obtain some alleviation of his punishment. Songyun responded cautiously that such a request would need to come from the head of the English company and invited Staunton to dinner in a few days' time.[25]

At the dinner Songyun began asking Staunton why British warships were coming to China and why they had come to Macao in 1808, forcing Staunton to attempt to explain the British occupation. He then asked Staunton to kneel to him in the Chinese style. The provincial governor and Manchu general, all the hong merchants, several of the linguists, and one of Staunton's junior East India Company colleagues were all present, and Staunton was taken aback. He said that English custom forbade it and, when Songyun pressed him, burst out that he would not kneel even if the whole trade were at stake. Apparently unruffled, Songyun dropped the subject and everyone sat down to dinner. Warm milk was handed round, another reminder of the Macartney embassy. After the dinner, Staunton tried to hand over his revised document, but Songyun would not take it, saying that this was just a social occasion. He did accept with approval the booklet on vaccination on which the now bankrupt and imprisoned Zheng Chongqian had cooperated.[26]

Afterward Staunton, still desperate to please Songyun, wrote to apologise, explaining that not kneeling was simply a matter of custom, not at all because he did not respect Songyun. Songyun accepted this and asked to see Staunton again. This time he was alone when Staunton arrived. He took Staunton's hand, told him that he was not at all offended, then launched into a string of advice. When Staunton mentioned plans for another British embassy, he was emphatic: "The emperor knows it is a long way and does not wish you to trouble yourselves. Besides the climate doesn't agree with you—you may catch infectious distempers. No your nation must not send an embassy. I will not allow it."[27]

Later Songyun came down to Macao where he visited the East India Company's residence. To everyone's amazement, he sat down to drink tea with the English and spoke to each of them in turn with Staunton interpreting. Most of Songyun's report on this is taken up with a speech he made about opium, which was becoming a major issue at court:

> When you merchants from all the European countries come to Canton to trade, you should continue to bring useful goods as you did in the past. That way you will make a profit and also win the blessing of happiness. As for opium, it is something that no one really knows how to

make up properly. You people bring it into Canton and simmer it down to a paste for smoking. When people smoke it their minds are instantly affected so that they can do all kinds of terrible things. It is so bad that when they get used to smoking it they cannot quit even if they want to, so that very many families are ruined and lives are lost. Think about it! If you harm people like this for the sake of profit it is sure to anger Heaven and one day your family will be ruined and your property lost. The retribution will be even worse than what happens to the people who smoke the opium. Each of you should write to your country asking them to strictly ban the trade in this poisonous stuff, and then you may be able to escape disaster.[28]

Songyun said that after this speech the English looked embarrassed and fearful. As so often, the emotions of the interpreter appeared to be the emotions of the group. Elphinstone had dismissed his remarks as merely pro forma, but some months later when Staunton got hold of a copy of this letter and translated it he left out the tea party and this speech altogether.[29]

Staunton must have known that Songyun's moral persuasion had no hope of success with his colleagues. In fact the opposite happened. There was already a shortage of silver in Canton due to an American embargo on silver exports, and now Songyun's personal inspection had made it impossible for the opium importers to offload their incoming cargoes. As a result the committee of senior English merchants (of which Staunton was not yet a member) decided for the first time to accept opium as security for credit notes. They debated the issue but went ahead on the grounds that London was in need of silver for the war and the deal would also "contribute generally to the advantage of the opium trade of Macao, a trade in whose success connected as it is with an important branch of the Honourable Company's revenue we cannot with propriety be wholly indifferent."[30] The logic of this was that the company's monopoly on opium production in Bengal had become a major revenue stream essential to pay for its wars and fund its rule in India, so it was essential for them to support the price of opium. Within a month the English Factory was holding opium worth half a million dollars from both Portuguese and British traders.[31]

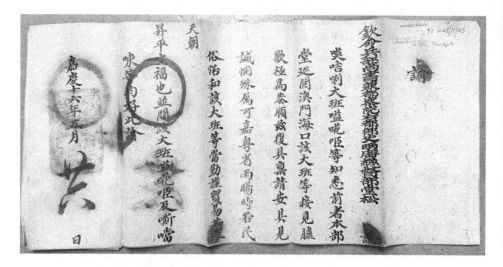

FIGURE 14.2. A formal letter from Songyun ending with an enquiry after the health of Elphinstone and Staunton. Songyun has added the date in the red ink that marks his formal pronouncements as governor general and circled the character 福 meaning "blessings." He folded the paper up straightaway, so that the red ink has stained through to the facing pages. The result is characteristic of his flamboyant style.

Songyun, meanwhile, was thinking about Staunton's concern for Wu Yacheng. When the English arrived back in Canton, he sent a message to say that he would like to meet with Elphinstone and Staunton in his residence immediately. Elphinstone did not like the style of this and said that he was not feeling well. Songyun then sent an officer to enquire after his health; the officer asked to speak privately to Elphinstone and Staunton and proposed to them that the foreign debts of the two failed merchants should be rescheduled over sixteen years rather than ten in return for the release of Wu Yacheng and Zheng Chongqian. Elphinstone, who had large personal debts as a result of Zheng's bankruptcy, flatly refused.[32] Staunton saw his efforts for Wu Yacheng destroyed by his English colleagues.

Songyun, however, had not finished with the English: in accordance with Jiaqing's orders he was paying attention to Canton's maritime defences, and in particular the forts that controlled the entrance to the river. When Elphinstone issued an invitation to him to visit the English ships, he accepted. No one had expected this, but the visit took place successfully a few days later. Songyun went aboard the *Perseverance*, with every British ship in the area firing gun salutes and a unit of marines presenting arms. The *Perseverance* was a forty-gun East Indiaman, with nothing like the fire power of the British warships, but she was still far more heavily armed than any Chinese ship. Songyun did nothing more than sit on the deck and make polite conversation, mainly to Staunton, and he reported the event to Jiaqing as an example of English respectful behaviour.[33] He had, however, seen the British ships firsthand. By the time he moved on to a new post that winter, the British were delighted, and he was also much better informed.

Staunton, however, had announced that he was ill and quite unexpectedly returned to England. It was common enough for the English merchants to use their health as an excuse to leave Canton, but there had been no earlier sign of Staunton having health problems. It seems more likely that he was finding his situation in China increasingly uncomfortable. Songyun's gifts reached him, along with a letter from Li Zibiao, in the spa town of Tunbridge Wells.[34]

Staunton had been working on a translation of the Yongzheng emperor's *Sacred Edict*, a simple distillation of the official Confucian philosophy with which Songyun was so closely identified. In Staunton's version the values of a Confucian scholar and those of the English gentleman are melded together so that it is impossible to tell whether Staunton is imposing his own values on the Chinese text or whether he has simply come to share the Confucian ideas. On the establishment of schools, Staunton's translation might well be his own view of his role in China: "Among the four classes of the people, the student holds the first rank.—All men ought therefore to have a due consideration for his profession, and he ought to have a due consideration for it himself."[35] When he left China he abandoned the translation suddenly at item 9: "Attend each to your proper employment that the people may be fixed in their purposes."[36] He never returned to it.

Operating between the Chinese and the English had become much harder than before the occupation of Macao, and Staunton's learning and his translations that would help the British understand the thinking of Qing officials no longer seemed to provide an answer. Wu Yacheng had paid the price, and when Staunton tried to rescue him he was let down by Elphinstone. Staunton wrote later that although the social life of the English Factory was easier by this time, his "distaste for my position in China" returned "with redoubled force."[37]

Back in London he took part in the debate on the renewal of the East India Company's charter, which resulted in India being opened to British merchants, but the company's monopoly in Canton being extended for another twenty years. Along with other company employees he defended the company's position in Canton against the advocates for free trade and was interviewed by the parliamentary select committee. He explained to them the logic of the Qing position: they have a system of strict control in which senior officials bear extensive individual responsibility, and for them this is a sign of good government. The root of the problem, as he saw it, was not the failings of the company's institutions in Canton but the "constant and increasing provocation" from British naval vessels.[38] The world in which he had lived and made his translations was coming to an end.

CHAPTER FIFTEEN

A Linguist and His Troubles

STAUNTON ARRIVED BACK IN CHINA, where, as he wrote to his mother, "I am in some degree, at Home," in the summer of 1814.[1] That sense of belonging was soon to be entirely destroyed in disputes with the Qing authorities over the arrest of another of his Chinese friends, the linguist Li Yao. The risks for anyone acting as an intermediary with the British were about to become abundantly clear. Li Yao was caught between increasing British power and the Jiaqing emperor's growing awareness of the threat. Information was filtering through to the emperor not only from his officials but also from the Chinese merchants with their immense wealth and global links. When Staunton took action to protect his friend he too was soon in danger.

At the root of these problems lay the wars of the French Revolution and the expansion of British naval power. Tensions between Britain and its former colony the United States of America led to Thomas Jefferson's Embargo Act against British trade, then a British naval blockade of American trade, and then the War of 1812, which brought British warships back to the south China coast to blockade the American trade there. However, the ongoing wars were not only leading to incidents off the China coast and causing Britain and France to develop new weapons but also absorbing all their attention. In this context the policy of controlling those who acted as intermediaries with the British appeared to Qing officials to be working.

The Chinese merchants had been using the Americans as a way to avoid the monopoly power of the East India Company, so the naval blockade affected them too. When the blockade began to cut into the profits of the American merchants, the Chinese merchants lent money to them to help them through. They were then badly affected when the Americans became insolvent and defaulted on the loans. Pan Changyao and the young Wu Bingjian, who had become one of the wealthiest in part through his close links to the Americans, had hired American lawyers and were pursuing their losses through the courts. Pan even tried to appeal his case to President Madison.[2] As a banker Staunton did well out of these pressures, which were exacerbated by the arrival of a new customs superintendent, Xiangzhao, who had failed to collect the taxes due in his previous posting and now refused to take over the post from his predecessor until all tax arrears had been paid up. Interest rates in Canton shot up as merchants tried to borrow the silver to pay their tax bills, and some of the resulting loans were at annual rates of nearly 40 percent.[3]

At the same time the prizes to be won by capturing the American merchant vessels leaving Canton were a huge inducement to British naval officers. Soon a British warship, HMS *Doris*, was hovering off the coast. First she attacked and wrecked an American ship in the river not far from Canton with crowds of spectators looking on. Then a few months later she seized a ship trading from India that had put into Macao for protection. This ship was originally British but had been captured by the Americans, leading to a major dispute as to who now owned its valuable cargo.[4]

The governor general at this time was Jiang Youxian, a clever and cautious man descended from one of the Chinese families that had fought for the Manchus before their invasion of China. He announced that actions like this in China's territorial waters were entirely unacceptable and stopped the trade until a resolution could be reached. He reported to the emperor that Britain was dependent on trade and China did not need British exports. This sounds like conventional Chinese rhetoric, but Jiang had just explained that Britain was at war with America, information he had learned from the Chinese merchants. Those same Chinese merchants had been badly hit by the Embargo Act and may very well have known that the Americans had used this strategy on the same grounds that Britain was dependent on trade. As the dispute intensified Elphinstone, now the senior English merchant, in consultation with Staunton, who had finally been appointed to the committee that ran the Factory, responded by refusing to allow incoming English vessels to sail upriver and unload their cargoes.[5]

Jiang Youxian also decided to pursue Li Yao, one of the linguists who was particularly close to the British. Li Yao and Staunton had known each other since they were both in their late teens. Li Yao was sharp, with an intelligence that could match Staunton's. Both were very talkative, but Staunton had always lacked confidence, whereas Li Yao was ambitious and flashy. In the years since they first met Li had gone abroad as servant to the captain of one of the East India Company ships. It was presumably at this stage that he learned to write a good English hand. He returned in 1808 during the British occupation of Macao. Quite what his role was that year is unclear, but an intelligent Chinese servant with good English could have been useful in any number of ways, and he seems to have known Admiral William Drury personally.[6]

When he returned to China Li Yao married the daughter of a comprador and took up a post as a linguist. He also bought a house and an official degree.[7] Clearly he was making money. Since it is obvious that he was not telling the truth in his statements to the officials who later interrogated him, it is not entirely clear what he was doing, but it seems that the company was using him very much on the model of the Indian *dubash*. In other words his role combined interpreting where necessary with political advice and acting as a financial agent. He said that he was being paid by the company to price tea at source. The English were not allowed to travel up country, which made them very dependent on their suppliers for the quality of their tea. Li Yao went, against all the rules, on their behalf to inspect the crop and fix its price. For this he received a significant cut of the profits. Qing officials thought that Li Yao had also made money as the middleman for British loans to the merchant Li Xiefa whose business was one of several in financial difficulties because of the shortage of credit.[8] When the British wanted to send gifts to Songyun in Beijing to cement their relationship after his departure, it was Li Yao who took them. He also used the opportunity to purchase an honorific post in the central government.[9]

Li Yao's arrest was basically speculative: the county magistrate reported that he had dealings with foreigners and appeared suspicious. The trip to Beijing had made him conspicuous. There were various rumours as to what he might have been up to, but Songyun's cautious reaction to the gifts (he reported everything to the emperor) had made it very hard to act on these. So instead the magistrate had Li's house searched, his wife and servants beaten and interrogated, and the hong merchants and linguists questioned. This failed to uncover opium smuggling, which was what officials had hoped. Instead they had to rely on information given by Liu Dezhang, who reported that Li had been a servant on one of the English ships.[10] This meant he could be punished for the obscure crime of purchasing a government post having once been a menial servant. "This," as he wrote to Staunton from prison, "is what will get me."[11]

The British had retired to Macao for the summer, and Staunton was receiving almost daily letters from Li Yao. Both of them were rich enough to bribe the prison staff, and Li Xiefa, who knew everyone in the bureaucracy because he had previously held an official post himself, was also involved. Later, when Li Yao began to appreciate the risks for Staunton, he addressed them to Elphinstone and even wrote Elphinstone's name in English on the cover, but since the content was in Chinese it was still Staunton who was reading them.[12]

Staunton thought of appealing to the emperor, but who would write the appeal? He did not want to and nor did Morrison; both of them remembered what had happened to James Flint, who had been imprisoned for interpreting fifty years earlier, and Rodrigo da Madre de Dios, now in Brazil. Morrison replied bluntly that "at this moment, as in some other cases, the duties of Chinese Translator are attended with some personal hazard."[13] However, he did agree to appeal for mercy for Li and to inform officials that the company would not authorise the new season's trade to start until he was released.[14]

This only made the investigating officials even more suspicious. Li Yao was questioned about spying and confessed to informing the British and Americans about the positions of each other's ships, though he insisted that he had never spied against the Qing. He was also interrogated about the loans. On this occasion he was so severely beaten that he thought he would die and confessed to everything that was put to him. He realised he was facing the same accusations made against Wu Yacheng two years earlier. His letter to Elphinstone and Staunton ends: "This evening back in the lockup, I kept thinking it all over. Each day's questioning was different so I could see clearly that they are using the same method as the year before last. I really don't dare implicate my friends. I know now that it is all to repay the kindness of the two of you to me. If it is like this tomorrow morning and I am lucky enough to survive, it will also be because of your good fortune."[15] The Chinese term he uses for friend, *pengyou*, is both stronger and less commonly used than its equivalent in English.

Elphinstone was now comfortably settled in Macao for the summer and had no intention of returning to the heat of Canton. Staunton, desperate, persuaded him to give him authority to negotiate with officials and went up to Canton. But this was only half the problem, Staunton also needed grounds for negotiation that he could put forward not only to Qing officials but also to the directors of the East India Company in London and the English merchants in China, and indeed to justify his actions to himself. He stated these in a letter to his mother as "improving our situation" and "maintaining the honor of our Country."[16] In practice, both these were about Li Yao. He depicted Li's arrest as an attempt to tighten control over the trade by restricting the use of Chinese agents. He pointed out that the English Factory needed large numbers of Chinese servants as porters, gatekeepers, cooks, and so on. To the officials sent to negotiate with him this argument was simply perverse. They had no problem with the idea that large numbers of Chinese were employed in these kind of roles by the English Factory and ships. What was not allowed was *shawen*, a transliteration of the English word "servant," which to them meant someone like Li Yao with a close personal relationship to the English.[17] Staunton's second point, about maintaining British honour, referred to the gifts to Songyun, which included a portrait of the Prince Regent: Li should not be punished for delivering these. Staunton summed up his objectives to the London directors, "It must be proved to the Chinese, that, to desert those who have rendered them service is no part of the English character."[18]

To these central goals Staunton added various ongoing sources of irritation to the British, mainly to do with the idea that the Qing officials were favouring the Americans in the various disputes involving HMS *Doris*. He also objected to offensive language in Chinese official documents, in particular the use of the term "barbarian" (*manyi*) to refer to the English. Actually this particular compound was hardly ever used in relation to the English, and these questions of terms were usually more of a problem for Morrison, who believed in the power of certain words to influence behaviour. The Qing negotiators explained that *man* referred to people from the south and *yi* to people from the west. They might have pointed out that the English had occasionally used the term *yi* for themselves.[19]

After hearing all this, Jiang Youxian reported to the emperor on the need to pursue any cases of people whose relations with foreigners were too close. No one should be allowed to act as a personal servant to the foreigners and then become a linguist for the trade. He mentioned both Wu Yacheng and Li Yao. Jiaqing, reading the document, added the words "Yes, indeed."[20]

Li, in prison, was touched by Staunton's loyalty but worried that it might make his situation worse. He was clearly in the habit of giving Staunton instructions and wrote endless advice as to what he should say, drafting whole speeches that would focus on the insult to England and depict Li himself merely as a sincere linguist or someone who had been unjustly treated.[21]

Staunton was also in trouble from the British side. As the new season's ships began to arrive, Jiang Youxian lifted his ban on the trade, leaving Staunton and Elphinstone responsible for the captains being unable to unload their cargoes. Many of the ships were leaking from the long voyages, and almost all were facing fees for failing to make their next voyage on time for reasons not covered by their insurance. The captains came in person to protest, alleging damages of several hundred thousand pounds, and threatening to sue Staunton and Elphinstone personally for their losses. Central to their objections was that Staunton's main goal appeared to be to rescue an acknowledged criminal from the law of his own country.[22]

Under all this pressure Staunton lost his temper and drafted a Chinese letter in which he spoke of the Qing as a country (*da Qing guo, Zhongguo*), accused it of failures of ritual propriety (*li*), and got to the heart of the problem from his point of view: how could a linguist visiting the English be accused of being a traitor making nefarious connections (*jianmin gouchuan*) if the English were good people?[23] This so infuriated Jiang Youxian that the investigating magistrate threatened to cut off Li Yao's head and display it in front of the English Factory if trade was not restarted.[24]

Li reassured Staunton that he did not really believe they would carry out this threat, and "even if they cut off the heads of my whole family it isn't important."[25] Instead he was desperately worried about Staunton. What would happen if the British captains resisted his orders and the hong merchants refused to help? "I keep thinking about it and when I get to this point I feel shattered. I can only beg you, sir, not to think about me. Consider how to open the holds of the ships and come up with some other way to rescue me. You really must not delay any longer, causing trouble for the Honourable Company and wasting more money. I am also afraid that your anxiety for me is making you ill, and that makes me feel even more desperate."[26]

Jiang Youxian wrote to Staunton, personally punctuating the letter in red ink, complaining about his demands and saying that Li was being punished only because he had been a servant and had then bought political office. Any further enquiries into his case would be proof that Li did indeed have nefarious connections and would increase his punishment.[27] Then Xiangzhao, the customs superintendent, wrote to the hong merchants, pointing out that the negotiations had lasted half a month and so far the English had done nothing but send in petitions on behalf of "that traitor Li Yao."[28] He also demanded an investigation of Staunton's personal connections with Li Yao.[29]

Staunton took a huge gamble. He got help from the senior British naval officer in the area, ordered all the British ships to sail out of the port, and threatened to sail north and appeal the case to the emperor. This would have wrecked the career of every Qing official involved. Li Yao was exhilarated by the news. Despite being interrogated and beaten repeatedly by furious officials after the news came through, he wrote to Staunton, "Your Company is quite something! Even though I may be executed I like it!"[30] Jiang Youxian responded by circulating a message to the English captains blaming the entire dispute on Staunton: ships with cargoes worth many thousands of taels were rotting in the water because of a single Chinese criminal. There was no way given the distance that the British king could possibly know about or have approved such a policy.[31]

Both sides had now pushed the dispute as far as they could go. Wu Bingjian was sent to persuade Staunton to return and restart negotiations. And while the official in charge was the Canton prefect, the discussions were actually led by Zeng Ao, the provincial treasurer who was an eminent scholar and a friend of Pan Youdu's family. In these propitious circumstances for Staunton, the discussions were handled with great tact and Zeng conceded several minor points, most of which involved confirming existing practices: the British were allowed to write their letters to officials in Chinese, they could employ staff (but not "servants"), and so on.[32] This was enough for Staunton to claim to the East India Company that his negotiations had succeeded, but on the issue at the heart of the dispute, Li Yao, he failed.

Failure had in fact been inevitable from the moment that Jiaqing had approved the arrest, though the emperor understood that punishment would be difficult because no serious crime had been committed. Jiaqing had begun to make connections between Christianity and the British naval threat: now he suggested that Li should be asked to tread on a cross. If he refused he could be exiled as a Christian. Jiang Youxian complied, but, as he had expected, Li Yao trod on the cross straightaway showing no concern at all: he was clearly not Christian. So he was sentenced to exile in Xinjiang on the charge of buying political office having been a menial servant.[33]

It seemed that the case was finished, but then in January of 1815 two more imperial edicts arrived in Guangdong, and these dealt not with Li Yao but with Staunton. The first covered the activities of British warships and the problem of foreign loans to the hong merchants. Then Jiaqing went on,

> There is also an Englishman Staunton who came along to the capital when that country presented tribute. He was crafty even in his child-hood and on the journey home he carefully drew a set of pictures showing all the landscape along the route. Also, after he arrived in Guangdong he did not return to his own country but has stayed on in Macao for twenty years. He is able to speak Chinese. There is a regulation that the foreigners living in Macao are not allowed to enter the provincial capital, but when Songyun took up the position of Governor General of Guangdong and Guangxi, because he had once escorted the English ambassador Staunton came to the provincial capital and requested a meeting. And when Jiang Youxian took office Staunton came again to the provincial capital but Jiang Youxian refused to see him. Because Staunton has been in Guangdong for a long time the English who come there are often taken in by him and there has long been a fear that he will make trouble. The hong merchants owe too much money to this foreigner for their purchases and are under his control which is also inappropriate. Jiang Youxian must immediately report the full story of how the English warship entered the port in detail. He should also clarify whether when he was in Guangdong Staunton ever made trou-ble, had secret communications, or profited from fraud. If proof can be found perhaps he should be relocated into exile.[34]

Most imperial statements begin with a reference to incoming corre-spondence, but in this case Jiaqing does not explain how he knows about Staunton. It cannot have been from Songyun, who was far off on China's western frontier, and in any case the emperor's source appears to have been hostile to Songyun, criticising him for meet-ing Staunton. Apparently news of British activities was reaching Jiaqing through other channels.

Li Yao, still in prison in Canton, heard that Liu Dezhang had paid a spectacular bribe to the province's top military officer to enable him to have a face to face meeting with the emperor. As it turned out this may not have been quite how Liu's influence worked. Staunton and Elphinstone later heard that it was one of the other censors who brought the topic up with the emperor. Liu Dezhang's son Liu Chengshu, who had a position in the Board of Revenue in Beijing, had failed to prevent a massive fraud in which clerical officers had been extracting silver from the treasury and allowing outsiders to read sensitive tax information, in both cases by using faked authorization slips. Liu Chengshu managed to extricate himself from any serious punishment but lost his position and was sent back to Canton. Now Liu Dezhang was setting him up to take over the trade with the East India Company. They were joined by Li Zhongzhao, a famously daring Cantonese censor who had accused some of the wealthy salt merchants of Tianjin of embezzling a huge amount of tax money and won the case. However, he had lost his position after being caught obtaining secret documents from the Board of Revenue on behalf of one of the Canton merchants in the foreign trade (again using faked authorization slips). Li Zhongzhao had been the court patron of Liu Dezhang's nephew (who had also recently been dismissed from the Board of Revenue) and was taken on by the family as a high class tutor to their sons, so he too might have been involved in the allegations against Staunton. Whatever the exact machinations that led to the emperor's statement, people in Canton were convinced that Liu Dezhang was working with officials to reduce the total number of merchants registered to deal with the British so that he could pick up the business of those who failed and ultimately form a Chinese monopoly that could compete with the East India Company.[35]

Jiang Youxian responded cautiously. He sent Wu Bingjian to check the details of Staunton's career and submitted a statement of exactly which years Staunton had actually been in China. The outrage with which Staunton pointed out that he had never been any good at drawing comes through even in the version that reached the emperor. Jiang ended by assuring the emperor that he had no leads on Staunton making trouble, having secret communications, or profiting from fraud. To this Jiaqing responded, "Keep up the investigation and don't overlook it!"[36]

Meanwhile, another imperial edict had arrived, marked as secret and addressed only to Jiang Youxian and the customs inspector. This too focussed on the need to drive British warships off the coast and prevent large debts or other personal connections to foreigners. At the end Jiaqing rebuked Jiang for not having reported on Staunton earlier. He goes on, "I find that since childhood Staunton has been crafty, and has a deep understanding of Chinese affairs. If he is not very safe and proper in his conduct in Macao, then you should certainly not order him to return to his country, but you should handle the matter by getting a grip on his crimes, take advice, and exile him to another place where he can be suitably guarded and controlled."[37] This edict too came into Staunton's hands. To be sent into exile in China, perhaps even in Xinjiang, was a much more serious threat than being sent back to England. When the directors of the company in London were informed, they noted that the intention was "to detain him, remove him to the interior etc."[38] Everyone assured Staunton that officials would not dare carry out their threat, but that autumn the Qing authorities had actually executed Gabriel Dufresse, a Frenchman caught spreading Christianity in Sichuan province.[39]

Staunton avoided speaking of these edicts if he possibly could, but he was both upset and furious.[40] When the subject was brought up by English critics of the company, he dismissed it as court infighting: "No person who has the most distant idea of the spirit of intriguing among the Chinese, the system of *espionage* that is kept up, and hanging over all the officers of the government, and the allegations and retractions that are continually passing amongst them, would ever think of building any opinion or argument whatever upon such a basis."[41] This is a sophisticated response, reflecting the depth of his knowledge of the Qing state. Five years earlier it was that knowledge that had enabled him to publish his translation of the Qing legal code in which he defended the Chinese government and its legal system. Since then he had lived day by day through first Wu Yacheng and then Li Yao's prosecution. By now Li Yao's money was gone. He had reached a low point at the end of the year, writing in one particularly desperate note, "Those dog officials just say anything. They're none of them human."[42] When he thought of the long journey into exile during which he would have to enter 150 local government lockups he contemplated suicide.[43] Staunton could hardly fail to be affected.

Staunton had battled above all against the idea that Li Yao's relation with him as an Englishman was inherently immoral and illegal. Living and working where the two cultures met, he wanted Qing officials to acknowledge him, and the English in general, as good people. But the British had already attempted to occupy Macao, and there were British warships off the Chinese coast, which Li Yao had eventually concluded lay at the root of his own problems.[44] And Staunton was in fact making large loans to the hong merchants, though with the emperor's edict threatening him he now felt unable to collect the money owed.[45] Moreover, whatever his personal opinions on the subject, as a senior merchant of the English Factory he was complicit in the smuggling of large quantities of a dangerous drug into China. Staunton understood all this, but that did not make his own personal experience caught between the two states any easier. His faith in the Qing state was shattered. He now considered it "totally corrupt and unprincipled in all its ramifications."[46]

Li Yao finally set off on his journey into exile the following summer. He was a resilient character, and by the time he left he was quite cheerful again: the East India Company paid generously for his travel expenses so he did not have to wear shackles but could travel "just like a normal person" and did not have to enter any prisons on the way.[47] However, Staunton now knew that he too must leave. He began to send hints to his mother that he would be coming home for good soon and also to discourage the plans for a British embassy that he knew Barrow was promoting.[48] However, that embassy, led by Lord Amherst, was in fact already about to depart for China. The opportunity for diplomatic engagement that Staunton had been working toward all his life had finally come, but only when he no longer wanted it.

CHAPTER SIXTEEN

The Amherst Embassy

IN THE EMBASSY that followed issues that had been emerging over the past few years came together. On the British side there was a negative set of attitudes toward China that had grown out of the experience of rule in India. On the Chinese side there was a new emphasis on orthodox Confucian rituals. Jiaqing was also very much aware of the narrow constraints within which he could act because of the state's financial difficulties and as a result increasingly determined to control the individuals who mediated with the British. What became obvious during the embassy was just how dangerous mediation, and indeed any knowledge of the West, had become. The scrupulously precise translations of Robert Morrison contributed to the problems by exaggerating the differences between the two sides.

Barrow had been promoting the idea of a new British embassy to China for years with the hope that Staunton would be the ambassador. With the end of the wars with France, Barrow had written to the Earl of Buckinghamshire, president of the Board of Control of the East India Company, proposing an embassy to develop British exports.[1] William Elphinstone, then chairman of the directors, backed the plan and added as goals solutions to the previous year's problems through written confirmation of the company's privileges and a British diplomat resident in Beijing. The directors expressed the hope that the mission would consist of a good-looking military member of the aristocracy plus John Elphinstone (the son of the chairman) and Staunton. They then wrote to Canton to inform them of the plans.[2]

William Pitt Lord Amherst of Montreal, a pleasant but indecisive man whose uncle had won his title when he conquered Canada, was appointed ambassador. However, Buckinghamshire decided to appoint as the second member of the embassy Henry Ellis, his own illegitimate son. Staunton could be the interpreter.[3] But after many years of complaining about his poor health, failing to make money, and never quite leaving, Elphinstone suddenly departed for England just days before the company's letter announcing the embassy arrived. Presumably he had heard of the plans in a private letter, realised the dangers he might face, and fled.[4] So only Staunton went out to sea to meet the embassy. This was the opportunity he had been working toward all his life, and he was expecting to follow in his father's footsteps as a diplomat. He took with him his Cantonese cook, $468 worth of best Brazil snuff for gifts, a Cambridge academic gown specially made in Macao (to cover his knees during the rituals), and the small embroidered purse that the Qianlong emperor had given him.[5]

When the embassy arrived Staunton found to his fury that he had been appointed not as a diplomat but merely as the interpreter and worse still that this had been done partly on the grounds that he was a merchant and the Chinese court looked down on merchants. Ellis later explained that although in both China and Europe trade was a source of revenue it was "never reputed honourable."[6] Staunton insisted that he was *not* a merchant but, in a wildly exaggerated version of his role, "a public functionary who represents the British nation and possesses supreme control over all British subjects and British commerce within the Chinese territories."[7] He also pointed out that he had brought Morrison and several other British members of the Canton staff to do the interpreting. Amherst, characteristically, gave in and declared both Staunton and Ellis to be his commissioners.[8]

Ellis was part of a new generation whose attitudes toward China were shaped by experiences in British-dominated India. His father had been able to get him appointed to the China embassy on the grounds of his "acquaintance with the customs and languages of the East," which meant that he had spent time in India and been

FIGURE 16.1. This portrait of Lord Amherst by Thomas
Lawrence was commissioned for the Canton Factory of the
East India Company, which can be seen in the background.
In 1835 when the Factory was closed, the portrait was
presented to George Thomas Staunton.

on a mission to Persia.[9] Attitudes to other peoples can shape power
relations, but it is power that makes such attitudes possible. Alongside the fashion for China when Li Zibiao arrived in Naples, the
eighteenth century had seen British men operating as courtiers in
Indian settings and even contracting dynastic marriages with elite
Indian families, but as British power had expanded, boundaries
had hardened. In the twenty years since the Macartney embassy

the expansion of the East India Company's rule in India had transformed British attitudes toward Asia.

The implications of these changing attitudes were obvious from the moment the embassy arrived off the north China coast and was received by officials of the same rank as had been sent out to the previous embassy. Macartney had invited Wang Wenxiong and Qiao Renjie to dinner, where they all drank together, and later William Alexander had made his sympathetic portraits. Ellis's reaction to their successors was that their dress was unimpressive and their attendants smelled bad. Clarke Abel, the embassy's surgeon and scientist, found the smell so repulsive that it was some time before he could bring himself to go up and examine their dress. After landing Abel saw wretched naked men heave their barges upstream, the poverty of the farmers, the mud dwellings, and the lack of clothing. When he came across a group of well-dressed women he focussed on the shape of their eyes and eyelids. Staunton might be angry with the Qing government, but these comments irritated him: as they approached Tianjin he pointed out gardens, vines, fine large willow trees, crowds of well-dressed people, and splendid displays of troops.[10]

There had, of course, been changes in China: the fashion at court under the Jiaqing emperor was for a subdued frugality very different from the glamorous clothes and bright colours of the Qianlong period.[11] However, it is hardly likely that people smelled different or that trackers pulling barges wore fewer clothes. What had changed were British attitudes to race and class: Macartney and his retinue had been delighted to meet people whom they recognised as gentlemen and had paid little attention to impoverished bargemen. Now the English saw Eastern poverty and nakedness, and their scientist focussed on racial markers. Staunton came to the depressing conclusion that they were so prejudiced that not even seeing things with their own eyes could shake them.[12]

On the Chinese side the most obvious change was the emphasis on the kowtow, which was "the principal feature in every conference."[13] The poet who complimented Qianlong on Macartney's kowtow had described the English envoy as falling to his knees overawed by the very sight of the emperor. That was not what was asked of Amherst. Instead officials repeatedly told him that the emperor was the son of Heaven and other rulers owed him homage. The Macartney embassy had in fact never had to deal with the full regulations for a tribute mission because the imperial audience was held in Chengde and the embassy was handled almost entirely by members of Qianlong's inner court. After Qianlong's death Jiaqing had built his power in part by overthrowing these men with the help of Chinese officials who had come up through the examination system. When the Amherst embassy arrived Confucian literati were in the ascendant at court and the details of ritual had become far more important. What was expected of Amherst was not astonished awe at the sight of the emperor but a formally rehearsed ritual.

All this began almost as soon as the embassy arrived, when Jiaqing ordered his officials to offer the English an imperial banquet, tell the interpreter to explain to the ambassador that he must kowtow in thanks, and report back on whether or not he was willing to perform what he himself called "Chinese" ceremonies.[14] Macartney had not been asked to do this. The revitalisation of a conservative, morally inflected form of Confucianism had recently been intensified by the response to a religiously motivated rebellion in 1813, which led to an attempt to assassinate the emperor. However, Jiaqing was also drawing on a tactic that had worked well in 1805 when Russia, another powerful and threatening state, had sent an embassy but had been successfully turned back at the border.[15] When Jiang Youxian later pointed out that it was not English custom to kneel, Jiaqing replied, "I foresaw this problem and that is why when the envoy reached Tianjin I twice sent someone to investigate the situation. If they really could not kowtow, I originally ordered that they need not come to the capital. I would accept their offerings, present them with gifts, and send them back. It all sounded fine."[16] Jiaqing himself seems to have been more concerned about the British threat than his claims to cosmic rule. When one of his officials commented that the English wished to come because they admired China's virtue and might, he dismissed it as just the kind of thing foreigners often say; what he was worried about was that the English would make demands and in particular they might ask to be allowed to trade in other ports as they had on the previous embassy.[17]

The interpreter remained a major figure, but where Li Zib-iao and even Barrow had been manipulated through friendship, Staunton faced threats. Formally of course Morrison was the inter-preter, but Staunton knew that if he began to speak Chinese he would end up interpreting. He might claim that Morrison was a better scholar of the Chinese language, and in some ways that was true, but Morrison had learned the language painstakingly as an adult and had mostly spoken Cantonese.[18]

Qing officials focussed on Staunton from the start: Suleng'e, the president of the Board of Works who was put in charge of the embassy, was told to look out for him. Suleng'e had been the superintendent of customs in Canton at the time of the Macart-ney embassy and should, Jiaqing thought, be able to recognise Staunton. But the middle-aged man with a long nose and reced-ing hairline hovering in the background failed to catch his atten-tion. Eventually he had to ask about the British boy called Thomas Staunton who had come on the previous embassy and could speak Chinese. Morrison hesitated in his interpreting, and Staunton, who had been waiting with increasing anxiety for this moment, stepped forward. He explained that he had changed his name when he inherited his title and that his spoken Chinese was not so good these days because he had been away in England. Staunton was the kind of person who planned what he was going to say: the edict against him stated that he had been in Macao since the previ-ous embassy, so he emphasized that he had been back to England. Guanghui, the conductor to the embassy, said politely that he had heard a lot about Staunton from Songyun. He then complimented Staunton on how well he could draw. Staunton replied that he was no good at drawing at all, which Guanghui insisted on treating as mere modesty. This conversation of veiled threats and hinted rebut-tals was conducted in Chinese and completely passed Ellis by: he was told simply that Suleng'e had remembered meeting Staunton as a child.[19]

Staunton's difficulties were exacerbated by the difference between what had actually happened on that day he never spoke of, the day when Macartney was received by the Qianlong emperor, and the impression his father and Macartney had given on their return to England. When, during the interminable discussions about the kowtow, Amherst intervened to point to the previous embassy as a precedent, Suleng'e responded that Macartney *had* kowtowed; he had seen it and so had the present emperor. He turned to Staunton to confirm the statement. To Amherst's astonishment Staunton did not deny it. Instead, he said that he was a child of twelve at the time so he could hardly be expected to remember clearly, whereas Amherst's information came from the written records. When Jiaqing read this legalistic phrasing it confirmed his impression of Staunton. He wrote in red on the side, "Detestable equivocation!"[20]

In the end the imperial banquet did take place and the British did not kowtow. Staunton explained to Amherst that although Macartney had not prostrated himself he had in fact bowed nine times, and Amherst agreed to do the same. Suleng'e, feeling that progress had been made, then allowed the banquet to take place. Amherst was delighted to have achieved something that the Russians had not, while Staunton enjoyed the wonderful food and the positive atmosphere. The rest of the English struggled with sitting cross-legged and eating with chopsticks, and most of them did not like Chinese food.[21]

It was, however, only a brief respite for Staunton as pressure on the kowtow continued and the threats against him intensified. Jiaqing even wrote a speech for Suleng'e and Guanghui to deliver to him. This begins, "You came with the envoy in the 58th year of the Qianlong emperor. When you came to our court you saw all the ceremonies of the imperial audience, banquets and gifts with your own eyes."[22] It ends threateningly, "You have lived in Guangdong for many years and you are familiar with China's legal system. Perhaps the emperor will not accept the gifts and will send you back to your country or will suddenly become angry and arrest you as punishment. His mind is unpredictable. Then you would regret what you have done wouldn't you?"[23]

When none of this worked, Jiaqing sent his brother-in-law Heshitai to ensure that Amherst either rehearse the kowtow or depart. Heshitai was an impressive figure who had distinguished himself during the fighting in the palace in 1813. He launched into a prepared speech that included the words, "Heaven does not have two suns and the earth does not have two emperors. The great emperor is the son of heaven; before him all kings should bow down. You," here he looked directly at Morrison who was interpreting, "know it."[24] This rhetoric had ancient roots, but no one had ever faced Macartney with it. When it failed to persuade Amherst, Heshitai sent Zhang Wuwei, Qiao Renjie's successor, to continue the task using almost the opposite approach. Zhang referred to the kowtow for the imperial audience as a Manchu ritual of no concern to Chinese like himself. Such an argument was possible because much Chinese scholarship during this period focussed on the original meanings of the classical texts rather than grand cosmological theory, which seemed old-fashioned and was increasingly associated with the Manchu dynasty. Zhang said he understood that the English objected because they believed the kowtow was a sign of political dependence, but this was wrong: it was just a matter of court etiquette.[25]

Zhang Wuwei also renewed the threats against Staunton, this time speaking to Morrison and Amherst and producing documents to prove his point, including a letter from Guangdong saying that Staunton was a merchant and therefore not a proper member of an embassy and was said to have great wealth and a fine aviary. Staunton repeated to everyone that East India Company staff in Guangzhou were public officers and that it was the Cantonese-speaking private merchant Thomas Beale who had an aviary.[26] Nevertheless he was beginning to feel really afraid. He thought about Li Zibiao and how he had been threatened during the Macartney embassy and that the interpreter "is commonly the first object of their attack."[27] Staunton had made Morrison the interpreter, but he knew that in the eyes of the Qing officials that made little difference: he was the one who was at the centre of the negotiations. So he went to see Amherst and finally explained that he was facing the prospect of arrest.[28]

It was only at this point that Staunton finally explained to Amherst that Macartney had not merely bowed nine times but had gone down on one knee to do so. Amherst could see no real difference between this and the kowtow. Moreover, because the kowtow had been important for the Macartney embassy, it had been debated in England before they left, and the general feeling had been to emphasize practical goals over ceremonial forms. The Earl of Buckinghamshire had told Amherst that he was at liberty to perform the ceremony of prostration if he deemed it expedient. Now Ellis supported his father's position and said that claims of universal sovereignty were too ridiculous to bother about. They decided they would kowtow if they believed that it would bring other benefits.[29]

However, having won the argument, the intimidating Heshitai proved a very poor negotiator. Amherst said he would send a final written decision by the end of the day, and the English debates continued, with Amherst and Ellis arguing for the kowtow and Staunton arguing against. Staunton cared more about the outcome and could emphasize his expertise, so that at the end of the day Amherst's note said that they would not after all kowtow but that they were willing to kneel on one knee and lower their heads. Heshitai, however, had taken their earlier note as decisive and had already arranged for the earliest possible imperial audience.[30]

The stage was now set for the final fiasco. Staunton, thinking his solution had been accepted, was delighted and even took over the interpreting as they set off for Beijing.[31] They travelled through the night, and Amherst, Ellis, Staunton, and a few others became separated from the rest of the party. Just before dawn they found themselves driving along the side of a park. The road opened up in front of what Staunton called "a very large building in the best Chinese taste" with crowds of officials.[32] They were ushered into a pavilion to rest. Amherst lay down while members of Jiaqing's court crowded in to see them and peered through the open windows. Zhang Wuwei appeared and told them that the imperial audience was about to begin. At this point Amherst himself made a decision. He might be willing to kowtow, but he was certainly not going to make a fool of himself at a foreign court, exhausted, without attendants, and in the clothes he had travelled in overnight. He announced that he was too tired. Heshitai reappeared and tried to pull him up. Amherst resisted and after a near brawl and some more delay the English were told could go to Songyun's house where they were to stay. Heshitai vented his fury by seizing a whip from one of his attendants and striking out on either side as he saw them to their carriage.[33]

Even at this moment of humiliation for the British, when they felt they were being treated like wild beasts in a menagerie,

Staunton still wanted to defend the Chinese: he said afterward that the problem was that these people at court were Manchus: "I doubt whether any assembly of the superior class, or indeed any class, of Chinese, would have shown themselves so totally regardless, not merely of the considerations of courtesy, but even of the common feelings of humanity."[34] It was nevertheless immediately clear that this was the end of the embassy's hopes for an imperial audience. The next day Jiaqing composed a letter to the English king explaining that his letter had not been delivered because of the discourtesy of the ambassador who had pretended to be ill. He demoted Sulenge and Guanghui, accepted some of the British gifts, and wrote to Jiang Youxian to warn him against Staunton.[35]

Four days later the embassy was on its way back to Guangdong, travelling overland like Macartney, since to the considerable annoyance of the Qing officials Amherst had sent their ships away. On the journey south they were accompanied for a while by Shengtai, the Zhili provincial judge, a stout middle-aged man who turned out to their surprise to be an enthusiast for knowledge of the West. He had read extensively in the Jesuits' Chinese publications and talked about Russia, France, and Italy. He infuriated Staunton by telling him that although the British might be superior by sea, the French were more powerful by land and also better at manufacturing. He was not a good listener, and Staunton had difficulty getting a word in at all.[36]

Shengtai also took Staunton aside to point out to him confidentially that having spent so long in Guangdong he ought to understand Chinese protocol. He went on to say that when writing to the emperor Staunton should have referred to himself as "your minister Staunton" (*chen ming Sidangdong*).[37] This is quite surprising since, although it does have broader meanings, *chen* was usually used in this period by officials for themselves when they were addressing the emperor. Like Jiaqing's plan to send Staunton into exile inside China, it hints at how those dealing with Staunton sometimes saw him as someone who ought to be drawn into the political structures of their own world rather than a foreigner who should be kept out. This was intended, and experienced by Staunton, as a threat.

Staunton did not tell the others much about this encounter, merely complaining that the man was quite intolerable. Unfortunately for

Shengtai the emperor had much the same response when he met him later in the year. Shengtai told Jiaqing that he had asked about the size of the British navy and discussed the wording of their correspondence. Jiaqing condemned him as a bold, arrogant busybody, who had interfered in matters beyond his position and sent him off to do forced labour beyond the Great Wall. There he spent the next twelve years mostly as a petty official until the Daoguang emperor recalled him and put him in charge of Tibet. Shengtai was a high-ranking Mongol bannerman with no foreign language skills, and Jiaqing was relatively open to expressions of opinion from his officials, but the British were beyond the line of what could safely be discussed. Shengtai's enthusiasm for knowledge about foreign countries had wrecked what looked like a promising career, and his fall became a well-known story at court.[38]

Amherst and his suite travelled on south. When they passed near Mount Lu in Jiangxi, Staunton, who had evidently brought a Chinese guidebook with him, noted that it was "celebrated in Chinese classic writings."[39] Morrison was moved by the ravine where the twelfth-century philosopher Zhu Xi had gone fishing. Ellis, however, thought that although it was a fine landscape, "in vain will the man of honour look for a friend, and still more in vain would amiable woman look for a companion on the banks of the Yang-tse-kiang; what is not mere manner is barbarism, and what is not barbarism is deceit."[40] Ellis's views were shared by most of the other members of the embassy, but Staunton continued to defend China: when they saw mud huts he admitted that they were worse than "our English cottages," but at least they had chimneys and windows, which was better than the cabins of the poor in Ireland.[41]

Meanwhile Jiaqing was writing to Jiang Youxian in Guangdong over how to prevent future British embassies, how to handle Staunton, and whether it would be financially viable to stop the British trade. He asked Jiang Youxian exactly what proportion of the total tax revenue from the trade was paid by the British. Jiang replied that the annual revenue was more than 1.2 million taels, of which the English were paying over 70 percent.[42] This was a huge sum, and Jiaqing accepted the inevitable.

Keeping control of those who mediated with the British was one of the few things Jiaqing actually could do. He also, rightly, held Staunton responsible for Amherst's changes of mind on the kowtow. He told Jiang to order him to return to England. Jiang agreed, but he was also worried about what Staunton might say or write once he was back in England. He drafted a letter criticising Staunton to be circulated to the captains of the English ships. Jiaqing decided against it: what Staunton might say in England was not a problem, and publishing his errors to foreign countries now would not really demonstrate the dynasty's greatness.[43]

Meanwhile HMS *Alceste*, which had brought the embassy, was making the English threat obvious. When Captain Murray Maxwell was not allowed to sail up the river to Canton, he simply blasted through the forts guarding the entrance. These had recently been reinforced so that they had 110 cannons and could keep up cross fire across the passage. Ships were sent out to block the entrance and a linguist to tell Maxwell to anchor. He replied that he would first pass the forts and then hang the linguist. When the wind got up, he sailed straight between the forts, which fired but failed to do serious damage. He then fired a broadside, leaving the linguist kneeling at his feet pleading for mercy and forty-seven men dead in the forts.[44]

When the embassy reached Guangdong, a letter Jiaqing had written to placate the Prince Regent was handed over to the English in Chinese, Manchu, and Latin copies. Amherst read the Latin and found it so conciliatory that he concluded that the Jesuit missionary translator in Beijing must have softened it. He told Morrison to translate it again from the Chinese.[45] For Morrison, whose entire experience of China was Canton with its complex institutional structures to control the English, it seemed obvious that the Qing state was simply hostile to foreigners. His version begins, "The supreme potentate who has received from Heaven and revolving Nature (the government of the World) issues an Imperial Mandate to the King of England."[46] He added two notes to this. The first explains that *huangdi*, which had hitherto always been translated simply as "emperor," is rendered as "supreme potentate" as more appropriate for the claims being made. The second note explains why he has added the words "the government of the world," which he says are "fully implied in the Chinese" because the emperor has presumed to write an "imperial Mandate" (*chiyu*) to the king of

England. Later in the text *gongshun* (literally respectful and sub-missive), which twenty years earlier Li Zibiao had transformed into the English king's "great good will," became his "respect and obedience."[47] Where Li's translations had turned Chinese texts into acceptable European diplomatic correspondence, Morrison's sought the root meanings of each Chinese word and thus empha-sized every difference. The words were accurate, but Jiaqing's intention to placate the Prince Regent was entirely lost.[48]

A rebuke Jiaqing had planned for Staunton was never delivered, but Staunton had known from the start that he could not continue to live in China. He set off for England, though not on the *Alceste*, since he did not trust the irascible Captain Maxwell: rightly as it turned out since the ship was wrecked before it reached Jakarta and the passengers survived only after a long journey on a tropical sea in open boats.[49] Jiang Youxian had not dared inform Jiaqing of the *Alceste*'s dramatic passage through the forts, but his letter reporting the embassy's departure ended,

> The foreigners are hard to predict. Perhaps in a year or two they will suddenly send warships to sail to Macao and the nearby islands as they did in 1802 and 1808. Their plans and demands are hard to anticipate. Even though that country is far across the sea we certainly cannot stop the trade for long and break off our own source of income, but we absolutely must prepare to defend our maritime border. We are now inspecting the forts at the mouth of the harbour and the situation of all of the islands.[50]

To this Jiaqing responded that tight defences were needed not only on ports but also on islands.[51]

PART IV

Exclusion

CHAPTER SEVENTEEN

Li Zibiao's Last Years in Hiding

WHILE LORD AMHERST'S EMBASSY was travelling south through China by boat, Li Zibiao was walking over the mountains toward western Shanxi. Although he had always been calm about the many dangers he faced, he had good reason to be anxious. Jiaqing had issued a stern order to provincial governors to follow up reports of Christian practice and sentence any who refused to recant to exile in Xinjiang. The governor of Shanxi province had pressed his subordinates to discover such cases to such an extent that for the first time even the remote southeast of the province was affected and Li was fleeing the crackdown.[1] The timing was probably not entirely coincidental: Jiaqing had come to see Christianity as linking the threat of sectarian rebellion with the Europeans on the southeast coast.

Back in 1805, when a church courier had been arrested and he suspected Western espionage, Jiaqing had decided to read some of the books that the missionaries had published himself. When he did so he was shocked not only by the Westerners' failure to abide by Confucian norms but also by their claims to cosmic rule: how could they say that their god was "the emperor of ten thousand lands" or that "Jesus is the emperor of every person in the whole world"?[2] He banned the remaining court missionaries from evangelising, publishing, or having any contacts with Chinese. Li Zibiao heard that two of the churches in Beijing had been destroyed and only three European missionaries were left in the city.[3]

Jiaqing's worries had intensified as a result of the arrest in 1811 of a Christian named Zhang Duode on a visit to his home village in Shaanxi province. Zhang was in fact a priest and one of Li's former pupils in Shanxi. The authorities did not find this out, but he did make an extensive confession with detailed descriptions of Christian practices and ideas. When, two years later, in the aftermath of the 1813 rebellion Jiaqing called for proposals to improve the government, people began to look closely at Zhang's reported confessions. One of Jiaqing's top specialists on sects pointed out that Christianity had its own "transforming emperor" (the pope), official posts, and ranks, all of which suggested an alternate state, and argued from this that foreigners were intending to stir up the Chinese against the government and must be controlled. The word he used for foreigners was not only *xiyangren* (literally Western Ocean people), which had long been used for the missionaries in Beijing and the Portuguese in Macao, but *yi*, which was closely associated with the British.[4] So when a Cantonese student was arrested in Beijing 1814 with opium in his possession, Jiaqing instantly drew a link with Christianity and added in vermilion ink to the draft edict on his case that Christianity was a religion that destroyed proper morals and was "far more harmful than the White Lotus teachings."[5] The student in question was not accused of being Christian, but for the emperor opium and Christianity were evils springing from the same sources in Guangdong province, which was why he had also suggested that Staunton's friend Li Yao might be Christian.

Then, in the spring of 1816 as Lord Amherst's embassy approached, the emperor strongly endorsed an anti-Christian pamphlet that not only made the link between Christianity and opium but also pointed to potential political threats from the Europeans. The author, Zhu Shiyan, a prominent scholar official, began by criticizing Christianity on the conventional grounds of Christians' failure to perform proper funerals. However, he also linked the problem with the European threat on the south coast. He argued that the reason behind the Christian emphasis on heaven is that the Western Ocean people want their converts to be willing to accept martyrdom for them, and this can be seen from the history of Gaerba (probably

Java) and Luzon (in the Philippines), where the Westerners enticed the people to follow Christianity and then seized the territory. As an alternative he cites the case of Japan where the Japanese realised what was going on with the missionaries and refused to pardon anyone who was unwilling to trample on the cross. This was not new information, indeed the events dated back to the seventeenth century, and Zhu had almost certainly found his material in Ming dynasty books, but the link with the Europeans in Guangdong was radical in its political implications.[6]

Li Zibiao lived on the fringes of this intellectual world. He wrote to Rome that because the 1813 rebellion had been started by members of a false religion, officials were trying to root out the problem of anything that looked like a sect, in other words any organisation whose members gathered together to say prayers.[7] Indeed he had come to believe that the Chinese nation's love of its ancient customs, "which will accept no religion, however suitable, as legitimate," was at the root of Christianity's failure to advance.[8] He noted, however, that the imperial family was "completely enslaved" to another religion, Tibetan Buddhism, and that the state tolerated what he called the superstition of the ignorant common people.[9]

Li himself held firmly to the Christian teachings that were at the core of his personal identity. He wrote to the Chinese students in Naples telling them not to be afraid if they heard that there was a new law ordering that Christians should be sent into exile and missionaries executed since it was not actually implemented all the time or in every place. Such a law should in fact encourage them "for whom to live is Christ, and to die is gain."[10] The year before the Amherst embassy he was still writing to Rome that due to God's mercy and protection there was not yet a savage persecution where he was but people's fears prevented them from receiving him into their homes.[11]

Nevertheless Li's life had been transformed. Missionaries were now treated as rebel leaders, and any mention of their names would lead to a reward being offered for their arrest. Two of his colleagues from the Naples College had been condemned to have a heavy wooden board clamped round their necks for the rest of their lives and exiled to Xinjiang. He himself was no longer able to live in comfort with the relatively well-off Christian families in Machang

FIGURE 17.1. The site of Zhaojialing village. The villagers lived in caves, some of which, now abandoned, can be seen, cut into the soft rock.

or to travel from one family to another. Christian rituals had to be performed secretly and at night. As had occurred throughout his life in times of great stress or unhappiness, he was again suffering from frequent periods of ill health. He was spending increasing amounts of time in Zhaojialing, a little village of about fifty families of poor farmers and petty traders up in the hills.[12]

The Zhaojialing villagers were all Catholics, and because the village was isolated and yet not too far from the road north to the centre of the province priests had occasionally stayed there in the past.[13] Li used money sent in memory of Cardinal Stefano Borgia, presumably by his friend Giovanni Borgia, to establish a room there where two young women and an older widow could live a Catholic religious life. It seems likely that at least one of these women came from one of the wealthier Catholic communities on the plain, and they were living in Zhaojialing because this kind of establishment might have caused trouble if it had come to the attention of local government. The villagers later preserved the story of a priest who persuaded a widow to donate three hundred strings of cash to build

FIGURE 17.2. The church that Li Zibiao built in Zhaojialing as it is today.
The two small archways toward the back lead to a tiny inner room.

a church. Later nineteenth-century European missionaries saw this
little chapel built with money from the whole district and donations
from Rome as the only real church in the area, since all the others
were chapels within people's homes, so they valued it highly and
paid for it to be rebuilt when it was damaged by an earthquake.[14]

Thus it survives today: a little brick-faced cave looking out over a quiet valley with birds singing and sheep braying in the distance. However, at the time the reason Li with all his abilities and European learning was living among poor farmers in a cave in the hills was that it was too dangerous for him to live anywhere else. Even here the villagers were almost certainly too frightened to allow him to live with them and instead helped him to build a cave of his own where he could read and pray.

When Li fled over the hills to the west of the province in 1816, it was because even in Zhaojialing the risk to himself and the villagers was simply too great. The crackdown had reached Dunliu county not far away, the place whose conversions had so delighted him when he first arrived in Shanxi fifteen years earlier. The Dunliu Christians were now arrested, beaten, and pressed to recant. Six refused and were sent into exile in Xinjiang, while twelve others who were willing to tread on a cross received lesser punishments. What is striking about this case as it is recorded in the Qing archives is that despite the months he had spent working with them in the past none of these men gave the least hint of Li's existence. When asked how they had come to believe in the religion, some said that they had learned it from their parents, others that they had heard about it from other villagers who had already died. Their answers were varied, plausible, and quite impossible to follow up so that the governor was unable to pursue the case any further.[15]

Li's skill in dealing with people, which had kept him safe when he was interpreting for the British at the court of the Qianlong emperor, was also what helped him to survive now. Over the years many European missionaries and many of his Naples classmates were betrayed and captured, often because disagreements within the Christian communities led to officials becoming aware of their existence. Li's survival depended on managing relationships among those he worked with, so that people were willing to take risks for him. A later Dutch missionary who saw a letter full of descriptions of local affairs that Li had written noted his astute comments on the character and behaviour of those he had to deal with including many who were not Christian.[16] Li's own opinion was that "if in each Christian community there is one Christian who knows how to manage things with the gentiles there will not be any danger."[17]

The respect for Li was shared by the European missionaries with whom he worked: Salvetti even recommended to become a bishop. A Chinese had been consecrated as a bishop in the seventeenth century, but no other Chinese bishop was created until the twentieth century. However, Jiaqing was not the only person thinking that Christianity might be wiped out in China as it had been in Japan. In Rome too people thought that they were looking at the total destruction of the China mission. The missionaries who had worked at the court in Beijing for more than a century were nearly gone, it was all but impossible to smuggle Europeans into the country, and the French missionary Dufresse had been executed rather than expelled. The church bureaucracy began to consider appointing Chinese as bishops and canvassed the opinion of the three surviving European bishops in China. The only Chinese actually suggested was Li Zibiao, though the bishop in Fujian supported the idea in general terms. Salvetti, however, wrote to say that Li Zibiao was "shrewd, and capable of anything, because of his intelligence, learning, zeal, and attachment to the Holy See."[18] When the committee considering the matter looked back through the files for other comments on him they found that Salvetti had earlier described him as "far the most shrewd and capable in everything because of his intelligence and learning" and that his only negative comment was that because of his "somewhat unreliable health his ministry does not always correspond to the readiness of his spirit."[19]

These proposals were never put into action, so Li Zibiao did not become a bishop, which would in any case almost certainly have led to his discovery and exile or death. Instead the member of the Li family who won glory that year was Li Zichang's son Li Jiong. Li Jiong was well known in Liangzhou for his rejection of Catholicism in favour of Confucian learning. That rejection had now become something leading officials were keen to celebrate. After a lifetime of study, he finally passed the highest level of the examinations in Beijing in 1817. When he died on the journey back from the capital, his life was written up for a set of studies of their hometown's eminent men.[20]

The crackdown on Christianity ended with the death of Jiaqing in 1820. Li Zibiao explained to Rome that the Daoguang emperor, who came to the throne, took no interest in the subject. Christians were still occasionally sent into exile but without much enthusiasm on the part of officials since the emperor was no longer involved. Instead Li saw grander spiritual powers at work, "for the enemy of the human race exerts all his infernal efforts and all his strength. This happens everywhere, but much more in these lands of infidels in order to blind their eyes lest the light of the Gospel having risen they should come to an understanding of the truth."[21] Li went back to living in Machang, where he was pleased to note that the number of Catholics had not shrunk and that although some people had recanted in the courts, this was merely a matter of weakness and timidity, and genuine intellectual apostasy was either nonexistent or extremely rare. He was sixty now and wrote to Rome that he was in good health, but that his hair was going white and he was aware of the approach of death.[22]

In Machang he picked up the threads of his correspondence. The Naples College was keen to find new Chinese students, and Li was almost their only surviving correspondent. He was cautious as one of the students he had sent to Naples at the end of the Macartney embassy had been a disaster and his behaviour was making him a serious danger to the mission. In the end Li sent two boys he knew really well. One of them was Wang Duolu, the fifteen-year-old son of the family with whom he usually lived when he was in Machang. When they arrived in Naples the head of the college wrote to describe the crowds as the two young men were taken to see the king and the huge festivities over their formal admission to the college, which "you who know what this place is like can have no difficulty imagining."[23] Thereafter Li's letters to the Chinese students in Naples are full of news for these young men, including a rather sad account of how a tablet honouring Confucius had been put up again in the little chapel in Zhaojialing to convert it into a local Confucian shrine in case anyone sent by the provincial governor should see it.[24]

He was most touched to receive a letter and gift from Giovanni Borgia. During the period of intense persecution, Li had corresponded only with Rome and the Chinese students in Naples, which he saw as his duty, but this had been hard. On one occasion he hinted to the students to tell him something of Borgia "whom I love greatly."[25] At the height of the persecutions when the danger was intense and he quoted Jesus's saying "Who loves his life let him lose it," he sent special greetings through the students to Borgia and Ignazio Orlando, another member of his own generation who had become the head of the college, telling them that "I would write to them many times each year if I were living outside this empire."[26] He asked the Chinese students to buy a Chinese gift for Borgia if they were passing through Canton and charge his own account with the procurator in Macao. Then, after many years, Yan Kuanren's nephew, who had completed his studies and was returning to China, brought a set of religious prints from Borgia and a letter also arrived.[27]

Li's reply, the only one of his letters written using the informal form of "you," bears witness to the strength of the friendships that still, more than thirty years after his return to China, bound him to Europe:

> Most beloved sir, I thought, perhaps rightly perhaps wrongly, that one or another of my letters written to our superiors or colleagues would be enough to preserve and suggest that joining of our souls which began in our earliest years, so I have not written to you separately without an urgent cause for many years. I have also failed to do this for many others who have deserved well of me. Your noble intelligence will have realised that the cause is the great difficulty of the route and the fear of danger, since the carrying of letters is often regarded as unacceptable in this region. And as for the rest, the desires of both of us to know of each other's good health and mutual affection were never denied.[28]

He goes on to thank Borgia for the prints, "But what delights me more is that not only in spirit but also in old age your bond with me is no less strong than it was in youth, so that you confirm what you once said to me, that what is not endured in youth will be endured in old age, and weak young men become stronger in old age, and the truth of these words is born out in us."[29] The rest of his letter tells of the struggles of his daily life in old age and his need for Borgia's prayers that "I may not fail in my mission until life itself fails me."[30]

Two years later, in 1828, Li Zibiao died and was buried in Machang village.[31] His exceptional ability in handling people meant that he was never arrested or exiled, but his great linguistic and intellectual abilities had led him to a life in hiding in a remote and isolated corner of the Chinese empire. He himself always understood his life as part of a great global exercise, writing in his last letter to Rome that he always thanked God that he had been able to fulfil his sacred ministry for more than thirty years, but he had done so with "really miniscule rewards," not because God in his infinite mercy did not increase the Christians' piety or convert some of the gentiles, but because his own sins and idleness impeded the task, so that "the spiritual fruits, for which you and the whole Sacred Congregation long, have not been harvested from this vineyard of the Lord that has been entrusted to me." [32]

After his death Salvetti wrote to Rome praising Li as "the person who had the firmest base in ability and in theory, more than anyone else. Spending just a little time with him every year for the most part was a great comfort to me because I could discuss things easily with him, both the ordinary course of events and anything unusual that had happened." [33] In the years to come young Chinese seminarians making especially good progress in their studies would be praised for following in his footsteps, because there had been no theologian in the province since Li's death. [34]

CHAPTER EIGHTEEN

Staunton in Parliament

STAUNTON HAD RETURNED to England in 1817 at the age of thirty-six as an exceedingly wealthy baronet. He knew more about China than anyone else in Britain and expected that his knowledge, wealth, and status would launch him into a career in diplomacy or government.[1] Such a career would have enabled him to influence British policy on China. That was not what happened. Instead he was excluded and mocked in ways that played on his links with China and exacerbated the social anxieties he had always felt as a result of his background and unusual education.

It was easy enough for Staunton to get a seat in Parliament. In the 1818 election he became the member for Mitchell, a Cornish village with eighteen voters. The going rate for such a seat was four or five thousand pounds, a sum Staunton could well afford. Indeed he probably paid a good price since Viscount Falmouth, the hard-line Tory who controlled the seat, agreed that Staunton should sit as an independent.[2] Like the Chinese merchants who made fortunes in the Canton trade and bought honorary degrees and government offices, Staunton was able to use his wealth to buy a position within the state.

However, also as in China, trade was despised by the aristocracy and land was the safest and most respectable form of investment. Staunton bought a country estate. Laying aside romantic ideas of buying an estate connected with medieval Stauntons or Byron's former home at Newstead Abbey, he purchased Leigh Park, a relatively modest house on the hills looking out over Portsmouth toward the

FIGURE 18.1. Leigh Park by Joseph Francis Gilbert. This is one of a series of paintings that Staunton commissioned for his London house. A coach is arriving with guests who can see two gardeners and the dog on the lawn: this is Staunton's ideal. The smoke rising from the chimney suggests warmth indoors as well as the heated conservatory for his hothouse plants. He added the gothic library in 1832.

sea. It had a modern stove in its elegant circular entrance hall to keep it warm, several wine cellars, and a large conservatory. It was also cheap since a previous sale had fallen through because of fears of dry rot.[3]

The final stage in setting up his life would have been to marry. One of the books he bought around this time was Jane Austen's *Mansfield Park*, where the plot revolves around the attractions of marrying a baronet with a good fortune. Austen, who had recently died, belonged to Staunton's world: her family home was a few miles north of Leigh Park, her nephew was the vicar of a nearby parish, and her brother had been Morrison's friend in China.[4] People had indeed been trying to arrange Staunton's marriage for years. There had been all those parties he so much enjoyed in Galway. Then on his last visit back to England, Jane Macartney had tried to set him up with Barrow's daughter who was still in her early teens but would be of marriageable age when he completed his time in China. Johanna was still talking about the pleasant days they had spent together when she was in her fifties. Staunton, however, started avoiding staying with the Barrows. He read romances and had always loved dancing, and he took part enthusiastically in the balls of his first London season, but he never married.[5]

At first he greatly enjoyed being a member of Parliament, agreeing with those who said "the House of Commons to be (though rather an expensive one) the best club in London!"[6] Proceedings began in the late afternoon, and Staunton would go along, take his seat on the back benches, and listen to the leading politicians as they opened the day's debate, returning later after dinner to listen to the closing stages of the debate. He enjoyed the "intellectual feast," listened carefully to the debates, and took the voting that ended the evening's proceedings extremely seriously.[7] But in eight years as MP for Mitchell he simply could not bring himself to face the ordeal of making a speech. Nor did he join a party or even a political campaign. He listened, dined, and voted, but "had literally *nothing to do.*"[8]

The House of Commons was dominated at this time by sons of aristocratic families. Benjamin Brodie described these kinds of people as men brought up to idleness from their boyhood who fill their lives as adults with politics, travelling, field sports, horse racing, or gambling.[9] Staunton and his cousins all felt uncomfortable in that world, but they were more successful in it than he was: Benjamin Brodie became doctor to the king, Peter Brodie a leading member of a commission on property law, and Thomas Denman Lord Chief Justice. Staunton never achieved the government office he longed for, but his problem was not simply one of social class: his background in China turned out to be a problem in itself.[10]

When Robert Morrison returned from China, both of them realised just how much they had in common. Morrison was famous by now but felt strangely out of place when he returned to Newcastle and Staunton was the person he knew would understand. Morrison's wife claimed that the only leisure he took in his two years in England was a visit to Leigh Park. He had already visited Staunton's house in Marylebone, a plain, quiet place where the decorations consisted of a few rather expensive old masters that Staunton had bought recently, portraits of members of his family (fig. 2.1), and paintings of his properties. At first sight Leigh Park seemed much the same, with a stained glass window in the hall-way showing Staunton's coat of arms and a view of his Irish estates alongside an oil painting of dead game. This was Staunton the English landed gentleman, as he tried to appear to his neighbours and constituents. In fact he did not shoot, and his sole contact with the local fox hunt was to complain vociferously when the hounds trampled his garden.[11]

It was not until they entered the billiard room, a space where Staunton could retire with close friends, that any reference to China appeared. There the walls were covered with Chinese paintings. In pride of place over the fireplace hung the portrait of Pan Youdu (fig. 12.2), flanked by two paintings of the trial of the *Neptune* sailors (fig. 13.2). Staunton could also point out Alexander's sketch of him kneeling before the Qianlong emperor and the cushion in the window seat covered with satin presented to him during that embassy.[12]

He had invited Manning, who had been with them in China, to meet Morrison, and the three of them stayed up late into the evening talking. The next morning they walked round the gardens. Not far from the house they came to a classical temple (fig. 18.2) that Staunton had built after his mother's death in 1823. Inside were memorials to his parents, but what touched Morrison was a tablet commemorating other friends and relatives. The list, which was simply arranged by the date of death, included several people they had both known in China: two of the older East India Company merchants, two of the Catholic missionaries from Macao, George Millet the ship's captain who had been Staunton's first investor, and Pan Youdu.[13]

Afterward Staunton bought a spectacularly expensive silver gilt inkstand and matching candlestick and had it engraved with the words "To the Rev.d Robert Morrison D.D. from his affectionate friend, George Thomas Staunton."[14] He sent it to Morrison just as he was leaving for China. Staunton and Morrison had worked together and respected each other for years, but the barriers of class were powerful, and both had regarded Staunton as Morrison's patron. For Staunton to give Morrison all his titles and to describe himself just as an affectionate friend was something quite different, and Morrison was overwhelmed, writing in his letter of thanks,

FIGURE 18.2. Temple Lawn by Joseph Francis Gilbert, 1832. The temple looked out to sea and contained memorials to Staunton's parents and friends, including Pan Youdu. Gardeners are busy cutting and sweeping the lawn.

"You have for twenty years condescended, I may say, (considering my humble circumstances) to favour me with your friendship. . . . Accept of my best thanks for this parting expression of your 'affectionate' friendship. May the divine blessing of God our Saviour rest upon you!"[15]

Many years later, when Staunton wrote his memoirs, he claimed that he had stopped his Chinese studies when he returned to England because he did not have time and could not translate without the assistance of Chinese scholars. This was only partially true, and it certainly was not what he intended when he first returned. He brought back a library of more than three thousand Chinese volumes (*juan*) that occupied a whole room of his London house.[16] In 1821 he issued *Narrative of the Chinese Embassy to the Khan of the Tourgouth Tartars by the Chinese Ambassador*, an annotated translation of Tulisen's *Record of Foreign Regions* (*Yi yu lü*), which told of a journey undertaken at the command of the Kangxi emperor to make contact with the Torghut Mongols living in the Volga region of Russia. The text had been partly translated into French and published a hundred years earlier as a source of geographical data along with the astronomical observations of the Jesuit missionaries who first brought Christianity to Li Zibiao's home town of Liangzhou. Staunton chose it for another reason: as his title suggests, he saw Tulisen's journey as an embassy. He understood that this was due to the circumstances of Kangxi's reign, but he argued that the work nevertheless showed that "the anti-social system of the Chinese" was not an essential characteristic, but a policy.[17] It was the display of British naval power off the south coast that was making impossible for the Chinese government to abandon this policy "without, in some degree, compromising its own security."[18] The following year he backed his arguments up with *Miscellaneous Notices Relating to China and Our Commercial Intercourse with That Country*, which began with some translations but consisted mainly of his own essays on the trade.[19]

These books were intended to show that diplomacy with China was possible and to prove Staunton's expertise, but the reception was discouraging. China was isolated from the struggles between the European states over the balance of power, so that nothing that happened there was likely to make any real difference to politics in London, and there was little interest. Staunton wrote to Morrison that it was "almost throwing away time to attempt to inform the public on the subject of China."[20] The books maintained his position as a minor celebrity, but they did not result in government interest, let alone an appointment. In 1823 he was so discouraged that he made a grand gesture of donating all his Chinese books to the newly established Royal Asiatic Society.[21]

So in 1826, when Staunton lost his parliamentary seat over his support for Catholic religious freedom, he set out to try and turn himself into something other than an expert on China. He had been approached about joining the Society of Dilettanti but needed to have done a grand tour, so he set off for Italy where he "rush'd round palaces and churches," grumbled about the winter weather, enjoyed the local wines, and bought some expensive artworks.[22] He also launched into improvements of his gardens at Leigh Park, adding a lake, developing his hothouses, and even getting a banana plant to fruit.[23] In Ireland he designed a new house and garden on the banks of Loch Corrib and provided himself with an heir in accordance with his late father's wishes: George Lynch, the eldest son of his Galway cousins. He gave the young man an allowance and installed him in the new house.[24]

In London society people wanted to hear about the Macartney embassy and the kowtow, not Staunton's views on Britain's current relations with China. The way he bowed when he met people fitted with this idea and was a topic for lighthearted amusement, as if he were a figure who had emerged from a chinoiserie landscape. Henry Crabb Robinson was delighted to be seated next to Staunton at a dinner, but was primarily interested in George Leonard's account of the Macartney embassy. His comment on George Thomas was that his bows gave him "a ludicrous air; but he is perfectly gentlemanly, and I believe in every way respectable."[25] The Irish novelist Maria Edgeworth, who met him at a party given by a woman who liked to invite celebrities, wrote, "I never saw anything so droll as his bows and I thought they would never cease at every fresh word I said on meeting him." She described him as "chou-chouing in quick time" like a jack-in-the-box being pressed down into a box and popping up again.[26] Bowing was in everyone's mind when they met him because of the Macartney embassy. Precise degrees of etiquette had also been endlessly contested in negotiations with Qing officials in Canton. Now, uncomfortable in the aristocratic society he was trying to enter, he bowed too much, and being laughed at as a kind of Chinese toy behind his back can only have contributed to his anxieties.

One real friend he made was Sir Martin Archer Shee, a portrait painter, adept at setting people at their ease, with a very similar Irish background. They met through the Society of Dilettanti, and when Shee was in trouble Staunton commissioned him to paint a grand and very expensive portrait for his London house (fig. 18.3). Shee and his family became regular visitors at Leigh Park and continued to come for long stays even after he became seriously ill and disabled. His son later described Staunton as someone "whose engaging vivacity, varied knowledge, and genuine kindness of heart, communicated to the social atmosphere of Leigh a peculiar charm, that can never be effaced from the memory of those who were so fortunate as to experience the exhilarating influence."[27]

Staunton returned to Parliament in the 1830 general election and nerved himself up to give a maiden speech apparently under

FIGURE 18.3. Sir Martin Archer Shee's portrait of George Thomas Staunton, 1833.

pressure from his Galway relations: it was on the extension of the local electoral franchise to Catholics in Galway. However, the great political issue of the day was parliamentary reform. This was complex for Staunton, who had inherited his Irish father's liberal views but held one of the rotten boroughs that the reformers aimed to abolish. Torn between his own contradictory opinions in a tightly divided Parliament, he became one of the crucial swing voters.[28]

He was charged with vacillating, but relativism might have been more appropriate: his opinions about the British state emerged from ideas that he had developed as an interpreter and translator in China. As he pondered his votes, he wrote in his private notebook, "In systems of government there is no such thing as right or wrong independent of men's friends."[29] He went on to say that no wise statesman would wish to change the government of a country whether "by a democracy, an aristocracy or an absolute monarchy."[30] Characteristically, he then qualified this by saying that a system might be changed if it did not work well and the change would be likely to make it work better. This interpreter's ability to engage with entirely different viewpoints produced some very erratic votes from a party-political viewpoint.

However, at the crucial moments Staunton voted for Reform, and since he still hardly spoke in Parliament his opinions were private. So when he stood in the 1832 general election for the newly created seat of South Hampshire (which was to elect two members of Parliament) he and Lord Palmerston came together as the Reform ticket. The two men were about the same age with a shared interest in foreign affairs, and both had previously held purchased seats, but Palmerston was a viscount, a major local landowner, and the foreign secretary. The election focussed on Palmerston and Staunton was criticised mainly for aligning himself with him: the attack that most upset him, presumably because of the sexual innuendo, accused him of being "a *consenting* if not a *soliciting companion*" to Palmerston.[31]

Criticism of Staunton also drew on popular images of China. A relative of the Baring family who came from very much the social world that laughed at Staunton in London wrote flippantly to a friend "we shall be represented I fear by Sir G. Staunton who goes bowing unopposed through the county like a Chinese Mandarin."[32] In the press this chinoiserie imagery was taken further. Verses in the *Hampshire Advertiser* contrasted Staunton's refusal to kowtow to the tea-pot king (the Jiaqing emperor) during the Amherst embassy with his willingness now to support the Reformers under Lord Grey:

"Knock your head nine times on the floor," said Tea
   "I'm the brother of Sun and Moon";
Says Staunton "I shall do no such thing–
   No, I will be d___d as soon."

The present Staunton is very unlike–
 About five feet high and a span;
"Knock your head on the floor to me," said Lord Grey,
 And down went the little man.[33]

But this was the year of the Reformers, and Staunton and Palmerston won the election on a wave of popular enthusiasm. When Staunton came home he found the local towns decorated and twenty-six young men, dressed in white with purple ribbons round their waists and laurel leaves in their caps, who insisted on unharnessing his horses and pulling his carriage through the crowded streets of Havant.[34]

So Staunton returned to Parliament, suddenly inspired with confidence, at a moment when the East India Company's monopoly on the China trade was about to expire and with it the Company's role in relations with the Qing. He decided to make a huge effort to persuade Parliament that a unilateral change without any prior agreement from the Chinese government would be disastrous. No one who was not "absolutely seeking" an excuse to go to war with China would think of putting a British representative in such a potentially humiliating situation.[35] These arguments were seen as special pleading by the East India Company, there was very little interest in China, and Staunton had great difficulty getting his resolutions timetabled for parliamentary debate.

When Staunton's resolutions did come up late one evening, Palmerston had just made a rousing speech on relations with Portugal. China was of very little interest to anyone, and Staunton was paralysed by nerves. Up in the gallery, the newspaper reporters could just hear the beginning of some of Staunton's sentences before his voice was lost in the rising swell of conversation. As he struggled on with his speech, one of the officers moved that there should be a count to check that the house was quorate. The required forty members were found to be present, but this was a strong hint to them to leave. Members began to walk out. Fifteen minutes later the House was counted again and found to be inquorate and the debate was adjourned, leaving Staunton utterly humiliated.[36]

The next year, when new elections were announced, the Tories had an even better target. Staunton took to using a speaking

trumpet, which Palmerston politely tried to discourage.[37] A broadside ballad titled *The Lamentation of Sir G. Stan-ching-quot, Mandarin of the Celestial Empire* had him lamenting his lost hopes
of profit from the tea trade and being counted out "like a beaten
cock."[38] When the Tories won, the results list in the local newspapers called Palmerston, who was a famous womaniser, Cupid and
Staunton Koo Too.[39] The victorious Tory candidate made a victory
speech that referred to an end to "the sway of protocols and hieroglyphics."[40] Staunton pasted the newspaper clipping into his notebook and drafted a letter to the newspaper. The chinoiserie imager
was now getting to him: protocols clearly referred to Palmerston's
negotiations as foreign secretary, but what about hieroglyphics?
Did the author "mean to insinuate that literary acquirements and
a knowledge of Foreign languages is a *disqualification* for a seat in
Parliament!"[41]

Meanwhile events in China were turning out as Staunton had
foreseen. In 1834 Lord Napier was sent out to Canton as the representative of the British government under the title superintendent
of trade. During a lengthy standoff with the Qing authorities, Napier's health collapsed and he died on the journey back to Macao.
Soon the British merchants in Canton began to call for war.

For Staunton these events were overshadowed by Morrison's
death at the start of the negotiations. Morrison had been appointed
interpreter to Napier, a role he felt he had to take because his family
would need the money after his death. His letters to Staunton were
full of his anxieties about acting as interpreter in negotiations that
could not possibly succeed. After many years in Canton Morrison
was also worried about China: what would be the impact of free
trade given the Qing government's financial problems? As he wrote
to Staunton, "I am not that patriot who would wish to aggrandize
my own country by the injury or ruin of another."[42]

Staunton wrote privately to government officials, offering to
negotiate with the Chinese, despite the personal risk, in the hope
of averting war.[43] For the first time in years, he also turned to Chinese documents, writing rough translations of two statements from
Governor General Lu Kun to the British in his private notebook.
His translations, evidently written rapidly but with occasional cor-
rections as he pondered how to phrase a sentence in English, are

strikingly different from Morrison's versions, which were put on record by the British government.[44] As Staunton had done all his life he made the Chinese officials sound like Europeans. Where Morrison, exhausted and not at his best, has Lu Kun say, "I, the Governor, looking up, embody the heaven-like benevolence of the Great Emperor," Staunton writes, "I act in the spirit of the benevolent intentions of my Sovereign."[45] He is also clearly sympathetic to Lu Kun's arguments. He adds underlining when Lu Kun argues that what China values "is the subjection of men by <u>reason</u>" and inserts the word "invaders" to make a sentence about driving the British out work grammatically in English.[46] Later in his notebook he picked up Lu Kun's language himself, describing Napier's actions as "unprovoked and violent aggressions upon the Chinese, defying their laws, attacking their forts, and killing their people."[47]

One of the British merchants in Canton, Hugh Lindsay, had written a public letter calling on Palmerston to coerce the Chinese to obtain access to ports other than Canton and a commercial treaty, on the grounds that the Chinese were uncivilised and did not treat the English as equals.[48] Staunton, outraged, responded in a pamphlet arguing that China is not a place to which different rules apply but a state just like a European one. He began with a practical point: Lindsay had claimed that a war against China would need only twelve ships and six hundred troops. Given the huge size of the Chinese army, Staunton argues, this could be true only if the Chinese were extremely cowardly, which they are not. Apparently writing this made Staunton think that perhaps he had contributed to this mistaken view of the Chinese in his garden at Leigh Park, where the lake had a bridge with Chinese gateways and inscriptions as well as a Chinese pavilion and boathouse. He now added a large fort, modelled on those that guarded the river below Canton, over which he flew the Qing flag.[49]

However, the main point of Staunton's pamphlet is not military but legal. He argues that while access to northern trading ports and a commercial treaty are desirable, they are certainly not a justification for war. To fight for these would "reflect only disgrace and dishonour on our flag and name."[50] Britain should treat China in accordance with international law, just as it would a European country. Napier was wrong to send warships up the river to Canton,

Leigh Water   *West View*

FIGURE 18.4. The lake at Leigh Park by Joseph Francis Gilbert showing the Chinese fort and boathouse. From this view the Chinese bridge is hidden behind the trees.

and any other government would have responded as the Chinese did: after all, how would the British respond if French frigates were to force their way up the Thames?[51]

Lindsay had argued that international law was not relevant because the Chinese did not treat the British as equals but called them barbarians. Staunton debates Lindsay's translation of the term in question (*yi*), saying that although it is not the most positive term, it is also not as strongly negative as the English word "barbarian." He mocks Lindsay for referring to how Confucius used the word—the Chinese may not change much, but even so one certainly cannot assume that a word means what it did more than two thousand years ago. Moreover, translating words in "their most offensive sense" in itself creates hostility.[52] However, what really annoyed him was the translation of *yimu*, a term the Chinese had used for Napier, as "barbarian eye." To him *yimu* is a reasonable Chinese term for a foreign superintendent. Translating it "barbarian eye" may sound like a harmless joke, but when it results in inflaming people's minds "with indignation at imagined insults, which nothing but the sword and bayonet can expiate, it cannot be too severely reprobated."[53] In other words Staunton dismisses the idea that the true meanings of words are to be found in the classical past and argues that the translation should be judged in terms of its contemporary political impact.

Staunton cared deeply that China should be treated like any other country and the Chinese as ordinary people, not laughed at because they referred to a superintendent of trade as a barbarian eye. No doubt some of this passion is due to the fact that he is writing a pamphlet and some to Morrison's death, but his own experience of being treated as an oriental amusement rather than listened to as an authority was probably also relevant. And yet, despite all this, two years later Staunton, by then back in Parliament, was to vote for the Opium War.

CHAPTER NINETEEN

The Opium War

IN 1839 BRITAIN DECLARED WAR on China after a series of events precipitated by the Daoguang emperor's adoption of a radical new policy on opium smuggling. Given Britain's growing imperial power and the Qing state's weakness, such a war was probably inevitable, but it was a war that, despite Jiaqing's orders about maritime defence and Staunton's claims about the size of the Chinese army, the Qing had no hope of winning. The Qing state simply did not have the financial resources to fund the kind of military that could have defeated the British.

Many people in Canton and some of the Qing officials who had served there must have known this, just as Wu Xiongguang had thirty years earlier when the British occupied Macao. However, none of it was written down: even in the imperial archives there were only the briefest of hints, and published Chinese sources provided no meaningful information at all about the British. Lin Zexu, who arrived in Canton to implement the new policy, was eager to learn and was soon employing a whole team of translators, but by that time he had gone too far to turn his back on the policy he had promoted. Moreover, the suspicion of people with long-standing links to the British was such that few were willing to offer their services as interpreters even when Lin first arrived in Canton. By the end of the war the distrust and dangers were such that no Chinese interpreters at all were present for the final treaty negotiations.

The immediate cause of the war was opium, something that Staunton had not really anticipated. The abolition of the East India

Company encouraged a host of new British traders to enter the market by undercutting prices. By the late 1830s the drug's widespread use was causing anxieties about the fighting capacity of the army, and some senior Chinese officials were worrying that the outflow of silver used to pay for it was leading to economic problems and popular unrest. Crackdowns had been tried before and might provoke British naval action or, in the classical terms in which these issues were debated, border disputes. Now, with growing anxiety about the impact of the drug, the Daoguang emperor chose to back a proposal for a far tougher crackdown than any previously implemented: the plan was to go after drug users as well as dealers and to execute those who did not change their ways.[1]

The proponents of this policy were primarily Chinese who had come up through the examination system, and they treated the opium trade as a moral and economic issue, not one of foreign relations, in which they had little expertise. Lin Zexu, who was sent to implement the new policy, had risen from a relatively humble background through the examination system to the rank of governor general. He was known for being hardworking and incorruptible, which made him a good choice for a job where he was bound to meet significant resistance. Reports from foreigners who met him in Guangdong, not to speak of the veneration in which he was held by subsequent generations of Chinese scholar officials, suggest that he could also be charming and very good company.

As Lin Zexu travelled south he was already reading through archives and ordering the arrest of major dealers. Eight days after his arrival he ordered the foreigners to hand over all their opium and sign a bond promising not to sell it in the future on penalty of death. The British stalled, and Lin, following Wu Xiongguang's tactics in 1808, ordered all Chinese servants out and stopped the delivery of food supplies. Charles Elliot, the British government's superintendent of trade, told the British traders to formally surrender all their opium to him and handed it over to Lin, who personally oversaw its destruction in seawater and lime. Lin then allowed the trade to restart.[2] Both Lin and Elliot were aware that British naval action was likely, but with shipping still dependent on the annual monsoon winds, there would be no response from London for several months.

In the meantime it was clear that Lin needed to learn as much as he could about the British so that he could face the threat when it came. He did have a translator: Yuan Dehui, who had been employed by the Imperial Household Department as a Latin translator for some years. He came from a Catholic family and, like Li Zibiao, had gone abroad to study for the priesthood. He spent several years at a seminary in the British-controlled Straits Settlements (Singapore, Penang, and Malacca). Then in his mid-twenties he apparently gave up studying for the priesthood and transferred to the Protestant Anglo-Chinese College in Malacca. This had been founded by Robert Morrison with the help of a sizable donation from Staunton. It was then funded by the East India Company and combined training future missionaries and running a Christian printing press with professional Chinese and English language training for paying students. Yuan already had good Latin and now applied himself diligently to learning English. The American and British students found him boring, but the Chinese language teachers, who were not very highly educated themselves, were impressed by his Chinese. They employed him to translate from English into Chinese and to do the calligraphy for the Christian books they were printing. After two years he returned to Canton presumably to work in the trade. He had been sent to Beijing by the governor general in 1829 in response to a request for a Latin translator to replace the last of the former Jesuits for formal communications with the Russian court. In practice, however, he appears to have been used as an English translator and interpreter: the next year he reappeared in Canton with two officials sent to deal with the case of some shipwrecked British sailors and bought English books. In 1836 he took indefinite leave of his job on the grounds of his mother's ill health, and the next time we meet him he is in the entourage of Lin Zexu, which suggests that he also had contacts with those interested in the opium problem.[3]

Written translation is a slow task, and Yuan Dehui helped Lin Zexu to build a team of translators and interpreters. He appears to have turned for help to one of the teachers from the Anglo-Chinese College Liang Fa who had been one of Morrison's earliest converts (and is now best known as the author of the Christian pamphlet that inspired the great Taiping Rebellion). Liang Fa's son Liang

Jinde, who had also been to school in Singapore, became Lin Zexu's most trusted translator.[4] Peter Parker, the American missionary doctor strongly opposed to opium, who had previously employed Liang Jinde was also invited to translate for Lin.[5] There was also a young man educated by missionaries in America and the son of a Chinese father and Bengali mother who had studied with British missionaries in India. A British surgeon, one of a group of ship-wreck survivors who were taken to be questioned by Lin in person, found among the linguists in attendance yet another possible inter-preter, "a very intelligent young man" who spoke English "remark-ably well" as a result of spending eight years in London working for John Elphinstone.[6]

Lin Zexu appears to have employed Yuan Dehui and Liang Jinde primarily as translators. For general background Liang Jinde trans-lated parts of a geographical encyclopaedia, selecting the sections on Britain and America and focussing on government and the mili-tary. For the legal framework within which the British were operat-ing Yuan Dehui translated the relevant sections of the classic *Law of Nations* by Emmerich Vattel. As a check on Yuan's accuracy Lin then asked Parker to translate some of the same material. Lin him-self annotated the final version with comments linking ideas in the text to recent Chinese cases. For the likely British response to his policies he had a translation made of parts of Algernon Thelwall's *Iniquities of the Opium Trade in China.* (Thelwall was a paid edi-tor, and the book was put together by former East India Company employees, very likely including Staunton who shared its goals and might have known Thelwall from his other job as a public speaking coach.)[7] For information on recent events Lin had his staff translate selections from Canton's two English-language newspapers, which reprinted reports from London, India, and beyond. He circulated copies of the resulting *Macao News Sheet* (*Aomen xinwen zhi*) to sympathetic colleagues, and information from them found its way into his correspondence with the emperor.[8]

Lin also conducted interviews with his translators and others. Only a tiny fraction of the interview notes that he took while he was in Guangdong survive, but these include extracts from interviews with Yuan Dehui, Rong Lin who had been in England, and Wen Wenbo from Bengal, as well as Robert Thom, a trader who was interpreting for the British.[9] Between them these men had a great deal of general knowledge of the expanding British Empire.

And yet Lin was capable of arguing to the emperor that because the British wore tight clothing that made it difficult for their knees to bend they would not be able to fight well on land. Even the most limited discussion of the conquest of India should have made it obvious that the British were capable of fighting on land and that this was a major risk: the forts that protected Canton had been designed to deal with British ships blasting their way through the channel, as had happened at the end of the Amherst embassy, but they were totally unprotected from the land.[10] To make matters worse Lin made this entirely specious argument six months after he arrived in Canton in a letter written to persuade the emperor to let him enforce his new regulations on the new season's opium imports and if necessary execute one or two foreigners, an action that was bound to exacerbate the crisis. His letter summarises the agreed policy as one of stopping the opium at source while avoiding border disputes. He says that he has been conducting secret investigations and has concluded that the British can in fact be defeated. As all the Americans have told him, the British are extremely aggressive, have occupied a series of cities in Southeast Asia, have no sense of right and wrong, and will only listen to force. The letter is structured to respond to opponents within the government who fear British naval power and wealth. Lin argues that this is wrong; there is no need for fear as long as the Chinese are careful to avoid any sea battles. The point about their tight clothing making them unsuited to fight on land is made in this context.[11]

Lin Zexu was no fool, but he had come to Canton already committed to the line of action he was going to take. The knowledge he needed had not been part of the policy-making process in Beijing, which had centred on how to deal with the drug, skirting round the issue of British naval power. While officials who had served in Guangdong, as many had, were very likely aware of the potential threat from British warships, this was not part of the written Chinese learning that shaped public debate. Such knowledge remained in the domain of the spoken and indeed the unspoken, and that was especially true for the scholarly Chinese world from which Lin Zexu came, which was still nervous of touching the Manchu privilege of foreign affairs. The story of Shengtai, who had been sent into exile for many years as a result of his curiosity about the British during the Amherst embassy, was well known, and he was not even Chinese but a Mongol bannerman who could speak to the emperor.

Instead of rethinking his policy as a result of what he learned after he arrived in Guangdong, Lin picked the information he needed to back his own position. So, he had his translators select newspaper articles from the relatively sympathetic *Canton Press*, focussing on debates about the opium trade, which was a matter of huge controversy in Britain. He collected very little information about the British navy; indeed his only lengthy translation about the British military was an article on the dreadful state of the British troops taking part in the ongoing Afghan campaign. This naturally tended to back up his idea that the British were dangerous only at sea.[12] The British surgeon who met him described how interested he was in the English costume, telling his secretary to lead one of the ship's officers round first in one direction and then in another. Lin put on his spectacles to get a good look and made little exclamations of surprise, all the time laughing and joking with his colleagues.[13] Apparently this firsthand view of British naval dress either reinforced what Lin already knew about its inconvenience for fighting or was an opportunity to reinforce it for others

The news that Lin Zexu had confined the British merchants to their compound and that Elliot had handed over the stocks of opium reached London in early August 1839. On 1 October the cabinet decided on war with China in a two-day private meeting that also declared war on the Ottoman Empire. The deciding factor was that the opium surrendered was said to be worth the staggering sum of over two million pounds. The government would certainly not be able to raise taxes to compensate drug smugglers, but the cabinet all agreed that the sum was too large just to let the markets suffer. So they decided to use military force and make the Chinese pay instead. Lin Zexu, who had been reading Vattel, might have argued that the law of nations hardly justified the payment of compensation to smugglers, but the cabinet were swayed by politics rather than law and a passionate speech on the imprisonment of British merchants and the importance of national honour provided cover. Palmerston, as foreign secretary, was authorised to send instructions to China and India, but in London the decision remained a secret.[14]

It was not until spring and the arrival of the next season's ships from India that news began to filter through. Staunton was back in Parliament as one of the members for Portsmouth, a stronghold of East India Company influence. Two years earlier he had pushed back against a bill of Palmerston's creating extraterritorial British legal jurisdiction in China by insisting it must contain a provision that the British court could not infringe on the jurisdiction of the Chinese courts without the consent of the government of China. The bill was dropped.[15] Now Palmerston, who was foreign secretary for a very weak Whig government, realised that he needed to keep Staunton on side. He consulted him on how to write to the Qing court, sent him polite notes, and arranged little informal meetings in the House of Commons.[16] Staunton continued to see events in China through the lens of his own experiences in China and particularly in negotiating what he now called the Provincial Treaty in 1814, but also his ongoing battle for China to be treated like any other foreign power. He advised that the British negotiating stance should be founded on "common sense, and common practice, which are understood in all countries, however imperfectly observed in any" and, his mind going back to Li Yao or possibly even his own position during the Amherst embassy, that "not even the humblest individual should be trusted within the grasp of the Chinese without a hostage."[17] A second letter warned Palmerston that although his letter had not discussed the question of opium he had a "strong feeling against it" and had promised to second a motion against it in the House of Commons.[18]

Then in April 1840 when the opposition brought a vote of no confidence over the government's handling of events in China, Palmerston offered Staunton the honoured position of speaking second in defence of the government. This was a major debate on which the continuation of the government in power depended. Finally, China was a matter of real concern for British politics and Staunton was to be at the centre of the debate. The House of Commons was packed, the debate lasted three days, and all the great political figures of the day spoke. Staunton was finally to be acknowledged as the great expert on China.

Staunton took the bait, but he was not just speaking in favour of the war because he had been flattered; as always he could see both sides of the case. He spent much of his speech expressing his opposition to opium and his belief that China should be treated according to the law of nations. One of the later speakers complained that all he could make out was that Staunton did not think there should be interference of any kind with the people or government of China. Staunton had in fact given a justification for the war: how could it be right for the Chinese to threaten to execute the traders of the new season's opium who could not have known about his policy before they set off from India? This was scarcely the mood of the House of Commons that day, but it *was* one of the problems that Lin Zexu had placed before the Daoguang emperor. Staunton, with his knowledge of China and his lawyer's mind, which Qing officials had always hated, had picked on one of the technical weaknesses in the Chinese case from their own point of view. At an emotional level Staunton identified with Elliot, whom he knew and liked and saw as facing the same dangers he himself had done in 1814.[19]

During the debate Staunton's opinions and writings were repeatedly referenced by both sides: Sir James Graham's opening speech attacking the government accused them of failing to treat Staunton's earlier warnings with the respect they deserved. Other speakers complimented him on his prescience, used the arguments from his antiwar pamphlet, and criticized him for supporting the government. But Staunton's pleasure in all this recognition was spoiled by a remark that showed that attitudes toward him had not in fact changed: John Hobhouse had raised a laugh at Staunton for taking the debate too seriously: what mattered after all was the party politics. He declared that hereafter he was going to refer to Staunton as his "excellent and innocent friend the member for Portsmouth" because he "had lived so long in China that he did not know the practise of the House of Commons."[20] Palmerston, wrapping up the debate, sat down to thundering applause after defending his actions using facts about Chinese law from Staunton's speech. However, the next day Staunton was so upset that he wrote a formal letter asking Hobhouse not to repeat his expression.[21] Six months later when Staunton wrote to Palmerston to ask if perhaps the government might consult him in a more formal capacity, Palmerston replied that he did not understand what Staunton meant.[22]

Lin Zexu had the newspaper reports of this debate translated as soon as they reached China. The translators focussed on Sir James Graham's criticisms of the government and omitted almost all the support for the war. Staunton's contribution was reduced to a single sentence warning that the war was likely to be a long one.[23] Since different characters were used for his name, no one could have recognised him as the same figure who had aroused the anger of the Jiaqing emperor twenty years earlier. In any case, by this point the British fleet was already sailing up the Chinese coast.

Rather than targeting Macao, the British were heading for Zhoushan off Ningbo, which the British government had seen as a possible base since before the Macartney embassy. After capturing the main island, they sailed on north to the sandy gulf off Tianjin, where they submitted Palmerston's letter of demands to the horrified court. Lin Zexu was dismissed, ordered into exile, and replaced with the Zhili governor general, the Manchu Qishan, who was sent south to negotiate.

Qishan, like Macartney all those years ago and Qing officials for some time to come, distrusted everyone involved in the trade. Allowing the linguists or hong merchants to interpret for him would give them and the local officials far too much power. He was also a political opponent of Lin Zexu's and had been sent partly to investigate him. He was later said by Lin's supporters to have been dismissive of Lin's translation project, but in any case the team of translators were at risk after Lin's fall: Liang Jinde quickly took refuge in Macao.[24]

Instead Qishan chose as his interpreter a man named Bao Peng who had been employed by one of the major British opium traders. Bao, who had made a significant amount of money and bought a low-ranking honorary official post, had fled north to Shandong province to avoid the crackdown on the opium trade. There he joined the staff of a man he knew who was a county magistrate. When a British warship arrived he was naturally called on to interpret. The British turned out to know him and to have come ashore merely in order to buy provisions, so Bao had little difficulty getting them to leave without causing trouble. Qishan passing through the province on his way south heard of Bao's achievement and asked for him as an interpreter.[25]

With this background no one trusted Bao Peng, but Qishan evidently intended to control him through threats. For his crucial personal meeting with Elliot in November 1840, which took place on board a British ship, he brought only Bao Peng with him. The merchants, linguists, and others who could have understood were left on other boats. The outcome of these negotiations was that the Chinese agreed to pay a huge indemnity and to allow the British to occupy the island of Hong Kong, but not to change the terms of the trade, a result that infuriated both the Daoguang emperor and Palmerston. Qishan was sentenced to death (though later reprieved), and Bao Peng was sent into military slavery in Xinjiang.[26]

Palmerston replaced Elliot with Henry Pottinger, who was sent out with orders for a far more aggressive campaign. In the autumn of 1841 the British fleet sailed north up the coast and occupied the cities of Xiamen and Ningbo. When this too failed to bring the Qing to terms, they brought in further reinforcements from India and took their fleet up the Yangzi river, where they took the town of Zhenjiang and in the summer of 1842 threatened the great city of Nanjing.

During this lengthy second stage of the war the main negotiations were handled by Robert Morrison's son John, who had been born in Macao. He had spent his childhood partly there and partly at school in England. Then he had studied at the Anglo-Chinese College in Malacca. He knew both Yuan Dehui and Liang Jinde from his schooldays, but even before the war his beliefs were very much those of the British of his generation: unlike Staunton he thought that international law could not be applied to the Chinese because they did not share the religious and moral principles of Christendom. He was much liked by the British leaders. The Chinese held him responsible for many of their policies and were said to have put a fifty-thousand-dollar reward on his head.[27]

The British had few alternatives to the overworked Morrison because the trade had continued to rely heavily on the linguistic skills of the Chinese merchants and their staff. The most highly rated were Karl Gützlaff, who had been a missionary in

Southeast Asia and could speak the Fujian dialect but was a Prussian national, and Robert Thom, who had been diligently studying Chinese but often had to communicate in writing. On the ground there were Chinese compradores, who were accustomed to working for the British but knew that they would be executed if they were captured.[28]

So the negotiations for the Treaty of Nanjing, which concluded the war, and the subsequent commercial arrangements signed in Canton were interpreted and in effect conducted by John Morrison. The Qing officials brought no interpreters of their own, and John Morrison referred significant decisions back to Pottinger who remained on Hong Kong Island, several days' journey away. John Morrison's influence was such that both sides came to distrust him, and when differences emerged between the Chinese and English versions of the commercial arrangements there were rumours that the Chinese had bribed him to allow this to happen.[29] When Staunton, as one of the very few people in England capable of understanding the translation issues, asked the new Conservative government for authorisation to examine the treaty to see what had happened, his letter was annotated "This may go to sleep."[30]

After the Opium War interpreting and translating in China would take place either in the new colonial context or as part of a Chinese nationalist endeavour to resist British imperialism. In Hong Kong and the new treaty ports, interpreters were a necessary part of the British colonial establishment. John Morrison was given several high positions in Hong Kong but died the following year of a fever thought to have been brought on by the anxieties of his situation during the treaty negotiations. Gützlaff was put in charge of Zhoushan for several years. Staunton was also finally able to get backing for his long-standing campaign to establish a university lectureship in Chinese in England. Liang Jinde, after a short spell in Hong Kong, went back to Canton to work for one of the major Chinese merchants. He was outspoken in his criticism of the British both for the war and for the behaviour of British police in Hong Kong. After his father's death he left the church having earlier told one missionary that Christianity could not be respected until the English were kinder. He ended up with a position in the Imperial Maritime Customs, a Qing institution that employed

British administrators, where he became one of the new generation of English-speaking Chinese who would spearhead China's late
nineteenth-century modernisation efforts.[31]

Meanwhile, as Lin Zexu set off into exile he gave a copy of the
geography Liang Jinde had translated to Wei Yuan, a friend who
edited and published it as part of a much larger work on foreign
countries. This was only one of a number of works on Western
countries published in the years immediately after the war, many of
them by people closely associated with Lin. Almost no Chinese had
dared even to mention the Macartney embassy in private writings,
but now the barriers that kept Han Chinese away from the study of
foreign affairs had been broken while the war itself had made many
people realise the urgency of that study.[32]

Months later, travelling at walking pace across China, Lin Zexu
reached Gansu province and an old friend Chen Depei came out to
keep him company, walking beside the little cart toward Liangzhou,
the same route that Li Zibiao had followed seventy years earlier
when he first left the town as a boy to go to Naples. Together the
two men talked and drank together, laughed, and sighed over the
events of the war. Afterward Chen copied out and carefully preserved extracts from Lin's interview notes with his English translators. Lin wrote to thank Chen for his sympathy in a poem that ends,

> I've gone ten thousand miles and crossed the mountain passes but I
>   have nightmares,
> I still hear the sound of the war drums east of the Yangzi.[33]

CHAPTER TWENTY

Forgetting

IN THE RUN-UP to the 1852 general election, which was to bring Palmerston to power as prime minister, George Thomas Staunton was pushed out of his Portsmouth parliamentary seat. When he tried to stand for South Hampshire, a letter in the local newspaper described him as someone whose long career "leaves no greater trace upon a country or neighbourhood than the shadow of a passing cloud."[1] It depicted him as entirely out of touch with the times, seeing the country only from the windows of his drawing room and carriage. "Without family, without friends in the proper acceptation of the word," he is surrounded by people hoping only to inherit his money, who flatter him and avoid any chance of offending him, so that his "ideas and opinions are never brought into contact and collision with the world as it is."[2] There was enough truth in this to upset Staunton, and no doubt it contributed to the hostility to the press in his memoirs, but like many political attacks it missed half the story: Staunton did know about this new high Victorian age and its ideas, but he was now in his seventies and, like many older people, did not always agree with them.

The thirty years since Staunton returned from China had been a period of extraordinarily rapid change. The Industrial Revolution, whose earliest stages he had seen when he toured England as a small boy with his father in the 1780s, had by this time transformed almost every aspect of life. In 1841 he took on a new confidential servant and with his help made a series of tours of Germany and Italy. These included his first railway journey, which inspired "sensations

of anxious surprise and curiosity."[3] Only a few years later his visitors
at Leigh Park were arriving from London on the train, and revolutions across Europe had shown the political impact of all these
changes.

His ideas, which were now so old-fashioned, can be seen in
a pamphlet he had recently published on the best way to translate "God" in the new Chinese Bible that was being produced in
Shanghai. The pamphlet combines Staunton's Anglican piety with
an openness to other Christian denominations and indeed other
religions that was common enough when Macartney and George
Leonard Staunton expressed it in the eighteenth century, but which
George Thomas Staunton's Hampshire constituents found hard
to accept. In it he argues that Protestant translators should use
the same Chinese terminology as Catholics because the Catholic
missionaries too have promoted the Christian faith and that even
Chinese who do not believe in Christianity may have some natural
"knowledge and worship of the true God."[4] This argument from
natural theology had provided the basis for the seventeenth-century
Jesuit policy of accommodation toward Confucianism, but was now
certainly not shared by most Protestant missionaries. Finally, in a
point about translation that he had made so often throughout his
career, he argues that "words are nothing but the symbols of ideas,"
so it is wrong to expect that any Chinese word will fully and correctly convey the idea of the English word "God."[5] All these were
ideas he had held since the early 1800s and which had made it possible to work between Chinese and European culture, but they were
very much at odds with the new age of European confidence and
imperialism.

When he was not working in his library, Staunton spent pleasant hours chatting at his clubs, not only the Dilettanti but also the
Athenaeum and the Royal Society Club, where he could meet many
of the leading intellectuals of the day. He was an active member of
the new British Association for the Advancement of Science as well
as the Royal Asiatic Society.[6] In the evenings he was free to indulge
his appetite for good food and wine. Johannes Hüttner, his former
tutor, could never quite believe it when he found himself at dinner
in Devonshire Street, sitting there beneath the portrait of Macartney and George Leonard Staunton after their return from Madras

(fig. 2.1), and on the opposite wall George Thomas returning to his
mother after the embassy (fig. 12.1) "quaffing half-a-dozen of the
choicest wines, and regaling on venison, vol-au-vent, patties, and
delicacies, the very name of which makes my mouth water."[7]

For three months every summer Staunton moved down to
Leigh Park, where a succession of visitors came to stay to enjoy and
admire the gardens. The lake and the temples he had built twenty
years earlier were all still there, but these days the garden was best
known for its tropical plants grown in heated greenhouses. This
was cutting-edge horticulture, and in 1845 the garden was covered
in the *Gardener's Chronicle*. A diagram showed the main glass-
house, which was kept at sixty-five degrees Fahrenheit or above
all year round by an elaborate coal-fired hot-water system. In the
centre were tropical fruit trees including eight different types of
banana, oranges, lychee and longan, avocado, and date palms as
well as spice trees such as cinnamon and nutmeg and many more.
Flowering climbers were trained up the columns, while ferns grew
in pots on the heated shelves.[8] When Staunton's gardeners succeeded in getting a mango to fruit and the fruit turned out to be
delicious, he added a special new mangosteen house to grow a
larger crop. Orchids flourished in the warm, moist atmosphere,
including the great Bee Swarm orchid (*Cyrtopodium punctatum*)
from Florida, which was the first to flower in England and which
Staunton exhibited at Kew Gardens in 1844. When Joseph Paxton,
working for the Duke of Devonshire at Chatsworth, succeeded in
getting the giant Amazonian water lily (*Victoria regia*) to flower
in 1849, Staunton was keen to try to do the same. He built a new
hexagonal glass house, in which it flowered for the first time in
1853 (fig. 20.1).[9]

The pleasure grounds Staunton had built earlier were now also
full of rare and special plants. When the huge *Agave americana*
from the deserts of the southern United States sent up its twenty-
four-foot spikes and flowered, Staunton printed a flyer for visitors
and sent a copy to the directors of Kew Gardens. His cousin Benjamin Brodie used the striking contrast between its mass of pale
flowers and the dark conifers behind as part of the setting of the
popular science book he was writing and a hint as to the identity of
its characters.[10]

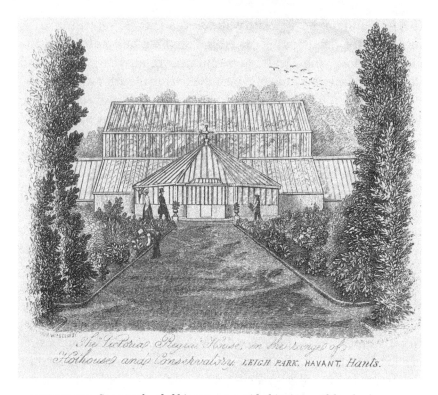

The Victoria Regia House, in the range of Hothouses and Conservatory, LEIGH PARK, HAVANT, *Hants.*

FIGURE 20.1. Staunton headed his notepaper with this picture of the glasshouses. Visitors are approaching and gardeners are hard at work on the carefully tended borders of the walled garden.

Benjamin Brodie's *Psychological Inquiries* was an introduction to many of the big scientific and political issues of the day presented as a dialogue between three characters, Eubulus the wise counsellor, Crites the lawyer, and Ergates the doctor, as they walk through Eubulus's beautiful gardens and sit in his library. Brodie published the book anonymously, but it sold very well, running to three editions in just two years, and he was quickly identified. Even in the first volume it is easy enough to identify Ergates as Benjamin Brodie himself, Eubulus as Staunton, and Crites as Benjamin's brother Peter. In a second volume, written after both Staunton and Peter Brodie had died, not only is Eubulus's garden described in detail but he is asked about the Chinese language. The conversations are, of course, fictional, but at least for the first volume Brodie could be sure that his brother and Staunton would read it and recognise themselves and that other members of the family would do so too. In fact a large part of the book's attraction is the characterisation, which draws the reader in to imagine walking in this beautiful place talking about these interesting topics with people whose knowledge is broad and opinions varied, but who are clearly close friends and always generous to each other's point of view.[11]

Staunton talks of the beauty of the landscape, and his enjoyment of the alterations of light and shape, the development of buds and flowers, the growth of the trees, and the habits of birds and insects. He argues that one should not overlook the goodness in other people and ought to make an effort to be cheerful even in painful circumstances. His positive attitudes provide a contrast to Peter Brodie, the cynical lawyer, always aware of "the vices, caprices and vagaries of mankind."[12]

Their discussions begin with the difficulties of retiring after a long and busy working life. Benjamin and Peter Brodie have arrived on the train from London. The fresh air of the garden is especially pleasing to Peter, who has been cooped up in his chambers with a headache from breathing the polluted London fog. As they sit on a fallen tree in a beech wood, they cannot help thinking that this would be a lovely place to retire, but Staunton assures them that this idea would not last long. Unlike Peter Brodie, he does not wish to live in retirement from the rest of mankind, since he is sure that the social instinct is "as irresistible as that of hunger."[13]

This leads them into the new sciences of the mind, or as George Henry Lewes put it in a characteristically cutting review, "some agreeable remarks on Memory, Sleep, Dreams, Phrenology, Drowning, and other attractive topics."[14] Much of the text is a vehicle for Brodie's experimental and anecdotal knowledge, but Staunton is given a wide knowledge of natural history and a special fondness for dogs: he tells stories about dogs that find their way home, rejoice in being your companion, and can be seen dreaming as they lie by the fire.[15]

From the sciences of the mind, the discussion moves on to political philosophy. Here Peter Brodie is the proponent for the fashionable new ideas of the day. He puts forward the popular science of phrenology, based on the idea that the shape of the head reveals character, which was being applied to the physical characteristics of races. Benjamin Brodie argues against this on the basis of a comparison with the brains of animals. Then he gives Staunton a long speech arguing for the many and varied elements that shape human character: original human instincts, habits, education and childhood training, health, and even age. The central idea is that it is not race or biology that shapes national character, but government: people who have "an uncertain tenure of life or liberty, or property, under an arbitrary and oppressive government" will tend to become low-minded and cunning, whereas those who have the advantage of living in a free and well-regulated community will be open and manly.[16] Elsewhere he argues that the best form of civilisation is the result of a mixture of natural human instincts, habits, and intelligence, but these are so mixed up that the problem of a civilisation's ultimate cause is "too complicated for a satisfactory solution."[17]

Staunton also applies these ideas to social class. He argues that the working classes are just as intelligent as others but that their situation means that they have little opportunity to learn. He learns a great deal of natural history from talking to the older men in the nearby villages. As with those who belong to what are called the higher classes of society: "There are some who are stupid, and many who are careless, and who never much learn to observe or think for themselves. But there are still others who make their own observations on what comes under their notice, and reason upon them with perfect accuracy."[18]

The second volume of Benjamin Brodie's *Psychological Enquiries* was issued shortly after Darwin's *Origin of Species*. Sitting in the library Peter Brodie comments on Staunton's collection of books on natural theology. This leads into a debate on the idea of evolution and its implications. Peter Brodie asks whether or not Negroes should be seen as members of a different species. Benjamin responds, "I know that this is a hypothesis that has been propagated in the slave states of America; I cannot, however, admit it to be well founded."[19] Staunton concludes that there are so many different causes that can promote or retard the progress of civilisation that it is impossible to answer the question other than to say that change takes generations. The causes he lists are the form of government, the climate, and the influence of peace and war. (Climate was a classic explanation of human difference, but the emphasis on government and war was close to his own experiences in China.) Later, pushed to say that the highest degree of civilisation is in modern Europe, he replies that the men of the Middle Ages were just as intelligent, the only difference is that people today have a greater knowledge of science and certain other subjects.[20]

Staunton was not out of touch with the popular ideas of the age, but he did not sympathise with them. He had been educated by a father deeply imbued with the ideals of the Enlightenment, then spent most of the formative years of his life in China. His friendships with Chinese colleagues of his own age, with Catholic missionaries, and with the working-class Protestant dissenter Robert Morrison were some of the closest in his life. Interpreting between English and Chinese had forced him to shift mentally between the ideas of the two very different cultures, and his translation work had made him think through the intellectual choices he made when he did this.

Although in his memoirs Staunton depicted himself after his return to London simply as an English gentleman, that former life never entirely left him. In 1853 he included in his list of visitors to Leigh Park the name "Mr Hochee."[21] This was He Zhi who had belonged to the same circles as Staunton in Canton. After Wu Yacheng and Li Yao were exiled and Staunton departed from Canton, He Zhi repeatedly took positions travelling overseas and in 1822 settled permanently in England. He married an English girl and got a job working for John Elphinstone. Elphinstone had continued to employ Chinese servants after his return to Britain, but He Zhi was something more than a servant: he had a large house of his own, ran one of Elphinstone's farms, and was treated as a friend by both Elphinstone and several local doctors. It seems likely that he managed Elphinstone's opium addiction and possibly also smoked with him. Now Elphinstone had promised to leave He Zhi his English property, and he needed recommendations to become a naturalised British subject in order to inherit.[22] It is impossible to know why he came to visit at this moment. Both he and Staunton liked to play chess and had won prizes for their garden flowers. We can only hope they enjoyed eating Staunton's lychees or mangoes together as they chatted about old times. The one thing, however,

FIGURE 20.2. An early coloured photograph of He Zhi playing chess with his son
John Elphinstone Fatqua Hochee.

that is clear from the mention of the name in this list of visitors is
that Staunton treated He Zhi as a gentleman of his own class.

However, the people most often around Staunton now were the
younger generation of his family. George Lynch, Staunton's acknowledged heir, who lived in Galway visited Leigh Park from time to
time, but there were others who came more regularly: George's
younger brother Henry; George Simcockes, an Irish godson who

had been paid for all his life by Staunton; and the daughters of one of his Salisbury relatives who had fallen on hard times. Behind them there was also George Belsey, Staunton's butler, and his son. It was these people, with their complicated relations between each other and their benefactor, whom the newspaper described as speculating on the elderly Staunton "as a matter of property."[23]

Staunton died in 1859, leaving his Irish property and the bulk of his investments to George Lynch, but his London house and the Leigh Park property to Henry Lynch. He also left substantial legacies to Simcockes, various cousins, and several old friends, a year's wages to his servants, a very large annuity to his butler Belsey, and pensions to thirteen other older and retired servants. Henry Lynch died suddenly of cholera six weeks later, and his son sold everything as soon as he was able to: the houses, the furniture, the paintings, the rare plants were all auctioned off. Within six years Leigh Park house had been demolished by its new purchaser and the garden entirely reconfigured. In the last years of his life George Thomas had donated to the Royal Asiatic Society the jade sceptre given to his father and the yellow silk purse he himself received from the Qianlong emperor. The sceptre was later transferred, with the rest of the society's collections, to the Victoria and Albert Museum. Everything else was gone.[24]

Around the same time Li Zibiao's legacy in Shanxi was also being dismantled. The Opium War created a new set of power relations between European missionaries and the Chinese priests and Christians. More than fifty years after Li had put in his request for Catholic toleration to the Qianlong emperor, it was in the aftermath of the Opium War that his successor Xianfeng finally issued a formal edict announcing the toleration of Christianity. The Shanxi Catholics were overjoyed at the news, but it was rapidly followed by the arrival of a new generation of European missionaries with a far more critical attitude to China and its people.[25] These new missionaries were no longer at risk of being imprisoned or exiled by the Qing state if they fell out with the local Chinese Catholics and were funded from their home countries rather than by local elites. They were also influenced by those same ideas of a hierarchy of civilisation and competition between races that Staunton argues against in Benjamin Brodie's *Psychological Inquiries*.

In Shanxi the new generation of missionaries was headed by a confident and autocratic new bishop Gabriele Grioglio, who condemned many Chinese practices and threw his energies into making the practice of Catholicism more similar to Europe. Chinese priests, led by those trained in Naples, protested to Rome, but without effect, and found themselves reduced to the role of assistants to the Europeans. Machang, where Li had been based, was a centre of several disputes as newly arrived Italian missionaries criticised local practices. They dismantled the institutions that Li had created, in the teeth of much opposition from local Catholics. The money from Li's dining club was taken from its members and used to build a new church with any remainder to be handed over to the parish priest.[26]

Toward the end of the nineteenth century Lu'an became a separate diocese under Dutch missionaries, who developed the tiny village of Zhaojialing, where Li had hidden during the persecutions of the 1810s, as a diocesan pilgrimage site. Li's cave chapel was preserved but was soon dominated by a massive new baroque church on the top of the hill. It was paid for by European money and was ultimately blown up by the communist Red Army during World War II.[27]

As a result of these changes Christianity came to be seen as a religion that had been introduced by foreigners and had always been controlled by them. In Machang Li's grave, which was moved in the late nineteenth century to the courtyard of a new Gothic church, has been lost, and elderly villagers in 2018 claimed to me that their ancestors converted to Christianity at the time of the Dutch missionaries. In Zhaojialing up in the hills people remembered Li as Father Mie, the unusual surname that he took after the embassy. A notice in the village church says that he was the first to bring the gospel to the area, and people associate him with the little cave chapel on the side of the hill that they have carefully preserved. However, so strong is the perception of Christianity as a foreign religion that, even though the notice in the church describes Li as having come from Gansu, people assume that he must have been a foreigner. He Tianzhang, the Chinese priest from Macao who most probably did make the first converts in the village but never stayed there long, is recorded only in the archives and the works of Italian missionary historians, while Li Zibiao's astonishing achievements as a Chinese who studied in eighteenth-century Europe and interpreted before the Qianlong emperor have disappeared.[28]

Neither George Thomas Staunton nor Li Zibiao was ever entirely forgotten, but the interconnected eighteenth-century world in which they operated became so irrelevant that it was hard even to imagine. By the late nineteenth century their stories no longer made sense in the larger narratives people told about the world, and they appeared only in the footnotes of careful historians. Their lives did indeed seem to be no more than the shadow of a passing cloud on a summer day.

Conclusion

LANGUAGES ARE IMPORTANT, and interpreters have power in diplomatic negotiations because translation is not a simple process. Some years ago Lydia Liu argued that the process of translation in nineteenth- and early twentieth-century China created super-signs, that is, paired Chinese-English words that gathered round them clusters of meanings in the two languages, and that these super-signs had a political impact. The pairing of the Chinese word *yi* and the English word "barbarian" is the powerful example with which she starts.[1] Looking at the history of interpreting illuminates the political nature of a much broader range of translation choices and their role in negotiations.

Li Zibiao and George Thomas Staunton were men formed in the eighteenth century, and their interpreting reflected their world. Li Zibiao interpreted for the Macartney embassy in terms intended to minimise differences and achieve a successful outcome for the negotiations. The Macartney embassy has usually been understood as a failure because it failed to achieve any British negotiating goals, but this was not Li's criterion for success. His aim was the much more balanced one of achieving an outcome acceptable to both sides, and when Macartney departed with plans for a future embassy and Li himself was able to go safely on to Macao he had succeeded. George Thomas Staunton shared a similar mindset as an interpreter. At his father's insistence, he learned both Latin and Chinese as a child primarily through being immersed in the spoken language, and as a young man his translations were guided by the Chinese merchants and their staff who had long facilitated the trade. His natural bent was for book learning, and he was far more successful as a written translator than an interpreter, but he translated before the existence of a Chinese-English dictionary and had to learn through conversation and discussion with his Chinese colleagues in the trade. The result was translation that minimised difference and emphasized what was shared between the two cultures.

Set against these two is the approach of Robert Morrison, who learned Chinese as an adult by sheer grit and determination in order to translate the Bible, which expressed a truth that he believed could not be paraphrased. Morrison began by creating a dictionary and for the purposes of his translation searched for the true meanings of words in China's classical philosophy. All this made him in time, as Staunton said, the better scholar of Chinese, but his precise and literal translations made Chinese strange and different to English readers. It was Morrison's approach that influenced the later nineteenth-century translators and interpreters: he trained several of them in their early days in the East India Company, others used his dictionary and its successors, and his method was much closer to English school methods of language teaching. The alienating effect of the resulting translations also fitted with ideas of cultural difference and political hierarchy.

Staunton and Morrison knew that there is no simple solution to these problems of expressing the ideas of one culture in the language of another. Choosing words in translation is more than a case of right and wrong. They worked together for the East India Company and were close friends partly because each was the only person who fully understood the difficulty of the tasks the other was undertaking.

In the twentieth century developing models of machine interpreting and the professionalisation and feminisation of interpreting had the effect of concealing the difficulties of these decisions and thus undervaluing the role of the interpreter. This is now very obvious for twenty-first-century China, where political debates are again conducted in an archaic jargon alien to English speakers. Where Qing officials debated policy in Confucian terms of border disputes and the respectful submission of the English king, contemporary Chinese bureaucrats argue in set phrases drawn from a

Chinese-inflected Marxism almost equally confusing when literally translated into English. Scholars have spent much time debating whether Chinese political decision makers actually believe these terms, a problem that intersects with important debates in international relations about the power of ideology in influencing foreign policy. However, how to convey these ideas in English remains a serious problem.

Because interpreters have power and successful diplomatic interpreting usually requires someone who has spent a considerable part of their life in another culture, interpreting has also continued to be dangerous when states come into conflict. Li Zibiao wrote after he finished interpreting for the Macartney embassy that only someone who was extremely stupid would have undertaken such a dangerous task—and that was before there was any real conflict between China and Britain. With the British navy becoming increasingly active on the south China coast, Staunton's friends Wu Yacheng and Li Yao ended up in exile in Xinjiang, and Staunton himself left China never to return after the Jiaqing emperor threatened to punish him in the same way. This book has argued that these dangers provide an answer to the question of why political decision makers in China were so ignorant of Britain in the mid-nineteenth century.

Knowledge is not something that simply spreads and increases. It is possible to lose knowledge, and there were strange absences of knowledge in Britain as well as in China. The Jesuit and other Catholic European missionaries of the seventeenth and eighteenth centuries had a deeply impressive knowledge of the Chinese language. Francesco Jovino, who lived with Li Zibiao's family, wrote several books in Chinese. And yet in London in the 1790s the Italian Antonio Montucci was trying to understand Chinese texts by decoding them from first principles even though there were Chinese seamen living by the docks at the other end of the city. Social class was a crucial factor here, as was the absence of knowledge in written form. Elite men with scholarly pretensions expected to learn from books. The reason George Thomas Staunton was the one English person who really learned Chinese successfully in this period was that his father had what was at the time a highly eccentric belief in learning all languages by childhood immersion.

In China the problems caused by the absence of knowledge were far more serious because in the early nineteenth century China faced a rich, technologically advanced, and structurally expansionist Britain emerging from the vast military struggles of the Napoleonic Wars. As in Britain lack of knowledge of foreign languages was a key issue, and social class and the absence of written texts were major reasons for this. In neither China nor Britain did adult elite men wish to study from seamen and servants. However, in China there was the added problem of danger. Fears about loyalty in a situation of military tension made it extraordinarily dangerous to be known to have extensive knowledge of the other side. Interpreters and translators were on the front line in facing these risks. And as in many political contexts, but particularly a highly centralised and autocratic system like Qing China, the problems were exacerbated by the fact that controlling what knowledge was presented to the decision maker was one of the most effective means of influencing his decisions. When we say that China was ignorant of the Western threat, we mean, above all, that the Daoguang emperor was ignorant, but the information he was presented with was inevitably partial.

These problems too exist in our own day, not so much with China but for people in parts of the Arabic-speaking world, where the United States has been at war. There too interpreters have been placed in positions of extreme risk because they are perceived to be too close to the other side. Many have fled their native countries. Moreover, major political decisions have been made without information that was known but not presented to the decision makers at the crucial moment, and there is rising academic interest in the study of these kinds of ignorance.

The story of Li Zibiao as a boy leaving his home in China's far northwest for Naples, learning Latin and Greek and Hebrew, making friends with a future duke, and travelling through Europe during the French revolutionary wars, is an extraordinary one. Staunton's experiences as a child meeting the Qianlong emperor, watching A Hiue flying a Chinese kite he had made in a Wiltshire village in the 1790s and putting together a Chinese pamphlet that helped introduce vaccination to China, are almost equally unexpected. These are stories that show us the origins of the globalised world that we live in. Experiences of living between two cultures, coming to understand them and forming lasting friendships across them, were rare then, but are shared by many people today.

Their tragedy was that the same process of contact and interaction ultimately produced the tensions between states that made their lives impossible. Li and Staunton were fortunate in that both lived on into old age. If their knowledge of foreign countries was not appreciated, at least they were alive and not living in exile. When Lin Zexu arrived in Li Zibiao's hometown of Liangzhou and wrote poems expressing the depth of his anger at the Opium War, this was no longer a world that allowed for Li Zibiao's story with his friendships that crossed the world and his deep belief in a philosophy that transcended differences between cultures. In the aftermath of the Opium War imperialism, and a nationalism focussed on resisting imperialism, were central to China's relations with the West. Imperialism and nationalism grew out of the complex interconnected eighteenth-century world in which Staunton and Li lived and worked. Imperialism was its shadow side even in the early nineteenth century, and imperialism and nationalism were its outcome. Their later domination meant that the far more complex world that preceded this time not only ceased to exist but was forgotten.

This book has been about the dangers of interpreting and how those dangers increased as the political situation between China and Britain became more hostile. Interpreters were at risk because their ability to empathise with the other side and, quite literally, speak their language meant that their loyalties could never be entirely clear, but complex identities should not prevent us from seeing the value of the interpreter's work. The lives of Li Zibiao and George Thomas Staunton remind us of the vital importance of languages and translation in our understanding of other cultures, and the value of the years of study that allow us to listen, empathise, and understand when others speak and to explain ourselves to them. It is only with this knowledge of other cultures that together we can build a future for the interconnected world that we live in today.

ACGOFM   Archivio della Curia Generalizia dell'Ordine
dei Fratri Minori, Rome

AION   Archivio Istituto Universitario Orientale
Napoli

APF   Archivio Storico di Propaganda
Fide, Rome

BL   British Library, London

GT   George Thomas Staunton Papers, Duke
University Library

FHA   First Historical Archives, Beijing

IOR   India Office Records, British Library

Macartney   George Macartney Papers, Cornell University
Cornell MS   Library

TNA   The National Archives, London

GLOSSARY

chen	臣
chen ming Sidangdong	臣名斯當東
chiyu	敕諭
da Qing guo	大清國
Da Qing lü li	大清律例
daban	大班
dufu	督撫
fan	番
gong	貢
gongshi	貢使
gongshun	恭順
huangdi	皇帝
jianmin gouchuan	奸民勾串
Jiating jianghua	家庭講話
jingbao	京報
jinshi	進士
juan	卷
kou	叩
koutou	叩頭
li	禮
man	蠻
manyi	蠻夷
mei	梅
pengyou	朋友
Qianziwen	千字文
Sanguo yanyi	三國演義
Sanzijing	三字經
shawen	沙文
shiqiang	恃彊
ting	聽
tongshi	通事
wo guo wang	我國王
xiyangren	西洋人
xunfu	巡撫
yi	夷
yimu	夷目
yuanchen	遠臣

yuanguan	遠官
yuefu gongshun	悅服恭順
Zhongguo	中國
Zhonghua	中華
zongdu	總督

Introduction

1. Macartney, *Embassy to China*, 122–23; G. L. Staunton, *Authentic Account*, 2:229–34.

2. *Qing Gaozong (Qianlong) yuzhi shiwen quanji*, 9:581; Evelyn S. Rawski, *The Last Emperors: A Social History of Qing Imperial Institutions* (Berkeley: University of California Press, 1998), 6.

3. India Office Records [IOR] G/12/92, Macartney to Dundas, 9 Nov. 1793; Archivio Storico di Propaganda Fide [APF], SOCP 68:623 Ly, 20 Feb. 1794.

4. GT Staunton Papers, Diary, 14 Sept. 1793.

5. Barrow, *Travels in China*, 7.

6. Harrison, "Qianlong Emperor's Letter to George III."

7. Fairbank, *Chinese World Order*; Tingyang Zhao, "Rethinking Empire from a Chinese Concept 'All-under-heaven' (Tianxia)," *Social Identities* 12, no. 1 (2006); Perdue, "Tenacious Tributary System."

8. Keliher, *Board of Rites*.

9. Wang, *Remaking the Chinese Empire*; Zhang Shuangzhi, *Qingdai chaoqin zhidu yanjiu*.

10. Amsler, Harrison, and Windler, "Introduction."

11. Wang, *White Lotus Rebels and South China Pirates*.

12. Wang Hongzhi, *Fanyi yu jindai Zhongguo*.

13. Torikai, *Voices of the Invisible Presence*.

14. G. T. Staunton, *Remarks on the British Relations*, 36; Liu, *Clash of Empires*; Chen, *Merchants of War and Peace*, 82–102.

15. Margareta Bowen et al., "Interpreters and the Making of History," in *Translators through History*, ed. Jean Delisle and Judith Woodsworth (Amsterdam: John Benjamins, 1995).

16. Nancy L. Hagedorn, "'A Friend to Go Between Them': The Interpreter as Cultural Broker during Anglo-Iroquois Councils, 1740–70," *Ethnohistory* 35, no. 1 (1988).

17. APF SOCP 68:612 Ly, 20 Feb. 1794.

18. Grégoire Mallard and Linsey McGoey, "Strategic Ignorance and Global Governance: An Ecumenical Approach to Epistemologies of Global Power," *British Journal of Sociology* 69, no. 4 (2018).

19. *Yapian zhanzheng dang'an shiliao*, 1:673; Mao, *Qing Empire and the Opium War*.

20. Fatica, "Gli alunni del *Collegium Sinicum* di Napoli."

21. Chen, *Chinese Law in Imperial Eyes*.

22. Jami, *Emperor's New Mathematics*; Nicolas Standaert, *The Intercultural Weaving of Historical Texts: Chinese and European Stories about the Emperor Ko and His Concubines* (Leiden: Brill, 2016).

23. Van Dyke, *Canton Trade*; Wong, *Global Trade in the Nineteenth Century*; May Bo Ching, "The Flow of Turtle Soup from the Caribbean via Europe to Canton, and Its Modern American Fate," *Gastronomica* 16, no. 1 (2016).

24. Chen Guodong, *Qingdai qianqi de Yue haiguan*; Lai Huimin, *Qianlong huangdi de hebao*; Hanser, *Mr. Smith Goes to China*.

Chapter 1: The Li Family of Liangzhou

1. ACGOFM MH 23–4 Libro della recezione de collegiali alla prima pruova, 33; ACGOFM Missioni 53 Raccolta di lettere, Liu 1781.

2. G. L. Staunton, *Authentic Account*, 1:389.

3. *Tang shi sanbai shou* 唐詩三百首 [Three hundred Tang poems], ed. Qiu Xieyou 邱燮友 (Taibei: Sanmin shuju, 1973), 357; Li Dingwen 李鼎文, *Gansu wenshi conggao* 甘肅文史叢稿 [Collected essays on Gansu literature and history] (Lanzhou: Gansu renmin chubanshe, 1986), 130.

4. Li Yukai, *Li Yukai yigao jicun*, 26; *Ming Qing shilu, juan* 1003 QL 41/2/14; ACGOFM Missioni 53 Raccolta di lettere, Kuo to Ly 1787.

5. Archivum Romanum Societatis Iesu, Jap.Sin. 105 II Sinarum Historia 1681–1707, 319, 341.

6. Souciet, *Observations mathématiques*, 1:35, 176–77; Louis Pfister, *Notices biographiques et bibliographiques sur les Jésuites de l'ancienne mission de Chine 1552–1773* (Shanghai: Imprimerie de la Mission Catholique, 1932), 1:530–34, 584–86.

7. Giovanni Battista Maoletti da Serravalle 葉宗賢, APF SC Indie 12:136, Serravalle, 2 Aug. 1712; APF SOCP 27:319, Serravalle, 4 Aug. 1704.

8. Gianstefano Remo, *Della Nolana ecclesiastica storia* (Napoli: Stamperia Simoniana, 1757), 526; APF SC Indie 14:597 Serravalle, 8 Aug. 1719; APF SC Indie 14:577 Ottaiano, 20 July 1720; APF SC Indie 16:305–6 Ottaiano, 10 Aug. 1722; APF SC Indie 16:840 Memorie dalla Cina dell anno 1724; APF SC Indie 19:711 Supplemento delle Memorie 1728; APF SC Indie 18:413 Memorie degli affari concernenti varie occorenze delle missioni, 20 Dec. 1726.

9. Remo, *Della Nolana ecclesiastica*, 526–27; Zetzsche, *Bible in China*, 26–27; Francesco Jovino 参傳世, *Moxiang shengong lüeshuo* 默想神工略說 [A brief account of the spiritual task of meditation], Österreichische Nationalbibliothek MS.

10. *Wuwei shi minzu zongjiao zhi*, 229. This wrongly identifies the missionary concerned as Etienne Lefevre, who did not work in Liangzhou.

11. *Qing zhongqianqi xiyang tianzhujiao*, 1:123–24; APF SC Indie 31:297 Liu, 1766.

12. Fu Boquan 傅伯泉, "Wuwei lidai de shangye maoyi" 武威歷代的商業貿易 [Wuwei's trade through the ages], *Wuwei wenshi* 武威文史 3 (2006): 58; *Wuwei jianshi*, 140–42.

13. Zeng Jiwei 曾繼衛, "Ouyang Yongqi yu qi 'Dun jielian tiaoyue'" 歐楊永椅與其 《敦節儉條約》, *Wuwei wenshi* 2 (2004): 207.

14. Vitalis Josephus Kuo郭元性, APF SC Indie 30:248 Kuo, 15 Oct. 1761; Margiotti, *Cattolicismo nello Shansi*, 300–304; Di Fiore, *Lettere di missionari*, 169, 272.

15. ACGOFM MH 23–4 Libro della recezione de collegiali, 33.

16. ACGOFM Missioni 53 Raccolta di lettere, Kuo to Ly 1787; First Historical Archives 02-01-006-003082-0002 Guo Shixun QL 56/10/17; Pan Yikui, *Wuwei qijiu zhuan*, 4:14; *Wuwei jianshi*, 134–35.

17. APF SOCP 55:6 Lieu, 17 June 1764; Archivio Istituto Universitario Orientale Napoli (AION) 16.1.8 Kuo 1792.

18. Perdue, *China Marches West*, 368; Li Dingwen, *Gansu wenshi conggao*, 214; *Wuwei tongzhi. Da shi juan* 武威通志. 大事卷 [Wuwei gazetteer. Major events volume] (Lanzhou: Gansu renmin chubanshe, 2007), 33.

19. Pan Yikui, *Wuwei qijiu zhuan*, 2:8–9, 4:14–15; Li Yukai, *Li Yukai yigao jicun*, 26.

20. Liang Fen 梁份, *Qinbian jilue* 秦邊紀略 [Notes on the borders of Qin], 2:1–2, 20; Li Dingwen, *Gansu wenshi conggao*, 175.

21. *Wuwei jianshi*, 40.

22. Xiangyun Wang, "Tibetan Buddhism at the Court of Qing: The Life and Work of lCang-skya Rol-pa'i-rdo-rje (1717–86)" (PhD diss., Harvard University, 1995), 48.

23. *Wuwei shi minzu zongjiao zhi*, 126–27.

24. Pan Yikui, *Wuwei qijiu zhuan, juan* 2:9–11.

25. Fatica, *Matteo Ripa e il Collegio*, 325–26.

26. ACGOFM Missioni 53 Raccolta di lettere, Vita compendiosa D. Cajetani Siu; APF SOCP 59:480–3 Simonetti, Memorie per l'occurrenze 1772; *Elenchus alumnorum*, 2–4; APF SC Collegi vari 10, Nota degli alunni Cinesi del Coll. Della S.F. di Gesu 1773; APF SC Collegi vari 10, Nota degli alunni esistenti nel Collegio della S. Familia di Gesu Cristo, 30 Nov. 1776; APF SOCP 59:500 Simonetti, 16 Jan. 1773.

27. APF SOCP 59:483 Simonetti, Memorie per l'occurrenze, 1772; AION 42.2 Corrispondenza dell' Europa, Fatigati, 5 Feb. 1783; APF SC Indie 33:490 Palladini, 20 June 1773; APF SC Indie 33:506 Palladini, 26 July 1773; AION 6 Borgia to Fatigati, 9 Nov. 1773.

Chapter 2: George Leonard Staunton of Galway

1. G. T. Staunton, *Memoirs of the Chief Incidents*, 191.

2. G. T. Staunton, *Memoir of the Life and Family*, 2, 143; AION 16.1.15 Ly to Massei, 14 May 1792; McNulty, "Genealogy of the Anglo-Norman Lynches"; G. A. Hayes-McCoy, "A Relic of Early Hanoverian Rule in Galway," *Journal of the Galway Archaeological and Historical Society* 23, nos. 1/2 (1948): 62–63.

3. G. T. Staunton, *Memoir of the Life and Family*, 10; National Archives of Ireland, Documents re Stauntons' interest in the tithes of the parish of Cargine and property in Grenada 999/241/1/4A.

4. G. T. Staunton, *Memoir of the Life and Family*, 11, 160–65, 176; James Hardiman, *History of the Town and County of Galway* (Dublin: Folds and Sons, 1820), 318.

5. G. T. Staunton, *Memoir of the Life and Family*, 12–13; McNulty "Genealogy of the Anglo-Norman Lynches," 32.

6. GT Staunton Papers, G. L. Staunton to sister 1 Dec. 1774; Sir George Leonard Staunton papers, BL, G. L. Staunton to Margaret Staunton, 26 July 1768.

7. *Public Advertiser*, 12 Sept. 1772.

8. G. T. Staunton, *Memoir of the Life and Family*, 200–201; Brodie, *Works of Sir Benjamin Collins Brodie* (London: Longman, Green, Longman, Roberts & Green, 1865), 1:3; GT Staunton Papers, Brodie to G. L. Staunton, 3 June 1781.

9. Barrow, *Some Account of the Public Life*, 1:2–6, 37–38, 327; Roebuck et al., *Macartney of Lisanoure*, 1, 12, 16–20, 23, 57, 61–62, 131; Bodleian Library, George Macartney Papers, Eng. lett. c. 385 Macartney to Jane Macartney, 22 Mar. 1784.

10. Christine Y. Ferdinand, *Benjamin Collins and the Provincial Newspaper Trade in the Eighteenth Century* (Oxford: Oxford University Press, 1997), 28–47.

11. G. T. Staunton, *Memoir of the Life and Family*, 17 (date corrected from correspondence), 393; Sir George Leonard Staunton Papers, BL, Jane Staunton's marriage portion, 22 July 1771, George Leonard Staunton Will; National Archives of Ireland, Stauntons' interest in the tithes of the parish of Cargine, 999/241/2/3 Collins to Staunton, 27 Jan. 1778.

12. G. T. Staunton, *Memoir of the Life and Family*, 57.

13. G. T. Staunton, *Memoir of the Life and Family*, 271.

14. G. T. Staunton, *Memoir of the Life and Family*, 57.

15. National Archives of Ireland, Stauntons' interest in the tithes of the parish of Cargine 999/241 2/3 Collins to Staunton, 27 Jan. 1778.

16. G. L. Staunton, *Authentic Account*, 1:172–73.

17. Bodleian Library, George Macartney Papers, Eng. misc. f. 533:2 Commonplace book.

18. Sir George Leonard Staunton Papers, BL, Staunton to parents, 5 Feb. 1780; G. T. Staunton, *Memoir of the Life and Family*, 22.

19. Sir George Leonard Staunton Papers, BL, Staunton to parents, 5 Feb. 1780.

20. Lucy S. Sutherland, "Lord Macartney's Appointment as Governor of Madras, 1780: The Treasury in East India Company Elections," *English Historical Review* 90 (1975).

21. Bodleian Library, Papers of Lady Louisa Stuart, Eng lett. c. 387 Jane Macartney to Caroline Dawson, 18 May 1785.

22. G. T. Staunton, *Memoir of the Life and Family*, 268.

23. GT Staunton Papers, Brodie to G. L. Staunton, 3 June 1781.

24. GT Staunton Papers, Jane Staunton to G. L. Staunton, 30 June 1781.

25. GT Staunton Papers, Jane Staunton to Margaret Staunton, 6 Sept. 1781.

26. GT Staunton Papers, Margaret Staunton to Jane Staunton, 5 Apr. 1784.

27. Hanser, "From Cross-Cultural Credit to Colonial Debt."

28. Bodleian Library, George Macartney Papers, Eng. misc. b. 162: 56 Short account of affairs on the Coromandel Coast. See also Davies, *Private Correspondence of Lord Macartney*, ix.

29. G. T. Staunton, *Memoir of the Life and Family*, 264.

30. Bodleian Library, George Macartney Papers, Eng. hist. c. 66:2 Coote to Macartney, 15 Aug. 1781, 25 Aug. 1781, 2 Sept. 1781; Eng. hist. c. 68 Tourndary to Coote, 28 Nov. 1781; Barrow, *Some Account of the Public Life*, 1:188–91.

31. Davies, *Private Correspondence of Lord Macartney*, xi; G. T. Staunton, *Memoir of the Life and Family*, 272–76; Barrow, *Some Account of the Public Life*, 1:174–97.

32. G. T. Staunton, *Memoir of the Life and Family*, 37.

33. Journal of the Commissioners, 1:95, 2:7, 2:169–70; *Minutes of Evidence Taken before the Right Honourable House of Lords, in the Lords Committees Appointed to Take into Consideration So Much of the Speech of His Royal Highness the Prince Regent as Relates to the Charter of the East India Company* (London, 1813), 96–97; Sinnappah Arasaratnam, *Merchants, Companies and Commerce on the Coromandel Coast 1650–1740* (Delhi: Oxford University Press, 1986), 257–58.

34. Journal of the Commissioners, 1:86.

35. Journal of the Commissioners, 1:89.

36. Journal of the Commissioners, 2:170.

37. Journal of the Commissioners, 2:170.

38. Journal of the Commissioners, 2:169.

39. Barrow, *Some Account of the Public Life*, 1:604–5; Bodleian Library, George Macartney Papers, Eng. lett. c. 386:106 Macartney to Jane Macartney, Eng. misc. f 533:14 commonplace book.

40. GT Staunton Papers, G. T. Staunton to Jane Staunton, 30 Dec. 1805; Barrow, *Some Account of the Public Life*, 1:321, 1:334–35; G. T. Staunton, *Memoir of the Life and Family*, 10.

Chapter 3: Li Zibiao's Education in Naples

1. Carlo Antonio Pilati, *Voyages en différens pays de l'Europe en 1774, 1775 et 1776* (A La Haye: C. Plaat et Comp., 1772), 2:160–62; Helen Hills, "Cities and Virgins: Female Aristocratic Convents in Early Modern Naples and Palermo," *Oxford Art Journal* 22, no. 1 (1999): 45; Romeo De Maio, *Società e vita religiosa a Napoli nell'età moderna (1656–1799)* (Napoli: Edizioni scientifiche italiane, 1971), 14–20, 104–5, 340–46; John Moore, *A View of Society and Manners in Italy* (Dublin: Price, W. Watson et al., 1781), 2:226.

2. Ugo Di Furia, "Arte e storia nella chiesa e collegio della Sacra Famiglia ai Cinesi"; Michele Fatica, "I percorso della mostra," in Fatica, *Matteo Ripa e il Collegio*.

3. Tiziana Iannello, "Il collegio dei cinesi durante il decennio francese (1806–15)," in Fatica and D'Arelli, *La missione cattolica in Cina*, 268–69; Michele Fatica, "Per una mostra bibliografica ed iconografica su Matteo Ripa, il Collegio dei Cinesi e il Real Collegio Asiatico (1682–1888)," in Fatica and D'Arelli, *La missione Cattolica in Cina*, 13; APF SC Collegi vari 9:63 Fatigati, 20 Mar. 1762.

4. *Elenchus alumnorum.*

5. APF SC Collegi vari 10:296 Alunni levantini, 26 Nov. 1773; APF SC Collegi vari 10:289–91 Fatigati, 19 Dec. 1773.

6. Fatica, "Gli alunni del *Collegium Sinicum* di Napoli," 535; *Elenchus alumnorum*, 4.

7. Giacomo Di Fiore and Michele Fatica, "Vita di relazione e vita quotidiana nel Collegio dei Cinesi," in Fatica, *Matteo Ripa e il Collegio*, 37–39; APF SC Collegi vari 10:126 Avvisi dalla Consulta, 1767.

8. APF SC Collegi vari 9:181 Fatigati, 27 Oct. 1764; APF SC Collegi vari 10: 173 Fatigati, 25 May 1770; APF SC Collegi vari 10: 291 Fatigati, 19 Dec. 1773; APF SC Collegi vari 11:142 Fatigati, 19 Jan. 1782; APF SC Collegi vari 11:294 Palladini, 15 Oct. 1785; Di Fiore and Fatica, "Vita di relazione"; Elio Catello, *Cineserie e Turcherie nel '700 napoletana* (Napoli: Sergio Civita Editore, 1982), 12.

9. APF SC Collegi vari 12:150 Massei, 15 Mar. 1794.

10. Alfredo Zazo, *L'Istruzione pubblica e privata nel Napoletana (1767–1860)* (Castello: Il Solco, 1927), 28–29; Giuseppe Maria Galanti, *Breve descrizione della città di Napoli e del suo contorno*, ed. Maria Rosaria Pelizzari (Napoli: Di Mauro, 2000), 235.

11. APF SC Collegi vari 10:296 Alunni levantini, 26 Nov. 1773.

12. AION 42.2 Corrispondenza dell'Europa, Marrini, 26 July 1795; APF SRC Collegi vari 10:557 Fatigati, 5 Dec. 1778.

13. AION 16.1.15 Ly to Borgia, 10 Sept. 1826; Luigi Borgia, "Famiglia Borgia" (Nobili Napoletani), www.nobili-napoletani.it.

14. ACGOFM MH 23-2 Variae erudit (this is the notebook of a Chinese student at the college that includes both Chinese and Latin writing; a poem on a portrait of Jacobus Nien 嚴雅谷, a student from Zhangzhou in Fujian who died in 1762, suggests that it was probably compiled in the later 1760s); APF SC Collegi vari 10:240 Nota degli alunni 1771; ACGOFM Missioni 53 Raccolta di lettere 95, Wan, 4 Sept. 1772; Cappello, *Progymnasmatum eloquentiae*; Cappello, *Hieropaedia Catholica*; Giambattista Vico, *On the Study Methods of Our Time*, ed. and trans. Elio Gianturco (Indianapolis: Bobbs-Merrill, 1965).

15. APF SC Collegi vari 10:142 Sersale, 24 June 1767; ACGOFM MH 10-1:13 Regole e costituzione della Congregazione e Collegio della Sacra Famiglia di Gesù Cristo.

16. APF SC Collegi vari 10:275 Nota degli alunni cinesi; APF SC Collegi vari 11:147 Stato di signori alunni cinesi del 1782.

17. These are Lin Yunming 林雲銘, ed., *Guwen xiyi* 古文析義 [Principles of classical prose], 1682 (Standaert, "Jean François Foucquet's Contribution," 415) and Lü Yunzhuang 呂芸莊, ed., *Kaojuan jingrui* 考卷精銳 [Selected examination essays], 1842 (Fatica, *Matteo Ripa e il Collegio*, 324).

18. APF SRC Collegi Vari 10:142 Sersale, 24 June 1767.

19. ACGOFM MH 23-2 Variae erudit.

20. APF SC Collegi vari 11:6 Fatigati, 16 Dec. 1779; APF SC Collegi vari 11:147 Stato di signori alunni cinesi del 1782.

21. Elvira Choisi, "Intellectuals and Academies," in *Naples in the Eighteenth Century: The Birth and Death of a Nation State*, ed. Girolamo Imbruglia (Cambridge: Cambridge University Press, 2000), 127–28.

22. Cappello, *Hieropaedia Catholica*.

23. APF SC Collegi vari 10:514–5 Nota d'alunni cinese nota d'alunni levantini 1778.

24. Cappello, *Progymnasmatum eloquentiae*, 1; ACGOFM Missioni 53 Raccolta di lettere, Wan, 8 Oct. 1784.

25. APF SC Collegi vari 10:442 Nota degli alunni, 30 Nov. 1776.

26. APF SC Collegi vari 10:515 Nota d'alunni cinese, 6 Jan. 1778; APF SC Collegi vari 11:6 Fatigati, 16 Dec. 1779.

27. APF SC Collegi vari 11:95 Fatigati, 31 Mar. 1781.

28. ACGOFM MH 7–7 Libro degli aggregati, Ignazio Orlando "D. Gennaro Fatigati."

29. ACGOFM MH 7–7 Libro degli aggregati, 1791 Giovanni Maria Borgia; ACGOFM MH 7–7 Libro degli recezione de novizii, Giovanni Maria Borgia; Luigi Borgia, "Famiglia Borgia" (Nobili Napoletani), www.nobili-napoletani.it.

30. APF SC Collegi vari 11:5–6 Fatigati, 16 Dec. 1779.

31. APF SC Collegi vari 11:94 Fatigati, 31 Mar. 1781.

32. Michele Fatica, *Seats and Palaces of Università degli Studi di Napoli "L'Orientale" (1729-2005)* (Napoli: Università degli Studie di Napoli "L'Orientale," 2005), 19; Fatica and D'Arelli, *La missione cattolica in Cina*, 234.

33. *Elenchus alumnorum*, 2–5.

34. APF SC Collegi vari 12:62 Massei, 31 Oct. 1789.

35. APF SC Collegi vari 10:136–42 Sersale, 24 June 1769; John A. Davis, *Naples and Napoleon: Southern Italy and the European Revolutions (1780-1860)* (Oxford: Oxford University Press, 2006), 25–26.

36. ACGOFM Missioni 53 Raccolta di lettere, Wan, 8 Oct. 1784.

37. P. Ovidi Nasonis, *Tristium Libri Quinque; Ibis; Ex Ponto Libri Quattuor; Halieutica Fragmenta*, ed. S. G. Owen (Oxford: Oxford University Press, 2015), *Epistulae ex Ponto*, 1:4, 1:8, 3:5, 5:9.

38. Di Fiore and Fatica, "Vita di relazione," 41.

39. APF SC Collegi vari 12:18 Massei, 27 Feb. 1787.

40. AION 16.1.15 Ly, 23 Mar. 1806; *Elenchus alumnorum*, 4.

41. APF SC Collegi vari 12:281–92 Phan, 29 Nov. 1816.

42. APF SC Collegi vari 10:136–42 Sersale, 24 June 1769; *Elenchus alumnorum*, 24–25; ACGOFM Missioni 53 Raccolta di lettere, Ly, 24 Aug. 1792.

43. *Elenchus alumnorum*, 23; APF SC Collegi vari 10:136–42 Sersale, 24 June 1769; APF SC Collegi Vari 10:123 Avvisi dalla consulta della congregazione, 1767; Di Fiore, *Lettere di missionari*, 11.

44. APF SC Esami dei missionarii 3:59, 9 Jan. 1791; APF SOCP 67:183 Cho 19 Feb. 1791; ACGOFM Missioni 53 Raccolta di lettere, Ly, 28 Dec. 1790, 14 Jan. 1791.

Chapter 4: George Thomas Staunton's Peculiar Childhood

1. G. T. Staunton, *Memoirs of the Chief Incidents*, 7, 187–88.

2. Sir George Leonard Staunton Papers, BL, G. L. Staunton to Ann Staunton, 6 Nov. 1782.

3. GT Staunton Papers, [Peter Brodie] Verses presented to my Dear Wife on Her Birthday 1782.

4. GT Staunton Papers, Margaret Staunton to Jane Staunton, 5 Apr. 1784.

5. Sir George Leonard Staunton Papers, BL, G. L. Staunton to Collins, 28 Jan. 1785; GT Staunton Papers, Blake to Jane Staunton, 1 Oct. 1784.

6. G. T. Staunton, *Memoir of the Life and Family*, 3, 316.

7. National Archives of Ireland 999/241/2/4 Last Will and Testament of Benjamin Collins; *A Pretty Book of Pictures for Little Masters and Misses, or, Tommy Trip's History of Beasts and Birds with a Familiar Description of Each in Verse and Prose to Which Is Prefix'd the History of Little Tom Trip Himself, of His Dog Jouler, and of Woglog the Giant*, 14th ed. (London: B.C. Collins, 1787).

8. G. T. Staunton, *Memoir of the Life and Family*, 319; Anna Barbauld, *Lessons for Children. Part I. For Children from Two to Three Years Old* (London: J. Johnson, 1800), 9–10.

9. G. T. Staunton, *Memoir of the Life and Family*, 316–17.

10. G. T. Staunton, *Memoir of the Life and Family*, 319.

11. *The Times*, 23 June 1792, 2.

12. Bodleian Library, George Macartney Papers, Eng. Lett. c. 385:136 Jane Macartney to Pitt, 31 July 1785.

13. Bodleian Library, George Macartney Papers, Eng. Misc. b. 162:39 Commonplace book.

14. Bowen, *Business of Empire*; Hanser, *Mr. Smith Goes to China*, 120–26, 140–43.

15. G. T. Staunton, *Memoir of the Life and Family*, 305; Sir George Leonard Staunton Papers, BL, Staunton to Menzies, 10 Apr. 1788.

16. Pritchard, "Crucial Years of Early Anglo-Chinese Relations," 237.

17. Sir George Leonard Staunton Papers, BL, Staunton to Menzies, 10 Apr. 1788.

18. Old Bailey Proceedings Online, June 1789, trial of Leonard Wilson (t17890603-2); GT Staunton Papers, Curtis to G. L. Staunton, 1 Feb. 1788.

19. GT Staunton Papers, G. L. Staunton to Egan, Jan. 1790; G. T. Staunton *Memoir of the Life and Family*, 324.

20. National Archives of Ireland, Documents re Stauntons' interest in the tithes of the parish of Cargine 999/241/2/12.

21. Old Bailey Proceedings Online, June 1789, trial of Leonard Wilson (t17890603-2).

22. GT Staunton Papers, Beck to G. L. Staunton, 10 Mar. 1791.

23. Barrow, *Auto-biographical Memoir*, 43, see also 5, 8–13, 17, 40, 45.

24. GT Staunton Papers, Diary, 6 June 1791.

25. GT Staunton Papers, Diary, 15 June 1791.

26. Berg, "Britain, Industry and Perceptions of China."

27. GT Staunton Papers, Diary 21, 30 June 1791.

28. Smith, *Memoir and Correspondence*, 382–83.

29. Linnean Society of London, Correspondence of Sir James Edward Smith, Hope to Smith, 28 Sept. 1792.

30. Barrow, *Some Account of the Public Life*, 1:391.

Chapter 5: Finding an Interpreter for an Embassy to China

1. IOR G/12/91:28 Macartney to Dundas, 4 Jan. 1792. Punctuation added for clarity.

2. G. L. Staunton, *Authentic Account*, 1:40; GT Staunton Papers, Diary, 24 Jan. 1792 and 15, 22, 25 Jan. 1792.

3. G. T. Staunton, *Memoir of the Life and Family*, 348.

4. GT Staunton Papers, Hamilton to G. L. Staunton, 21 Feb. 1792.

5. APF SC Collegi vari 12:131 Massei to Antonelli, 17 Mar. 1792; APF SC Collegi vari 10:276 Nota degli Alunni Cinesi [1773].

6. ACGOFM Missioni 53 Raccolta di lettere, Ly [1792]. Li refers to a "dictionarium sinicolatinum" suggesting that this was probably the manuscript *Dictionarium Latino-Italico-Sinicum* compiled by Carlo Orazi da Castorano in Beijing in 1732 and later presented by G. T. Staunton to the Royal Asiatic Society (RAS George Thomas Staunton Box 1). See Hui Li, Il Dictionarium Latino-Italico-Sinicum di Carlo Orazi da Castrorano O.F.M. (1673–1755) (Sapienza PhD diss. 2014/2015), 4, 66.

7. APF SC Collegi vari 10:442 Nota degli alunni, 30 Nov. 1776; APF SC Collegi vari 12:18 Massei, 27 Feb. 1787.

8. *Elenchus alumnorum*, 4; APF SC Collegi vari 11:95 Fatigati, 31 Mar. 1781.

9. APF Collegi vari 12:133 Massei to Antonelli, 27 Mar. 1792; APF SOCP 67:518 Cho, 4 Apr. 1792.

10. AION 42.2.8 Cho and Ly, 23 Mar. 1792; Sir George Leonard Staunton Papers, BL, Staunton to Macartney, 11 Aug. 1792.

11. ACGOFM Missioni 53 Raccolta di lettere, Ly, 26 Mar. 1792.

12. ACGOFM Missioni 53 Raccolta di lettere, Ly, 26 Mar. 1792, 13 Apr. 1792; APF SOCP 67:518 Cho, 4 Apr. 1792.

13. ACGOFM Missioni 53 Raccolta di lettere, Ly, 13 Apr. 1792.

14. ACGOFM Missioni 53 Raccolta di lettere, Ly, 13 Apr. 1792; Sir George Leonard Staunton Papers, BL, Staunton to Macartney, 11 Aug. 1792.

15. G. T. Staunton, *Memoirs of the Chief Incidents*, 11; G. T. Staunton, *Memoir of the Life and Family*, 341–42.

16. ACGOFM Missioni 53 Raccolta di lettere, Ly, 14 May 1792.

17. ACGOFM Missioni 53 Raccolta di lettere, Ly, 14 May 1792.

18. ACGOFM Missioni 53 Raccolta di lettere, Ly, 14 May 1792.

19. AION 16.1.15 Ly to Massei, 14 May 1792.

20. AION 16.1.15 Ly to Massei, 14 May 1792.

21. G. T. Staunton, *Memoir of the Life and Family*.

22. AION 16/1/16 Cho and Ly, 22 May 1792.

23. *General Evening Post*, 9 June 1792, 8; Barrow, *Auto-biographical Memoir*, 43; *Morning Herald*, 31 Jan. 1792, 4.

24. ACGOFM Missioni 53 Raccolta di lettere, Ly, 7 July 1792.

25. ACGOFM Missioni 53 Raccolta di lettere, Ly, 7 July 1792, 24 Aug. 1792.

26. ACGOFM Missioni 53 Raccolta di lettere, Ly, 24 Aug. 1792.

27. For clothing and Christianity as markers of identity, see Roxann Wheeler, *The*

Complexion of Race: Categories of Difference in Eighteenth-Century British Culture (Philadelphia: University of Pennsylvania Press, 2000), 7; Dror Wahrman, *Making of the Modern Self: Identity and Culture in Eighteenth-Century England* (New Haven, Conn.: Yale University Press, 2004), 93, 177.

28. *Gazetteer and New Daily Advertiser*, 3 May 1792, 6.

29. Bodleian Library, George Macartney Papers, Eng. Misc. b. 162:81 Commonplace book.

30. Burney, *Journals and Letters*, 1:195.

31. AION 16/1/16 Cho and Ly, 22 May 1792; Roebuck et al., *Macartney of Lissanoure*, 21; Basil Gray, "Lord Burlington and Father Ripa's Chinese Engravings," *British Museum Quarterly* 22, nos. 1/2 (1960); IOR/G/12/91: 28–9 Macartney to Dundas, 4 Jan. 1792.

32. ACGOFM Missioni 53 Raccolta di lettere, Ly, 7 July 1792.

33. Toyo Bunko, Japan, MS-42 Macartney Papers, Dundas to Macartney, 29 July 1792; Baring Archives NPI C.22.7 Baring to Dundas, 28 Aug. 1792.

34. William Shepherd, "Ode on Lord Macartney's Embassy to China," in *New Oxford Book of Eighteenth Century Verse*, ed. Roger Lonsdale (Oxford: Oxford University Press, 1984), 787–88.

35. ACGOFM Missioni 53 Raccolta di lettere, Nien, 24 Aug. 1792, Ly to Borgia, 24 Aug. 1792; APF SOCP 67:517 Nien, 3 July 1792.

36. Pritchard, "Instructions of the East India Company," 375–77; G. L. Staunton, *Authentic Account*, 1:41–42.

37. ACGOFM Misisoni 53 Raccolta di lettere, Ly to Borgia, 24 Aug. 1792; Macartney, *Embassy to China*, 64.

38. Barrow, *Auto-biographical Memoir*, 50.

39. Barrow, *Some Account of the Public Life*, 2:501.

40. GT Staunton Papers, Reeves to G. L. Staunton, 4 July 1792.

41. Antonio Montucci, *Proposals for Publishing by Subscription a Treatise on the Chinese Language with an Answer to the Reviewers* (London, 1801), 2, 8; Antonio Montucci, *De studiis sinicis in imperiali athenaeo petropolitano* (Berlin: Ludovicus Quien, 1808), 9–11; Villani, "Montucci, Antonio." For Fourmont, see Stephanus Fourmont, *Meditationes Sinicae* (Paris: Lutetiae Parisiorum, 1737), xi–xxvi, 8–9, 19–22; Leung, *Etienne Fourmont*, 146–55.

42. Wu, *Traduire la Chine au XVIIIe siècle*, 75–83.

43. Stifler, "Language Students," 48–50.

44. IOR/L/MAR/C/902:33 Statement of the circumstances attending the maintenance and return of Lascars and Chinese, 11 Feb. 1811; *Morning Chronicle and London Advertiser*, 29 July 1782, 4; Old Bailey Proceedings Online, Dec. 1804, trial of Ann Alsey, Thomas Gunn (t18041205-56), Sept. 1800, trial of William Rayer and Charles Moren (t18000917-29); Fisher, *Counterflows to Colonialism*, 151; Price, *Chinese in Britain*, 18–28, 31–33.

45. Steven Shapin, *A Social History of Truth: Civility and Science in Seventeenth-Century England* (Chicago: University of Chicago Press, 1994).

Chapter 6: Crossing the Oceans

1. GT Staunton Papers, Diary, 15 and 16 Sept. 1792; Macartney, *Embassy to China*, 23; Macartney, Journal of a Voyage, 1–2; G. H. Williams, "The Western Defences of Portsmouth Harbour 1400–1800," *Portsmouth Papers* 30 (1979).

2. *General Evening Post*, 19–21 June 1792, 5; Macartney, Journal of a Voyage, 1–2; Bodleian Library, George Macartney Papers, Eng. misc. f. 534:32–3 Commonplace book; Burney, *Journals and Letters*, 1:193, 207; National Library of Ireland MS 8799 (3) Documents relating to the pedigree of the Winder family.

3. *Biographical Memoir of Sir Erasmus Gower*, 3–6, 11–14, 50.

4. Barrow, *Auto-biographical memoir*, 45.

5. Barrow, *Auto-biographical Memoir*, 49.

6. Bodleian Library, George Macartney Papers, Eng. misc. f. 534:32–3 Commonplace book; Proudfoot, *Biographical Memoir of James Dinwiddie*, 130–31.

7. G. L. Staunton, *Authentic Account*, 1:88; Baring Archives NP1.C25 Nepean to Baring, 3 Sept. 1792; IOR L/MAR/B 267 GA Henry Lindeman Journal, 1 Nov. 1793; Macartney, Journal of a Voyage, 2; Bodleian Library, George Macartney Papers, Eng. misc. b. 162:79 List of persons belonging to the China embassy; H. V. Bowen, "Privilege and Profit: Commanders of East Indiamen as Private Traders, Entrepreneurs and Smugglers, 1760–1813," *International Journal of Maritime History* 19, no. 2 (2007).

8. Sir George Leonard Staunton Papers, BL, Staunton to Pigott, 23 Sept. 1792.

9. G. L. Staunton, *Authentic Account*, 1:55, 195–96, 319; Anderson, *Narrative of the Embassy*, n.p.; Macartney, Journal of a Voyage, 2; Alexander, Journal, 2 July 1793; *Biographical Memoir of Sir Erasmus Gower*, 90.

10. G. L. Staunton, *Authentic Account*, 1:58; *Lloyds Evening Post*, 29–31 Aug. 1792, 214; J. C. Hüttner, *Voyage a la Chine* (Paris: J.J. Fuchs, 1798), 32–33, 61–63, 79, 147, 245.

11. G. L. Staunton, *Authentic Account*, 1:58 (this translation is not G. L. Staunton's English version but is closer to George Thomas's simple Latin); G. T. Staunton, *Memoirs of the Chief Incidents*, 18–19.

12. GT Staunton Papers, Diary, 25 Sept. 1792.

13. G. L. Staunton, *Authentic Account*, 1:195; GT Staunton Papers, Diary, 14 Apr. 1793.

14. GT Staunton Papers, Diary, 13 Jan. 1793.

15. G. L. Staunton, *Authentic Account*, 1:195; Barrow, *Travels in China*, 105–6; Alexander, Journal, 88.

16. Wellcome Trust MSS 3352 Macartney Journal of a Voyage, 3–9.

17. GT Staunton Papers, Diary, 13 Oct. 1792.

18. Bodleian Library, George Macartney Papers, Eng. misc. f 533 Commonplace book, 29; Peyrefitte, *Collision of Two Civilisations*, 35 (I have been unable to identify Peyrefitte's source, but it seems likely to have been a different transcription of Macartney's journal).

19. Gower, Journal of His Majesty's ship Lion, 11; G. L. Staunton, *Authentic Account* 1:87; Bodleian Library, George Macartney Papers Eng. misc. f. 533:21

Commonplace book; Karen Harvey, "Ritual Encounters: Punch Parties and Masculinity in the Eighteenth Century," *Past and Present* 214 (2012).

20. GT Staunton Papers, Diary, 19 Nov. 1792.

21. GT Staunton Papers, Diary, 3, 8, 13 Dec. 1792; Macartney, Journal of a Voyage, 75–94.

22. G. L. Staunton, *Authentic Account*, 1:174; Barrow, *Voyage to Cochinchina*, 91.

23. Gower, Journal of HMS Lion, 19–20; G. L. Staunton, *Authentic Account* 1:193.

24. GT Staunton Papers, Diary, 10 Jan. 1793 and 7 Jan. 1793.

25. GT Staunton Papers, Diary, 12, 20, and 21 Jan. 1793.

26. Gower, Journal of HMS Lion, 31.

27. GT Staunton Papers, Diary, 25 Jan. 1793; Gower, Journal of HMS Lion, 31.

28. Macartney, Journal of a Voyage, 72; J. K. Laughton and Andrew Lambert, "Ommanney, Sir John Acworth," in *Oxford Dictionary of National Biography* (2004), www.oxforddnb.com.

29. *Hampshire Advertiser*, 29 Sept. 1832.

30. GT Staunton Papers, Diary, 18, 22, 25, and 28 Feb. 1793.

31. GT Staunton Papers, Diary, 5 Mar. 1793; Barrow, *Voyage to Cochinchina*, 169, 203.

32. Alexander, Album, BL WD 959, 280–82; Bodleian Library, George Macartney Papers, Eng. misc. f. 533:9 Commonplace book.

33. Barrow, *Voyage to Cochinchina*, 203; GT Staunton Papers, Diary, 6 Mar. 1793; Alexander, Journal, 11 June 1793; IOR/G/12/93 2:220–1 Secret Committee, 31 June 1793; Kwee, *Political Economy of Java's Northeast Coast*, 14, 162–71.

34. Bodleian Library, George Macartney Papers, Eng. misc. f. 533:15 Commonplace book. See also Mcgee, "Putting Words in the Emperor's Mouth."

35. Macartney, Journal of a Voyage, 111–12; Barrow, *Voyage to Cochinchina*, 204–6.

36. GT Staunton Papers, Diary, 1 Mar. 1793; Macartney, Journal of a Voyage, 113–18; Barrow, *Voyage to Cochinchina*, 208.

37. Macartney, Journal of a Voyage, 128.

38. ACGOFM Missioni 53 Raccolta di lettere, Nien, 13 Apr. 1793.

39. Gower, Journal of HMS Lion, 62; AION 27/10/5 Nien, 13 Apr. 1793; Bodleian Library, George Macartney Papers, Eng. misc. f. 533:29 Commonplace book; G. L. Staunton, *Authentic Account*, 1:283.

40. AION 27/10/5 Nien, 13 Apr. 1793.

Chapter 7: Other Possible Interpreters

1. *Elenchus alumnorum*, 2; ACGOFM Missioni 53 Raccolta di lettere, Zen, 15 Mar. 1786; Wu Weiwei 吳巍巍, "Mingmo Ai Rulüe zai Zhangzhou de chuanjiao huodong yu shehui fanxiang" 明末艾儒略在漳州的傳教活動與社會反響 [Giulio Aleni's missionary activities in Zhangzhou in the late Ming and society's response], *Zhangzhou shifan daxue xueyuan xuebao (zhexue shehui kexue xueban)* 漳州師範學院學報 (哲學社會科學版) 3 (2010); Erik Zürcher, ed., *Kouduo Richao Li Jiubiao's Diary of*

Oral Admonitions: A Late Ming Christian Journal (Sankt Augustin: Institut Monumenta Serica, 2007), 94–97.

2. For the original text, see Morse, *Chronicles of the East India Company*, 2:244–47. The Chinese version referred to here is the National Archives (TNA), London, FO 1048/1 King's letter to Kienlung, Sept. 1793 (with many thanks to Xu Maoming who found this document). For evidence that this translation was made by Yan Kuanren, see G. L. Staunton, *Authentic Account*, 1:388; Macartney Cornell MS DS117, 329 Credentials to King of Vietnam. See also Ji Qiufeng, "Majiaerni shi Hua shijian," who argues convincingly that the letter was translated during the voyage, but not having seen the version in the British archives assumes this applies to the version in the Qing archives (for which see chapter 8).

3. Macartney, Journal of a Voyage, 196–202.

4. IOR G/12/93 3:33 Macartney to Dundas, 18 June 1793; Barrow, *Voyage to Cochinchina*, 270; Wang, *White Lotus Rebels and South China Pirates*, 210–20.

5. Macartney, Journal of a Voyage, 209; Gower, Journal of HMS Lion, 62–64; Alexander, Journal, 28 May 1793.

6. Macartney, Journal of a Voyage, 217–29; Barrow, *Voyage to Cochinchina*, 291–92; Anderson, *Narrative of the Embassy*, 54.

7. Wang Hongzhi, "Magaerni shi Hua de fanyi wenti"; Macartney Cornell MS DS116 vol. 11 Edicts communicated by Thomas Fitzhugh QL20/3/25.

8. AION 42/2/8 Ly, 16 May 1793.

9. APF SOCP 68:611 Ly, 20 Feb. 1794; AION 42/2/8 Ly, 16 May 1793.

10. APF SOCP 68:487 Marchini, 3 Nov. 1793; *Qingdai Taiwan guanxi yuzhi dang'an huibian* 清代台灣關係諭旨檔案彙編 [Collected and edited archives relating to Qing dynasty Taiwan], ed. Taiwan shiliao jicheng bianji weiyuanhui 台灣史料集成編輯委員會 (Taibei: Xingzhengyuan wenhua jianshe weiyuanhui, 2004), 2:163–65; *Qinding pingding Taiwan jilue* 欽定平定台灣紀略 [Imperially authorised account of the pacification of Taiwan] (1788) (Wenyuange siku quanshu edition), 42:21, 50:20, 54:24, 56:13; *Ping Tai jishi benmo* 平臺紀事本末 [A full account of the pacification of Taiwan], ed. Taiwan yinhang 臺灣銀行 (Taibei: Zhonghua shuju, 1958), 46, 49, 62; FHA 02-01-006-003082-0002 Guo Shixun QL56/10/17.

11. G. L. Staunton, *Authentic Account* 1:389.

12. AION 27/10/5 Nien 8 July 1793.

13. Yin Guangren 印光任 and Zhang Rulin 張汝霖, *Aomen jilue* 澳門記略 [Brief notes on Macao], repr., *Sikuquanshu cunmu congshu, shi 221* 四庫全書存目叢書。史 221 (Jinan: Qilu shushe, 1996), 1:35, 2:53.

14. Li Changsen, *Jindai Aomen fanyi shigao*, 70–82; Liu Fang and Zhang Wenqin, *Qingdai Aomen zhongwen dang'an huibian*.

15. English text: Pritchard, "Instructions of the East India Company," 2:375–77. See also Li Changsen, *Jindai Aomen fanyi shigao*, 69; IOR G/12/93 2:33–9 Secret Committee, 11 Oct. 1792.

16. Chinese text: *Yingshi Magaerni*, 216. See also Chen Xianpo, "Zhuti wenhua dui yizhe"; Liu Li, "Zhong Ying shouci zhengshi."

17. Chen Guodong, *Qingdai qianqi de Yue haiguan*, 171–97.

18. Pritchard, "Instructions of the East India Company," 376.

19. IOR G/12/93 2:21–2 Browne, 25 Nov. 1792.

20. Chinese text: *Yingshi Magaerni*, 217. See also *Yingshi Magaerni*, 279; Liu Fang and Zhang Wenqin, *Qingdai Aomen zhongwen dang'an huibian*, 1:357–58 (which illustrates the use of the Macao translators' office in similar circumstances).

21. Chinese text: *Yingshi Magaerni*, 91–92.

22. IOR G/12/93 2:204 Secret Committee, 1 June 1793, 2:227–28 Secret Committee, 22 June 1793, 2:318 Secret Committee, 29 Sept. 1793 (arrangements were presumably the same for Antonio as for his brother); *Yingshi Magaerni*, 309–10; G. L. Staunton, *Authentic Account*, 2:14; Barrow, *Some Account of the Public Life*, 1:346.

23. APF SOCP 68:485–6 Marchini, 3 Nov. 1793; IOR/G/12/92:141, Macartney to Dundas, 9 Nov. 1793; Macartney Cornell MS DS117, 252 Macartney journal notes, 22 June 1793.

24. FHA 02-01-006-003087-0006 Agui QL56/12/16; APF SOCP 68:487 Marchini, 3 Nov. 1793.

25. Guo Chengkang 郭成康, *Shiba shiji de Zhongguo zhengzhi* 十八世紀的中國政治 [Chinese politics of the eighteenth century] (Taibei: Zhaoming, 2001), 319–20.

26. *Yingshi Magaerni*, 309–13; Alexander, Journal, 22 July 1793.

27. Barrow, *Travels in China*, 55. See also Alexander, Journal, 2 July 1793; Macartney, *Embassy to China*, 65; Macartney Cornell MS DS117, 252 Macartney journal notes, 3 July 1793; *Yingshi Magaerni*, 314–15.

28. *Yingshi Magaerni*, 314; Barrow, *Auto-biographical Memoir*, 59.

29. G. L. Staunton, *Authentic Account* 1:416–17.

30. *Yingshi Magaerni*, 320–21; G. L. Staunton, *Authentic Account*, 1:417. See also Chen, *Chinese Law in Imperial Eyes*, 25–65.

31. G. L. Staunton, *Authentic Account*, 1:432.

32. G. L. Staunton, *Authentic Account*, 1:432–33; *Yingshi Magaerni*, 396, 65.

33. Macartney, *Embassy to China*, 67; *Yingshi Magaerni*, 336.

34. Macartney Cornell MS DS117, 265 Narrative of Events, 21 July 1793; Lai Huimin, *Qianlong huangdi de hebao*, 150; Li Huan, *Guochao qi xian leizheng chubian*, 96:38–39; *Yingshi Magaerni*, 82, 340–41.

35. Wang Wenxiong: G. L. Staunton, *Authentic Account*, 1:485–87; *Qing shi gao xiaozhu*, 12:9553. Qiao Renjie: Liu Wenbing 劉文炳 *Xugou xian zhi* 徐溝縣志 [Xugou county gazetteer] (Taiyuan: Shanxi renmin chubanshe, 1992), 432; *Haocun Qiao shi jiapu* 郝村喬氏家譜 [The genealogy of the Qiao family of Hao village] (2005), 27; Macartney, *Embassy to China*, 98, 248; Lai Huimin, *Qianlong huangdi de hebao*, 150.

36. G. L. Staunton, *Authentic Account*, 1:488.

37. G. L. Staunton, *Authentic Account*, 1:488–89.

38. *Yingshi Magaerni*, 374; G. L. Staunton, *Authentic Account*, 1:489.

39. Barrow, *Travels in China*, 105–6, 267.

40. Alexander, Journal, 28 July 1793; IOR G/12/92:27–32 Macartney's Instructions to his Attendants; Macartney Cornell MS DS117, 252 Macartney journal notes, 22 July–3 Aug. 1793.

41. Bodleian Library, George Macartney Papers, Eng. misc. f. 533:9 List made out by Sir George Staunton.

42. Macartney Cornell MS DS117, 271 Gower to Macartney, 16 Sept. 1793.

43. IOR/G/12/93 2:347–8 Macartney, 6 Aug. 1793.

Chapter 8: Li Zibiao as Interpreter and Mediator

1. APF SOCP 68:611–2 Ly, 20 Feb. 1794.

2. Macartney Cornell MS DS117, 265 Narrative of events, 21 July 1793; Anderson, *Narrative of the Embassy*, 58.

3. Macartney Cornell MS DS117, 265 Narrative of events, 21 July 1793.

4. *Yuzhi shi wuji* 御製詩五集, in *Qing Gaozong (Qianlong) yuzhi shiwen quanji*, vol. 9 *juan* 83:23, see also 80:26–27.

5. *Yuzhi shi wuji*, 83:23a.

6. *Yingshi Magaerni*, 347–48; Wang Zhonghan 王鐘翰, ed., *Qing shi liezhuan* 清史 列傳 [Biographies for Qing history] (Beijing: Zhonghua shuju, 1987), 7:2078.

7. *Yingshi Magaerni*, 343–45; Li Huan, *Guochao qi xian leizheng chubian*, 8:4451–52.

8. Macartney, *Embassy to China*, 248; *Ming Qing gong cang Zhong xi shangmao dang'an*, 4:2153–60; Preston M. Torbert, *The Ch'ing Imperial Household Department: A Study of Its Organization and Functions, 1662-1796* (Cambridge, Mass.: Council on East Asian Studies, Harvard University, 1977), 122–23; Chang Te-Ch'ang, "The Economic Role of the Imperial Household in the Ch'ing Dynasty," *Journal of Asian Studies* 31, no. 2 (1972); Lai Huimin, *Qianlong huangdi de hebao*, 112–13, 140–51, 232.

9. Macartney, *Embassy to China*, 71.

10. Macartney, *Embassy to China*, 71.

11. Macartney, *Embassy to China*, 74–76; National Library of Ireland MS8799(1) E Winder papers, Account by Edward Winder of a journey in China, 1; *Yingshi Magaerni*, 360.

12. Fairbank, *Chinese World Order*; John E. Wills, *Embassies and Illusions: Dutch and Portuguese Envoys to K'ang-hsi 1666-1687* (Cambridge, Mass.: Council on East Asian Studies, Harvard University, 1984); James L. Hevia, *Cherishing Men from Afar: Qing Guest Ritual and the Macartney Embassy of 1793* (Durham, N.C.: Duke University Press, 1995), 9–15; Wang, *Remaking the Chinese Empire*, 3–9.

13. Anderson, *Narrative of the Embassy*, 67; *Qinding da Qing huidian shili*, 505:2, 7–8.

14. *Qinding da Qing huidian shili*, 514:6, 10–12; Li Nanqiu, *Zhongguo kouyi shi*, 441–47; Kim, "Foreign Trade and Interpreter Officials"; Chan, "'Chinese Barbarian Officials.'"

15. Alexander, Album, BL WD 959, 60, 155; IOR G/12/93:368 Macartney to Dundas, 9 Nov. 1793; *Yingshi Magaerni*, 40.

16. *Qinding da Qing huidian shili*, 56:4–6.

17. IOR G/12/91:85 Macartney to Dundas, 17 Mar. 1792.

18. National Portrait Gallery, London, James Gillray, "The Reception of the Diplomatique and his Suite at the Court of Pekin," 1792; Macartney, *Embassy to China*, 84–85; Bodleian Library, George Macartney Papers, Eng. misc. f. 533:16 Commonplace book (undated note).

19. Macartney, *Embassy to China*, 86–87; Mosca, *Frontier Policy to Foreign Policy*, 129–53.

20. The conversation took place on 16 Aug. 1793. It is unclear whether Fukang'an had reached Beijing at this point. FHA 03-0260-008 Fukang'an QL 58/7/5; Barrow, *Travels in China*, 115–16.

21. Macartney, *Embassy to China*, 86.

22. Macartney, *Embassy to China*, 90; Anderson, *Narrative of the Embassy*, 94.

23. Macartney, *Embassy to China*, 90.

24. Barrow, *Travels in China*, 88; Hüttner, *Voyage a la Chine*, 31.

25. Barrow, *Travels in China*, 102, 108; Macartney, *Embassy to China*, 93; Proudfoot, *Biographical Memoir of James Dinwiddie*, 44.

26. *Yingshi Magaerni*, 1; Macartney, *Embassy to China*, 80; APF SOCP 68:609 Ly, 20 Feb. 1794.

27. Proudfoot, *Biographical Memoir of James Dinwiddie*, 46; IOR G/12/92:58–9 Macartney to Dundas, 9 Nov. 1793.

28. Proudfoot, *Biographical Memoir of James Dinwiddie*, 46; IOR G/12/92:59 Macartney to Dundas, 9 Nov. 1793.

29. APF SOCP 68:612 Ly, 20 Feb. 1794.

30. Macartney, *Embassy to China*, 92; APF SOCP 68:612 Ly, 20 Feb. 1794; *Yingshi Magaerni*, 375.

31. APF SOCP 68:609 Jacobus Li, 25 Dec. 1793 and 68:612 Ly, 20 Feb. 1794.

32. IOR G/12/92:57 Macartney to Dundas, 9 Nov. 1793.

33. Macartney, *Embassy to China*, 99–100; G. L. Staunton, *Authentic Account*, 142–43; Wang Hongzhi, "Magaerni shi Hua de fanyi wenti."

34. Barrow, *Some Account of the Public Life*, 2:422; Macartney, *Embassy to China*, 99–100; G. L. Staunton, *Authentic Account*, 142–43; GT Staunton Papers, G. T. Staunton to G. L. Staunton, 27 Mar. 1800.

35. APF SOCP 68:611 Ly 20 Feb. 1794.

36. Barrow, *Travels in China*, 422.

37. *Yingshi Magaerni*, 50–51.

38. Georg Simmel, *The Sociology of Georg Simmel*, trans. Kurt H. Wolff (London: Collier-Macmillan, 1950), 145–50.

Chapter 9: Speaking to the Emperor

1. *Yingshi Magaerni*, 562; Anderson, *Narrative of the Embassy*, 120–21.

2. Macartney, *Embassy to China*, 114; Hüttner, *Voyage a la Chine*, 61–63.

3. Macartney, *Embassy to China*, 114.

4. APF SOCP 68:610 Ly, 25 Dec. 1793.

5. Macartney, *Embassy to China*, 117, 124; Anderson, *Narrative of the Embassy*, 138; GT Staunton Papers, Diary, 8 Sept. 1793; Millward et al., *New Qing Imperial History*; Daniel Mark Greenberg, "A New Imperial Landscape: Ritual, Representation, and Foreign Relations at the Qianlong Court" (PhD diss., Yale University, 2015).

6. GT Staunton Papers, Diary, 8 Sept. 1793; Macartney, *Embassy to China*, 118–21; G. L. Staunton, *Authentic Account*, 2:209–13; APF SOCP 68:612 Ly, 20 Feb. 1794.

7. Original English text: Morse, *Chronicles of the East India Company*, 2:244. Yan Kuanren version: TNA FO 1048/1 King's letter to Kienlung, Sept. 1793. Almeida version: *Yingshi Magaerni*, 162–64. For the attributions, see Qin Guojing 秦國經, "Cong Qing gong dang'an kan Yingshi Magaerni fang Hua lishi shishi" 從清宮檔案看英使馬嘎爾尼訪華歷史事實 [Looking at the historical facts of the British envoy Macartney from the archives in the Qing palace], in *Yingshi Magaerni*, 74; Wang Hongzhi, "Magaerni shi Hua de fanyi wenti," 128.

8. *Yingshi Magaerni*, 148–49; Durand, "Langage bureaucratique et histoire," 97–98.

9. *Yingshi Magaerni*, 535.

10. APF SOCP 68:609 Ly, 25 Dec. 1793; AION 27/10/9 Ly, 20 Feb. 1794. See also G. L. Staunton, *Authentic Account*, 2:215; Macartney, *Embassy to China*, 119; Huang Yilong, "Yinxiang yu zhenxiang."

11. IOR G/12/93 3:72 Macartney to Dundas, 9 Nov. 1793. See also G. L. Staunton, *Authentic Account*, 2:220–22; Macartney, *Embassy to China*, 120–21; Yoon, "Prosperity with the Help of 'Villains.'"

12. Macartney, *Embassy to China*, 121; IOR G/12/92:68 Macartney to Dundas, 9 Nov. 1793.

13. *Yingshi Magaerni*, 51.

14. *Yingshi Magaerni*, 150–51; Macartney, *Embassy to China*, 121.

15. Greenberg, "New Imperial Landscape," 91–182; Keliher, *Board of Rites*, 72; Stephen H. Whiteman, "From Upper Camp to Mountain Estate: Recovering Historical Narratives in Qing Imperial Landscapes," *Studies in the History of Gardens & Designed Landscapes* 33, no. 4 (2013).

16. Macartney Cornell MS DS117, 371 Parish, 28 Feb. 1794; G. L. Staunton, *Authentic Account*, 2:225–29; Zhaolian, *Xiaoting zalu*, 375–76.

17. Keliher, *Board of Rites*, 154. For the Wanshu yuan ciyan tu 萬樹園賜宴圖, see Greenberg, "New Imperial Landscape," 113–16, 128.

18. Macartney, *Embassy to China*, 122.

19. GT Staunton Papers, Diary, 14 Sept. 1793.

20. GT Staunton Papers, Diary, 14 Sept. 1793.

21. G. L. Staunton, *Authentic Account*, 2:230–38; APF SOCP 68:610 Ly, 25 Dec. 1793; APF SOCP 68:613 Ly, 20 Feb. 1794; IOR/G/12/92:71 Macartney to Dundas, 9 Nov. 1793; Hüttner, *Voyage a la Chine*, 85–89; Macartney, *Embassy to China*, 124.

22. Anderson, *Narrative of the Embassy*, 148; GT Staunton Papers, Diary, 14 Sept. 1793.

23. GT Staunton Papers, Diary, 17 Sept. 1793.

24. GT Staunton Papers, Diary, 18 Sept. 1793.

25. *The Times*, 29 Sept. 1794, 3.

26. National Library of Ireland MS 8799 E Winder papers 1 Account by Edward Winder of a journey in China, 1793.

27. National Library of Ireland MS8799 (4) Wiley (illeg.) to Winder, 17 Feb. 1797.

28. Guan Shiming 管世銘, *Yunshantang shiji* 韞山堂詩集 [Collected poems of the Yunshan hall] (1802), 16:3. See also Liu Jiaju 劉家駒, "Yingshi Magaerni jinjian Qianlong huangdi de liyi" 英使馬戞爾尼覲見乾隆皇帝的禮儀 [The rituals for the English ambassador Macartney's meeting with the Qianlong emperor], in *Jindai Zhongguo chuqi lishi yantaohui lunwenji* 近代中國初期歷史研討會論文集 [Collected essays on the early history of modern China] (Taipei: Zhongyang yanjiuyuan, 1989).

29. Guan Shiming, *Yunshantang shiji*, 16:3.

30. *Qing Gaozong (Qianlong) yuzhi shiwen quanji*, vol. 9, *Yuzhi shi wuji*, 84:10–13.

31. Macartney, *Embassy to China*, 124–26; G. L. Staunton, *Authentic Account*, 2:240–48; Anderson, *Narrative of the Embassy*, 149.

32. Macartney, *Embassy to China*, 127–28; G. L. Staunton, *Authentic Account*, 2:343 (undated but this is the most likely occasion); IOR G/12/92:75 Macartney to Dundas, 9 Nov. 1793.

33. Mosca, *Frontier Policy to Foreign Policy*, 137–54; FHA 03-0259-066 Fukang'an QL58/6/22, 04-01-13-0093-007 QL58/6/11.

34. Macartney, *Embassy to China*, 127; *Song Wenqing gong sheng guan lu*, 119:257–68; Li Huan, *Guochao qi xian leizheng chubian*, 36:31; Ma Zimu, "Lun Qing chao fanyi."

35. Zhaolian, *Xiaoting zalu*, 318; *Song Wenqing gong sheng guan lu*, 275; Yoon, "Prosperity with the Help of 'Villains,'" 497.

36. Lai Huimin, *Qianlong huangdi de hebao*, 478–79; Chen Kaike, *Jiaqing shi nian*, 100–103.

37. *Song Wenqing gong sheng guan lu*, 285; *Qing shi gao xiaozhu*, 7:5420.

38. Macartney Cornell MS DS117, 17 Copy of a dispatch from the Ruling Senate, 1791; *Song Wenqing gong sheng guan lu*, 284; Fu, *Documentary Chronicle*, 309–16, 320–22; Afinogenov, *Spies and Scholars*, 177, 200.

39. Macartney, *Embassy to China*, 127. See also G. L. Staunton, *Authentic Account*, 256–57.

40. Gregory Afinogenov, "Jesuit Conspirators and Russia's East Asian Fur Trade, 1791–1807," *Journal of Jesuit Studies* 2, no. 1 (2015).

41. Anderson, *Narrative of the Embassy*, 149. See also Macartney, *Embassy to China*, 125; Hüttner, *Voyage a la Chine*, 93; GT Staunton Papers, Diary, 15 Sept. 1793.

42. Macartney, *Embassy to China*, 136–39; GT Staunton Papers, Diary, 18 Sept. 1793; Xiaoqing Ye, "Ascendant Peace in the Four Seas: Tributary Drama and the Macartney Mission of 1793," *Late Imperial China* 26, no. 2 (2005).

43. Hüttner, *Voyage a la Chine*, 112–17; Macartney, *Embassy to China*, 135; G. L. Staunton, *Authentic Account*, 256–58.

44. IOR/G/12/92 Macartney to Dundas, 9 Nov. 1793, 79, 83; Lai Huimin, *Qianlong huangdi de hebao*, 357–409.

45. Macartney Cornell MS DS117, 278 Macartney to Cho-chan-tong [Heshen], 3 Oct. 1793 Latin version.

46. *The Times*, 29 Sept. 1794, 3; Macartney Cornell MS DS117, 278 Macartney to Cho-chan-tong, 3 Oct. 1793.

47. Macartney, *Embassy to China*, 150; Macartney Cornell MS DS117, 278 Macartney to Cho-chan-tong, 3 Oct. 1793.

48. APF SOCP 68:613 Ly, 20 Feb. 1794; Fatica, "Gli alunni del *Collegium Sinicum di Napoli*."

49. *Yingshi Magaerni*, 59.

50. APF SOCP 68:610, Jacobus Ly, 25 Dec. 1793. See also Macartney, *Embassy to China*, 141.

51. *Yingshi Magaerni*, 59. For a later English translation, see Edmund Trelawney Backhouse and John Otway Percy Bland, *Annals and Memoires of the Court of Peking* (London: W. Heinemann, 1914), 322–31.

Chapter 10: Becoming an Invisible Interpreter

1. APF SOCP 68:620 Ly, 20 Feb. 1794.

2. GT Staunton Papers, Diary, 26 Sept. 1793; Macartney Cornell MS DS117, 259 Irwin to Macartney, 2 July 1793; Bodleian Library, George Macartney Papers, Eng. misc. f. 533:11 Commonplace book (undated note on Li Zichang's official dress suggests that Macartney met him and might need to identify him again); Barrow, *Travels in China*, 112–13.

3. APF SOCP 68:484 Marchini, 17 Dec. 1793.

4. William Jardine Proudfoot, *"Barrow's Travels in China": An Investigation* (London: George Philip and Son, 1861), 39.

5. Macartney, *Embassy to China*, 149.

6. APF SOCP 68:609–10 Ly, 25 Dec. 1793.

7. Macartney, *Embassy to China*, 150, 155–56.

8. *Yingshi Magaerni*, 60–62; GT Staunton Papers, Diary, 20 Oct. 1793.

9. Yang Zhongxi 楊鐘羲, *Xueqiao shihua xuji* 雪橋詩話續集 [Snowy Bridge poems and talk, additional collection] (1857), 6:85.

10. *Yingshi Magaerni*, 176–77.

11. *Yingshi Magaerni*, 405. See also Macartney, *Embassy to China*, 159.

12. *Yingshi Magaerni*, 405. See also Macartney, *Embassy to China*, 159–60.

13. Macartney, *Embassy to China*, 160–61, 178; G. L. Staunton, *Authentic Account*, 2:358.

14. Macartney, *Embassy to China*, 163.

15. Macartney, *Embassy to China*, 179; Yao Ying 姚瑩, *Shi xiao lu, Cunyin conglu* 識小錄, 寸陰叢錄 [A record of learning on minor matters, Collected records from spare moments], ed. Huang Jigeng 黃季耕 (Hefei: Huangshan shushe, 1991), 101.

16. *Yingshi Magaerni*, 415, 443; Macartney, *Embassy to China*, 177.

17. Macartney Cornell MS DS117, 308 Poirot to Macartney, 29 Sept. 1794; Macartney, *Embassy to China*, 166–67; *Yingshi Magaerni*, 437–40; IOR G/12/92:102, Macartney to Dundas, 9 Nov. 1793.

18. *Yingshi Magaerni*, 438.

19. *Yingshi Magaerni*, 438.

20. IOR G/12/92:353 Note for Cho-chan-tong, 9 Nov. 1793.

21. APF SOCP 68:614 Ly, 20 Feb. 1794.

22. AION 27/10/9 Ly, 20 Feb. 1794.

23. *Yingshi Magaerni*, 459.

24. *Yingshi Magaerni*, 478.

25. Zhaolian, *Xiaoting zalu*, 347, 459–60; *Qing shi gao xiaozhu*, 12:9479–81; Li Huan, *Guochao qi xian leizheng chubian*, 5:2960.

26. Macartney, *Embassy to China*, 176.

27. G. L. Staunton, *Authentic Account*, 2:470–71; FHA 03-0428-043 Changlin QL 53/5/27; Macartney, *Embassy to China*, 190.

28. Barrow, *Auto-biographical Memoir*, 114.

29. GT Staunton Papers, Diary, 11 Nov. 1793; Barrow, *Travels in China*, 523; Barrow, *Auto-biographical Memoir*, 139. Note: the identification of Zhu Gui depends on Barrow's 1847 memoir.

30. Barrow, *Auto-biographical Memoir*, 133.

31. Macartney, *Embassy to China*, 180–81; AION 27/10/9 Ly, 20 Feb. 1794.

32. IOR G/12/92:399 Macartney to Dundas, 23 Nov. 1793.

33. Macartney, *Embassy to China*, 184–85; APF SOCP 68:617 Ly, 20 Feb. 1794; Gower, Journal of HMS Lion, 96–97; *Yingshi Magaerni*, 198–99.

34. Macartney Cornell MS DS117, 333 Interpretatio verbalis responsi Imperatoris dictante Ciaan Zun tu.

35. Macartney, *Embassy to China*, 193.

36. *Yingshi Magaerni*, 198–99; Macartney Cornell MS DS117, 333 Interpretatio verbalis.

37. *Yingshi Magaerni*, 198–99; Macartney Cornell MS DS117, 333 Interpretatio verbalis.

38. Macartney, *Embassy to China*, 193.

39. Macartney, *Embassy to China*, 193; *Yingshi Magaerni*, 198–99.

40. Macartney, *Embassy to China*, 210.

41. *Zhanggu congbian* 掌故叢編 [Collected Historical Documents] 1 (1928; repr., Taibei: Guofeng chubanshe, 1964), 23; Wang Hongzhi, "Magaerni shi Hua de fanyi wenti," 134.

42. APF SOCP 68:618 Ly, 20 Feb. 1794; Macartney, *Embassy to China*, 205; *Ming Qing gong cang Zhong xi shangmao dang'an*, 4:2390–400; Fu, *Documentary Chronicle*, 327–31; IOR G/12/92:471–483 Viceroy's 1st and 2nd edicts; IOR G/12/93 3:316 Representation of Lord Macartney to the Viceroy.

43. IOR G/12/93 3:317 Representation of Lord Macartney; IOR G/12/93 3:289 Macartney to Browne, 22 Jan. 1794; Xu Dishan 許地山, ed., *Dazhong ji (Yapian zhanzheng qian Zhong Ying jiaoshe shiliao)* 達衷集 (鴉片戰爭前中英交涉史料) [Dazhongji (Historical documents from interactions between China and Britain before the Opium War)] (Shanghai: Shangwu yinshuguan, 1928), 169.

44. IOR G/12/92:445 Macartney to Dundas, 7 Jan. 1794.

45. Macartney, *Embassy to China*, 216–17.

46. Macartney Cornell MS DS117, 290 Draft journal, 13 Jan. 1794; Macartney, Journal of a Voyage, 47; IOR G/12/93 Macartney to Dundas, 25 Mar. 1793, 18 June 1793.

47. AION 27/10/9 Ly, 20 Feb. 1794.

48. APF SOCP 68:620 Ly, 20 Feb. 1794.

49. Proudfoot, *Biographical Memoir of James Dinwiddie*, 71.

50. Bodleian Library, George Macartney Papers, Eng. misc. f. 533:8 Commonplace book.

51. G. T. Staunton, *Memoir of the Life and Family*, 49–50.

52. APF SOCP 68:616 Ly, 20 Feb. 1794.

53. APF SOCP 68:620 Ly, 20 Feb. 1794; AION 27/10/9 Ly, 20 Feb. 1794.

54. APF SOCP 68:616 Ly, 20 Feb. 1794.

Chapter 11: Li Zibiao after the Embassy

1. APF SOCP 68:484 Marchini, 17 Dec. 1793.

2. *Biographical Memoir of Sir Erasmus Gower*, 38; Macartney Cornell MS DS 117, 290 Journal draft, 6, 12, and 24 Feb. 1794; APF SOCP 68:635 Marchini, 2 Mar. 1794; AION 27/10/9 Ly, 21 Feb. 1794; ACGOFM Missioni 53 Raccolta di lettere, Nien, n.d.

3. GT Staunton Papers, G. T. Staunton to G. L. and Jane Staunton, 25 Jan. 1800, G. T. Staunton to G. L. Staunton, 27 Mar. 1800, G. T. Staunton to Jane Staunton, 7 May 1801; TNA FO 1048/11/87 Copies of Chinese official documents about the Ashing case 1811. The link made here and later in this book between the Assing who went to England with the Stauntons and the later Assing (Wu Yacheng) known from the Qing and East India Company archives is circumstantial. All available details of their careers fit closely, and it is clear that the later Assing had a very close relationship with G. T. Staunton. However, Assing would have been a common name, and we do not have the surname of the young man who went to England, so it could also be that they are two different people.

4. APF SOCP 68:635 Marchini, 2 Mar. 1794. See also APF SOCP 68:621–8 Marchini, 17 Jan. 1794 (in Li's handwriting).

5. APF SOCP 69:153–4 Marchini, 17 Nov. 1794.

6. APF SOCP 69:254 Mandello, 18 Oct. 1794.

7. APF SC Indie 39:483 Ly, 3 Oct. 1795.

8. Margiotti, *Cattolicismo nello Shansi*, 89–114; APF SOCP 63:809 Kuo 1781; APF SOCP 69:385 Conforti, 30 Aug. 1799; *Tianzhujiao Changzhi jiaoqu jianshi*, 67. Machang is known to English readers as Horse Square Market in William Hinton, *Shenfan* (London: Secker & Warburg, 1983).

9. APF SC Cina 3:412 Landi, 2 Oct. 1807. See also ACGOFM Missioni 53 Raccolta di lettere, Guo to Li, 16 Mar. 1787; Bernward H. Willeke, ed., "The Report of the Apostolic Visitation of D. Emmanuele Conforti on the Franciscan Missions in Shansi, Shensi and Kansu (1798)," *Archivum Franciscanum Historicum* 84, nos. 1–2 (1991); APF SOCP 63:750 di Osimo, 26 Aug. 1782. It is possible that Li's new surname was a

translation back into Chinese of his English surname Plum as Mei (梅), but the records all give the Chinese character Mie (乜).

10. FHA 02-01-006-003213-0024 Changlin QL 60/1/21; APF SC Cina 2:142 Mandello, 1 Sept. 1803; Pan Yikui, *Wuwei qijiu zhuan*, 4:14–15; APF SC Indie 39:483 Ly, 3 Oct. 1795.

11. Willeke, "Report of the Apostolic Visitation," 265; ACGOFM Missioni 53 Raccolta di lettere, Ly, 15 Sept. 1798; *Qing shi gao xiaozhu*, 12:9553; Wang, *White Lotus Rebels and South China Pirates*, 41–80.

12. Wang, *White Lotus Rebels and South China Pirates*, 124–57.

13. *Qing shi gao xiaozhu*, 12:9468–69, 9480; Wang, *White Lotus Rebels and South China Pirates*, 151–53.

14. APF SC Cina 1a:440 Ly, 20 Dec. 1801. See also APF SC Cina 10:312 de Donato, 30 Oct. 1841.

15. ACGOFM Missioni 53 Raccolta di lettere Ly, 14 Aug. 1799; APF SC Cina 1a:552 Ly, 4 July 1802.

16. APF SOCP 69:387 Conforti, 30 Aug. 1799; APF SOCP 70:52 Indie Orientali Cina Ristretto 1802; APF SC Indie 39:826–7 Conforti 1799; APF SC Cina 1a:441 Ly, 20 Dec. 1801; APF SC Cina 2:131 Mandello, 9 Oct. 1803; Willeke, "Report of the Apostolic Visitation," 216–17; Henrietta Harrison, *Missionary's Curse*, 48.

17. APF SC Cina 1a:441 Ly, 20 Dec. 1801; APF SOCP 70:111–2 Indie Orientali Cina Pekino ristretto 1803; Willeke, "Report of the Apostolic Visitation," 216; Margiotti, *Cattolicismo nello Shansi*, 615–16.

18. APF SC Cina 14:275 da Moretta, 1851.

19. APF SC Cina 1a:441 Ly, 20 Dec. 1801.

20. AION 27/10/9 Ly, 21 Feb. 1794.

21. APF SC Cina 2:131–2 Mandello 1803; APF SC Cina 2:165 Ciang, 1803; APF SC Cina 3:603 da Signa 1808; APF SC Cina 3:789–90 U and Li, 4 Oct. 1810; APF SOCP 70:1 Conforti 1802.

22. ACGOFM Missioni 53 Raccolta di lettere Ly, nd.

23. AION 16/1/15 Ly, 3 July 1802.

24. AION 16/1/15 Ly, 3 July 1802.

25. ACGOFM Missioni 53 Raccolta di lettere Ly, 14 Aug. 1799; *Elenchus alumnorum*, 4.

26. AION 16/1/15 Ly, 7 Aug. 1799.

27. AION 16/1/15 Ly, 25 Feb. 1801.

28. ACGOFM Missioni 53 Raccolta di lettere, Ly, 30 July 1803.

29. Public Record Office of Northern Ireland, D572 Macartney Papers, 7/77 Ly, 25 Feb. 1801.

30. Public Record Office of Northern Ireland, D572 Macartney Papers 8/174 Plum, July 1802.

31. *Qing shi gao xiaozhu* 12:9554; Zhaolian, *Xiaoting zalu*, 92.

32. APF SC Cina 2:83–7 Mandello, Sept. 1803. Fan Tiancheng was also known as Simone Ciang.

33. ACGOFM Missioni 53 Raccolta di lettere, Ly, 14 Aug. 1797.

34. APF SC Cina 2:245 Ly, 28 Jan. 1804.

35. APF SC Cina 2:245 Ly, 28 Jan. 1804.

36. APF SC Cina 2:245–58 Ly, 28 Jan. 1804; APF SC Cina 2:417 Landi, 7 Nov. 1804.

37. APF SOCP 70:313–4 Ciao, 1 Aug. 1704; APF SC Cina 2:418 Landi, 7 Nov. 1804; AION 16/10/15 Ly, 30 Aug. 1804. Guo Ruwang was also known as Camillus Ciao.

38. APF SC Cina 2:418 Landi, 7 Nov. 1804.

39. APF SOCP 70:373 Indie Orientali Cina Ristretto, 1806.

40. APF SC Cina 3:412 Landi, 2 Oct. 1807.

41. APF SC Cina 3 Ly, 23 Mar. 1806; APF SC Cina 3:376 Ly, 9 Feb. 1807 APF SC Cina 3:419 Landi, 2 Oct. 1807; *Qingdai waijiao shiliao Jiaqing chao*, 1:24–26; Stefano Gitti, *Mons. Gioacchino Salvetti O.F.M. (1769-1843) e la missione dei francescani in Cina* (Florence: Studi Francescani, 1958), 14–23.

42. ACGOFM Missioni 53 Raccolta di lettere Ly, 24 Oct. 1808.

43. APF SC Cina 3:695 Ly to Ciu, 24 Oct. 1809.

Chapter 12: George Thomas Staunton Becomes an Interpreter

1. GT Staunton Papers, G. T. Staunton to parents, 21 June 1799, 7 May 1801; IOR B/123:375 Court Minutes, 6 July 1796.

2. G. T. Staunton, *Memoirs of the Chief Incidents*, 200; Smith, *Memoir and Correspondence*, 303.

3. Andrew West, "The Staunton Collection," www.babelstone.co.uk/Morrison /other/Staunton.html.

4. GT Staunton Papers, G. T. Staunton to G. L. Staunton, 15 Aug. 1796. English text: IOR G/12/93 3:327–30 George III to Emperor of China, 20 June 1795. Chinese text: *Yingshi Magaerni*, 230–34.

5. *Yingshi Magaerni*, 493.

6. G. T. Staunton, *Memoirs of the Chief Incidents*, 18–19; Brodie, *Works of Sir Benjamin Collins Brodie*, 1:5; GT Staunton Papers, G. T. Staunton to parents, 5 Aug. 1796, 15 Aug. 1796, 29 Aug. 1796, 19 Sept. 1796, 7 Oct. 1796; G. T. Staunton, *Memoir of the Life and Family*, 366–67.

7. Arnould, *Life of Thomas, First Lord Denman*, 1:3, 9–10.

8. G. T. Staunton, *Memoirs of the Chief Incidents*, 20–22.

9. IOR B/122: 1249 Court of Directors minutes, 10 Feb. 1796; G. T. Staunton, *Miscellaneous Notices*, 201; Baring Archive, NP1 C.22.11 G. L. Staunton to Francis Baring, 16 Mar. 1796, NP1 B.3.3 William Baring, 18 Nov. 1802.

10. G. L. Staunton, *Authentic Account*, 2:234; GT Staunton Papers, Duke of Portland, 28 July 1797, Lord Mornington, 28 July 1797, Marquis of Lansdown, 15 Aug. 1797, 8 Mar. 1798; IOR B/126: 1229 Court of Directors minutes, 5 Apr. 1798, 1276–7, 10 Apr. 1798; G. T. Staunton, *Memoir of the Life and Family*, 373.

11. GT Staunton Papers, G. T. Staunton to parents, 28 July 1799.

12. GT Staunton Papers, G. T. Staunton to parents, 26 June, 22 Oct. 1799.

13. GT Staunton Papers, G. T. Staunton to parents, 28 July 1799, 25 Jan. 1800.

14. GT Staunton Papers, G. T. Staunton to G. L. Staunton, 18 Apr. 1801.

15. GT Staunton Papers, G. T. Staunton to parents, 25 Jan. 1800.

16. IOR G/12/136:106 Canton consultations, 3 Dec. 1801; Ch'en, *Insolvency of the Chinese Hong Merchants*, 352–53; Mao Yike 毛亦可, "Qingdai liubu siguan de 'wubu'" 清代六部司官的'烏布' ['Ubu' administrative associates in the Six Ministries in the Qing dynasty], *Qing shi yanjiu* 清史研究 3 (2014), 83; Zhongguo di yi lishi dang'anguan 中國第一歷史檔案官, "Jiaqing shisinian shuli maoling kuxiang an dang'an" 嘉慶十四年書吏冒領庫項案檔案 [Archives of the case in which clerks forged treasury withdrawal slips in the 14th year of Jiaqing], *Lishi dang'an* 歷史檔案4 (2018), 17; Hilary J. Beattie, *Land and Lineage in China: A Study of T'ung-ch'eng County, Anhwei, in the Ming and Ch'ing Dynasties* (Cambridge: Cambridge University Press, 1979).

17. GT Staunton Papers, G. T. Staunton to G. L. Staunton, 27 Mar. 1800; IOR G/12/128:30–1, 50–1, 56 Canton Consultations 1800; Chen, *Chinese Law in Imperial Eyes*, 25–41, 79–82.

18. Pan Jianfen, *Guangzhou shisanhang hangshang Pan Zhencheng*, 14, 60, 101; Jenkins, "Old Mandarin Home"; IOR G/12/134:78 Canton Consultations 1801.

19. Morrison, *Memoirs of the Life and Labours*, 1:468.

20. GT Staunton Papers, G. T. Staunton to G. L. Staunton, 27 Mar. 1800.

21. GT Staunton Papers, G. T. Staunton to G. L. Staunton, 27 Mar. 1800.

22. GT Staunton Papers, G. T. Staunton to G. L. Staunton, 26 May 1800.

23. GT Staunton Papers, G. T. Staunton to G. L. Staunton, 27 Mar. 1800.

24. IOR G/12/128:211 Canton Consultations 1800.

25. IOR G/12/128:105–7 Canton Consultations 1800; GT Staunton Papers, G. T. Staunton to G. L. Staunton, 27 Mar. 1800.

26. GT Staunton Papers, G. T. Staunton to G. L. Staunton, 27 Mar. 1800.

27. Zhaolian, *Xiaoting zalu*, 110.

28. IOR G/12/128:209 Canton Consultations 1800. See also GT Staunton Papers, G. T. Staunton to G. L. Staunton, 26 May 1800.

29. GT Staunton Papers, G. T. Staunton to G. L. Staunton, 26 May 1800.

30. IOR G/12/136:107–8 Canton Consultations 1801–2; GT Staunton Papers, G. T. Staunton to G. L. Staunton, 27 Mar. 1800.

31. G. T. Staunton, *Memoirs of the Chief Incidents*, 25–26.

32. Elphinstone Collection, BL MSS Eur F89/4 JF Elphinstone to mother, 26 Feb. 1801, 31 July 1801; Guy Duncan, "Hochee and Elphinstone" (unpubl. MS, 2004), 34, 54.

33. GT Staunton Papers, G. T. Staunton to J. Staunton, 20 Dec. 1806; Cai Hongsheng, "Qingdai Guangzhou," 70–76.

34. GT Staunton Papers, G. T. Staunton to parents, 21 June and 19 Oct. 1799, 25 Jan. and 27 Mar. 1800, 7 May 1801.

35. TNA FO 1048/14/67 Li Yao to G. T. Staunton JQ19/10/13.

36. Duncan, "Hochee and Elphinstone," 33–34; Ch'en, *Insolvency of the Chinese Hong Merchants*, 348–49.

37. William C. Hunter, *The "fan kwae" at Canton before Treaty Days, 1825-1844* (London: Kegan Paul, Trench & Co, 1882), 50–53; Van Dyke, *Canton Trade*, 77–94.

38. GT Staunton Papers, G. T. Staunton to G. L. Staunton, 20 Jan. 1800, 27 June 1800.

39. GT Staunton Papers, G. T. Staunton to G. L. Staunton, 27 June 1800, 9 Aug. 1800, 29 Feb. 1801; G. T. Staunton, *Ta Tsing Leu Lee*, 493–509, 540–43; G. T. Staunton, *Narrative of the Chinese Embassy*, 258–318; IOR G/12/133:38–49 Canton Consultations 1801; IOR G/12/134:48–52 Canton Consultations 1801.

40. IOR G/12/134:13–4, 52, 110–23, 125, 148 Canton Consultations 1801; IOR/G/12/136:101, 107, 115–20 Canton Consultations 1801–2.

41. G. T. Staunton, *Memoir of the Life and Family*, 387; IOR G/12/136:209 Canton Consultations 1801–2; GT Staunton Papers, G. T. Staunton to J Staunton, 5 Oct. 1801.

Chapter 13: Sir George Staunton, Translator and Banker

1. Sir George Leonard Staunton Papers, BL, Will.

2. Coutts Bank Archive, London, Coutts Ledgers S 1805–6 Sir George Thomas Staunton.

3. Brodie, *Works of Sir Benjamin Collins Brodie*, 1:16, 18, 23, 32; Charles Butler, *Reminiscences of Charles Butler, Esq. of Lincoln's Inn* (London: John Murray, 1822), dedication.

4. GT Staunton Papers, G. T. Staunton to Jane Staunton, 9 Sept. 1802, and also 14 Sept. 1802.

5. *Yingjiliguo xinchu zhongniudou qishu*; IOR G/12/150 Canton Consultations 1805:11, 37.

6. *Yingjiliguo xinchu zhongniudou qishu*, 6; Leung, "Business of Vaccination," 26; Zhang Jiafeng, "Shijiu shiji chu niudou."

7. Hariharan, "Relations between Macao and Britain"; Liu Fang and Zhang Wenqin, *Qingdai Aomen zhongwen dang'an huibian*, 2:744–46.

8. *Qingdai waijiao shiliao Jiaqing chao*, 1:11–13.

9. Zhaolian, *Xiaoting zalu*, 110.

10. IOR G/12/148 Canton Consultations 1805:78.

11. Chinese text: *Qingdai waijiao shiliao Jiaqing chao*, 1:18–19. English text: IOR G/12/148 Canton Consultations 1805:135–9.

12. IOR G/12/148 Canton Consultations 1805:135.

13. IOR G/12/148 Canton Consultations 1805:77.

14. IOR/G/12/148 Consultations 1805:78.

15. TNA FO 1048/5/1 Wood to Viceroy, 1805.

16. Coutts Bank Archive, Ledgers S 1805–1817 Sir George Thomas Staunton. The graph was compiled by adding up the holdings that regularly paid interest into the account and the figures should be taken as an indication only. The holdings recorded in this way were mainly in British government 3, 4, and 5 percent consols and 5 percent navy stocks. £8,107 came from the Nawab of Arcot's debts inherited from his father. From 1809 sums increasing to approximately £16,000 were held in his mother's name. The figures do not include $63,000 (ca. £13,000) in U.S. stock

transferred in George Leonard's will. They also do not include the sums invested in Canton, so George Thomas was undoubtedly considerably wealthier than appears here.

17. GT Staunton Papers, G. T. Staunton to G. L. Staunton, 9 Aug. 1800, 18 Apr. 1801; Coutts Bank Archive, Ledgers S 1805–1817 Sir George Thomas Staunton. For Pan Youdu, see G. T. Staunton, *Tablets in the Temple*, 8.

18. GT Staunton Papers, G. T. Staunton to G. L. Staunton, 27 Mar. and 26 May 1800, 26 Feb. 1801; Grant, *Chinese Cornerstone of Modern Banking*, 78–82; Hanser, *Mr. Smith Goes to China*, 83.

19. GT Staunton Papers, G. T. Staunton to G. L. Staunton, 5 May 1801.

20. GT Staunton Papers, G. T. Staunton to Jane Staunton, 6 June 1804, 1 Mar. 1805, 30 Dec. 1805, 26 Feb. 1806, James Mackintosh to G. T. Staunton, 15 Aug. 1805; Coutts Bank Archive, Ledgers S 1805 and 1812 Sir George Thomas Staunton; Bank of England Archive, London, Personal communication, 23 Dec. 2019; Weng Eang Cheong, *Mandarins and Merchants: Jardine Matheson & Co., a China Agency of the Early Nineteenth Century* (London: Curzon Press, 1979), 27–32.

21. G. T. Staunton, *Memoirs of the Chief Incidents*, 40.

22. G. T. Staunton, *Select Letters*, 48; Wong, "'We Are as Babies under Nurses'"; Morrison, *Memoirs of the Life and Labours*, 2:305.

23. Morrison, *Memoirs of the Life and Labours*, 1:153.

24. Morrison, *Memoirs of the Life and Labours*, 1:214. See also Morrison, *Memoirs of the Life and Labours*, 1:1–2, 77; Marshall Broomhall, *Robert Morrison: A Master-Builder* (London: Student Christian Movement, 1927), 32–33; Yang Huiling, *19 shiji Han Ying cidian*, 102.

25. G. T. Staunton, *Memoirs of the Chief Incidents*, 35.

26. Morse, *Chronicles of the East India Company*, 3:40–43; G. T. Staunton, *Miscellaneous Notices*, 262–79; Royal Asiatic Society, Thomas Manning Archive TM 1/1/40 Manning, 24 Feb. 1807.

27. G. T. Staunton, *Miscellaneous Notices*, 271.

28. Royal Asiatic Society, London, RAS 01.001 Chinese Court of Justice in the Hall of the British Factory at Canton, 9 Apr. 1807; G. T. Staunton, *Notices of the Leigh Park Estate*, 6; Morse, *Chronicles of the East India Company*, 3:52–53.

29. G. T. Staunton, *Ta Tsing Leu Lee*, 517.

30. GT Staunton Papers, G. T. Staunton to Jane Staunton, 5 Nov. 1805.

31. GT Staunton Papers, G. T. Staunton to Barrow, 25 Aug. 1807; G. T. Staunton, *Ta Tsing Leu Lee*, xxix–xxx.

32. G. T. Staunton, *Ta Tsing Leu Lee*, title page (original in Latin).

33. Royal Asiatic Society, George Thomas Staunton collection, 28–29.

34. G. T. Staunton, *Ta Tsing Leu Lee*, 148, 528.

35. G. T. Staunton , *Ta Tsing Leu Lee*, xxxii.

36. GT Staunton Papers, G. T. Staunton to G. L. Staunton, 26 May 1800; Pan Jianfen, *Guangzhou shisanhang hangshang Pan Zhencheng*, 38–41, 97.

37. G. T. Staunton, *Miscellaneous Notices*, 57–58; Royal Asiatic Society, George Thomas Staunton Collection, 33; Jenkins, "Old Mandarin Home"; BL IOR Neg 11666

1857 Madeleine Jackson Papers, Memoir compiled c 1871 by James Molony (1795–1874), 30; G. T. Staunton, *Notes of Proceedings*, 9; Duncan, "Hochee and Elphinstone," 25.

38. Chen, *Chinese Law in Imperial Eyes*, 127–28.

39. Ong, "Jurisdictional Politics in Canton."

40. St. André, "'But Do They Have a Notion of Justice?,'" 14.

41. Chen, *Chinese Law in Imperial Eyes*, 113.

42. G. T. Staunton, *Ta Tsing Leu Lee*, ix–x.

43. G. T. Staunton, *Ta Tsing Leu Lee*, x–xi.

44. G. T. Staunton, *Memoirs of the Chief Incidents*, 51–53.

Chapter 14: The British Occupation of Macao and Its Aftermath

1. BL Elphinstone Collection BL MSS Eur F89/4 JF Elphinstone to WF Elphinstone, 14 Dec. 1810.

2. For detailed narratives, see Wakeman, "Drury's Occupation of Macau"; Wang, *White Lotus Rebels and South China Pirates*, 240–46.

3. Liu Fang and Zhang Wenqin, *Qingdai Aomen zhongwen dang'an huibian*, 2:749; *Qingdai waijiao shiliao Jiaqing chao*, 2:23–24, 33–35.

4. IOR G/12/164 Consultations 1808:62.

5. *Qingdai waijiao shiliao Jiaqing chao*, 2:27.

6. *Qingdai waijiao shiliao Jiaqing chao*, 2:34.

7. *Qingdai waijiao shiliao Jiaqing chao*, 2:28.

8. *Qingdai waijiao shiliao Jiaqing chao*, 3:2. This argument is made by Wang, *White Lotus Rebels and South China Pirates*, 244.

9. IOR/G/12/164 Consultations 1808, 143; *Qingdai waijiao shiliao Jiaqing chao*, 2:36, 3:13–16.

10. GT Staunton Papers, G. T. Staunton to parents, 20 Jan. 1800; IOR G/12/269 Secret Consultations: 21–22 and 27 Feb. 1809, 25 Sept. 1805, 7 Jan. 1808 (re unnamed spy), 11 Jan. 1809; IOR G/12/164 Consultations 1808: 168–70, 191–92; António Aresta, "Portuguese Sinology: A Brief Outline," *Review of Culture* 31 (n.d.), http://icm.gov.mo.

11. IOR G/12/269 Secret Consultations: 27 Feb. and 7 May 1809.

12. G. T. Staunton, *Miscellaneous Notices*, 69.

13. Morrison, *Memoirs of the Life and Labours*, 1:395.

14. Morrison, *Memoirs of the Life and Labours*, 1:293. See also G. T. Staunton, *Notes of Proceedings*, 332; Kitson, *Forging Romantic China*, 161–62.

15. Morrison, *Memoirs of the Life and Labours*, 1:293; IOR G/12/170:23–7.

16. IOR G/12/170 Canton Consultations 1810:81–2. Chinese text: TNA FO 1048/10/34 Ruling by governor on Austin's petition, 1810.

17. IOR G/12/174 Canton Consultations 1810:149–51.

18. Ch'en, *Insolvency of the Chinese Hong Merchants*, 235–38.

19. TNA FO 1048/11/87 Sewn bundle of copies of Chinese official documents about the Ashing case; *Qingdai waijiao shiliao Jiaqing chao*, 3:31–33.

20. *Qingdai waijiao shiliao Jiaqing chao*, 3:18; Li Huan, *Guochao qi xian leizheng chubian*, 5:2979, 2981; FHA 03-1671-020 Songyun JQ16/3/22; IOR G/12/20 Staunton to Barrow, 16 July 1811; IOR G/12/269 Secret Consultations: 19 Oct. 1811; Ch'en, *Insolvency of the Chinese Hong Merchants*, 93.

21. IOR G/12/176 Canton Consultations 1811:95, 99, 109; TNA FO 1048/11/18 Manhop's hong to Sir G Staunton.

22. IOR G/12/176 Canton Consultations 1811:116–7; IOR G/12/20 Staunton to Barrow 16 July 1811; TNA FO 1048/11/22 G. T. Staunton to Songyun 9 May (draft apparently kept as notes to speak from).

23. IOR G/12/176 Canton Consultations 1811: 116–7.

24. English text: IOR/G/12/176 Consultations 1811, 120–26; Chinese text: TNA FO 1048/11/26 Document which Staunton tried to present. Staunton's holdings: GT Staunton Papers, G. T. Staunton to Jane Staunton, 7 Apr. 1815.

25. IOR G/12/176 Canton Consultations 1811:117–9. See also Zhaolian, *Xiaoting zalu*, 88.

26. IOR G/12/176 Canton Consultations 1811:127–30.

27. IOR G/12/269 Secret Consultations: 7 June 1811. See also IOR/G/12/176 Canton Consultations 1811: 133–37.

28. *Qingdai waijiao shiliao Jiaqing*, 3:42–43.

29. IOR G/12/176 Canton Consultations 1811:167; IOR G/12/269 Secret Consultations: 23 Dec. 1811.

30. IOR G/12/176 Canton Consultations 1811:188–89.

31. IOR G/12/176 Canton Consultations 1811:186, 198, 208.

32. IOR G/12/269 Secret Consultations: 19–20 Oct. 1811; IOR G/12/178 Canton Consultations 1811:45; Duncan, "Hochee and Elphinstone," 22–23.

33. FHA 02-01-008-002876-006 Songyun JQ 16/7/1; FHA 03-1681-098 Songyun JQ 16/9/24; IOR G/12/178 Canton Consultations 1811:48–49, 80–81.

34. GT Staunton Papers, G. T. Staunton to Jane Staunton, 26 July 1812.

35. G. T. Staunton, *Miscellaneous Notices*, 31.

36. G. T. Staunton, *Miscellaneous Notices*, 55.

37. G. T. Staunton, *Memoirs of the Chief Incidents*, 54.

38. G. T. Staunton, *Miscellaneous Notices*, 136. See also *Minutes of Evidence Taken before the Committee of the Whole House, and the Select Committee, on the Affairs of the East India Company* (London, 1813), 739.

Chapter 15: A Linguist and His Troubles

1. GT Staunton Papers, G. T. Staunton to Jane Staunton, 14 Aug. 1814.

2. Wong, *Global Trade in the Nineteenth Century*, 72, 82–84, 95–97; Grant, "Failure of the Li-ch'uan Hong."

3. Ch'en, *Insolvency of the Chinese Hong Merchants*, 135, 168; GT Staunton Papers, G. T. Staunton to Jane Staunton, 22 Sept. 1814.

4. Morse, *Chronicles of the East India Company*, 3:214–19.

5. Liu Fang and Zhang Wenqin, *Qingdai Aomen zhongwen dang'an huibian*, 2:771–72; *Qingdai waijiao shiliao Jiaqing chao*, 4:23; IOR G/12/270 Secret Consultations, 1 Oct. 1814; *Qing shi gao xiaozhu*, 12:1970.

6. TNA FO 1048/14/67 9th of 10 letters from Ayew in prison, FO 1048/14/68 10th of 10 letters from Ayew in prison, FO 1048/15/2 Ayew to Elphinstone, FO 1048/15/7 Ayew from prison to Elphinstone (Drury was the only Admiral of the White to visit the south China coast in this period).

7. TNA FO 1048/14/72 The confessions of Ayew and of his wife.

8. TNA FO 1048/14/108 Ayew from prison to Elphinstone, FO 1048/14/68 10th of 10 letters from Ayew.

9. TNA FO 1048/13/3 Letter to [?Elphinstone] from linguist Ayou in Peking, FO 1048/14/68 10th of 10 letters from Ayew.

10. TNA FO 1048/14/72 Another copy of FO 1048/14/71 with a report on the case by the Nan-hai magistrate, FO 1048/14/68 10th of 10 letters from Ayew, FO 1048/14/58 Letter from Ayew to Elphinstone; IOR/G/12/197:40–1 Amherst Embassy. For a detailed account of the case focusing on Li Yao's role as a linguist, see Wang Hongzhi, "1814 nian 'Ayao shijian.'"

11. TNA FO 1048/14/68 10th of 10 letters from Ayew.

12. IOR G/12/270 Secret Consultations, 4 and 11 Dec. 1814; TNA FO 1048/14/57 Part of a letter from Ayew.

13. Morrison, *Memoirs of the Life and Labours*, 1:421.

14. TNA FO 1048/14/58 Letter from Ayew to Elphinstone.

15. TNA FO 1048/14/58 Letter from Ayew to Elphinstone.

16. GT Staunton Papers, G. T. Staunton to Jane Staunton, 14 Dec. 1814. For the importance of these negotiations, see Wang Hongzhi, "Sidangdong yu Guangzhou tizhi."

17. G. T. Staunton, *Miscellaneous Notices*, 216–17; IOR G/12/197 Lord Amherst's Embassy, 37; TNA FO 1048/14/96 Statement from Select Committee delivered to Sub-prefect Fu, FO 1048/14/73 Petition to viceroy and provincial treasurer.

18. IOR G/12/197:41 Lord Amherst's Embassy.

19. IOR G/12/197: 34–7, 42 Lord Amherst's Embassy; TNA FO 1048/14/96 Statement from Select Committee, FO 1048/14/73 Petition to viceroy, FO 1048/10/21 Petition from Capt. Austin to viceroy.

20. *Qingdai waijiao shiliao Jiaqing chao*, 4:23.

21. TNA FO 1048/14/59 1st of 10 letters from Ayew in prison to Staunton, FO 1048/14/60 2nd of 10 letters from Ayew in prison to Staunton.

22. G. T. Staunton, *Miscellaneous Notices*, 213–15, 297; TNA FO 1048/14/63 5th of 10 letters from Ayew in prison to Staunton; IOR G/12/190:168–72 Canton Consultations 1814; G. T. Staunton, *Corrected Report of the Speeches*, 38–39.

23. TNA FO 1048/14/80 Statement submitted to sub-prefect for Macao.

24. TNA FO 1048/14/63 5th of 10 letters from Ayew in prison to Staunton.

25. TNA FO 1048/14/65 7th of 10 letters from Ayew in prison to Staunton.

26. TNA FO 1048/14/65 7th of 10 letters from Ayew in prison to Staunton.

27. TNA FO 1048/14/82 Order from Viceroy and Hoppo to Select Committee.

28. FO 1048/14/87 Order from Hoppo to hong merchants.

29. FO 1048/14/87 Order from Hoppo to hong merchants.

30. G. T. Staunton, *Miscellaneous Notices*, 214–15; TNA FO 1048/14/66 8th of 10 letters from Ayew in prison to Staunton.

31. TNA FO 1048/14/89 Order from viceroy to Canton prefect.

32. TNA FO 1048/14/94 Senior hong merchants to Staunton; Morrison, *Chinese Commercial Guide*, 48–53; Liang Tingnan, *Yue haiguan zhi*, 560–62; Pan Jianfen, *Guangzhou shisanhang hangshang Pan Zhencheng*, 225.

33. *Qingdai waijiao shiliao Jiaqing chao*, 4:24, 27.

34. *Qingdai waijiao shiliao Jiaqing chao*, 4:24–25.

35. TNA FO 1048/15/4 Ayew to Elphinstone; IOR G/12/270 Secret Consultations, 3 and 5 Mar. 1815, 17 June 1815; Ch'en, *Insolvency of the Chinese Hong Merchants*, 354–55; Zhaolian, *Xiaoting zalu*, juan 2; *Ming Qing shilu*, JQ14/7 12190–2 and 12219, JQ17/8 15339; Zhongguo diyi lishi dang'anguan, "Jiaqing shisinian shuli maoling kuxiang an." Liu Dezhang's nephew was Liu Yang 劉洋.

36. *Qingdai waijiao shiliao Jiaqing chao*, 4:28.

37. *Qingdai waijiao shiliao Jiaqing chao*, 4:25. Translation adapted from IOR G/12/270, 3 Mar. 1815.

38. IOR G/12/20:298 Board of Control Miscellaneous.

39. *Qing zhongqianqi xiyang tianzhujiao*, 3:1058.

40. Morrison, *Memoirs of the Life and Labours*, 1:424–25.

41. G. T. Staunton, *Miscellaneous Notices*, 244–45.

42. TNA FO 1048/14/108 Ayew from prison to Elphinstone and others.

43. TNA FO 1048/14/113 Ayew to Elphinstone.

44. TNA FO 1048/14/113 Ayew to Elphinstone.

45. GT Staunton Papers, G. T. Staunton to Jane Staunton, 14 Dec. 1814.

46. IOR G/12/196:191 Lord Amherst's Embassy (Select Committee with Staunton as president).

47. FO 1048/15/9 Ayew from San-shui hsien.

48. GT Staunton Papers, G. T. Staunton to Jane Staunton, 8 July 1815, 21 Sept. 1815.

Chapter 16: The Amherst Embassy

1. G. T. Staunton, *Memoirs of the Chief Incidents*, 41–43; IOR G/12/197:1–6 Barrow to Buckinghamshire, 14 Feb. 1815.

2. IOR G/12/196 Letter to China, 27 Sept. 1815; IOR G/12/196:7–8 Elphinstone to Buckinghamshire, 3 Mar. 1815, 38–44 Grant to China, 27 Sept. 1815, 75–6 Secret Commercial Committee to Amherst, 17 Jan. 1816.

3. IOR G/12/196:36 Buckinghamshire, 21 Sept. 1815, 100–2 Secret commercial committee to Amherst, 17 Jan. 1816; Douglas M. Peers, "Amherst, William Pitt, First Earl Amherst of Arracan" and R. M. Healey, "Ellis, Sir Henry (1788–1855)," in *Oxford Dictionary of National Biography* (2004), www.oxforddnb.com.

4. IOR G/12/196:189–91 Canton Secret Consultations, 12 Feb. 1816; GT Staunton Papers, G. T. Staunton to Jane Staunton, 21 Feb. 1816.

5. G. T. Staunton, *Notes of Proceedings*, 423; Davis, *Sketches of China*, 1:84; IOR G/12/196:274 Secret consultations, 17 June 1816; GT Staunton Papers, G. T. Staunton to Jane Staunton, 7 Aug. 1816.

6. Ellis, *Journal of the Proceedings*, 2:219. See also IOR G/12/196:112 Secret Commercial Committee to China, 26 Jan. 1816.

7. IOR G/12/196:215 Staunton to Amherst, 11 July 1816.

8. G. T. Staunton, *Notes of Proceedings*, 3; IOR G/12/196:217 Amherst to Staunton, 11 July 1816.

9. IOR G/12/196:36 Buckinghamshire, 21 Sept. 1815. See also Healey, "Ellis, Sir Henry."

10. Ellis, *Journal of the Proceedings*, 1:111, 1:113; Clarke Abel, *Narrative of a Journey in the Interior of China, and a Voyage to and from That Country in the Years 1816 and 1817* (London: Longman, Hurst, Rees, Orme & Brown, 1819), 70, 76, 87–88; G. T. Staunton, *Notes of Proceedings*, 39–40.

11. Zhaolian, *Xiaoting zalu*, 423.

12. G. T. Staunton, *Notes of Proceedings*, 206.

13. IOR G/12/196:367 Secret consultations, 1 Jan. 1817. See also Wang Hongzhi 王宏志, "1816 nian Ameishide shituan de fanyi wenti" 1816年啊美士德使團的翻譯問題 [Translation problems of the 1816 Amherst embassy], *Fanyixue yanjiu* 翻譯學研究 2015.

14. *Qingdai waijiao shiliao Jiaqing chao*, 5:3.

15. Zhang Ruilong, *Tianlijiao shijian*, 144–56; Chen Kaike, *Jiaqing shi nian*, 330–52, 456–57.

16. *Qingdai waijiao shiliao Jiaqing chao*, 6:20.

17. *Qingdai waijiao shiliao Jiaqing chao*, 5:5.

18. G. T. Staunton, *Notes of Proceedings*, 44.

19. *Qingdai waijiao shiliao Jiaqing chao*, 5:15; G. T. Staunton, *Notes of Proceedings*, 43–44; *Yingshi Magaerni*, 512; Ellis, *Journal of the Proceedings*, 1:133.

20. *Yingshi Magaerni*, 512. See also IOR G/12/197:223 Amherst to Canning, 12 Feb. 1817; G. T. Staunton, *Notes of Proceedings*, 46–47.

21. IOR G/12/197 p 223, 234 Amherst to Canning, 12 Feb. 1817; *Qingdai waijiao shiliao Jiaqing chao*, 5:29; G. T. Staunton, *Notes of Proceedings*, 50; Morrison, *Memoir of the Principal Occurrences*, 20–21; Abel, *Narrative of a Journey*, 74.

22. *Yingshi Magaerni*, 210.

23. *Yingshi Magaerni*, 211.

24. Morrison, *Memoir of the Principal Occurrences*, 32 (adapted). See also Morrison, *Memoir of the Principal Occurrences*, 29, *Yingshi Magaerni*, 211.

25. *Qingdai waijiao shiliao Jiaqing chao*, 5:50; Morrison, *Memoir of the Principal Occurrences*, 34; Ellis, *Journal of the Proceedings*, 1:235.

26. Ellis, *Journal of the Proceedings*, 1:239–40; G. T. Staunton, *Notes of Proceedings*, 85–86, 88–89, 91. See also *Yingshi Magaerni*, 515.

27. G. T. Staunton, *Notes of Proceedings*, 89, see also 85–89.

28. G. T. Staunton, *Notes of Proceedings*, 93.

29. G. T. Staunton, *Notes of Proceedings*, 30, 94; Ellis, *Journal of the Proceedings*, 1:167, 231–32, 255.

30. Morrison, *Memoir of the Principal Occurrences*, 37; G. T. Staunton, *Notes of Proceedings*, 100–103; Ellis, *Journal of the Proceedings*, 1:258–60; Davis, *Sketches of China*, 1:138–39; *Yingshi Magaerni*, 213.

31. G. T. Staunton, *Notes of Proceedings*, 103–4.

32. G. T. Staunton, *Notes of Proceedings*, 116.

33. G. T. Staunton, *Notes of Proceedings*, 118–22; Abel, *Narrative of a Journey*, 104–5; IOR G/12/197:286–8 Amherst to Canning, 8 Mar. 1817; Morrison, *Memoir of the Principal Occurrences*, 40.

34. G. T. Staunton, *Notes of Proceedings*, 121. See also Ellis, *Journal of the Proceedings*, 1:271; Abel, *Narrative of a Journey*, 106.

35. *Qingdai waijiao shiliao Jiaqing chao*, 5:55–60.

36. G. T. Staunton, *Notes of Proceedings*, 57–58, 162–63; Duke University Library, Henry Hayne papers, Diary, 7 Sept. 1816.

37. *Qingdai waijiao shiliao Jiaqing chao*, 6:25.

38. G. T. Staunton, *Notes of Proceedings*, 162; *Qingdai waijiao shiliao Jiaqing chao*, 6:25; *Ming Qing shilu*, DG8/6 9582, DG8/10 9958; Yigeng 奕賡, *Jia meng xuan congzhu* 佳夢軒叢著 [Collected writings from the pavilion of beautiful dreams], ed. Lei Dashou 雷大受 (Beijing: Beijing guji chubanshe, 1994), 39.

39. G. T. Staunton, *Notes of Proceedings*, 330, see also 323.

40. Ellis, *Journal of the Proceedings*, 2:64.

41. G. T. Staunton, *Notes of Proceedings*, 150.

42. *Qingdai waijiao shiliao Jiaqing chao*, 5:59–60, 6:12.

43. *Qingdai waijiao shiliao Jiaqing chao*, 5:59–60, 6:19–20, 6:25.

44. John McLeod, *Voyage of His Majesty's Ship Alceste along the Coast of Corea to the Island of Lewchew* (London: John Murray, 1818), 152–53, 155–57, 163.

45. IOR G/12/197:365 Amherst to Canning, 21 Apr. 1817.

46. English text: IOR G/12/197:391–9 Translation of letter to Regent. Chinese text: *Yingshi Magaerni*, 213 (draft).

47. English text: IOR G/12/197:391–9 Translation of letter to Regent. Chinese text: *Yingshi Magaerni*, 213 (draft).

48. Wang Hongzhi, "1816 nian Ameishide shituan." Wang approves Morrison's translation for its accuracy.

49. GT Staunton Papers, G. T. Staunton to Jane Staunton, 3 Jan. and 8 July 1817.

50. *Qingdai waijiao shiliao Jiaqing chao*, 6:38.

51. *Qingdai waijiao shiliao Jiaqing chao*, 6:38.

Chapter 17: Li Zibiao's Last Years in Hiding

1. APF SOCP 73:316 Ly, 22 Nov. 1816; *Qing zhongqianqi xiyang tianzhujiao*, 3:1085–87.

2. *Qingdai waijiao shiliao Jiaqing chao*, 1:28.

3. *Qingdai waijiao shiliao Jiaqing chao*, 1:23; ACGOFM Missioni 53 Raccolta di lettere degli alunni Cinesi, 184 Ly, n.d.

4. *Qing zhongqianqi xiyang tianzhujiao*, 3:994–95. The specialist was Gan Jiabin 甘家斌. For Zhang Duode, see *Qing zhongqianqi xiyang tianzhujiao*, 2:901–2; APF SC Cina 3:859–65 Salvetti, 25 Sept. 1811; APF SC Cina 2:165 Ciang, 15 Oct. 1803; APF SC Cina 3:871 Ly, 29 Oct. 1811. See also Zhang Ruilong, *Tianlijiao shijian*, 275–76.

5. *Qing zhongqianqi xiyang tianzhujiao*, 3:1004.

6. *Qing zhongqianqi xiyang tianzhujiao*, 3:1075–76; Sachsenmaier, *Global Entanglements*, 130–35.

7. APF SOCP 73:315 Ly, 22 Nov. 1816.

8. ACGOFM Missioni 53 Raccolta di lettere degli alunni Cinesi, 171 Ly, 2 Oct. 1810.

9. ACGOFM Missioni 53 Raccolta di lettere degli alunni Cinesi, 171 Ly, 2 Oct. 1810.

10. ACGOFM Misioni 53 Raccolta di lettere degli alunni Cinesi, 173 Ly, 26 Sept. 1815.

11. APF SOCP 73:248 Ly, 29 Sept. 1815.

12. APF SOCP 73:316 Ly, 22 Nov. 1816; APF SOCP 70:4 Ciao 1801; APF SC Cina 4:362–3 Salvetti, 15 Sept. 1814; Timmer, *Apostolisch Vicariaat van Zuid-Shansi*, 18–20; *Zhaojialing shengmutang jianjie* 趙家岭聖母堂簡介 [A brief introduction to Zhaojialing Marian shrine] (2013).

13. Léon de Kerval, *Deux Martyrs Francais de l'ordre des frères mineurs le R.P. Théodoric Balat et le Fr. André Bauer massacrés en Chine le 9 Juillet 1900* (Rome: Lemière, 1914), 119–20.

14. APF SC Cina 6:120 Salvetti 1825; APF SC Cina 10:306 De Donato, 30 Oct. 1841, *Zhaojialing shengmutang jianjie*. Giovanni Borgia was not at all closely related to the cardinal, but the connection was important to the Naples Borgia.

15. *Qing zhongqianqi xiyang tianzhujiao*, 3:1085–87.

16. Timmer, *Apostolisch Vicariaat van Zuid-Shansi*, 20.

17. APF SC Cina 4:365 Li, 15 Sept. 1814.

18. APF SOCP 73:71, 75 Garofalsi [1817]. See also APF SOCP 73:153–5 Memoria sopra la necessità [1817].

19. APF SOCP 73:208–9 Salvetti, 28 Sept. 1813.

20. Pan Yikui, *Wuwei qijiu zhuan*, 4:15.

21. APF SC Cina 6:310 Ly, 10 Sept. 1826.

22. APF SC China 5:151 Ly, 8 Sept. 1821; AION 16/1/15 Ly, 22 Apr. 1825 (Petrus Van was from Machang).

23. AION 1/5 to Ly, Jan. 1822. See also AION 16/1/15 Ly, 13 Sept. 1821; *Elenchus alumnorum*, 4.

24. ACGOFM Missioni 53 Raccolta di lettere degli alunni Cinesi, 182 Ly, 18 Sept. 1826.

25. ACGOFM Missioni 53 Raccolta di lettere degli alunni Cinesi, 175 Ly, 26 Sept. 1815.

26. ACGOFM Missioni 53 Raccolta di lettere degli alunni Cinesi, 178, 2 Sep 1818.

27. AION 16/1/15 Ly to Borgia, 10 Sept. 1826.

28. AION 16/1/15 Ly to Borgia, 10 Sept. 1826.

29. AION 16/1/15 Ly to Borgia, 10 Sept. 1826.

30. AION 16/1/15 Ly to Borgia, 10 Sept. 1826.

31. Timmer, *Apostolisch Vicariaat van Zuid-Shansi*, 93.

32. APF SC Cina 6:310 Ly, 10 Sept. 1826.

33. APF SC Cina 6:659 Salvetti, 28 Oct. 1828.

34. ACGOFM Missioni 53 Raccolta di lettere, 204 Vam Minor, 19 Sept. 1832.

Chapter 18: Staunton in Parliament

1. G. T. Staunton, *Memoirs of the Chief Incidents*, 74–75.

2. G. T. Staunton, *Memoirs of the Chief Incidents*, 109–10; R. G. Thorne, "Mitchell," in *The History of Parliament: The House of Commons 1790–1820*, ed. R. Thorne (London: Secker & Warburg, 1986) (History of Parliament Online); Brown, *Palmerston*, 50.

3. Kitson, *Forging Romantic China*, 99; Gladwyn, *Leigh Park*, 30–34.

4. G. T. Staunton, *Catalogue of the Library at Leigh Park*, 13. Austen lived in the village of Chawton north of Leigh Park, and her nephew George is commemorated in Saint John's church at Rowland's Castle.

5. G. T. Staunton, *Select Letters*, 56–57; GT Staunton Papers, Jane Macartney to G. T. Staunton, 18 Mar. 1812; John Sweetman, "Robert Batty, 1788–1848," in *Oxford Dictionary of National Biography*, www.oxforddnb.com; GT Staunton Papers, G. T. Staunton to Jane Staunton 9 Aug. 1812, 3 June 1818.

6. G. T. Staunton, *Memoirs of the Chief Incidents*, 118.

7. G. T. Staunton, *Memoirs of the Chief Incidents*, 117.

8. G. T. Staunton, *Memoirs of the Chief Incidents*, 118; O'Neill and Martin, "Backbencher on Parliamentary Reform."

9. Brodie, *Works of Sir Benjamin Collins Brodie*, 1:122; "The Members," in Fisher, *History of Parliament*.

10. Brodie, *Works of Sir Benjamin Collins Brodie*, 1:xvii, 68, 93; C. C. Boase and Beth F. Wood, "Brodie, Peter Bellinger (1778–1854)," in *Oxford Dictionary of National Biography*, www.oxforddnb.com; Arnould, *Life of Thomas*, 1:19; Nechtman, *Nabobs*.

11. Morrison, *Memoirs of the Life and Labours*, 2:259–62, 304–6; G. T. Staunton, *Notices of the Leigh Park Estate*, 12–13, 42–44; GT Staunton Papers, G. T. Staunton, Nov. 1828; G. T. Staunton, *Memoirs of the Chief Incidents*, 141.

12. G. T. Staunton, *Notices of the Leigh Park Estate*, 6–11. By 1836 when this book was published, Staunton had given the original Neptune trial painting to the Royal Asiatic Society.

13. Morrison, *Memoirs of the Life and Labours*, 2:305; G. T. Staunton, *Tablets in the Temple*, 6.

14. British Museum, London, Inkstand by Robert Hennell (1979,1008.1).

15. Morrison, *Memoirs of the Life and Labours*, 2:343, see also 325.

16. G. T. Staunton, *Memoirs of the Chief Incidents*, 101; Royal Asiatic Society, George Thomas Staunton Collection, 27–29; Andrew West, "The Staunton Collection," www.babelstone.co.uk/Morrison/other/Staunton.html; Morrison, *Memoirs of the Life and Labours*, 1:523.

17. G. T. Staunton, *Narrative of the Chinese Embassy*, v. Chinese: Tulichen (Tulisen) 圖理琛, *Yiyu lu* 異域錄 [Record of foreign regions] (Shanghai: Shangwu yinshuguan, 1936). (Staunton was working from the Chinese version of the Manchu text.) French: Souciet, *Observations mathématiques*, 148–65.

18. G. T. Staunton, *Narrative of the Chinese Embassy*, v.

19. G. T. Staunton, *Miscellaneous Notices*.

20. Morrison, *Memoirs of the Life and Labours*, 1:522–23.

21. G. T. Staunton, *Memoirs of the Chief Incidents*, 173; Morrison, *Memoirs of the Life and Labours*, 2:231.

22. GT Staunton Papers, Diary, 4 Dec. 1826, and Oct. 1826 to Feb. 1827 passim; G. T. Staunton, *Notices of the Leigh Park Estate*, 13, 43.

23. Gladwyn, *Leigh Park*, 53–57, 65–66.

24. Sir George Leonard Staunton Papers, BL, George Leonard Staunton Will; G. T. Staunton, *Memoirs of the Chief Incidents*, 147–50.

25. Henry Crabb Robinson, *Diary, Reminiscences and Correspondence of Henry Crabb Robinson, Barrister-at-Law F.S.A.*, ed. Thomas Sadler (London: Macmillan, 1869), 2:403. Cf. Nechtman, *Nabobs*, 234–35.

26. Maria Edgeworth, *Letters from England 1813–1844*, ed. Christina Colvin (Oxford: Clarendon, 1971), 450.

27. Martin Archer Shee, *The Life of Sir Martin Archer Shee, President of the Royal Academy, F.R.S. D.C.L.* (London: Longman, Green, Longman & Roberts, 1860), 2:247–48. See also William Fraser, ed., *Members of the Society of Dilettanti 1736–1874* (London: Chiswick Press, 1874), 32; GT Staunton Papers, Visitors to Leigh Park.

28. Farrell, "Staunton, Sir George Thomas," in Fisher, *History of Parliament*; O'Neill and Martin, "Backbencher on Parliamentary Reform."

29. GT Staunton Papers, Diary, 14 July 1831.

30. GT Staunton Papers, Diary, 14 July 1831.

31. Palmerston Papers BR 195/71A To Sir G.T. Staunton Bart.; GT Staunton Papers, Diary, 25 Oct. 1832 (newspaper clipping). See also David Brown, "Palmerston, South Hampshire and Electoral Politics, 1832–1835," *Hampshire Papers* 26 (2003).

32. Keele University, Sneyd Archive GB172 SC17/182 Baring Wall to Sneyd, 15 Aug. 1832.

33. *Hampshire Advertiser*, 10 Nov. 1832.

34. *Hampshire Telegraph*, 7 Jan. 1833.

35. G. T. Staunton, *Corrected Report of the Speeches*, 32.

36. *The Times*, 5 June 1833, 4 and 23 May 1834, 4.

37. GT Staunton Papers, Palmerston to G. T. Staunton, 7 Jan. 1834.

38. Lamentation of Sir G. Stan-ching-quot, Mandarin of the Celestial Empire (Portsea: Moxon, 1834), broadside held in BL.

39. GT Staunton Papers, Diary, 18 Jan. 1835.

40. GT Staunton Papers, Diary, 21 Jan. 1835 (newspaper clipping) and draft, 19 Jan. 1835.

41. GT Staunton Papers, Diary, 21 Jan. 1835 (newspaper clipping) and draft, 19 Jan. 1835.

42. Morrison, *Memoirs of the Life and Labours*, 2:505.

43. GT Staunton Papers, Diary, 5 and 7 Mar. 1835 (drafts).

44. Staunton: GT Staunton Papers, Diary, 7 Mar. 1835 (edicts). Morrison: *Sessional Papers Printed by Order of the House of Lords or Presented by Royal Command in the Session 1840* (1840) 8:35–39.

45. GT Staunton Papers, Diary, 7 Mar. 1835.

46. GT Staunton Papers, Diary, 7 Mar. 1835.

47. GT Staunton Papers, Diary, 13 May 1835.

48. Hugh Hamilton Lindsay, *Letter to the Right Honourable Viscount Palmerston on British Relations with China* (London: Saunders & Otley, 1836), 4.

49. G. T. Staunton, *Remarks on the British Relations*, 8; GT Staunton Papers, Diary notes for Leigh Park, 1836.

50. Staunton, *Remarks on the British Relations*, 28.

51. Staunton, *Remarks on the British Relations*, 16, 24.

52. Staunton, *Remarks on the British Relations*, 35–36. See also Dilip K. Basu, "Chinese Xenology and the Opium War: Reflections on Sinocentrism," *Journal of Asian Studies* 73, no. 4 (2014).

53. Staunton, *Remarks on the British Relations*, 38.

Chapter 19: The Opium War

1. Polachek, *Inner Opium War*; Mao, *Qing Empire and the Opium War*, 74–78.

2. Glenn Melancon, *Britain's China Policy and the Opium Crisis: Balancing Drugs, Violence and National Honour, 1833–1840* (Aldershot: Ashgate, 2003), 74–79; Yang Guozhen 楊國楨, *Lin Zexu zhuan* 林則徐傳 [Biography of Lin Zexu] (Beijing: Renmin chubanshe, 1981), 144.

3. Hunter, *Bits of Old China*, 260–62; Chen Depei, "Lin Zexu Yangshi zalu," 23; "Letter to the Editor," *Canton Press*, 14 Nov. 1840, 17–18; FHA 05-08-003-000166-018 Duyusi 都虞司 DG 20/8/27, 04-01-12-0408-113 Li Hongbin 李鴻賓 DG 9/6/12; Tan Shulin, "Ying Hua shuyuan yu wan," 66.

4. McNeur, *Liang A-fa*, xiv, 71, 82–83, 88; Su Jing, *Lin Zexu kanjian de shijie*, 35–37.

5. George B. Stevens and W. Fisher Markwick, *The Life, Letters and Journals of the Rev. and Hon. Peter Parker, M.D. Missionary, Physician, and Diplomatist* (Boston: Congregational Sunday-School and Publishing Society, 1896), 175.

6. Su Jing, *Lin Zexu kanjian de shijie*, 24, 29–35; "Loss of the British Bark Sunda," *Chinese Repository*, 1 Jan. 1840, 484.

7. Chen Shunyi 陳順意, "Fanyi yu yishixingtai: Lin Zexu fanyi huodong yanjiu" 翻譯與意識形態：林則徐翻譯活動研究 [Translation and ideology: A study of Lin Zexu's translation activities] (PhD diss., Wuhan daxue 武漢大學, 2016), 46–47, 54–56, 81–83, 94, 107–10, 170–73; Algernon S. Thelwall, *The Iniquities of the Opium Trade with China* (London: W.H. Allen, 1839), ix; M. C. Curthoys, "Thelwall, Algernon Sydney (1795–1863)," in *Oxford Dictionary of National Biography*, www.oxforddnb.com.

8. Su Jing, *Lin Zexu kanjian de shijie*, 3; Chen Shunyi, "Fanyi yu yishixingtai," 95–96.

9. Chen Depei, "Lin Zexu Yangshi zalu"; Chen Shenglin, "Lin Zexu 'kaiyan shijie' de zhengui jilu," 1, 3.

10. Mao, *Qing Empire and the Opium War*, 122.

11. *Yapian zhanzheng dang'an shiliao*, 1:673–75; Wang Hongzhi, "Di yi ci yapian."

12. Su Jing, *Lin Zexu kanjian de shijie*, 17–18, 43, 58–60.

13. "Loss of the British Bark Sunda," *Chinese Repository*, 1 Jan. 1840.

14. Hobhouse, *Recollections of a Long Life*, 5:227–28. For an alternative interpretation, see Melancon, *Britain's China Policy*, 104–7.

15. G. T. Staunton, *Memoirs of the Chief Incidents*, 139–41; Palmerston Papers GC/ST/36 G. T. Staunton to Palmerston, 3 May 1838, GC/ST/38 G. T. Staunton to Palmerston, 12 June 1838; GT Staunton Papers, Palmerston to G. T. Staunton, 12 May 1838, 10 June 1838.

16. G. T. Staunton, *Memoirs of the Chief Incidents*, 87–88; GT Staunton Papers, Palmerston to G. T. Staunton, 2 Apr. 1840. For an alternative interpretation, see Guan Shipei, "Ying Fa 'Nanjing tiaoyue' yizhan."

17. TNA FO 17/41:116 G. T. Staunton to Palmerston, 17 Feb. 1840.

18. TNA FO 17/41:145 G. T. Staunton to Palmerston, 20 Feb. 1840.

19. G. T. Staunton, *Corrected Report of the Speech of Sir George Staunton on Sir James Graham's Motion on the China Trade in the House of Commons, April 7, 1840* (London: Edmund Lloyd, 1840), 7; *The Times*, 7 Apr. 1840, 4–6; *Yapian zhanzheng dang'an shiliao*, 1:669; GT Staunton Papers, Visitors to Leigh Park.

20. *The Times*, 10 Apr. 1840, 4. See also *The Times*, 7 Apr. 1840, 4–6, 8 Apr. 1840, 4.

21. Hobhouse, *Recollections of a Long Life*, 5:257–58.

22. GT Staunton Papers, Palmerston to G. T. Staunton, 24 Oct. 1840.

23. Su Jing, *Lin Zexu kanjian de shijie*, 445.

24. Wang Hongzhi, "Di yi ci yapian," 99; Ji Yaxi and Chen Weimin, *Zhongguo jindai tongshi*, 158, 178; Li Wenjie, *Zhongguo jindai*, 203, 340–41; Porter, "Bannermen as Translators"; McNeur, *Liang A-fa*, 88.

25. Ji Yaxi and Chen Weimin, *Zhongguo jindai tongshi*, 163–67.

26. Ji Yaxi and Chen Weimin, *Zhongguo jindai tongshi*, 169–70, 185; Wang Hongzhi, "Di yi ci yapian," 102.

27. Morrison, *Chinese Commercial Guide*, vi; Wang Hongzhi, "Di yi ci yapian," 25, 28–29; Guan Shipei, "Fanyi yu tiaojie chongtu," 64.

28. Wang Hongzhi, "Di yi ci yapian," 17, 24; Platt, *Imperial Twilight*, 277–78.

29. Wang Hongzhi, "Di yi ci yapian," 52, 57; Guan Shipei, "Ying Fa 'Nanjing tiaoyue,'" 153–54.

30. TNA FO 17/63 G. T. Staunton, 19 Dec. 1842.

31. Barton Starr, "Morrison, John Robert," in *Oxford Dictionary of National Biography*, www.oxforddnb.com; Wang Hongzhi, "Di yi ci yapian," 18, 91; Guan Shipei, "Ying Fa 'Nanjing tiaoyue,'" 161–63; McNeur, *Liang A-fa*, 93, 97, 116.

32. Leonard, *Wei Yuan and China's Rediscovery*, 97–98; Wang Hongzhi, "Di yi ci yapian," 94; Chen Shunyi, "Fanyi yu yishixingtai," 47.

33. Lin Zexu 林則徐, *Lin Zexu quanji* 林則徐全集 [Complete works of Lin Zexu] (Fuzhou: Haixia wenyi chubanshe, 2002), 6:3086; Chen Shenglin, "Lin Zexu kaiyan de shijie," 1.

Chapter 20: Forgetting

1. *Hampshire Advertiser*, 17 Apr. 1852, see also 22 Feb. 1851.

2. *Hampshire Advertiser*, 17 Apr. 1852, see also 22 Feb. 1851.

3. G. T. Staunton, *Memoirs of the Chief Incidents*, 163, see also 162–66.

4. G. T. Staunton, *Inquiry into the Proper Mode of Rendering the Word "God,"* 31. See also *Hampshire Advertiser*, 24 Feb. 1838, 3 and 29 June 1839, 3.

5. G. T. Staunton, *Inquiry into the Proper Mode of Rendering the Word "God,"* 42.

6. G. T. Staunton, *Select Letters*, 4, 12, 14, 66.

7. G. T. Staunton, *Memoirs of the Chief Incidents*, 206.

8. *Gardeners' Chronicle and Agricultural Gazette*, 26 Apr. 1845, 275; Richard Carter, "Notes on the Different Kinds of Banana Cultivated at Leigh Park, the Seat of Sir G.T. Staunton, Bart," *Gardener's Magazine and Register of Rural and Domestic Improvement* 8 (1832): 506–7.

9. Jones, "Timeline of Leigh Park History," 19, 22, 25.

10. Royal Botanic Gardens, Kew, Archives: Directors' Correspondence 38/3 "Floriculture"; Brodie, *Works of Sir Benjamin Collins Brodie*, 1:262.

11. Brodie, *Works of Sir Benjamin Collins Brodie*, 1:119–377; G. H. Lewes, "Brodie's Psychological Inquiries," *Saturday Review* 1, no. 21 (22 Mar. 1856): 422–23.

12. Brodie, *Works of Sir Benjamin Collins Brodie*, 1:228, see also 1:262–63.

13. Brodie, *Works of Sir Benjamin Collins Brodie*, 1:228, see also 1:122, 299.

14. Lewes, "Brodie's Psychological Inquiries."

15. Brodie, *Works of Sir Benjamin Collins Brodie*, 1:194, 202, 244.

16. Brodie, *Works of Sir Benjamin Collins Brodie*, 1:240.

17. Brodie, *Works of Sir Benjamin Collins Brodie*, 1:225.

18. Brodie, *Works of Sir Benjamin Collins Brodie*, 1:333.

19. Brodie, *Works of Sir Benjamin Collins Brodie*, 1:372.

20. Brodie, *Works of Sir Benjamin Collins Brodie*, 1:373, 376–77.

21. GT Staunton Papers, Visitors to Leigh Park.

22. Janet H. Bateson, "Ho Chee, John Fullerton Elphinstone and the Lowdell Family" (RH7 History Group, 2008), www.rh7.org; Ch'en, *Insolvency of the Chinese*

Hong Merchants, 348–51; Duncan, "Hochee and Elphinstone," 40, 53, 54, 58; Price, *Chinese in Britain*, 86.

23. Duke Staunton Papers, Visitors to Leigh Park; *Hampshire Advertiser*, 17 Apr. 1852, 3.

24. Hampshire Record Office, Winchester, Copy/628/4 Will of Sir George Thomas Staunton of Leigh Park, 30 Jan. 1852; Steve Jones, "William Henry Stone of Leigh Park His Life, Including His Political Career and the Changing Face of the Leigh Park Estate," *Havant Borough History Booklet* 65 (n.d.): 8–15; Royal Asiatic Society, George Thomas Staunton Collection; Victoria and Albert Museum, London, A.17–1925 Ruyi sceptre.

25. AFP SC Cina 11:775 Grioglio 1845, 11:604 Agostino 1845.

26. APF SC Cina 14:275–6 Grioglio 1851; ACGOFM Missioni 53 Raccolta di lettere Wang 1832; Harrison, *Missionary's Curse*, 65–91.

27. *Tianzhujiao Changzhi jiaoqu jianshi*; *Zhaojialing shengmutang jianjie*; *Shanxi tongzhi Minzu zongjiao zhi*山西通志. 民族宗教志 [Shanxi gazetteer. Ethnic minorities and religions] (Beijing: Zhonghua shuju, 1997), 405.

28. Timmer, *Apostolisch Vicariaat van Zuid-Shansi*, 93; Margiotti, *Cattolicismo nello Shansi*, 173; APF SOCP 43:587 Serrati, 16 Sept. 1739; APF SOCP 63:809 Kuo 1781.

Conclusion

1. Liu, *Clash of Empires*, 31–86.

Abbatista, Guido, ed. *Law, Justice and Codification in Qing China: European and Chinese Perspectives*. Trieste: Edizioni Università di Trieste, 2017.

Afinogenov, Gregory. *Spies and Scholars: Chinese Secrets and Imperial Russia's Quest for World Power*. Cambridge, Mass.: Harvard University Press, 2020.

Alexander, William. Journal of Lord Macartney's Embassy to China 1792–94. British Library, Add MS 35174.

———. Album of 379 drawings of landscapes, coastlines, costumes and everyday life made during Lord Macartney's embassy to the Emperor of China (1792–94). British Library, India Office Records, Prints, Drawings and Photographs, WD959.

Amsler, Nadine, Henrietta Harrison, and Christian Windler. "Introduction: Eurasian Diplomacies around 1800: Transformation and Persistence." *International History Review* 5 (2019).

Anderson, Aeneas. *A Narrative of the Embassy to China, in the Years 1792, 1793, and 1794*. London: J. Debrett, 1795.

Archivio della Curia Generalizia dell'Ordine dei Fratri Minori (ACGOFM). Rome.

Archivio Istituto Universitario Orientale Napoli (AION). Naples.

Archivio Storico di Propaganda Fide (APF). Rome.

Archivum Romanum Societatis Iesu. Rome.

Arnould, Joseph. *Life of Thomas, First Lord Denman, Formerly Lord Chief Justice of England*. 2 vols. Boston: Estes & Lauriat, 1874.

Baring Archive. London.

Barrow, John. *Auto-biographical Memoir of Sir John Barrow, Bart., Late of the Admiralty*. London: John Murray, 1847.

———. *Some Account of the Public Life and a Selection from the Unpublished Writings of the Earl of Macartney*. London: T. Caddell & W. Davies, 1807.

———. *Travels in China*. London: T. Cadell & W. Davies, 1804.

———. *A Voyage to Cochinchina in the Years 1792 and 1793*. London: T. Cadell & W. Davies, 1806.

Basu, Dilip K. "Chinese Xenology and the Opium War: Reflections on Sinocentrism." *Journal of Asian Studies* 73, no. 4 (2014).

Berg, Maxine. "Britain, Industry and Perceptions of China: Matthew Boulton, 'Useful Knowledge' and the Macartney Embassy to China 1792–94." *Journal of Global History* 1, no. 2 (2006): 269–88.

Biographical Memoir of Sir Erasmus Gower, Knt. Portsea: W. Woodward, 1815.

Bowen, H. V. *The Business of Empire: The East India Company and Imperial Britain, 1756–1833*. Cambridge: Cambridge University Press, 2006.

British Library (BL). London.

Brodie, Benjamin. *The Works of Sir Benjamin Collins Brodie*. London: Longman, Green, Longman, Roberts & Green, 1865.

Brown, David. *Palmerston: A Biography*. New Haven, Conn.: Yale University Press, 2010.

Burney, Fanny. *The Journals and Letters of Fanny Burney*. Edited by Joyce Hemlow et al. Oxford: Oxford University Press, 1972–84.

Cai Hongsheng 蔡鴻生. "Qingdai Guangzhou hangshang de xiyang guan—Pan Youdu 'Xiyang zayong' pingshuo" 清代廣州行商的西洋觀— 潘有度《西洋雜咏》[The attitudes towards the West of a Qing dynasty Guangzhou hong merchant—Pan Youdu's *Miscellaneous songs on the Western Ocean*]. *Guangdong shehui kexue* 廣東社會科學 1 (2003).

Cappello, Felice. *Hieropaedia Catholica sive sacra instructio de diversis sacerdotii ordinibus in modum examinis exarata*. Neapoli: Petrus Perger, 1804.

———. *Progymnasmatum eloquentiae*. Neapoli: Fratres Simonii, 1763.

Chan Hok-Lam. "The 'Chinese Barbarian Officials' in the Foreign Tributary Missions to China during the Ming Dynasty." *Journal of the American Oriental Society* 88, no. 3 (1968).

Chen Depei 陳德培. "Lin Zexu Yangshi zalu" 林則徐《洋事雜錄》[Lin Zexu's *Miscellaneous Notes on Foreign Affairs*]. *Zhongshan daxue xuebao (zhexue shehuikexue ban)* 中山大學學報(哲學社會科學版) 3 (1986).

Chen Guodong 陳國棟. *Qingdai qianqi de Yue haiguan yu shisan hang* 清代前期的粵海關與十三行 [The Guangdong customs and the cohong in the early Qing]. Guangzhou: Guangdong renmin chubanshe, 2014.

Chen Kaike 陳開科. *Jiaqing shi nian: shibai de Eguo shituan yu shibai de Zhongguo waijiao* 嘉慶十年: 失敗的俄國使團與失敗的中國外交 [1805: The defeat of the Russian embassy and the defeat of China's foreign policy]. Beijing: Shehui kexue wenxian chubanshe, 2014.

Ch'en, Kuo-tung Anthony. *The Insolvency of the Chinese Hong Merchants 1760–1843*. Taipei: Academia Sinica, 1990.

Chen, Li. *Chinese Law in Imperial Eyes: Sovereignty, Justice and Transcultural Politics*. New York: Columbia University Press, 2016.

Chen Shenglin 陳勝粦. "Lin Zexu 'kaiyan shijie' de zhengui jilu: Lin shi *Yangshi zalu* pingjia" 林則徐'開眼世界'的珍貴記錄— 林氏《洋事雜錄》評價 [A precious record of the broadening of Lin Zexu's horizons—An evaluation of Mr Lin's *Miscellaneous notes on foreign matters*]. *Zhongshan daxue xuebao (Zhexue shehuikexue ban)* 中山大學學報(哲學社會科學版) 3 (1986).

Chen, Song-chuan. *Merchants of War and Peace: British Knowledge of China in the Making of the Opium War*. Hong Kong: Hong Kong University Press, 2017.

Chen Xianpo 陳顯波. "Zhuti wenhua dui yizhe de yingxiang—yi Folanxisi Bailing zhi Liangguang zongdu xinjian fanyi wei li" 主體文化對譯者的影響— 以佛朗西斯百靈至兩廣總督信件翻譯為例 [The influence of subjective culture on translators—A case study of the translation of the letter from Francis Baring to the governor general of Guangdong and Guangxi]. *Jiamusi daxue shehui kexue xuebao* 價木斯大學社會科學學報 29, no. 5 (2011).

Coutts Bank Archive. London.

Davies, C. Collin, ed. *The Private Correspondence of Lord Macartney Governor of Madras (1781–85).* London: Offices of the Royal Historical Society, 1950.

Davis, John Francis. *Sketches of China.* London: Charles Knight, 1841.

Di Fiore, Giacomo. *Lettere di missionari dalla Cina (1761–1775): La vita quotidiana nelle missioni attraverso il carteggio di Emiliano Palladini e Filippo Huang con il Collegio dei Cinesi in Napoli.* Napoli: Istituto Universitario Orientale, 1995.

Di Fiore, Giacomo, and Michele Fatica. "Vita di relazione e vita quotidiana nel Collegio dei Cinesi." In *Matteo Ripa e il Collegio dei Cinesi di Napoli (1682–1869): Percorso documentario e iconografico,* edited by Michele Fatica. Napoli: Università degli Studi di Napoli "L'Orientale," 2006.

Durand, Pierre-Henri. "Langage bureaucratique et histoire: Variations autour du Grand Conseil et de l'ambassade Macartney." *Études chinoises* 12, no. 1 (1993).

Elenchus alumnorum, decreta et documenta quae spectant ad Collegium Sacrae Familiae Neapolis. Chang-hai: Typographia Missionis Catholicae, 1917.

Ellis, Henry. *Journal of the Proceedings of the Late Embassy to China.* 2 vols. London: John Murray, 1818.

Elphinstone Collection. British Library.

Fairbank, John King, ed. *The Chinese World Order: Traditional China's Foreign Relations.* Cambridge, Mass.: Harvard University Press, 1968.

Farrell, Stephen. "Staunton, Sir George Thomas, 2nd bt. (1781–1859), of Leigh Park, Hants and 17 Devonshire Street, Portland Place, Mdx." In *The History of Parliament: The House of Commons 1820–1832,* edited by D. R. Fisher. Cambridge: Cambridge University Press, 2009.

Fatica, Michele. "Gli alunni del *Collegium Sinicum* di Napoli, la missione Macartney presso l'imperatore Qianlong e la richiesta di libertà di culto per i cristiani cinesi [1792–1793]." In *Studi in onore di Lionello Lanciotti,* edited by S. M. Carletti, M. Sacchetti, and P. Santangelo. Napoli: Istituto Universitario Orientale, 1996.

———. *Matteo Ripa e il Collegio dei Cinesi di Napoli (1682–1869): Percorso documentario e iconografico.* Napoli: Università degli Studi di Napoli "L'Orientale," 2006.

Fatica, Michele, and Francesco D'Arelli, eds. *La missione cattolica in Cina tra i secoli XVIII–XIX: Matteo Ripa e il collegio dei cinesi: Atti del colloquio internazionale Napoli, 11–12 febbraio 1997.* Napoli: Istituto universitario orientale, 1999.

First Historical Archives 中國第一歷史檔案官 (FHA). Beijing.

Fisher, D. R., ed. *The History of Parliament: The House of Commons 1820–1832.* Cambridge: Cambridge University Press, 2009.

Fisher, Michael H. *Counterflows to Colonialism: Indian Travellers and Settlers in Britain 1600–1857.* Delhi: Permanent Black, 2004.

Fu, Lo-Shu. *A Documentary Chronicle of Sino-Western Relations (1644–1820).* Tucson: University of Arizona Press, 1966.

Gao, Hao. *Creating the Opium War: British Imperial Attitudes towards China, 1792–1840.* Manchester: Manchester University Press, 2020.

Gladwyn, Derek. *Leigh Park: A 19th Century Pleasure Ground.* Midhurst: Middleton Press, 1992.

Gower, Erasmus. *A Journal of His Majesty's Ship Lion beginning the 1st October 1792 and ending the 7th September 1794.* British Library, Add MS 21106.

Grant, Frederic D. *The Chinese Cornerstone of Modern Banking: The Canton Guaranty System and the Origins of Bank Deposit Insurance 1780–1933.* Leiden: Brill, 2014.

———. "The Failure of the Li-ch'uan Hong: Litigation as a Hazard of Nineteenth Century Foreign Trade." *American Neptune* 48, no. 4 (1988).

Guan Shipei 關詩珮. "Fanyi yu tiaojie chongtu: diyici yapian zhanzheng de Ying fang yizhe Feilun (Samuel T. Fearon, 1819–1854)" 翻譯於調解衝突: 第一次鴉片戰爭的英方譯者費倫 (Samuel T. Fearon, 1819–1854) [Translation and conflicts over mediation: Samuel T. Fearon (1819–1954) an interpreter for the British during the First Opium War]. *Zhongyang yanjiuyuan jindaishi yanjiusuo jikan* 中央研究院近代史研究所集刊 76 (2012).

———. "Ying Fa 'Nanjing tiaoyue' yizhan yu Yingguo hanxue de chengli—Yingguo hanxue zhi fu Sidangdong de gongxian 英法《南京條約》譯戰與英國漢學的成立—英國漢學之父斯當東的貢獻 [The translation war between Britain and France over the Treaty of Nanking and the establishment of British Sinology—The contribution of the father of British Sinology Staunton]. *Fanyishi yanjiu* 翻譯史研究 3 (2013).

Hanser, Jessica. "From Cross-Cultural Credit to Colonial Debt: British Expansion in Madras and Canton, 1750–1800." *American Historical Review* 124, no. 1 (2019): 87–107.

———. *Mr. Smith Goes to China: Three Scots in the Making of Britain's Global Empire.* New Haven, Conn.: Yale University Press, 2019.

Hariharan, Shantha. "Relations between Macao and Britain during the Napoleonic Wars: Attempt to Land British Troops in Macao, 1802." *South Asia Research* 30, no. 2 (2010).

Harrison, Henrietta. *The Missionary's Curse and Other Tales from a Chinese Catholic Village.* Berkeley: University of California Press, 2013.

———. "The Qianlong Emperor's Letter to George III and the Early-Twentieth-Century Origins of Ideas about Traditional China's Foreign Relations." *American Historical Review* 122, no. 3 (2017).

Hobhouse, John Cam. *Recollections of a Long Life.* 6 vols. London: John Murray, 1911.

Huang Yilong 黃一農. "Yinxiang yu zhenxiang—Qing chao Zhong Ying liangguo de jinjian zhi zheng" 印象與真相—清朝中英兩國的覲見之爭 [Prints and the real picture—The contest over imperial audiences between China and Britain in the Qing Dynasty]. *Zhongyang yanjiuyuan lishi yuyan yanjiusuo jikan* 中央研究院歷史語言研究所集刊 78, no. 1 (2007).

Hunter, William C. *Bits of Old China.* London: Kegan Paul, 1855.

India Office Records (IOR), British Library. London.

Jami, Catherine. *The Emperor's New Mathematics: Western Learning and Imperial Authority during the Kangxi Reign (1662–1722).* Oxford: Oxford University Press, 2011.

Jenkins, Lawrence Waters. "An Old Mandarin Home." *Essex Institute Historical Collections* 71, no. 2 (1935).

Ji Qiufeng 計秋楓. "Magaerni shi Hua shijian zhong de Yingjili 'biaowen' kao" 馬戛爾尼 使華事件中的英吉利'表文'考 [An examination of the English "memorial" presented during Macartney's embassy to China]. *Shixue yuekan* 史學月刊 8 (2008).

Ji Yaxi 季壓西 and Chen Weimin 陳偉民. *Zhongguo jindai tongshi* 中國近代通事 [Interpreters in modern China]. Beijing: Xueyuan chubanshe, 2007.

Jones, Steve. "Timeline of Leigh Park History." *Borough of Havant History Booklet* 97 (n.d.).

Journal of the Commissioners appointed by the President and Select Committee of Fort St. George, Madras, to conclude a treaty of peace on behalf of the East India Company with Tipu Sultan. British Library, Add MS 39857–8.

Keliher, Macabe. *The Board of Rites and the Making of Qing China*. Oakland: University of California Press, 2019.

Kim, Kyung-ran. "Foreign Trade and Interpreter Officials." In *Everyday Life in Joseon-Era Korea: Economy and Society*, edited by Michael D. Shin. Leiden: Brill, 2014.

Kitson, Peter J. *Forging Romantic China: Sino-British Cultural Exchange 1760–1840*. Cambridge: Cambridge University Press, 2013.

Kwee, Hui Kian. *The Political Economy of Java's Northeast Coast c. 1740–1800: Elite Synergy*. Leiden: Brill, 2006.

Lai Huimin 賴惠敏. *Qianlong huangdi de hebao* 乾隆皇帝的荷包 [Emperor Qianlong's purse]. Taibei: Zhongyanyuan jinshisuo, 2014.

Leonard, Jane Kate. *Wei Yuan and China's Rediscovery of the Maritime World*. Cambridge, Mass.: Council on East Asian Studies, Harvard University, 1984.

Leung, Angela Ki Che. "The Business of Vaccination in Nineteenth-Century Canton." *Late Imperial China* 29, no. 1, Supplement (2008).

Leung, Cécile. *Etienne Fourmont (1683–1745): Oriental and Chinese Languages in Eighteenth-Century France*. Leuven: Leuven University Press & Ferdinand Verbiest Foundation, 2002.

Li Changsen 李長森. *Jindai Aomen fanyi shigao* 近代澳門翻譯史稿 [A draft history of translation in modern Macao]. Beijing: Shehuikexue wenxian chubanshe, 2016.

Li Huan 李桓, ed. *Guochao qi xian leizheng chubian* 國朝耆獻類徵初編 [Classified biographies of notables of the dynasty first series]. 1883. Reprint, Taibei: Wenhai chubanshe, 1966.

Li, Hui. "Il Dictionarium Latino-Italico-Sinicum di Carlo Orazi da Castrorano O.F.M. (1673–1755)." Sapienza PhD dissertation, 2014–15.

Li Nanqiu 黎難秋. *Zhongguo kouyi shi* 中國口譯史 [A history of interpreting in China]. Qingdao: Qingdao chubanshe, 2002.

Li Wenjie 李文杰. *Zhongguo jindai waijiaoguan qunti de xingcheng (1861–1911)* 中國 近代外交官群體的形成 (1861–1911) [The emergence of modern Chinese diplomats (1861–1911)]. Beijing: Sanlian shudian, 2017.

Li Yukai 李于鍇. *Li Yukai yigao jicun* 李于鍇遺稿輯存 [Collected writings left by Li Yukai]. Lanzhou: Lanzhou daxue chubanshe, 1987.

Liang Tingnan 梁廷枏. *Yue haiguan zhi* 粵海關志 [Guangdong maritime customs gazetteer] (1839). Edited by Yuan Zhongren 袁鐘仁. Guangzhou: Guangdong renmin chubanshe, 2014.

Liu Fang 劉芳 and Zhang Wenqin 張文欽, eds. *Qingdai Aomen zhongwen dang'an huibian* 清代澳門中文檔案彙編 [Collected Chinese archives from Qing dynasty Macao]. 2 vols. Aomen: Aomen jijinhui, 1999.

Liu Li 劉黎. "Zhong Ying shouci zhengshi waijiao zhong Bailing zhi liang Guang zongdu xinjian de fanyi wenti" 中英首次正式外交中百靈致兩廣總督信件的翻譯問題 [The problem of the translation of Baring's letter to the Guangdong Guangxi governor general during the first formal diplomatic encounter between China and Britain]. *Chongqing jiaotong daxue bao (shehui kexue ban)* 重慶交通大學報(社會科學版) 16, no. 2 (2016).

Liu, Lydia H. *The Clash of Empires: The Invention of China in Modern World Making.* Cambridge, Mass.: Harvard University Press, 2004.

Ma Zimu 馬子木. "Lun Qing chao fanyi keju de xingcheng yu fazhan" 論清朝翻譯科舉的形成與發展 [On the formation and development of translation examinations in the Qing dynasty]. *Qing shi yanjiu* 清史研究 3 (2014).

Macartney, George. *An Embassy to China Being the Journal Kept by Lord Macartney during His Embassy to the Emperor Ch'ien-lung 1793–1794.* Edited by J. L. Cranmer-Byng. London: Longmans, 1962.

———. George Macartney Papers. Asia Collections, Cornell University Library, Ithaca, N.Y. (Macartney Cornell MS).

———. Journal of a Voyage from London to Cochin China 11/9/1792–15/6/1793. Copy ca. 1805. Wellcome Trust, MSS 3352

———. Papers of George Macartney, 1st Earl Macartney. Bodleian Library, Oxford.

Mao Haijian. *The Qing Empire and the Opium War: The Collapse of the Heavenly Dynasty.* Translated by Joseph Lawson et al. Cambridge: Cambridge University Press, 2016.

Margiotti, Fortunato. *Il cattolicismo nello Shansi dalle origini al 1738.* Rome: Edizioni "Sinica Franciscana," 1958.

Mcgee, Nicholas. "Putting Words in the Emperor's Mouth: A Genealogy of Colonial Potential in the Study of Qing Chinese Diaspora." *Journal of World History* 30, no. 4 (2019).

McNeur, George Hunter. *Liang A-fa: China's First Preacher, 1789–1855.* Edited by Jonathan A. Seitz. Eugene, Oregon: Pickwick, 2013.

McNulty, Paul. "The Genealogy of the Anglo-Norman Lynches Who Settled in Galway." *Journal of the Galway Archaeological and Historical Society* 62 (2010).

Millward, James A., et al., eds. *New Qing Imperial History: The Making of Inner Asian Empire at Qing Chengde.* London: RoutledgeCurzon, 2004.

Ming Qing gong cang Zhong xi shangmao dang'an 明清宮藏中西商貿檔案 [Ming and Qing palace archives on the Sino-Western trade]. Zhongguo di yi lishi dang'anguan 中國第一歷史檔案館 ed. Beijing: Zhongguo dang'an chubanshe, 2010. 8 vols.

Ming Qing shilu 明清實錄 [Veritable records of the Ming and Qing]. Reprint, Beijing: Airusheng shuzihua jishu yanjiu zhongxin, 2016.

Morrison, John Robert. *A Chinese Commercial Guide, Consisting of a Collection of Details Respecting Foreign Trade in China.* Canton: Albion Press, 1834.

Morrison, Robert. *A Memoir of the Principal Occurrences during an Embassy from the British Government to the Court of China in the Year 1816.* London, 1819.

Morrison, Robert, and Eliza A. Morrison. *Memoirs of the Life and Labours of Robert Morrison D.D.* 2 vols. London: Longman, Orme, Brown, Green and Longmans, 1839.

Morse, Hosea Ballou. *The Chronicles of the East India Company Trading to China, 1635–1834.* 5 vols. Oxford: Clarendon, 1926–29.

Mosca, Matthew William. *From Frontier Policy to Foreign Policy: The Question of India and the Transformation of Geopolitics in Qing China.* Stanford, Calif.: Stanford University Press, 2013.

———. "The Qing State and Its Awareness of Eurasian Interconnections 1789–1806." *Eighteenth-Century Studies* 47, no. 2 (2014).

The National Archives (TNA). London.

National Archives of Ireland. Dublin.

Nechtman, Tillman W. *Nabobs: Empire and Identity in Eighteenth-Century Britain.* Cambridge: Cambridge University Press, 2010.

Old Bailey Proceedings Online. www.oldbaileyonline.org.

O'Neill, Mark, and Ged Martin. "A Backbencher on Parliamentary Reform, 1831–1832." *Historical Journal* 23, no. 3 (1980).

Ong, S. P. "Jurisdictional Politics in Canton and the First English Translation of the Qing Penal Code (1810)." *Journal of the Royal Asiatic Society* 20, no. 2 (2010).

Palmerston Papers, Southampton University Archive. Southampton.

Pan Jianfen 潘劍芬. *Guangzhou shisanhang hangshang Pan Zhencheng jiazu yanjiu (1714–1911)* 廣州十三行行商潘振承家族研究（1714–1911）[The family history of Pan Zhencheng of the thirteen hong merchant houses of Guangzhou]. Beijing: Shehui kexue chubanshe, 2017.

Pan Yikui 潘挹奎. *Wuwei qijiu zhuan* 武威耆舊傳 [Biographies of Wuwei elders]. ca. 1820.

Perdue, Peter C. *China Marches West: The Qing Conquest of Central Eurasia.* Cambridge, Mass.: Harvard University Press, 2005.

———. "The Tenacious Tributary System." *Journal of Contemporary China* 24, no. 96 (2015).

Peyrefitte, Alain. *The Collision of Two Civilisations: The British Expedition to China in 1792–4.* Translated by Jon Rothschild. London: Harvill, 1993.

Platt, Stephen R. *Imperial Twilight: The Opium War and the End of China's Last Golden Age.* New York: Knopf, 2018.

Polachek, James. *The Inner Opium War.* Cambridge, Mass.: Harvard University Press, 1992.

Porter, David. "Bannermen as Translators: Manchu Language Education in the Hanjun Banners." *Late Imperial China* 40, no. 2 (2019).

Price, Barclay. *The Chinese in Britain: A History of Visitors and Settlers.* Stroud: Amberley Publishing, 2019.

Pritchard, Earl H. "The Crucial Years of Early Anglo-Chinese Relations, 1750–1800." *Research Studies of the State College of Washington* 4, nos. 3–4 (1936).

———. "The Instructions of the East India Company to Lord Macartney on His Embassy to China and His Reports to the Company 1792–4." *Journal of the Royal Asiatic Society of Great Britain and Ireland* 70, nos. 2–4 (1938).

Proudfoot, William Jardine. *Biographical Memoir of James Dinwiddie, LL.D.* Liverpool: Edward Howell, 1868.

Qinding da Qing huidian shili 欽定大清會典事例 [Imperially authorised collected statutes and precedents of the great Qing]. Edited by Kungang 崑岡 et al. 1,220 vols. Beijing: Waiwubu, 1899.

Qingdai waijiao shiliao Jiaqing chao 清代外交史料嘉慶朝 [Qing foreign affairs historical materials from the Jiaqing reign]. Edited by Gugong bowuyuan 故宮博物院. 1932–35.

Qing Gaozong (Qianlong) yuzhi shiwen quanji 清高宗(乾隆)御製詩文全集 [The collected poetry and prose of Qing Gaozong (Qianlong)]. 10 vols. Beijing: Zhongguo Renmin daxue chubanshe, 1993.

Qing shi gao xiaozhu 清史稿校註 [Draft Qing History annotated edition]. 15 vols. Taibei: Guoshiguan, 1986.

Qing zhongqianqi xiyang tianzhujiao zai Hua huodong dang'an shiliao 清中前期西洋天主教在華活動檔案史料 [Historical archives relating to the activities of Western Catholics in China in the early and mid-Qing]. Edited by Zhongguo di yi lishi dang'anguan 中國第一歷史檔案館. Beijing: Zhonghua shuju, 2003.

Roebuck, Peter, ed. *Macartney of Lisanoure, 1737–1806: Essays in Biography.* Belfast: Ulster Historical Foundation, 1983.

Royal Asiatic Society. George Thomas Staunton Collection in the RAS Library, May 1998 (unpublished MS).

Sachsenmaier, Dominic. *Global Entanglements of a Man Who Never Travelled: A Seventeenth-Century Chinese Christian and His Conflicted Worlds.* New York: Columbia University Press, 2020.

Smith, Pleasance, ed. *Memoir and Correspondence of the Late Sir James Edward Smith M.D.* London: Longman, Rees, Orme, Brown, Green & Longman, 1832.

Song Wenqing gong sheng guan lu 松文清公升官錄 [A record of Songyun's official career]. In *Beijing tushuguan zhenben nianpu congkan* 北京圖書館藏珍本年譜叢刊 (Beijing: Beijing tushuguan chubanshe, 1999).

Souciet, Etienne. *Observations mathématiques, astronomiques, geographiques, chronologiques, et physiques tirées des anciens livres chinois ou faites nouvellement aux Indes et à la Chine par les pères de la Compagnie de Jesus.* Paris: Rollin, 1729.

Standaert, Nicolas. "Jean François Foucquet's Contribution to the Establishment of Chinese Book Collections in European Libraries: Circulation of Chinese Books." *Monumenta Serica* 63, no. 2 (2015).

St. André, James. "'But Do They Have a Notion of Justice?' Staunton's 1810 Translation of the Great Qing Code." *The Translator* 10, no. 1 (2004).

Staunton, George Leonard. *An Authentic Account of an Embassy from the King of Great Britain to the Emperor of China.* 2 vols. London: W. Bulmer, 1797.

———. Sir George Leonard Staunton Papers, 1753–1804. British Library.

Staunton, George Thomas. *Catalogue of the Library at Leigh Park, 1842.* Adams, 1842.

———. *Corrected Report of the Speeches of Sir George Staunton on the China Trade in the House of Commons, June 4, and June 13, 1833.* London: Edmund Lloyd, 1833.

———. George Thomas Staunton Papers, 1743–1885. David M. Rubenstein Rare Book & Manuscript Library, Duke University. Reproduced in China through Western Eyes: Manuscript Records of Traders, Travellers, Missionaries & Diplomats, Adam Matthews.

———. *An Inquiry into the Proper Mode of Rendering the Word "God" in Translating the Sacred Scriptures into the Chinese Language.* London: Lionel Booth, 1849.

———. *Memoir of the Life and Family of the Late Sir George Leonard Staunton Bart.* Hampshire: Havant Press, 1823.

———. *Memoirs of the Chief Incidents of the Public Life of Sir George Thomas Staunton, Bart.* London: L. Booth, 1856.

———. *Miscellaneous Notices Relating to China and Our Commercial Intercourse with That Country Including a Few Translations from the Chinese Language.* London: John Murray, 1822.

———, trans. *Narrative of the Chinese Embassy to the Khan of the Tourgouth Tartars.* London: John Murray, 1821.

———. *Notes of Proceedings and Occurrences during the British Embassy to Pekin in 1816.* Hampshire: Havant Press, 1824.

———. *Notices of the Leigh Park Estate Near Havant 1836.* London: Edmund Lloyd, 1836.

———. *Remarks on the British Relations with China and the Proposed Plans for Improving Them.* London: Edmund Lloyd, 1836.

———, ed. *Select Letters Written on the Occasion of the Memoirs of Sir G.T. Staunton Bart. by His Private Friends.* London, 1857.

———. *Tablets in the Temple, Leigh Park.* 1840.

———, trans. *Ta Tsing Leu Lee; Being the Fundamental Laws, and a Selection from the Supplementary Statutes, of the Penal Code of China.* London: T. Cadell & W. Davies, 1810.

Stifler, Susan Reed. "The Language Students of the East India Company's Canton Factory." *Journal of the North China Branch of the Royal Asiatic Society* 69 (1938).

Su Jing 蘇精. *Lin Zexu kanjian de shijie: "Aomen xinwenzhi" de yuanwen yu yiwen* 林則徐看見的世界:《澳門新聞紙》的原文與譯文 [The world that Lin Zexu saw: Original texts and translations of the "Macao News sheets"]. Guilin: Guangxi shifan daxue chubanshe, 2017.

Tan Shulin 谭樹林. "Ying Hua shuyuan yu wan Qing fanyi rencai zhi peiyang—yi Yuan Dehui, Ma Ruhan wei zhongxin de kaocha" 英華書院與晚清翻譯人才之培養— 以袁德輝、馬儒翰為中心的考察 [The Anglo-Chinese College and the education of late Qing translation talent—An examination centred on Yuan Dehui and John Robert Morrison]. *Anhui shixue* 安徽史學 2 (2014).

Tianzhujiao Changzhi jiaoqu jianshi 天主教長治教區簡史 [A brief history of Changzhi Catholic diocese]. Edited by Jiaoyou shenghuo 教友生活 [1997].

Timmer, Odoricus. *Het Apostolisch Vicariaat van Zuid-Shansi in de eerste vijf-en-twintig jaren van zijn bestaan (1890–1915).* Leiden: G.F. Théonville, 1915.

Torikai, Kumiko. *Voices of the Invisible Presence: Diplomatic Interpreters in Post–World War II Japan*. Amsterdam: John Benjamins, 2009.

Van Dyke, Paul A. *The Canton Trade: Life and Enterprise on the China Coast, 1700–1845*. Hong Kong: Hong Kong University Press, 2005.

Villani, Stefano. "Montucci, Antonio." In *Dizionario biografico degli italiani (1960–)*. 2018. http://treccani.it.

Wakeman, Frederic. "Drury's Occupation of Macau and China's Response to Early Modern Imperialism." *East Asian History* 28 (2004).

Waley-Cohen, Joanna. "China and Western Technology in the Late Eighteenth Century." *American Historical Review* 98, no. 5 (1993).

Wang Hongzhi 王宏志 (Lawrence Wong). "Di yi ci yapian zhanzheng zhong de yizhe: shang pian: Zhongfang de yizhe" 第一次鴉片戰爭中的譯者: 上篇: 中方的譯者 [The translators/interpreters in the First Opium War. Part one: Translators/interpreters of the Chinese camp]. *Fanyishi yanjiu* 翻譯史研究 1 (2011).

———. "Di yi ci yapian zhanzheng zhong de yizhe: xia pian: Yingfang de yizhe" 第一次鴉片戰爭中的譯者: 下篇: 英方的譯者 [The translators/interpreters in the First Opium War. Part two: Translators/interpreters of the English camp]. *Fanyishi yanjiu* 翻譯史研究 (2012): 1–59.

———. *Fanyi yu jindai Zhongguo* 翻譯與近代中國 [Translation and modern China]. Shanghai: Fudan daxue chubanshe, 2014.

———. "Magaerni shi Hua de fanyi wenti" 馬戛爾尼使華的翻譯問題 [The translation problems of the Macartney embassy to China]. *Zhongyang yanjiuyuan jindaishi yanjiusuo jikan* 中央研究院近代史研究所集刊 63 (2009).

———. "Sidangdong yu Guangzhou tizhi Zhong Ying maoyi de fanyi: jianlun 1814 nian Dong Yindu gongsi yu Guangzhou guanyuan yi ci sheji fanyi wenti de huiyi" 斯當東與廣州體制中英貿易的翻譯: 兼論1814年東印度公司與廣州官員一次涉及翻譯問題的會議 [George Thomas Staunton and translation in Sino-British trade in the Canton system: With special reference to the 1814 meeting involving the translation issue]. *Fanyixue yanjiu* 翻譯學研究 17 (2014): 225–59.

———. "1814 nian 'Ayao shijian': Jindai Zhong Ying jiaowang zhong de tongshi" 1814年'阿耀'事件: 近代中英交往中的通事 [The 1814 "Ayew Incident": Linguists in Sino-British relations in the nineteenth century]. 中國文化研究所學報 / *Journal of Chinese Studies* 59 (2014).

Wang, Wensheng. *White Lotus Rebels and South China Pirates: Crisis and Reform in the Qing Empire*. Cambridge, Mass.: Harvard University Press, 2014.

Wang Yuanchong. *Remaking the Chinese Empire: Manchu-Korean Relations, 1616–1911*. Ithaca, N.Y.: Cornell University Press, 2018.

Wong, John D. *Global Trade in the Nineteenth Century: The House of Houqua and the Canton System*. Cambridge: Cambridge University Press, 2016.

Wong, Lawrence Wang-chi. "'We Are as Babies under Nurses': Thomas Manning (1772–1840) and Sino-British Relations in the Early Nineteenth Century." *Journal of Translation Studies* 1, no. 1 (2017).

Wu, Huiyi. *Traduire la Chine au XVIIIe siècle: les jésuites traducteurs de textes chinois et le renouvellement des connaissances européennes sur la Chine (1687–ca. 1740)*. Paris: Honoré Champion, 2017.

Wuwei jianshi 武威簡史 [A simple history of Wuwei]. Edited by Wuwei xianzhi bianzuan weiyuanhui 武威縣志編纂委員會. Wuwei: Wuwei xian yinshuachang, 1983.

Wuwei shi minzu zongjiao zhi 武威市民族宗教志 [Wuwei city nationalities and religions gazetteer]. Lanzhou: Gansu minzu chubanshe, 2002.

Yang Huiling 楊慧玲. *19 shiji Han Ying cidian chuantong—Malixun, Weisanwei, Zhailisi Han Ying cidian de puxi yanjiu* 19 世紀漢英詞典傳統—馬禮遜, 韋三畏, 翟理斯漢英詞典的譜系研究 [The tradition of 19th-century Chinese-English dictionaries—Research into the genealogy of the Chinese-English dictionaries of Robert Morrison, Samuel Wells Williams and Herbert Giles]. Beijing: Shangwu yinshuguan, 2012.

Yapian zhanzheng dang'an shiliao 鴉片戰爭檔案史料 [Historical archival materials on the Opium War]. Edited by Zhongguo diyi lishi dang'anguan 中國第一歷史檔案館. Tianjin: Tianjin guji chubanshe, 1992.

Yingjiliguo xinchu zhongdou qishu 英吉利國新出種痘奇書 [The extraordinary story of the newly discovered English method of inoculation]. 1805. Reprint, 1885. Bodleian Library Sinica, 1417.

Yingshi Magaerni fang Hua dang'an shiliao huibian 英使馬嘎爾尼訪華檔案史料匯編 [Collected archival materials on the English envoy Macartney's visit to China]. Edited by Zhongguo di yi lishi dang'anguan 中國第一歷史檔案館. Beijing: Guoji wenhua chuban gongsi, 1996.

Yoon, Wook. "Prosperity with the Help of 'Villains,' 1776–1799: A Review of the Heshen Clique and its Era." *T'oung Pao* 98, nos. 4/5 (2012).

Zetzsche, Jost Oliver. *The Bible in China: The History of the Union Version, or The Culmination of Protestant Missionary Bible Translation in China.* Sankt Augustin: Monumenta Serica Institute, 1999.

Zhang Jiafeng 張嘉鳳. "Shijiu shiji chu niudou de zaidihua—yi 'Yingjili guo xinchu zhongdou qishu,' 'Xiyang zhongdou lun' yu 'Yindou lüe' wei taolun zhongxin" 十九世紀初牛痘的在地化— 以《英吉利國新出種痘奇書》,《西洋種痘論》與《引痘略》為討論中心 [Localisation of vaccination in the early nineteenth century—based around "The Extraordinary Story of the Newly Discovered English Method of Inoculation," "On Western Inoculation" and "An Outline of Inoculation"] *Zhongyang yanjiuyuan lishi yuyan yanjiusuo jikan* 中央研究院歷史語言研究所集刊 78, no. 4 (2007).

Zhang Ruilong 張瑞龍. *Tianlijiao shijian yu Qing zhongye de zhengzhi xueshu yu shehui* 天理教事件與清中葉的政治、學術與社會 [The Tianli Sect incident and politics, academy and society in the mid-Qing]. Beijing: Zhonghua shuju, 2014.

Zhang Shuangzhi 張雙智. *Qingdai chaoqin zhidu yanjiu* 清代朝勤制度研究 [Research into the Qing tribute system]. Beijing: Xueyuan chubanshe, 2010.

Zhaolian 昭槤. *Xiaoting zalu* 嘯亭雜錄 [Miscellaneous records from the Sighing Wind Pagoda]. Edited by He Yingfang 何英芳. Beijing: Zhonghua shuju, 1980.

1.1.   George Ernest Morrison, *Liangchow from the Bell Tower Looking North*, 1910. Mitchell Library, State Library of New South Wales.

2.1.   Lemuel Francis Abbott, *George Macartney and George Leonard Staunton*, ca. 1785. © National Portrait Gallery, London.

3.1.   Gaspar Butler, *Panoramic View of the Bay of Naples*, eighteenth century. National Maritime Museum, Greenwich.

3.2.   *The Chinese Church and College*, nineteenth century. Santangelo Collection. Photo: Pedicini fotografi, Naples.

3.3.   Entrance hall of Chinese College. Author's photograph.

3.4.   Chinoiserie porcelain boudoir of Queen Maria Amalia. Courtesy of Italian Ministry of Cultural Heritage and Activities and Tourism—Museum and Royal Park of Capodimonte.

4.1.   George Thomas Staunton's Diary, 1791. David M. Rubenstein Rare Book & Manuscript Library, Duke University.

4.2.   Thomas Hickey, *George Thomas Staunton*, 1792. MOCA (Museum of Contemporary Art), Yinchuan. Photo: Martyn Gregory Gallery, London.

6.1.   John Barrow, *A General Chart on Mercator's Projection*, 1794. From George Leonard Staunton, *An Authentic Account of an Embassy from the King of Great Britain to the Emperor of China*. W. Bulmer, 1797. Adapted by David Cox.

6.2.   William Alexander, *HMS Lion*, 1792. © The Trustees of the British Museum. All rights reserved.

6.3, 7.1, 7.2, 7.4, 8.1, and 8.2.   WD959 William Alexander's Sketches of the Macartney Embassy to China 1793 by permission of the British Library.

7.3, 8.3, and 10.1.   WD961 William Alexander's Sketches of the Macartney Embassy to China 1793 by permission of the British Library.

9.1.   *Giving a Banquet at the Wanshuyuan* 萬樹園賜宴圖, 1753. Provided by the Palace Museum, Beijing.

9.2. William Alexander, *The Court of Chien-Lung*. The Huntington Library, Art Museum, and Botanical Gardens. Gilbert Davis Collection.

12.1. John Hoppner, *Jane Staunton and Her Son*, ca. 1794. Courtesy of Patrick Dingwall.

12.2. *Puankhequa II*. Collection of Hong Kong Museum of Art.

13.2. *The Trial of the Neptune Sailors in the English Factory*, 1807. National Maritime Museum, Greenwich.

13.3. Thomas Allom, *The Fountain Court in Consequa's House, Canton*. From Thomas Allom, *The Chinese Empire Illustrated*. Fisher, 1843.

14.1. Staunton's statement to Songyun. The National Archives, ref. FO1048/11/26.

14.2. Letter from Songyun. The National Archives, ref. FO1048/11/45.

16.1. Sir Thomas Lawrence (British, 1769–1830), *Lord Amherst*, 1821, oil on canvas, 93 × 57 1/2 in. (236 × 146 cm), Toledo Museum of Art (Toledo, Ohio). Purchased with funds from the Libbey Endowment, Gift of Edward Drummond Libbey, 1964.

17.1. and 17.2. Zhaojialing. Author's photographs.

18.1 and 18.2. Joseph Francis Gilbert, *Leigh Park* and *Temple Lawn*, ca. 1832. Reproduced by kind permission of Portsmouth Museum Service, Portsmouth City Council.

18.3. © Martin Archer Shee, *George Thomas Staunton*, 1833; Crown Copyright: UK Government Art Collection.

18.4. Joseph Francis Gilbert, *The Lake at Leigh Park*. Photo: Paul Carter, Southampton.

20.1. *The Victoria Regia House, Leigh Park, Havant*. Hampshire Record Office, ref. TOP 151/2/2.

20.2. *Hochee Playing Chess with His Son*. Courtesy of Celia Duncan.

A NOTE ON THE TYPE

THIS BOOK has been composed in Miller, a Scotch Roman typeface designed by Matthew Carter and first released by Font Bureau in 1997. It resembles Monticello, the typeface developed for The Papers of Thomas Jefferson in the 1940s by C. H. Griffith and P. J. Conkwright and reinterpreted in digital form by Carter in 2003.

Pleasant Jefferson ("P. J.") Conkwright (1905–1986) was Typographer at Princeton University Press from 1939 to 1970. He was an acclaimed book designer and AIGA Medalist.

The ornament used throughout this book was designed by Pierre Simon Fournier (1712–1768) and was a favorite of Conkwright's, used in his design of the *Princeton University Library Chronicle*.

Printed in the USA
CPSIA information can be obtained
at www.ICGtesting.com
JSHW081532170923
48425JS00001B/1